"*Plain Speaking* is the real thing; there has never been a book like it and never will be again. Not that future journalists won't be capable of matching Miller's efforts, but there will not ever again be a subject like Harry Truman, at least not in the White House."

Robert Alan Aurthur, *Esquire*

❖   ❖   ❖

". . . in a time of national psychic dislocation and trauma, PLAIN SPEAKING provides an instant and badly needed rehabilitation from the spreading sickness of cynicism; it restores us to our senses, to what we know, if for the moment only in our bones, to be true and right."

Eliot Fremont-Smith,
New York Magazine

❖   ❖   ❖

"How do you describe a book whose every page jumps at you with deliciously simple language about world-shaking events that happened several decades ago but which still affect all of us?
To borrow two favorite expressions of Harry Truman's: This book is a 'crackerjack,' and 'no two ways about it.'"

Fort Wayne News-Sentinel

"This is the Truman idiom, vigorous, without cant or inhibition and valid for no one could possibly make it up. It's a rich taste of a better past."

John Kenneth Galbraith

❀   ❀   ❀

"Congress may have to pass a law making it mandatory that before anyone can run for any office above Dog Catcher, he or she must read PLAIN SPEAKING and prove an understanding of it by passing an oral examination monitored by Diogenes."

Variety

❀   ❀   ❀

"I know of no other work in which an ex-President speaks so bluntly of his experiences from childhood to retirement, so candidly of his contemporaries and successors . . . the work is engagingly human."

Los Angeles Times

❀   ❀   ❀

"PLAIN SPEAKING is an 'oral biography' so alive it will seem warm to the touch. Both a human document and political history, there has never been another book quite like it. Its shrewdness would please Plutarch; its wit would delight Mark Twain."

Harriet Van Horne,
Book-of-the-Month Club News

DEDICATION

For DAVID W. ELLIOTT, *who has been urging me to do this book for almost ten years now, who became as familiar with and as fond of Harry Truman as I am and who, when the time came, did more than half the work and deserves more than half the credit.*

Also for Judy Freed, who insisted that I do it and even found a publisher.

And, of course, for Robert Alan Aurthur and David Susskind, without whom I would never have met Harry Truman or any of the other people who inhabit these pages. They are mostly gone now, and I miss them.

✿   ✿   ✿

A NOTE ON THE LANGUAGE

The diligent reader will notice that sometimes Mr. Truman is quoted as saying "fella" and sometimes "fellow," that sometimes he confuses "like" and "as" and sometimes does not, and that while he usually has "dinner" at twelve noon, he occasionally has "lunch" at that hour. There are other inconsistencies. Mr. Truman talked that way, inconsistently, like the rest of us.

He was a self-educated man, and he mispronounced a reasonable number of words, which in the beginning puzzled me. Then I realized that while he had often read them, he had seldom, if ever, spoken them aloud, not even in many cases heard them spoken aloud. It's like that if you're one of the few readers in town.

✿   ✿   ✿

For, the noblest deeds do not always shew men's virtues and vices, but oftentimes a light occasion, a word, or some sport makes men's natural dispositions and manners appear more plain, than the famous battles won, wherein are slain ten thousand men, or the great armies, or cities won by siege or assault.

—PLUTARCH, *Alexander the Great, i*

Plain Speaking
an oral biography of
Harry S. Truman
by
Merle Miller

A BERKLEY MEDALLION BOOK
published by
BERKLEY PUBLISHING CORPORATION

Berkley Publishing Corporation
200 Madison Avenue
New York, N.Y. 10016

SBN 425-03577-8

Library of Congress Catalog Card Number: 73-87198

*BERKLEY MEDALLION BOOKS are published by
Berkley Publishing Corporation
200 Madison Avenue
New York, N.Y. 10016*

BERKLEY MEDALLION BOOKS ® TM 757,375

Printed in the United States of America

Berkley Medallion Edition, OCTOBER, 1974
FOURTH PRINTING   March 1977
Parts of this book have appeared in ESQUIRE,
HOLIDAY, SHOW, *and* VISTA.

Grateful acknowledgment is made to the following sources for
permission to reprint:

Bernard Geis Associates: *Mr. Citizen* by Harry S. Truman ©
1960 by Harry S. Truman.
Harcourt Brace Jovanovich, Inc.: *The American Presidency*
by Clinton Rossiter © 1956, 1960 by Clinton Rossiter.
Harper & Row: *Sketches from Life, Of Men I Have Known*
by Dean Acheson © 1961 by Dean Acheson.
Dell Publishing Company, Inc.: *America Comes of Middle
Age* by Murray Kempton © 1967 by Murray Kempton.
Macmillan Publishing Co., Inc.: *Truman Presidency* by Cabell
Phillips, © 1966 by Cabell Phillips.
W. W. Norton and Company, Inc.: *Present at the Creation:
My Years in the State Department* by Dean Acheson © 1969
by Dean Acheson.
G. P. Putnam's Sons: *The Man from Missouri* by Alfred Steinberg © 1962 by Alfred Steinberg.
The Viking Press, Inc.: *The Patriot Chiefs: Chronicle of
American Indian Leadership* by Alvin M. Josephy, Jr. © 1961
by Alvin M. Josephy, Jr.

CONTENTS

Preface

It has been good to think about Harry Truman this spring and summer, the twentieth summer since he left the White House, the summer after his death, the summer of Watergate. The memory of him has never been sharper, never brighter than it is now, a time when menacing, shadowy men are everywhere among us.

There was never anything shadowy about old Harry, never anything menacing. He was never less than four-dimensional; he was always a person, a human being.

I once wrote that Harry Truman might be the last human being to occupy the White House, and considering, as he would say, "the four fellas that succeeded me," I see no reason to change my mind.

As you will see in reading this book, Harry's words were never fancy, but they were never obscure either. You never had to try to figure out what Harry was up to; he told you what he was up to. And, as they said of him back in Independence, he was a man of his word. There was not a duplicitous bone in his body. He was without guile, and when it was all over, when he and Bess came back home, after eighteen years in Washington, more than seven of them in an unbugged,* unshuttered White House, neither of them thought of bringing any of the trappings of the Presidency with them. In fact, that last day in Washington, in January, 1953, Harry had thought that since the relations between himself and the incoming

---

* The week it was revealed that Nixon's White House was extensively bugged Major General Harry Vaughan, Truman's military aide, remembered that during Truman's first week in office he took some FBI phone taps (an extensive practice during the Roosevelt years) to the new President and asked if he was interested. Harry took a look at two pages of transcript of the doings of the wife of one member of the White House staff and then told Vaughan, "I haven't time for any such foolishness as that. Tell them I don't authorize any such thing."

President were, to state it gently, strained, he and Bess might have to walk from the White House to the railroad station. Or perhaps take a taxi.

"But that wouldn't have bothered me," he told me years later. "I was there more or less by accident you might say, and I just never got to thinking that I was anything *special*. It's very easy to do that in Washington, and I've seen it happen to a lot of fellas. But I did my best not to let it happen to me. I tried never to forget who I was and where I'd come from and where I was going back to. And if you can do that, things usually work out all right in the end."

As nearly as he could remember, Harry's last act in the White House was returning a pencil or maybe it was a pen to the desk of the man he had borrowed it from.

"Everything," he said, "all of it belongs to the people. I was just privileged to *use* it for a while. That's all. And since it was only *lent* to me, and by that I'm includin' the power of the Presidency, such as it is, I had to try to use whatever it was with great care so that I could pass it on to the next fella in the best condition possible. And for the most part I think you can say I succeeded."

Mr. President, it's been said that the Presidency is the most powerful office in the world. Do you think that's true?

"Oh, no. Oh, my, no. About the biggest power the President has, and I've said this before, is the power to persuade people to do what they ought to do without having to be persuaded. There are a lot of other powers written in the Constitution and given to the President, but it's that power to persuade people to do what they ought to do anyway that's the biggest. And if the man who is President doesn't understand that, if he thinks he's too big to do the necessary persuading, then he's in for big trouble, and so is the country."

So Harry and Bess took the train back to Independence, and people in Independence found them unchanged; it was as if they had never been away, and as a neighbor says in this book, maybe Harry never really left Independence; maybe he just sort of commuted to Washington.

Anyway, people back home found that they were as

Bernard Berenson, yes, Bernard Berenson, said, "Both as natural, as unspoiled by high office as if he had risen no further than alderman of Independence, Missouri."

And you remember the day after Mr. Truman got back home, he took his usual morning walk, and Ray Scherer, the television reporter, asked him what was the first thing he did when he walked in the house at 219 North Delaware the night before, pausing for some monumental statement suitable for engraving on the side of Mount Rushmore.

"I carried the grips up to the attic," said Harry.

That house on North Delaware Street had served as the summer White House various times during the more than seven years that Harry Truman was President, but somehow it never occurred to him to have it all fancied up at the expense of the taxpayers. In fact, he didn't even own the place. He and Bess had put up with mother-in-law Wallace from the time of their marriage in 1919 until her death in 1952. They had fed her and clothed her and housed her, including in her last years a room of her very own in the White House. But Madge Gates Wallace never stopped ruminating, aloud and whenever possible in the presence of her son-in-law, about all the people who would have made better Presidents than Harry. And why did he have to fire that nice General MacArthur? The general was a man she could have felt socially at ease with; for one thing, he was a gentleman to the manor born. He was a five-star general, not like some dirt farmers who shall be nameless. And don't track up the kitchen with your muddy feet, Harry.

When she died, that impossible old woman, she didn't even leave the house to Harry. She left it to Bess and the Wallace boys, and Harry had to buy out their share.

But, as it says in these pages, in all those years, Harry never once complained. He never once answered back. Mrs. W. L. C. Palmer, who taught him Latin and mathematics, says, "You must remember Harry is a reticent man."

Ethel Noland, Harry Truman's first cousin, put it another way. She said that both of them grew up at a time when if people asked how you were, you said, "I'm fine. And you?" You wouldn't have *dreamed* of discussing with anybody, except possibly the family doctor, how you really were. One accepted one's fate, never bemoaned it. For one thing, you didn't have time.

Whatever happened to old-fashioned reticence, do you suppose? Is there any way of getting it back? I've looked everywhere, asked everybody; nobody seems to know; nobody seems to care even, and when you ask, it's difficult to keep the asked from telling you why he doesn't care and how he feels. None of them feels good, not ever.

All right then. This is a book about Harry Truman, and most of it is in his own words and the words of people who knew him before he went to Washington and after and while he was there. It should be said instantly that the words were not spoken with a book in mind. They were spoken in the hope that out of them would come ideas for God-alone-knew how many television programs that would explain to the eager millions what it had been like to be President and what as President Mr. Truman had done.

As Mr. Truman used to say, "I'm mostly interested in the children. The old folks, mostly they're too set in their ways and too stubborn to learn anything new, but I want the children to know what we've got here in this country and how we got it, and then if they want to go ahead and change it, why, that's up to them. But I want them to understand what it's all about first. I want to make a historical record that has never been made before in the history of this country, and if it turns out all right, I'll be very happy indeed."

The way it turns out comes later.

But it began in the summer of 1961, continued that fall and winter into the cold, very cold, never colder, months of 1962.

I first went to Independence as the writer and, as

my friend Robert Alan Aurthur* describes it, "the general organizer" of the series. As I say, the programs were to deal largely with Mr. Truman's years in the White House. We're inclined, I am anyway, to think of those years as being simpler times, but maybe we were only young. Maybe it was that things seemed soluble then, and who among us didn't think he would become what he dreamed of becoming?

But looking back on them, the years don't seem simple at all. Think of it—the dropping of the Bomb, the formation of the UN, the Korean decision, the Hiss case, the firing of MacArthur, the birth of Israel, NATO, the Marshall Plan, McCarthyism, Point Four, and so on and endlessly on. And through it all, for almost eight years, Harry Truman was *there,* not in the eye of the storm, he *was* the eye of the storm. He did it, all of it. He asked his associates to tell him how long he had to decide whatever was to be decided, and when the deadline came, the decision had been made. And no regrets, no looking back, no wondering if-I-had-to-do-it-all-over-again, would I have? Dean Ache-

---

* Aurthur's beady-eyed account of some parts of our involvement with Mr. Truman appeared in two issues of *Esquire* in 1971. He wrote, "You wonder how I ever got to hang around Mr. Truman . . . ? Simply put, I was supervising a series of films for television independently produced and financed by David Susskind and his company, Talent Associates. At the birth of the project, then uninvolved except as a friend, I had suggested to David that the man to bring the perfect creative spark as writer and general organizer was another close friend, Merle Miller. To supplement Merle's obvious literary qualifications I felt he and Mr. Truman had much in common: both were from the Midwest; both had strong mothers, weak eyes, and early dreams of glory—which only Mr. Truman had realized."

As Huck Finn says of Mark Twain and *The Adventures of Tom Sawyer* at the beginning of his own adventures, ". . . he told the truth, mainly. There was things which he stretched, but mainly he told the truth."

The things which Bob stretched largely had to do with me.

son wrote that Harry Truman was totally without what he called "that most enfeebling of emotions, regret."

Regret was self-indulgent, as bad as, maybe worse than, telling people how you *felt*. No time for it. "If you can't stand the heat, stay out of the kitchen." Like that sign on Harry's desk when he was in the White House. "The buck stops here," it said, and that's where it stopped. The mistakes were Harry's, and he never blamed anyone else for them.

The triumphs were Harry's, too, but he was a modest man. There was nothing of Uriah Heep about him; he was just genuinely modest. Speaking of what Winston Churchill has called "the most unsordid act in history," the Marshall Plan, Mr. Truman once told me, "I said to General Marshall, I said, 'General, I want the plan to go down in history with your name on it. And don't give me any argument. I've made up my mind, and, remember, I'm your Commander in Chief."

And that other sign on his desk, that quotation from Mark Twain that his sister had at the little house out at Grandview the last time I saw her: "Always do right. This will gratify some people & astonish the rest."

Harry Truman always did what he thought was right. Can you imagine a member of his Cabinet seriously telling a committee of the U.S. Senate that he had *shielded* Harry from the truth?

One's blood congeals at the thought of how far we have gone since those days, and it's been downhill all the way.

Once Harry found out that a couple of his appointees had been "influence peddling"—how archaic those guys on the take for 5 percent seem these days—and, without hesitation, he threw them downstairs, right out in front of God, the electorate, and everybody.

When the fella that succeeded him, *whatever* his name was, Harry never could remember that bird's name, but when he had to get rid of *five* of his appointees for more or less the same thing, he *accepted their resignations* with letters so flattering that the resigners no doubt had them framed in gold and hung on their living-room walls. For one the President-General even had the troops pass in review.

When Harry was asked what he thought of such goings-on, he said, "I see why he had to fire them, but I don't see why he had to kiss them on both cheeks."

You can see what I mean by four-dimensional and why the memory of him is so luminous. Take the business of what you are willing to do to win an election.

In October, 1948, less than a month before the election almost nobody but Harry thought he could win, plans were made to send his old friend Fred Vinson, then Chief Justice of the United States Supreme Court, on a dramatic special mission to Moscow "to find some common ground with the Russians."

The journey just before the election would demonstrate to the electorate that Harry was a President who could be counted on to do anything to keep the peace. For a generation? Hell, maybe forever.

The President was to announce the Vinson trip on a national radio hookup. In fact, the speech had already been written, and the Chief Justice was packing his bags. Harry's exuberant adviser—not very much exuberance up to then—told him that this was what they'd been hoping for all through the campaign. This would do it. There were millions, maybe tens of millions of votes in it.

Harry listened, and then he went off to the communications room of the White House to discuss the mission with General George C. Marshall, who was then his Secretary of State and was attending a meeting of the Foreign Ministers in Paris. The general said that he, of course, was a subordinate of the President and that he didn't *know* that such a trip as Vinson's might make his work more difficult, but it might. He left the decision up to the President.

Harry came back to the meeting of his associates and said no. There would be no Vinson mission to Moscow, politically appealing as the idea might be.

His advisers said he was crazy. They asked what was

more important, *maybe* making old Marshall's work more difficult or winning the election. Jonathan Daniels, who was there, has written: "They talked to him as President and more sharply as candidate, too.

"He listened. His magnified eyes seemed almost slate gray. Then he said very quietly, 'I have heard enough. We won't do it.'

"He got up and went out of the glass-paneled door to the terrace by the rose garden and walked alone—very much alone that day—back toward the White House. . . ."

When in 1961 I mentioned that lonely night to Mr. Truman, he said, "Why, of course, I didn't know for sure whether it would help win the election or not, but after talking to General Marshall, I decided it wouldn't be the right thing to do, and so I didn't do it."

I waited for more, but there wasn't any more, and there really didn't need to be.

Harry Truman, a buck-stopper, a doer-of-right, alone, but his own man, never anybody else's. They said he was Tom Pendergast's man, but that wasn't true either. You'll see. Harry Truman never belonged to anybody. He once said, "Old Tom Jefferson wrote that, 'Whenever you do a thing, though it can never be known but to yourself, ask yourself how you would act were all the world watching you, and act accordingly.' "

Old Harry was far too modest a man to make any comparison between himself and old Tom.

I first went to Independence in the summer of 1961, and I must confess that up to then Harry hadn't been anywhere near the top of my list of favorite ex-Presidents. True, I'd voted for him in 1948, but reluctantly, most reluctantly. I had never quite forgiven him for not being Franklin Roosevelt, for being plain instead of patrician. Besides, Bob Aurthur is perfectly right. There were a lot of things about Harry Truman that reminded me of things about me that I wanted to forget. My childhood, just to start out.

But then how many chances had I had to be the Boswell

of an ex-President? Besides which, Bob Aurthur had promised me that the project would make me very, very rich and my name a household word, two things I had had on my personal agenda for all of my life.

So I went to Independence, along with two associates; the associates kept changing, but they all had two things in common, incompetence and stupidity. We had been told before leaving New York that the President would not be able to see us until the next morning, but we went out to the Truman Library anyway, and while we were still looking at the huge Thomas Hart Benton mural just inside the public entrance to the library, a member of the staff came up and said that the President had heard we were there and wanted to see us.

We were taken into Mr. Truman's private office, and when he came in, he was wearing the familiar double-breasted suit with the usual neatly folded handkerchief in the breast pocket, a white shirt that could have come from J. C. Penney, and a Sulka—or was it Countess Mara? —tie. His skin was pink and healthy-looking, and his blue eyes were amused and active, enhanced rather than diminished by the thin-rimmed glasses. He looked just as feisty and mischievous and forthright as I'd expected. He looked like a man who enjoyed himself hugely and who, if he did not, kept that knowledge to himself. I'm fine. And you?

Since I hadn't expected to see Mr. Truman, I was wearing an unpressed pair of slacks and a sports shirt, and I apologized.

"Oh, that's all right," he said, a sentence he was to repeat many times in many different contexts.

"Besides," he added, "I'm just an old Missouri farmer, and you're just an Iowa farmer. So don't worry about a thing like that."

The President had taken the trouble to find out a good deal about all three of us. I doubt, though, that he had used whatever influence he had with the Kennedy administration to get any secret FBI reports on us or had detectives hired to bug our phones or our bedrooms. You will

see later how he felt about such things. He was a very
private man who respected the privacy of others, all others.

In my case he had taken the trouble to read two of my
novels, and I'm sure they weren't his kind of books. So
it was a measure of his forbearance that he was willing
to let me handle the series. He was a very forbearing man.
"You'll never find me in any way criticizin' or jumpin' on
the people who are trying to help me. If a fella can't be
patient and considerate of the people who are actually
doin' the work for him, then he's not any good, and I
don't like him."

David Susskind said that Mr. Truman was corny, and
it's true. He often was, and sometimes I deplored it. But
looking back now on those weeks we spent together, reading over and listening to his words, to the words of his
friends, it all comes out beautifully refreshing. We need
more of it.

David also said that Mr. Truman was an elemental man,
the most elemental he, David, had ever met, and that's true,
too. Mr. Truman was the most elemental man I've ever
met, except maybe for my grandfather, and I think we
could use more of that as well. My grandfather never
voted for a Democrat his whole life through, and I don't
know that he'd have voted for Harry Truman, but he'd
have liked him. They were both elemental, and they were
both men of whom it could be said that they never met a
stranger.

That first afternoon with Mr. Truman we talked for a
few minutes about plans for the television series, and then
I said, "Mr. President, could I ask you a question that you
might consider impertinent?"

"Go right ahead," he said. "If I want to stop you, I'll
stop you."

"Well, sir, I've been wearing glasses since I was three
years old, and I know you had to wear glasses when you
were a boy. I wonder, sir, did they ever call you *four-
eyes?*"

The President smiled. It was a good smile, warm and

welcoming, holding nothing back. I was never sure whether the even teeth were false.

"I've worn glasses since I was six years old," he said, "and of course, they called me *four-eyes* and a lot of other things, too. That's hard on a boy. It makes him lonely, and it gives him an inferiority complex, and he has a hard time overcoming it."

He paused a moment, still smiling, then said, "Of course, we didn't know what an inferiority complex was in those days. But you can overcome it. You've got to fight for everything you do. You've got to be above those calling you names, and you've got to do more work than they do, but it usually comes out all right in the end."

That last sentence was another the President was to repeat many times.

"I always had my nose stuck in a book," he said, "a history book mostly. Of course, the main reason you read a book is to get a better insight into the people you're talking to. There were about three thousand books in the library downtown, and I guess I read them all, including the encyclopedias. I'm embarrassed to say that I remembered what I read, too."

That was how our relationship, I like to think our friendship, began. It continued, as I say, until the winter months of 1962, when it ended, not because there was ever any trouble between the President and me but because the three television networks to which we all owe so much were having no part of a series on Mr. Truman's Presidency.

In the months after our meeting, however, Mr. Truman and I had days, sometimes weeks, of conversations, interviews if you insist, many of them on tape, many not. The more formal of them were in Mr. Truman's office, often with the inhibiting presence, inhibiting I felt to Mr. Truman and certainly inhibiting to me, of two associates. One was David Noyes, a wealthy former vice-president of Lord & Thomas who had been a speechwriter during the 1948 campaign. Except for Mr. Truman, he had been the

only man who that year thought he could win the election.
He clearly loved Mr. Truman and was very protective of
him. I felt he was too protective.

The other was William Hillman, a former foreign correspondent of the Hearst newspapers. He was a large, sham-
bling man, a cigarette forever dangling from his full lips,
his ample stomach forever covered with ashes. A somewhat more benign version of Sidney Greenstreet with a
suitably gravelly voice.

Bob Aurthur reports that he and Hillman once had
lunch at the airport restaurant in Kansas City, all by itself a hazardous undertaking, and while Hillman described the way he had got an exclusive interview with
Adolf Hitler, he ate *two* orders of pig's knuckles and
sauerkraut.

Noyes and Hillman, Hillman in particular, had worked
with Mr. Truman in writing the *Memoirs* and on his other
writing chores. I felt that they had dejuiced and dehuman-
ized him in everything that was written. They had laund-
ered his prose, flattened his personality, and made him
pontifical, which was the last thing I found him to be.
Their mere presence in a room made him self-conscious,
caused him to clean up his language and soften his opinions. With them around Mr. Truman came out bland, another thing he just wasn't.

But, happily, they were away a good deal of the time,
and the best of the conversations in this book were when
Mr. Truman and I were alone or were waiting for somebody to change the film in a camera or do something or
other to one of the tape machines. A lot more time was
spent doing things like that than was spent actually filming
or recording. Mr. Truman never understood why, and
neither did I. The crews all came from New York, union
rules, and they were all bumbling incompetents. All.

Mr. Truman was invariably patient with them, though,
and with me. The only time he ever got angry with me was
once in New York when we were filming an episode of the
series having to do with Korea. I had suggested that since
even then Korea was very vague in the minds of those in
the television audience who were under thirty, we should

perhaps try to *dramatize* what. . . . *Dramatize.* That did it. Mr. Truman's eyes grew cold, and he drew his mouth into a tight, unpleasant line and said—for a second I felt some sympathy for the late Douglas MacArthur—"Now you look here, young man, you asked me to tell you the facts, and I'll do it, but I'm not going to be any playactor. Now what's your next question?"

Anyway, I suppose the ineptitude of the technical crews had its value; it gave me a lot more time to talk with Mr. Truman and with the two dejuicers out of the room.

Most of the time I would suggest the day before what we would discuss the following day, hoping that that night he would bone up on whatever the subject was. For all I know he did, and we returned to some subjects again and again, amplifying, adding color and detail.

While I was working on this book, a reviewer in the *Village Voice* dismissed a book about Mr. Truman as well as Mr. Truman himself, "the one after FDR and before General Eisenhower." One of Mr. Truman's observations particularly infuriated him. He treated it as if it had been the raving of an idiot child. The sentence was: "There is nothing new in the world except the history you do not know."

And all by itself it doesn't make much sense. But as Mr. Truman explained it to me, the whole thing goes like this:

"There's nothing new in human nature. The only thing that changes are the names we give things. If you want to understand the twentieth century, read the lives of the Roman emperors, all the way from Claudius to Constantine. . . . And go back to old Hammurabi, the Babylonian emperor. Why, he had laws that covered everything, adultery and murder and divorce, everything.

"Those people had the same troubles as we have now. Men don't change. The only thing new in the world is the history you don't know."

Not the most profound idea in the world, perhaps, but it's true.

To Harry Truman history was the men who made it, and he spoke of Marcus Aurelius or Henry of Navarre or old Tom Jefferson or old Andy Jackson as if they were friends and neighbors with whom he had only recently discussed the affairs of the day, their day:

". . . his real name was Marcus Aleius Aurelius Antoninus, and he was one of the great ones. He was a great field general, and he was a great emperor, one of the six great emperors of Rome.

"Some people think they're old-fashioned, but I don't. What he wrote in his *Meditations,* he said that the four greatest virtues are moderation, wisdom, justice, and fortitude, and if a man is able to cultivate those, that's all he needs to live a happy and successful life. That's the way I look at it anyway." *

* Mr. Truman's copy of *Meditations,* which he lent to me to take back to the hotel one night, was by the look of it one of the most read books in his library. He was a great underliner, a great writer of marginal comments, usually about things with which he disagreed, *"Bunk!" "He doesn't know what he's talking about!"* "That's not True!!" "Where did he ever get a damn fool notion like that?" And so on.

I was interested to see that these passages in *Meditations* were underlined:

"If it is not right, do not do it; if it is not true, do not say it."

"First, do nothing thoughtlessly or without a purpose. Secondly, see that your acts are directed to a social end."

"Today I have got out of all trouble, or rather I have cast out all trouble, for it was not outside, but within, in my opinions."

"It is not fitting that I should give myself pain, for I have never intentionally given pain even to another."

"Always be sure whose approbation it is you wish to secure, and what ruling principles they have. Then you will neither blame those who offend involuntarily, nor will you want their approbation, if you look to the sources of their opinions and appetites."

"When another blames or hates you, or when men say injurious things about you, approach their poor souls, penetrate within, and see what kind of men they are. You will discover that there is no reason to take trouble that these men have a good opinion of you. However, you must be well disposed to-

About Mr. Truman's memory. In Cabell Phillips' book *The Truman Presidency*, he says that in 1951, when Hillman was interviewing the President for the book *Mr. President*, Mr. Truman was talking about Alexander the Great, who had, he said, made the mistake of overextending himself.

Phillips writes:

"And then the people around him," he told Hillman, "made him think he was immortal, and he found that thirty-three quarts of wine was too much for any man, and it killed him at Babylon."

Working over the proofs of his book later, Hillman paused to puzzle over the President's mention of the thirty-three quarts of wine. Obviously, he thought, it was some sort of allegory; he, himself, had never heard of it, nor was he sure what it meant. He called the Library of Congress and asked their scholarly assistance in running the item down. A few days later they called back to say, sorry, they could find no link, real or poetic, between Alexander and thirty-three quarts of wine. Hillman was convinced that the President had mixed either his metaphors or his kings and was about to challenge him on it when, a few days later, he received another call from the researcher at the Library. In the manner of librarians everywhere, this one had not given up the search after the first admission of failure. He had pursued his quarry behind the locked doors of the Rare Books Section, and into an obscure and long-out-of-print volume of the history of the ancient Greeks, and, by golly, the President was right after all!

"And you know what?" the researcher added. "That book has been checked out of the shelves only twice in the last twenty years, and the last time was for Senator Harry Truman in 1939."

wards them, for by nature they are friends. And the gods, too, aid them in all ways, by dreams, by signs, toward the attainment of their aims."

In the margin of this particular paragraph Harry Truman had written, *"True! True! True!"*

When I was talking with him, Mr. Truman's memory was best during the first two or three hours in the morning—we usually got started around eight—but frequently after lunch it was no good at all. That was partly due, I imagine, to the fact that an old man's mind tires easily. I'm sure another reason, though, was the fact that before going home for "dinner," always a few minutes before noon, he had I would have what he always called a "slight libation," scotch or bourbon. "The Boss doesn't think I ought to," he would say, winking. The Boss was Mrs. Truman. When we had lunch at the Howard Johnson's near the library, we would always have two or three before setting out, and they were never slight, although they were libational.

In any case, in the mornings we talked about history, that made by Mr. Truman and by other men, and in the afternoons we talked, if we talked at all, about more personal matters. Mr. Truman's views of people, large and small, that he'd been associated with. Adlai Stevenson, with whom he had long since become disenchanted. Stevenson was a man who could never make up his mind whether he had to go to the bathroom or not. And Henry Wallace was a fellow "who wanted to be a great man but didn't know how to go about it." And there were two men he hated, "held a grudge against." One of them was Richard Nixon. I don't think he hated "the fella that succeeded me in the White House." He thought he was a lousy President and a moral coward for, among other things, taking out praise for General Marshall that had been written into a speech Eisenhower was going to deliver in Wisconsin during the 1952 campaign. As you'll see, Harry Truman couldn't understand the kind of man who would do such a thing.

Or we'd talk about things like the day Eddie Jacobson, the man who'd been Mr. Truman's partner in the famous failed haberdashery, came to the Oval Room to persuade Mr. Truman to see Chaim Weizmann, who was to become the first President of Israel.

Or Mr. Truman's boyhood. His memory of that never

dimmed, and about his remarkable mother and, he insisted, his equally remarkable father. Or his sister, Mary Jane. Mr. Truman was very sentimental about the women in his life. Mary Jane, Bess, and Margaret. One day I asked him if he would read on camera one of the letters he had written during his first days in the White House to Mamma and Mary Jane.

The President didn't get angry, but I could see that I had made a suggestion almost as bad as asking him to *act*.

"I can't do a thing like that," he said. "You know I can't do a thing like that, and you shouldn't ask me."

He added that the letters belonged to Mary Jane, and he said that when he was President, "and we had three-cent stamps when I was in the White House," he had never franked the letters.

I asked him why, and he said, "Because they were personal. There was nothing official about them."

All clear?

Mr. Truman's memories were always cheerful, always. He had, God knows, had his share and more of frustration, of failure, of disappointment, of poverty, of mortgage foreclosures, of heartbreak. My God, at forty he hadn't succeeded at anything, and he had a wife and a baby and an insupportable mother-in-law to support. And he went ahead and did it. No job was too menial, if it was necessary.

Did he weep? Did he curse the fates? Did he shake his fist at the thunder? If ever he did, he did it in private. Lincoln was an outwardly melancholy man; Harry Truman was not. His melancholy, if any, was all buttoned up inside him. He never, to use a phrase several of his contemporaries used in describing him, wore his heart on his sleeve. How are you? I'm fine. And you?

Mr. Truman was cheerful, because who wants to have a grouch hanging around? He felt that he had lived a remarkable life, which he had, and he liked to talk about it, and I liked to listen. He was a remarkable man, and the fact that he had been President wasn't the only reason,

not even the most important reason. William Howard
Taft wasn't up to much when it came to making memorable observations, but he once said that in every American
town with a population of more than 5,000 there is at
least one man qualified to serve on the Supreme Court of
the United States. I think that's true, and in Independence,
Missouri, there was a man qualified to be President, and
he got to be it, and he turned out to be one of the great
ones. Remarkable.

In *The American Presidency* the historian Clinton Rossiter wrote:

> . . . I am ready to hazard an opinion, to which I
> came, I confess manfully, with dragging feet, that Harry
> S. Truman will eventually win a place as President
> alongside Jefferson and Theodore Roosevelt. There will
> be at least a half-dozen Presidents strung out below him
> who were more able and large-minded, but he had the
> good fortune to preside in stirring times and will reap
> large credit for having survived them. . . . Harry S.
> Truman is a man whom history will delight to remem-
> ber. Those very lapses from dignity that made him an
> object of scorn to millions of Republicans—the angry
> letters, testy press conferences, whistle stops, impossible
> sports shirts, and early-morning seminars on the streets
> of dozens of American cities—open his door to immor-
> tality. It is a rare American, even a rare Republican,
> who can be scornful about a man one hundred years
> dead, and our descendants will be chuckling over his
> Missouri wit and wisdom long after "the five-per-cen-
> ters" have been buried and forgotten. They will read
> with admiration of the upset he brought off in 1948,
> with awe of the firing of General MacArthur, and with a
> sense of kinship of the way he remained more genuinely
> "home folks" than any other President. . . . He was
> fascinating to watch, even when the sight hurt, and he
> will be fascinating to read about. The historians can be
> expected to do their share to fix him securely in history,
> for he provides a classic study of one of their favorite
> themes: the President who grows in office.

As I've said, I had hoped that the conversations in these pages would provide me with the material for a series of hour-long television programs with Mr. Truman and others talking about his years before, during, and after the White House and talking about this country and its past. But for reasons I'll explain in a minute, that was not to be.

I still had the tapes, though; I still had the mountains of notes I made at the earliest possible moment after each conversation, and I still had all those marvelously warm memories. I had planned in a vague sort of way to use them as the basis for a full-scale biography of Harry Truman, but at the time of his death last winter I decided I would never have the patience or make the time to do that. I am in my fifties, that dangerous decade (see the obituary pages of this morning's *Times*), and so, urged on by my friend Judy Freed, and with the assistance every step of the way of a brilliant young writer and friend, David W. Elliott,* I have organized them into this book.

It is a book about the thirty-second President of the United States in his own words and in the words of his friends; there is not an enemy anywhere in these pages. I have added a few observations here and there, and I asked all the questions, not that that was much of an accomplishment.

The justification for this volume, if such is needed, comes from Mr. Truman himself. He was talking about libraries, and he said, "The worst thing in the world is when records are destroyed. The destruction of the Alexandrian Library and also the destruction of the great libraries in Rome. Those were terrible things, and one was done by the Moslems and the other by the Christians, but there's no difference between them when they're working for propaganda purposes.

"Now as for the Presidency, every piece of paper a President signs, every piece of paper he touches even has

---

* Elliott is the author of the critically acclaimed *Listen to the Silence* and *Pieces of Night* and the forthcoming *A Flaw in My Character.*

to be saved. You take Lincoln and Fillmore. Millard Fillmore's son burned all his father's papers because he was ashamed of his father, who had come from the very bottom line right to the top. And Robert Todd Lincoln burned about half to two-thirds of his father's papers for the same reason, because he was ashamed of him. A thing like that ought to be against the law."

If every piece of paper the President signs or touches is important, surely these wide-ranging conversations with Harry Truman are essential to our history. I also happen to think, perhaps immodestly, that the voice of Harry Truman that emerges from these pages is louder and clearer than it has ever been.

And as I say, during the summer of Watergate, there is a special kind of purity in what he has to say. Mary McGrory wrote some years back: "Since Harry Truman left town almost nobody has spoken his mind. Mr. Truman took the tradition of plain speaking back to Missouri with him."

Now the purists may wonder how accurate Mr. Truman's memory was when we talked, and didn't he touch things up a bit at times to give himself a more heroic stance? The answer to both questions is yes, possibly. Mr. Truman told it the way he remembered it, no doubt giving himself the benefit of as much doubt as with his basic honesty he could. I figured ten years ago and do now that at seventy-seven a man who'd been through what Mr. Truman had been through was entitled.

So, as I think Mr. Truman would have said, the hell with the purists. There are already hundreds of books and there will be hundreds more to clear up those small details that Mr. Truman and his friends may have misremembered.

I should perhaps warn the unsuspecting that a possibly disproportionate part of this book deals with the memories of people who knew Harry Truman when he was growing up, knew him as a farmer, when he was a captain in Battery D, as an unsuccessful haberdasher, and as a man who needed a job and although he had no special aptitude or taste for it went into politics.

I do not apologize for that disproportion, if such it is. By listening to the voices of those people who knew Mr. Truman before 1935, when at the age of fifty he went off to Washington for the first time, the reader may gain some insight into why, being the kind of man he was, he was able to do what he did between that January and the January in 1953 when he and Bess came back to Independence.

In the Preface to the first volume of *Abraham Lincoln, The Prairie Years*, Carl Sandburg wrote, "Perhaps poetry, art, human behavior in this country, which has a need to build on its own tradition, would be served by a life of Lincoln stressing the fifty-two years previous to his Presidency. Such a book would imply that if he was what he was during those first fifty-two years of his life it was nearly inevitable that he would be what he proved to be in the last four."

To understand Harry Truman you must understand something about Independence, in particular the Independence in which he grew up. Mr. Truman was fond of saying that to him Independence was what Hannibal, Missouri, was to Mark Twain. He liked to quote what Twain said late in his life in a speech in India, "All the *me* in me is in a little Missouri village halfway around the world."

And Mr. Truman would add, "I wouldn't think much of a man that tried to deny the people and the town where he grew up. I've told you. You must always keep in mind who you are and where you come from. A man who can't do that at all times is in trouble where I'm concerned. I wouldn't have anything to do with him."

When Harry Truman was growing up, Independence was still pretty much of a frontier town. There were men who proudly said that they had helped Quantrill when he made his murdering raid on Lawrence, Kansas. There were others who remembered Jesse James, or said they

did. And people spoke fondly of Frank James, who for
a time was a prisoner in the town jail.

That jail changed hands five times in the bitter border
war between Kansas and Missouri that started long before
the rest of the Civil War. There were also people still alive
who had been in what Harry later in these pages calls
"concentration camps" in Kansas City, interned there by
the Federal troops. Harry's mother was among those
internees, and she, not surprisingly, thought it was a good
thing when Lincoln was shot, and when at ninety-two she
broke her hip and shoulder after tripping in her kitchen,
Harry, who was then President, flew out to see her. She
looked up at him from her bed of pain and said, "I don't
want any smart cracks out of you. I saw your picture in
the paper last week putting a wreath at the Lincoln Memorial."

Mary Jane Truman told me that when their mother said
things like that, she was joking. It doesn't really matter one
way or the other. She was a woman of great spirit. She
taught her son to do what was right, and he never forgot it.

But in his boyhood Independence was not an easy place
for a little boy who wore glasses, who always had his nose
stuck in a book, whose contemporaries can scarcely ever
remember seeing him without a music roll under his arm
(". . . of course, they called me *four-eyes* and a lot of
other things, too. That's hard on a boy"). The thing about
Harry Truman is that he never forgot what it was like
being a kid who was lonely, who was teased, who because
he might break his glasses never played any games with
his brother, Vivian, and the boys of the neighborhood.

And because he remembered, he was marvelous with
children. When I was in Independence, his favorite hours
were those spent in the auditorium of the library when it
was filled with children. He would, for instance, tell them
what it had been like during the summer of 1787 when
those fellas, the Founding Fathers, met to write the Constitution. The fellas really came alive when Harry de-

scribed them. Washington and Alexander Hamilton and
Madison and old John Adams. It was never like that in
school.

One day he read them the opening paragraphs of one
of his favorite books, Catherine Drinker Bowen's *John
Adams and the American Revolution:*

> "On the Fourth of July, 1826, America celebrated its
> Jubilee—the Fiftieth Anniversary of Independence.
> John Adams, second President of the United States, died
> that day, aged ninety, while from Maine to Georgia,
> bells rang and cannon boomed. And on that same day,
> Thomas Jefferson died before sunset in Virginia.
>
> "In their dying, in that swift, so aptly celebrated
> double departure, is something which shakes an Ameri-
> can to the heart. It was not their great fame, their long
> lives or even the record of their work that made these
> two seem indestructible. It was their faith, their bound-
> less, unquenchable hope in the future, their sure, im-
> mortal belief that mankind, if it so desired, could be
> free."

As he read that day, there was a grandeur in Mr. Truman's voice that I had never heard before and, for that
matter, never heard again. And while he was far too modest a man to say it, even to think it, there was at least one
person in the auditorium that day who thought that Harry
Truman shared with those two monolithic figures of our
past a feeling of indestructibility. I know that he shared
their hope in the future as well as their sure, immortal
belief that mankind, if it so desired, could be free.

At the end of Mr. Truman's speeches there was always
a question period, and on one day I like to remember the
last question came from an anxious small boy with red
hair whose ears had grown up, but not his face.

"Mr. President," he said, and his future and the world's
depended on the reply, "was you popular when you was
a boy?"

The President looked at the boy over the glasses that
always made him look like an irritated owl. "Why, no,"

he said, "I was never popular. The popular boys were the ones who were good at games and had big, tight fists. I was never like that. Without my glasses I was blind as a bat, and to tell the truth, I was kind of a sissy. If there was any danger of getting into a fight, I always ran. I guess that's why I'm here today."

The little boy started to applaud, and then everybody else did, too. It was an eminently satisfactory answer for all of us who ever ran from a fight, which is all of us.

Later the dejuicers asked me to—their wishes were often commands—see to it that that question and the answer be removed from the tape "before any public use is made of the tape." "Especially the sissy part," said one of them.

I refused. As I say, I'm fond of that moment. We need more Presidents who have run from fights and admit it. We must run from more fights. That's our only hope.

Yes, when Harry was growing up, Independence was a rough town, but having said that, I must add something else. It was also a town in which people read books and listened to music, and at "supper"—that was and is at five, five thirty at the latest—they discussed ideas. As Ethel Noland put it, "There was conversation. I mean by that talk about what was going on in the world, talk about ideas."

America was not then and is not now, as a high school classmate of mine once put it, "a great big, oblong statistical blur, which is what most people in New York seem to think."

True. Thought and literacy are not confined to a narrow strip of land on the Eastern seaboard. Read in these pages the weekly activities, since her retirement, of Miss Noland. And consider Mr. Truman's friends the three Chiles sisters, anxiously wondering why it is that nobody reads Dickens and Thackeray anymore.

In school Harry and Charlie Ross, who when Harry was President was to become his press secretary, were both fond of Latin, and during the whole of one April they spent every spare moment, along with Elmer Twyman, who came from a family of doctors, building a bridge that was said to be an exact replica of one of the bridges that Caesar built across the Rhine. They had found a description of the bridge in Caesar's *Commentaries*.

Harry and Charlie Ross and Elmer Twyman knew a lot about Caesar, and, of course, Harry went on to be President, and he was able to make some use of that knowledge:

"His [Caesar's] big trouble was that he didn't know when to stop. As I've told you, Alexander suffered from the same thing, and you'll find men like that all through history, most recently, of course, Hitler, and if we'd let him get away with it, Stalin had the same thing in mind."

I don't know about Elmer Twyman, who became a doctor, but Harry and Charlie Ross were also fond of the works of Cicero, and for a time they worked on their own translation of some of his works. "The good of the people is the chief law. . . . The harvest of old age is the recollection and abundance of blessings previously secured."

Harry and Charlie never finished the translation. Charlie went off to the University of Missouri, and Harry, whose father, John, had fallen on bad times—he was a man who failed at things—had to take a job in what was called "the zoo" of a bank in Kansas City, salary $35 a month.

"Old Cicero," as Harry called him, "his full name was Marcus Tullius Cicero, you know," wrote: "If you aspire to the highest place it is no disgrace to stop at the second, or even the third."

Harry never aspired to high place, but he got it, and he described it the way he described everything else in terms that were, I suppose, corny, but elemental as well, simple, pure: "That job I had in the White House, it wasn't so very different from other jobs, and I didn't let it worry me. Worrying never does you any good. So I've never worried about things much. The only thing that I ever do worry about is to be sure that where I'm responsible that the job is properly done. I've always tried my best and to some extent have succeeded in doing the job as well as it's been done before me.

"When I was in school, I used to always sit around for a week or two . . . I skipped a grade or two while I was going through school . . . before I found out what it was all about, and then I'd go on from there."

When you got that job as you call it in the White House, you didn't really have any time to sit around and find out what it was all about.

"No, no. Like I told you, I was sworn in one night, and the next morning I had to get right on to the job at hand. I was plenty scared, but, of course, I didn't let anybody see it, and I knew that I wouldn't be called on to do anything that I wasn't capable of doing. That's another thing you learn from reading your history. People in the past have had much bigger burdens than you've ever been asked to assume, and somehow, the best of them just went ahead and did what they were called upon to do. And they usually made out all right."

Yes, *remarkable.*

Early in 1962 it became painfully apparent that the networks were not interested in what we then called *The Truman Series.* A cardinal reason for the lack of interest on the part of the networks was that Harry Truman was then still "a controversial figure." The fearsome years of the blacklist were not yet quite over. And Mr. Truman somehow intuitively sensed that long before the rest of us were ready to admit it.

While I was still seeing him with some regularity in Independence, he made a trip to Los Angeles, where he spoke at one of the universities, and I had been briefed by Noyes on an incident that happened off campus. I said, *Mr. President, I understand that you had a little exchange with General Sarnoff* [then chairman of the board and president of the Radio Corporation of America, which, of course, includes the National Broadcasting Company] *out in Los Angeles.*

The President was delighted that I'd heard. He said,

"Yes. We both got on the same elevator at the Beverly Hilton Hotel out there, and I looked down, and he'd broken his leg. Or his toe. I forget which. But it was in a big cast and was all bandaged up.

"I just looked at him kind of sideways, and I said, 'Well, General, I guess now for a while you'll have to kick people in the ass with the other leg, won't you?' He was so nervous that he got off at the next stop, although I don't think that's what he had in mind doing."

That particular session ended with what I guess you'd call the sound of general merriment. The President laughed the most of all; he almost always did.

No, Harry Truman was not impressed with wealth and power. One day I said, *Mr. President, I understand you had a little exchange with Henry Luce at the time he published your* Memoirs *in* Life *magazine.*

"That's true. I did. His magazines never did tell the truth about me. And in 1948 during the campaign they took all those pictures at places I spoke trying to prove there weren't any crowds turning out for my speeches, which was a damn lie, of course. They say pictures don't lie, but they do. Pictures can lie just as much as words if that's what the big editors and publishers set out to do.

"And those Luce magazines are just too damn big anyway. They've got too much power over people and what they think, and I've always been against that. And the big publishers have always been against me. It started out with the Kansas City *Star*. It was always against me, and I guess it still is, although they had to admit when I was presiding judge that I'd done some good things for the county. But as I say, big publishers, I've always been against them, although maybe I shouldn't say that because my son-in-law, who is just the nicest boy he can be, is associated with a big paper himself, the New York *Times*.

"But what you asked me about. Old Luce and I met at the time *Life* magazine had agreed to buy the *Memoirs,* and there was a party given to celebrate.

"Luce and I were introduced, and he said he was very glad to meet me. I said, 'Mr. Luce, a man like you must

have trouble sleeping at night. Because your job is to inform people, but what you do is misinform them.'

"Well, old Luce got red in the face, and Sam Rosen-
man came up to me—he was Roosevelt's friend and mine
and he was one of the lawyers in charge of drawing up the
papers—and he came up to me and said, 'Harry, be careful. We haven't signed all the papers yet. If you make him
mad, maybe he won't sign up.' I said that wasn't true,
that Luce needed us a hell of a lot more than we needed
him, and in the end it turned out that was true.

"I talked to Luce once more that same night. A little
later, maybe when I was leaving. I don't remember. He
came over, and he said that he thought if he and I just had
the time to talk things over, we'd find we agreed on most
things.

"I told him I doubted that very much, and I did, and I
I still do."

The last time I talked with Mr. Truman was in a projec-
tion room in New York. I was leaving the following day
for Spain, and some friends were giving me a farewell
party that night. Without telling me, they had sent a note
to the Carlyle asking the President to attend.

They thought it would be great fun if he walked in un-
announced. "After two drinks," they said that night, "everybody would have thought he was that actor in *Call Me
Madam*. They'd have started slapping him on the back,
and. . . ."

When I found out about the invitation, I was embarrassed, but I needn't have been.

"I'd very much like to come," said the President. "But
the Boss and I are leaving for Independence this evening.
Please apologize to your friends for me.

"We don't get out very much when we're in New York,"
he said.

I almost had the feeling that maybe he would have liked
to come.

Was I going to Spain to write a book?

Well, I said, not exactly, though out of my experience

might, I hoped, come several books. Actually, though, I was just going to look and loaf.

For how long?

"Three months," I said, "maybe a little more, maybe a little less."

The President made no comment, but by then I knew enough about him to realize that he was shocked at the idea of a man in his forties taking three months off to "look around and loaf."

I thanked him for his patience and said that I hoped all the time we spent together wouldn't turn out to have been wasted.

"It couldn't possibly be," said the President. "I think you learned a little something, and I enjoyed teaching it to you. I've told you, if I hadn't got into this other business, I might have turned out to be a teacher, and if I do say so, I don't think I'd have been so bad at it."

That was the last time I spoke to the President. The last time I saw him was in September, 1969. I was in Independence to write a profile of the town for *Holiday,* and at the library I was told that he saw almost nobody anymore and except when the weather was good no longer went on his morning walks. Miss Sue Gentry, the gentle woman who until her recent retirement had been writing about the Trumans for the Independence *Examiner* since 1929, always with affection, had seen him a few mornings before, and the sight had saddened her. "He used to be such a joyful man. No matter where he was or what he had to do, even in the White House, he was never too busy to make a joke. But now——" She hesitated a moment to choose the exact words. "There is no smile in him anymore."

I saw the President the last day I was there.

It was a little after 8 A.M., and the September air was immaculate. About half a block from the Truman house I saw the President coming toward me. He had shrunk in size, as old men do (I was told he weighted fifty pounds less than when he was in the White House, less certainly

than when I had talked with him), and his clothes hung
loosely on the frail body. He was walking very slowly, no
longer the one hundred and twenty-two steps a minute
he'd learned in the Army and followed so many years
thereafter. He was leaning on the once-jaunty cane as if
without its support he would fall. His head was bowed, his
shoulders slumped; clearly, there was no smile in him
anymore.

I was across the street, and the President passed me,
and though shrunken, he still seemed to me to be very
large against the sky.

I did not call out to him. He would not have wanted
that. On the morning of his eightieth birthday he told
reporters, "Remember me as I was, not as I am."

Myself, I would remember a bitter cold morning in
November, 1961. It was below zero, and there was a hint
of snow in the air. The President had just returned from
visiting his old friend Sam Rayburn, who was Speaker of
the House longer than any man in American history. Mr.
Sam was dying of cancer at his home in Bonham, Texas.
The news had been an awful blow to the President. He had
said sometime before with, I felt, a mingling of rue and
regret, "It sometimes seems to me that all I do anymore
is go to funerals."

In any case, when he returned from Texas, he looked
very much older and sadder.

On this particular inhospitable morning the inept film
crew, every member of it, gathered outside the house at
219 North Delaware at 4:30 A.M.

Miss Gertrude Stein may have been perfectly right
when she said that a dawn can be very beautiful depending
on which end of the day you see it from. But surely she
was speaking of Parisian dawns, summer Parisian dawns.
A November dawn in Independence was not beautiful,
never ever.

But we were through some miracle ready when, as
planned, the light went on in the President's bedroom. A
few minutes later he was to appear at the front door, come

down the steps, pick up the morning newspaper, and go back inside the house.

When the door opened, however, Mrs. Truman came out on the porch. She said that the President was not feeling well, and she was afraid he wouldn't be on hand for the walk we had been planning to film later that morning. Moreover, she was certain that he would not be able to come to the library for the filmed interview we had set up for that afternoon.

The director thanked her and quietly dismissed the crew.

After I'd had breakfast, I went out to the library to do some research. I was sitting in a room next to the President's office when, at a few minutes after eight, he walked in.

The pink complexion was white, and his eyes were tired and faded. He came up to me and said, "I'm very sorry I wasn't out there this morning."

There were sudden tears in my eyes, but I managed to say, "That's all right, Mr. President. You were ill."

"I know," he said, "but I like to live up to my obligations."

1

The Happiest Childhood

One week in Independence I didn't talk to anyone who was less than seventy-five years old, and it was one of the pleasantest weeks of my life. People live a long time in and around Independence, and they have long memories. What's more they seem to have, all of them I talked to anyway, something in common with Mr. Truman. They have character.

I guess my favorite among them was Miss Ethel Noland, who was then seventy-nine years old, two years older than the President. She had lived her entire life in a house across the street from 219 North Delaware. Miss Noland, the Truman family historian, was a retired teacher, and if her sentences seem to have a certain sweep and grandeur to them that is perhaps because she not only read Gibbon's *Decline and Fall of the Roman Empire* with frequency, but also read, for pleasure, mind you, *The Iliad* and *The Odyssey* in the original Greek.

The only uneasy time I had with Miss Noland was when I had to tell her that it would be necessary for me to reach inside her bodice to hook up a throat microphone that she was to wear during one filming session.

I mentioned the matter to her with suitable diffidence, and after a moment she smiled and said, "Oh, that's quite all right. I do have a male doctor, after all, and this is almost the same thing, isn't it?"

I asked Miss Noland how she managed to keep busy since her retirement. That was not really a problem, she said. There was, first of all, her diary. She had been keeping it daily for more than sixty years. I said that that would surely be a valuable historical document, but Miss Noland said, "Oh, no, I have no intention of allowing it to be published, even should someone wish to do so. I kept it for my own satisfaction only, and that is the way it will remain. We are all very private people around here."

In addition to keeping the diary, Miss Noland went on, there were the meetings of the Historical Society, the Browning Society, the Tennyson Club, the group that discusses current events, and the Mary Paxon Study Class. That's for ladies who find themselves going stale."

In addition, she was taking a course in modern drama taught by a young professor from the University of Kansas City. She mentioned having read the plays of Beckett, Arthur Miller, John Osborne, and Ionesco. She liked both Miller and Beckett. Of Osborne she said only, "Are things really that bad in England?" Of Ionesco, "I'm very much afraid that he escaped me completely."

I asked if her class had yet read any of Tennessee Williams.

"No," said Miss Noland, with a saintly smile, "that we still have to look forward to."

One day I asked Miss Noland, *Do you think Harry Truman had a happy childhood?*

"Well, of course, happiness, that is not easy to say about anyone really, is it? It is so close to being an indefinable word, and one is never quite sure—is one?—whether one is really quite happy. But Mr. Truman and I are first cousins, and I have known him, have observed him all his life, and I should say that, yes, I believe he had a happy childhood and one that was secure. Secure in the love of those, his family first, of course, but all of those who knew him. His family were all of them loving people.

"It should, I believe, be pointed out that his early environment was not nearly as poverty-stricken as many of the biographers have for some reason felt it necessary to portray. I think he has suffered a little bit from the image that has been put before the public. The fact that he did not come from a very rich family has, I think, been exaggerated.

"What has not been pointed out is that they were always very comfortable, very free of financial anxiety.

"And, of course, the picture of Mr. Truman's mother that people have been given is simply not true at all. She has been portrayed as, I believe you could say, a country bumpkin, and that is simply not the case.

"Mr. Truman's mother studied art and music at the Baptist Female College down in Lexington, Missouri. She played the piano, and she had a most remarkable idea of the proper values in life. One of them was music. Another was books. If she thought that money should be spent for a piano or for music lessons, she spent it that way.

"She never deviated from her idea of what was right, and she didn't let her children do that either. She had just about the finest set of values I have ever known. She was the type of mother that you would think would furnish a President for the United States. Her principles were so sound. Her discipline was so fine that greatness seemed to grow out of it.

"These days more and more people are beginning to act like Jimmy Hoffa, and it sometimes seems to me that a great many people are beginning to look like him, too.

"There are many things about this modern time that are desirable and good and amazing. But there are things that are fine and substantial and eternal about the nineteenth century that we will do well to hold on to. And Harry Truman is very much a man of the nineteenth century. His mother I think represented the best of those values.

"She was a most unusual woman."

Mary Jane Truman: "I suppose all of us think that we have . . . a most unusual mother, but I think it truly can be said that our mother was a very fine woman. I don't believe that she had an enemy in the world, and even after my brother Harry got to be President, she couldn't resist inviting everybody in. If anybody came to our door, why, they were always welcome. Mamma would go to the door, and regardless of who they might be, she would ask them in. And sometimes we had a little difficulty because people who came were sometimes not what they should have been mentally. So we decided it was time to put up a fence and have the gate locked.

"Sometimes it wasn't really very convenient. But it was

really the best thing that could have been done under the circumstances because my mother was in her nineties, and we just had to protect her from everybody seeing her, although she didn't like it at all. She just wanted to be friendly with everybody in the entire world.

"When my mother and I went to Washington not long after Harry got to be President, my brother went to the plane to take her out, and when she saw all those people, she said, 'My goodness, Harry, if I'd known this was going to happen, I wouldn't have come.' Of course, everybody quoted that, and we all laughed at her, and everybody thought she was serious. But I saw that she had a twinkle in her eye, and she had a fine sense of humor just generally, and a lot of the time when people took her seriously, she was making a joke. I don't know why people couldn't see that."

Harry Truman: "When my mother and sister came to Washington at the time I was . . . in the White House, my brother had told my mother that the one bed that was not occupied was the one in the Lincoln Room, and she said, 'You tell Harry if he tries to put me in Lincoln's bed, I'll sleep on the floor,' and she would have. But I had reserved the Rose Room, which is where the queens and princesses and everybody stay, and I took her back there when she arrived, and my sister was with her. And I said, 'Mommy, here's your room.' And there was a great four-poster bed that takes a stepladder to get into—it's that high above the floor—and she looked at me and said, 'Harry, do you expect me to sleep in that thing? Is that the only bed you've got in this big house?' I said, 'No, there's several more.'

"She went around and looked in the adjoining room where the maid to the queens and princesses and that sort of thing stayed, and there was a nice little single bed in there. She said, 'That's where I'll stay,' and she did.

"She was always a woman who did the right thing, and she taught us, my brother and sister and I, that, too. We were taught that punishment always followed transgression, and where she was concerned, it always did. I was punished, and it hurt, and I tried never to do whatever it was again. They say that isn't the way to do it now, and they may be right. I don't know. All I know is that's the way I was brought up."

Judge Albert A. Ridge of the U.S. District Court in Kansas City and a veteran of Battery D: "Harry Truman grew up in a society in which a man's word was his bond. If a man's word could be trusted there was no place he couldn't go. Nobody around here ever doubted Harry Truman's word.

"When Harry was a boy, it seems to me there was more a sense of moral values than there is now, more a sense of community life. Harry Truman was brought up in that kind of life—as almost all of us were, even though we lived here in Kansas City instead of in Independence. What I'm getting at, when someone on the block got sick, my mother would go and take care of them. And if she would get sick, the neighbors would come and take care of her.

"And we weren't too proud to go next door and borrow a cup of sugar. And if we had anything that the people next door needed, why, they were welcome to it. That was the sort of era I'm talking about. Mr. Truman grew up to be a man who's devoid, I think—as men generally were in those days—of an ability to hide their faults and pretensions under that cloak of public attitude that so many public men take refuge in. Harry Truman never learned to put on a public face, and he never had a public manner. He just never learned how to be anybody except himself."

Mr. President, Judge Ridge says that in this part of the country a man's word was very important when you were a boy. A man had to stand by his word, and that's the way you were brought up.

"That's true. Unless you were a man who stood by what he said, you were not well thought of around here and you never got very far, never got anywhere at all in this part of the country.

"And you never had to sign a piece of paper when you made a bargain. If you made a trade with a man, if you said you'd take so much for so many head of cattle, why, that was what you agreed on, and if the fella you'd made the bargain with came along later, it never did matter how much time had passed or if the price might have changed in the meantime, you just lived up to what you had agreed on at that earlier time. That's what your word meant.

"In those days, in the time I was growing up and when I was a young man, people thought more of an honest man than any one thing, and if a man wasn't honest, he wouldn't stay long in the neighborhood. They would run him out.

"And I have never changed my mind since. You have to stick by your word. Trust is . . . why, it has always seemed to me that unless you can trust a man and he can trust you, why, everything breaks down."

You seem to be saying that trust is like a cement that holds everything together, holds society together.

"That's a very good way to put it, yes, trust is absolutely fundamental in every possible kind of relationship, and in government. . . . If the people can't trust their government, the people in their government, the whole works will fall apart."

Edgar Hinde, the former postmaster of Independence and a veteran of Battery D: "Around here if a man gives his word, we expect him to keep it, and Harry Truman always kept his word. I never heard of him breaking his word to anybody. When he told you something, you could go home and sleep on it. That was it."

Harry Truman: "I had just the happiest childhood that could ever be imagined. My brother, Vivian, and I and two or three of the neighborhood boys used to have a great time playing in the pasture south of the house out at Grandview. There was forty acres in bluegrass, and it had a little draw that ran through it, and there was a spring right in the middle. And we used to catch tadpoles and have a big time over that.

"It was a wonderful place for small boys to enjoy themselves. There wasn't any place they could go that they'd get lost, although once in a while one of them would wander over in the cornfield and get lost. I did myself. I had a dog, a little black and tan dog named Tandy, and I also had a big Maltese cat named Bob. The reason he was called Bob is that he was sleeping in front of the fireplace in the old house one time, and a coal popped out and burned off his tail.

"Bob and Tandy always followed me everywhere I went, so when I got lost over in the cornfield, my folks could watch this dog and cat working in and out among the cornstalks, catching field mice. I must have been three and a half or four years old, and I suppose I got a good spanking for running away. I don't remember the spanking, but I do remember the trip through the cornfield.

"Those were most pleasant periods of time. We had a great big swing out in the backyard in one of the big old elm trees that was there. It's gone now. And we had a hammock made out of barrel staves that hung on the north porch. And even after we moved to Independence and began to go to school, in the summertime we would go out to Grandview and spend some happy times during the vacation, my brother and I together and sometimes each one of us by himself.

"Then the rest of the kinfolk, cousins who were about our size, usually would come out there, and we would have a real time when that happened, celebrating the Fourth of July or Christmas or whatever it happened to be.

"I once read some place that a happy childhood is a very, very rare thing, and I'm sure that that is true, but I can honestly say I had one. . . . Of course, we didn't have all the places to go and things to do that kids do now, and a lot of them don't see how they can get along if they don't have them. But I guess if you don't know what you're missing, you don't miss it, and so, of course, when I was a boy, we didn't have cars and movies and television and radio, none of that. We played. My mother played, and my sister and I played the piano, and we always had a houseful of books, and we read.

"And of course, we all had our chores to do, and we went to bed early and got up early and were always busy."

Were you ever bored?

"Oh, my, no. We didn't know the meaning of the word, and I'll tell you another thing. I can't remember being bored, not once in my whole life. How in the world can you be bored if you have things to think about, which I must say I always have?"

Mr. President, do you think those were better times, when you were a boy?

"Oh, I don't know about that. Comparisons like that. They're so easy to make, but I'm not sure they're ever right."

He thought for a moment, and then he said, "The only thing I'm sure of: People weren't so *nervous* then. All these things people have now that are supposed to entertain them and all. They just seem to end up by making everybody *nervous*."

Mary Jane Truman: "I don't think I could have had two nicer brothers than my brother Vivian and my brother Harry. And I suspect that maybe I took advantage of it just a little. I think they used to think I was kind of hard to live with once in a while. But my brother Harry always saw to it that I could go where I wanted to go. If there wasn't anyone else to take me, he would take me. I sometimes think that's why I never did get married. I just never met anybody who was as nice to me as Harry.

"When I was a baby, Harry used to sit on a rocking chair and sing me to sleep, and he braided my hair, and when I was outdoors, he wouldn't let me out of his sight. He was so afraid I'd hurt myself.

"He just couldn't have been nicer—and Vivian, too, of course.

"We played almost all of the games that children played in those days, and we all three had a horse to ride and did quite a bit of horseback riding. I remember one horse in particular—we called him Old Bill—and he wouldn't let the boys catch him. But I could go out and catch him in the pasture or anywhere else because I usually carried a biscuit or a piece of cake or something for him. He'd eat anything.

"He was the old buggy horse, and we drove him for years. We still had him when my brother Harry went to the First World War, and I drove him all during that time and then bought a car in the spring of 1919, shortly after my brother came home. But Old Bill was still there. We kept him as long as he lived."

One sunny summer afternoon Miss Mary Jane and I were standing on the tiny plot of land that was all that was left of the Truman home place at Grandview.

Most of the land had been turned into a neon-lighted shopping center that, naturally, is called Truman Corners. It was dominated by a large electric cat over a drugstore. The cat had malevolent brown eyes that lighted up at night, and it revolved endlessly behind the old barn in which Mary Jane, Vivian, and Harry used to play.

As Miss Truman and I stood in the field near the barn, the cat eyed us menacingly. An old C-47 groaned overhead, and there were the sounds and smells of trucks on their way to the grime and smog of downtown Kansas City. A voice on a loudspeaker shouted out a then-popular rock-and-roll song, and there was the competing noise of a disc jockey from the radio in a TV appliance store.

Miss Mary Jane listened for a moment.

"It used to be so quiet," she said, "and you could plow the north eighty without taking the plow out of the ground. It's all changed so much."

She looked around again.

"Well," she said. "That's progress. At least they say it is."

Ethel Noland: "Of course, really to understand Mr. Truman's boyhood, you must be aware that he was always reading. Just everything. He had a real feeling for history, that it wasn't something in a book, that it was part of life —a section of life of a former time, that it was of interest because it had to do with people.

"And I think that Harry had a sense of history during his entire career, that what he was living through was making history, not in a spectacular way. It was just a section of life. I think he understood a great deal about what it meant to be President that a person would not understand who had not had his background and his sort of boyhood and young manhood—serious but not dull. Thoughtful is the word that I would use. Harry was always thoughtful."

Henry Chiles, a childhood neighbor of Harry Truman: "Kids are always having an argument, and any kind of knowledge—well, Harry generally had it, and we didn't. We'd save up questions for him when he wasn't there. We'd play Dalton and the James gang, and Harry would set us straight on how many bank robbers there was and how many Daltons got killed. He'd tell us that. We didn't know. We didn't care. We was just shooting each other.

"And Harry always got good grades. Now don't ask me about mine because I just got by. That's probably the reason Harry got to be President and I'm just an old dirt farmer."

Morton Chiles: "I'm ashamed to admit it now, but we used to call Harry a sissy. He wore glasses and didn't play our games. He carried books, and we'd carry a baseball bat. So we called him a sissy."

One afternoon when I was discussing the decision to intervene in Korea with *General Omar Bradley* he said:
"President Truman was always reading things. I've been at his office when he was President at practically all hours, from six in the morning to as late as eleven o'clock at night, Saturdays, Sundays, weekdays, and I almost always found him at a desk with a bunch of papers in front of him, studying those papers.

"Now I know some people think that's going into too much detail. But from my own experience I found that even though I might be commanding a large unit, I had to know enough of the details to get a true picture of the big picture—the big problem. And I think that that was one of the attributes of President Truman. He always knew enough of the details to know what the big problem was.

"I did find him one time not behind a desk. This was about eleven o'clock at night when I took a message over to get clearance on it. I found him in his dressing room, reading a book. Before I left, I commented that I was glad to find him not working but reading a book. And he held up the book for me to see. The subject of it was the economics of government. So I still didn't catch him dead-beating it. He was thinking about his job."

Dean Acheson, Mr. Truman's Secretary of State, said, "Mr. Truman read, I sometimes think, more than any of the rest of us. It was never necessary to *digest* anything for him, to simplify, to make it understandable to the . . . shall I say *meanest* intellect. Mr. Truman read the documents themselves, and he understood and acted on them. It was, I believe, the habit of reading and, moreover and possibly more important, of *understanding* that followed all through his life, from his boyhood on."

I mentioned to Mr. Acheson that I had read that General Eisenhower wasn't much of a reader except for the Western novels of Zane Grey, and he said, yes, he had heard that, too, and added, "I doubt very much if a man whose main literary interests are in the works of Mr. Grey, admirable as they be, is particularly well equipped to be chief executive of this country—particularly where *Indian* affairs are concerned.

"Of course literacy is not an absolute essential for the Presidency. So far as I know it is not anywhere written into the Constitution as a requirement, but somehow, I do feel more *relaxed* with a *literate* man in the White House."

Mr. President, can you remember a time when you haven't read?

"No, I can't, not unless I was sick, and even then if I could manage it, I'd prop up a book and read on the sickbed. I read the Bible clear through twice before I went to school. My mother taught me to read, and my father, too, of course. I guess I read the Bible because the type was large, but then it developed about the time I was six years old, it was then that we first noticed it, that I had flat eyeballs. So my mother took me to a doctor, and he tested my eyes and gave me a pair of glasses, and I've worn them ever since.

"But glasses or not, I never stopped reading. I've never regretted it either, and I suppose considering the fact that I became President of the United States, it wasn't time wasted.

"And as I think I told you yesterday, when I was about ten, my mother gave me a little blackboard on the back of which was a column of about four or five paragraphs on every President up to that time, which included Grover Cleveland. And that's how I started getting interested in the Presidency and in the history of this country."

I mentioned that someplace not too long before, President Kennedy had made a speech in which he listed a whole series of books he had read recently. I said that to my knowledge Mr. Truman had never done that.

"Well, no. I never thought reading was something you went around bragging about. It was just something you did. And when I was a boy you kept as quiet about it as you possibly could. Reading wasn't any too . . . wasn't the most popular thing to do around these parts."

Mr. President, tell me about your first job.

"Well, when I was ten, maybe eleven years old, I got a job at Jim Clinton's drugstore on the northeast corner of the square in Independence. I had to get there at six thirty in the morning and set up the place so that when Mr. Clinton came down, he would find everything in order. I'd mop the floor and dust off the bottles and wipe off the counters, and then I'd wake Jim Clinton at seven."

Did you ever have any early-morning customers?

"Oh, yes, a great many. The people who were church members, the high hats in town, the ones who were afraid to go into a saloon and buy a drink, they'd come in, and I'd have to set out a bottle of whiskey, and they'd pay a dime for a drink before most people were up and around to see them. They'd put their dimes on the counter, and I'd leave all those dimes there until Mr. Clinton came in, and he'd put them in the cash register.

"All those fancy high hats, they'd say, 'Harry, give me a drink,' and I'd do it. And that's where I got my idea of what prohibitionists and high hats are. That's the reason some of them didn't like me. Because they knew I knew their background and their history.

"There were saloons all around the square, and the tough old birds who didn't give a damn about what people think, they'd go into the saloons and buy a drink when they wanted it. But as I say, the so-called *good* people, the fancy ones, they'd come in and buy a drink behind the prescription counter from a boy who didn't have any right to sell it to them.

"But that's the way I got to . . . well, feel a lack of respect for the counterfeits, and I don't care where they are. In Washington or wherever. There's a story they tell about this high hat that got to be Postmaster General of the United States. I think Mark Twain told it on him.

"He got to be Postmaster General, and he came back to his hometown to visit, and there wasn't anybody at the station to meet him but the village idiot. And the high hat wanted to know what people in the town had said when they found out he was Postmaster General.

"And the village idiot said, 'They didn't say anything. They just laughed.'

"That's what happens if you're a high hat and start taking yourself too seriously."

Do you think you ever did that, Mr. President?

"I tried not to. I did my level best not to, and if I had, the Boss and Margaret wouldn't ever have let me get away with it."

Mr. President, I understand that when you were still a boy, you got a job working as timekeeper for the Santa Fe Railroad.

"I worked for an old fellow named Smith, L. J. Smith his name was, and he was head of the construction company that was building the double track for the Santa Fe Railroad down here from Eaton Falls to where the Missouri Pacific comes into the Santa Fe down at Sheffield.

"I was eighteen years old, and I'd just finished high school and knew I wasn't going to get to go to West Point. So I took this job as a timekeeper. I took it to help out at home, to keep my brother, Vivian, and my sister, Mary, in school. My father was having a hard time with finances just then.

"Old man Smith had three camps, and there were about a hundred hoboes in each camp, and I got very well acquainted with them. My job was to keep tabs on them, to keep track of how much time they put in, and then I'd write out their paychecks for them. I'd usually write those checks in a saloon on the north side of the square in Independence here, a saloon called Pogunpo's or in old man Schmidt's saloon in Sheffield. I used to sit there and pay off those hoboes. And they weren't bad fellows. They'd work for two weeks. They'd get discounted if they drew their checks before that time. So they'd work two weeks, and then they'd spend all their money for whiskey in the saloon and come back to work the next Monday morning. I'd pay them off on Saturday night.

"But they weren't bad fellows. Not in any way. Most of them had backgrounds that caused them to be hoboes. Either they'd had family troubles or they'd been in jail for some damn fool thing that wasn't a penitentary offense. But they weren't bad citizens at all. I remember one time I told the old man that ran the saloon, he was an old Dutchman and wore whiskers, I told him, I said, 'This old bastard is the blacksmith out there on the railroad, and we need him. So try to cut out on his whiskey.'

"Well, damn old Schmidt went out and told this blacksmith what I'd said, and I never got a better cussing in my life than I did for interfering with the freedom of an American citizen. And he was right. And that taught me something.

"But after that I guess the blacksmith was grateful for it because he took a file, a regular ordinary file about that long and made a butcher knife out of it and tempered it so that the edge would never come off. He made two of them for me, and I think one of them is still around the house somewhere. . . . So he didn't hold it against me that I was trying to keep him from getting drunk."

When you said camps, what were they, houses or tents?

"Tents mostly. There were tents, and I had a tricycle car on the railroad that I went up and down on. I had to make a list of the men that were working every morning at seven thirty, and then I had to go back at one thirty in the afternoon to be sure that they were still there. So when the time came for their being paid, I had the records. No one ever doubted the records I kept."

How much did those men make?

"They made eleven dollars for two weeks' work, and as I say, they'd get paid on Saturday, and by Monday morning most of them had drunk it all up. But it was one of the best experiences that I ever had because that was when I began to understand who the underdog was and what he thought about the people who were the high hats. They felt just like I did about them. They didn't have any time for them. And neither did I. I always liked the underdogs better than the high hats. I still do."

Weren't you ever uneasy? I mean, you were a reader of books and wore glasses and, as you say, you'd been called a sissy.

"No. No. I never had any trouble with those birds. They were just as nice as they could be, and when I left, the foreman down there in Sheffield said, 'Harry's all right from the navel out in every direction.' Which when you come to think of it is just about the highest compliment I ever have been paid.

"Some of those hoboes had better educations than the president of Ha-vud University, and they weren't stuck up about it either. The average of them was just as smart as the smartest people in the country, and they'd had experiences, and a lot of them told me about their experiences. I hope I profited from it, and I think I did. I had to quit at the end of the summer, but my goodness, that was a great experience for me."

I understand you learned a few cuss words that summer.

"I did. The words some of those men knew I'd never heard before, but later when I was in the Army, there was an occasion or two when those words came in handy, and I used them.

"That experience also taught me that the lower classes so called are better than the high hats and the counterfeits, and they can be trusted more, too.

"About this counterfeit business. My Grandfather Young felt the same way. We had a church in the front yard where the cemetery is now. And the Baptists and the Methodists and all of them used it. And Grandfather Young when I was six years old, he died when I was eight, he told me that whenever the customers in any of those denominations prayed too loud in the Amen corner, you'd better go home and lock your smokehouse.

"And I found that to be true. I've never cared much for the loud pray-ers or for people who do that much going on about religion."

Mrs. W. L. C. Palmer, retired teacher: "In 1898 Harry Truman came into my classes, taking Latin and mathematics, and also Bess Wallace was in the same class, and so was Charlie Ross, who was later Harry's press secretary.

"I had thought I was going to be a Greek teacher, but when it came time for me to go away to school myself, my

father asked me where I wanted to go, and I said I wanted
to go to Missouri University. 'Well,' he said, 'they dance.
and play cards down there, and you can't go.' So he sent
me to a little Methodist school where I took four years of
Greek and four of Latin and four years of mathematics,
which were required before you could graduate.

"I came as a teacher of Latin and mathematics, and I
remember in my first classes I had Nellie and Ethel Noland, cousins of Harry Truman, and they were both excel-
lent pupils and both took Latin. When I finished college,
I had thought I was going to be a Greek teacher, as I said,
but I found there was no Greek in the local high school.
But Nellie and Ethel were very much interested in Greek,
so they organized a little private class, so I did have Greek
for one year.

"I had Harry in my classes for the years 1898 and 1899
and 1900. And then I married the principal of the high
school, Professor W. L. C. Palmer. And there was a rule
against married teachers in the schools. So I'm sorry to
say I wasn't a teacher the year he graduated. That was in
1901.

"The night they were graduated from high school—
Harry, Bess, and Charlie Ross—Harry didn't get the highest grades, and he didn't win the English prize. Charlie
Ross did, and at the end of the program, Miss Matilda
Brown, the teacher of English, went up on the stage and
kissed Charlie Ross. Harry Truman was standing nearby,
and he said to Miss Brown, 'Don't I get one, too?' And
Miss Brown said, 'Not until you've done something to deserve it.'

"Well, after Harry Truman became President of the
United States, Charlie, who had been a correspondent for
the St. Louis *Post-Dispatch,* became his press secretary.
He wouldn't receive as high a salary, but nevertheless it
was such an honor that he couldn't turn it down. And the
first night they were together, Charlie said to Harry,
'Wouldn't Miss Tillie be glad to know we're together
again?' And Harry picked up the phone and put in a call
for Independence and Miss Matilda Brown, and he said,

'Miss Brown, this is the President of the United States. Do I get that kiss now?'

"And she said, 'Yes, come and get it.' But I understand that he never did go and get it, so Miss Brown told me. I think she was very much disappointed.

"The first high school paper was put out in 1901, and Harry had a good deal to do with seeing that it got out. When I think of the motto of that high school paper, *The Gleam,* from the poem *Merlin and the Gleam,* which had been published not too long before, in 18 and 89 I believe you will discover, when I think of that motto, I feel that Harry Truman all through the years of his life has followed that gleam, and I'd like to quote it for you:

> Not of the sunlight,
> Not of the moonlight,
> Not of the starlight!
> O young Mariner,
> Down to the haven,
> Call your companions, —
> Launch your vessel
> And crowd your canvas,
> And, ere it vanishes
> Over the margin,
> After it, follow it,
> Follow the Gleam.*

"I believe that that is what Harry Truman has done his whole life through."

* Alfred, Lord Tennyson

2

Some Ancestors

Mr. President, did your grandparents have slaves?

"Oh, yes. They all had slaves. They brought them out here with them from Kentucky. Most of the slaves were wedding presents."

Was that a custom at the time, to give slaves as wedding presents?

"Yes, it was quite common. When a young couple got married, they got a few slaves to start out housekeeping with."

How many would an average family have, would you say?

"Five or six. They'd have a cook and a nurse for the children and a maid-of-all-work. Then maybe they'd have a couple of field hands to go along with them."

Why do you think your grandparents came here?

"I don't know why except that they thought it was a good place to start a new life. As it turned out to be. . . . In those days, I'm speaking of the 1840's now, Independence was where people who were going West made their equipment secure and got ready to start. The trails all began here, the Santa Fe Trail and the Oregon and the Mormon trails. They all started here in Independence."

Why here?

"It was convenient. The Missouri River makes a big bend up here, about ten miles from here, and there was a landing place a little east of what is now Courtney. Then it was called Blue Hills.

"Then they had a landing place west of Courtney called Wayne City Landing, and Independence built a railroad from Wayne City Landing to the city up here. That was the first railroad west of the Mississippi River. We used to play out there when I was a youngster. They only tore up the last part of that old railroad in the 1890's."

Mr. President, what kind of people came up and down the river in steamboats? Or were there steamboats?

"All the best sort of people came here by steamboat. All my ancestors came out here that way. The steamboats plied regularly between Wayne City Landing and St. Louis, and my grandparents got on the Ohio River at Louisville, and the steamboats ran from Louisville to St. Louis. Then they changed boats, and the Missouri River boats ran from St. Louis to Wayne City Landing and eventually to Westport Landing at the foot of Grandview Avenue in Kansas City.

"Solomon Young and grandmother, Harriet Louisa Young, came here in 1841, and my other grandfather, Anderson Shippe Truman, came a few years later."

I read in Jonathan Daniels' book, The Man of Independence, *that it was in 1846.*

"That book is filled with a lot of bunk; I don't know what got into Daniels. He used to work for me when I was President, and he worked for Roosevelt, and I liked him. But when he wrote that book, he just seemed to go haywire in places.

"But if he said it was 1846, it probably was. He got most things like that right. . . . Now they say my grandmother, my maternal grandmother, Mary Jane Holmes, got here first and went all the way back to Shelbyville to find my grandfather and marry him. . . . Anyway, they got married back there, although they say my great-grandfather, William Truman, was against it. I don't know the truth of it.

"But all four of my grandparents did originally come here from Kentucky. They may have known each other back there. I'm not sure. They came from Shelbyville in Shelby County. But whether they knew each other or not, they became very well acquainted when they got here. They eventually settled as neighbors no more than three or four miles apart. And a distance like that made them close neighbors in those days.

"In those days you could enter land, buy it for a dollar twenty-five an acre, and most of those old pioneers entered a hundred and sixty acres, but both my grandfathers entered more than that.

"Grandfather Young kept buying land wherever he could get his hands on it, and at one time he owned five thousand acres out in the southwest corner of Jackson County. He also owned almost the whole of what later became Sacramento, California. He owned about forty thousand acres of land, although it was in Spanish leagues, I don't know how many leagues it was. But forty thousand acres, and if you go back far enough you'll find his name on the title of nearly every lot in Sacramento. It was just a bit ranch at the time he owned it, and he had to sell it because one of the partners of his wagon train went broke, and my Grandfather Young had to pay off his debts."

Mr. President, if he hadn't sold that land, I guess you would have been born rich.

"I guess that's true, but people who spend too much time thinking about things like that are likely to wind up feeling sorry for themselves. So I haven't given it much thought. . . . Anyway, if I'd been rich, I wouldn't have wound up President."

And given a choice. . . .

"I didn't have a choice. What's your next question?"

Yes, sir. How did your Grandfather Solomon Young get out all the way to Sacramento, California?

"Well, he was quite a man, a great big man with a beard, and he could do pretty much anything he set his mind to, and mostly he did. He ran a wagon train from here, from Independence and Westport to San Francisco and Salt Lake City and places like that. He'd have a wagon pulled by a dozen oxen or maybe that many mules, a huge wagon that could haul tons of freight, and there would be as many as twenty-four or thirty of them in a train. And the train would take all that goods to the West."

I believe Chief Justice Warren referred to that in his speech dedicating the library.

"He did. He spoke of my Grandfather Young, and he said that on trips like that, and I can quote him, on trips like that 'the timid never started and the weak died along the way.' And I don't see how it can be denied. Those trips took a year at a time. They'd start one spring and they wouldn't get back until the next. But Solomon Young did it time and again."

Did he ever have any trouble with the Indians?

"I never heard him say that they bothered him. There were two or three trainmasters that the Indians didn't disturb, and he was one of them. They were afraid of him. That's why. They knew he had the ammunition and the guns and he would shoot them if they commenced to bother him."

Did he ever take your Grandmother Young with him?

"No, she never did go. She stayed here and raised a family. They had nine children, seven of whom lived to be grown. My Grandfather Young was out West in 1861 when she had to cook all those biscuits for Jim Lane's Red Legs.*

"She was a strong woman, had the prettiest red hair I ever saw on anybody, and there wasn't a thing in the world that ever scared her. She lived until I was more than twenty-one years old. She was ninety-one, and she was one of the most charming ladies I have ever encountered."

The other day Miss Ethel Noland said that your Grandmother Young was just as stern a taskmaster as your mother. Taskmaster is Miss Noland's word.

"As she always is, Miss Noland was perfectly right. My Grandmother Young laid down the law, and nobody ever questioned it. There was no need to. In those days what was right was right, and what was wrong was wrong, and you didn't have to *talk* about it. You accepted it."

You never argued with either your mother or your grandmother when they told you to do something?

"Never. Not once. Oh, maybe when I was very young, but I always got spanked for it."

Your mother spanked you?

"Of course she did. When I misbehaved, she switched

* See Chapter 4, *Independence and the War Between the States.*

me, and I never thought anything of it. She didn't do it unless I deserved it."

Did your father ever spank you?

"No, never, but he got mad at you over something or other, he could give you a scolding that would burn the hide off of you. I'd rather have taken the licking."

How about your Grandmother and Grandfather Truman?

"Well, of course, my Grandmother Truman had been dead a long time. She died in 1879, and so none of us ever knew her. My Grandfather Truman was a farmer. He had two hundred acres of land out at Hickman's Mills. He was a very quiet man, and the two of us were very fond of each other. I was very fortunate when it came to my family. We were all very close.

"My Grandfather Anderson Shippe Truman had three girls and two boys, and when they were all married off, he sold his farm and went to live with my mother and father until he died. He died when they were running Solomon Young's old farm. And then we moved to Independence.

"We moved to Independence in 1890, and we came here so that Mary and Vivian and I would have the benefit of graded schools. They just had an old one-room schoolhouse out at Grandview, and my mother wanted us to go to graded schools, which, of course, we did. When we moved, I was six years old; my brother, Vivian, was three, and Mary Jane was one year old.

"We lived in a house on Crysler Street, and we always had a lot of livestock, cows and chickens and pigeons and everything of that kind, and the boys in the neighborhood always liked to congregate in our yard, front and back. My mother was always kind to them. She was always on the side of the boys if any of them got in trouble."

Did you ever get in trouble when you were a boy?

"Very, very seldom. I was too busy. I told you I'd read all three thousand books in the library by the time I was fourteen years old. And I went through the grade schools of Independence and the high schools, and I must have learned something that prepared me for what happened later."

Did you have any juvenile delinquency when you were growing up in Independence?

"We never heard of it. We didn't know anything about it because there was no advertising medium to tell us about something like that.

"We had bad boys but no bad girls. The girls were all above reproach and decent, but we had boys who were terrible. They usually came through all right, though, and some of them graduated at the head of their classes.

". . . But I was too busy reading books to be bad. Now the only reason you read books is so you'll get a better insight into people. The thing I found out from reading was that there is damn little information in most schoolbooks that was worth a damn. If you wanted to find out why France was against England during the Revolution and the why and wherefore of Jefferson's being able to buy Louisiana, you had to go and look it up for yourself. It didn't matter how good your teachers were. They never taught you things like that.

"And you had to find out for yourself that no two smart men ever agree on anything. Never. No two historians ever agree on what happened, and the damn thing is they both think they're telling the truth.

"But you had to find that out for yourself and that somebody with authority has to make them understand that their viewpoint and the other viewpoint can be brought together and an agreement can be reached.

"It takes a politician to do that, not a historian."

How would you define a politician?

"Why, a politician is a man who understands free government. That's all the definition there is. When he understands free government, he's a politician. If he doesn't understand it, he's a Mugwump or something, somebody who likes to cause trouble."

It seems odd, feeling as you do, that you didn't want to get into politics.

"Well, I never did. I got into politics by accident. In

1922 I had gone broke trying to run a haberdashery store, and I had to have a job. And I had a lot of good friends in Jackson County and was kin to everybody else, and so I ran for eastern judge, one of five, and I licked all the rest of them because I knew more people in the county than they did. That's all. . . . It's getting lunchtime, and the Boss is expecting me. I have time for one question more."

Mr. President, getting back to your Grandfather Solomon Young for a moment, I understand that in 1948, when you were speaking in towns of the West, you often mentioned that he had stopped his wagon train in that town. Somebody, some newspaperman, said that if Solomon Young had made that many stops, it's a wonder he ever got to Sacramento at all.

The President laughed. "Well, he never kept a record of where he stopped that I know of, and so I may have let my imagination go a little wild there every once in a while."

After all, he made several trips.

"Yes, he did, and on one of them he made a deal to sell some goods to Brigham Young, the founder of the Mormons. That was in Utah, and you can bet I made some use of that incident when I was campaigning in that state."

Do you think your grandfather would have minded?

"Of course not. He was a horse trader, you remember, and so was my father."

I understand that in 1940, when you were running for reelection to the Senate, one of your opponents said that Solomon Young was a Jew.

"Yes, they did. It wouldn't have mattered a speck if he had been, but he wasn't. They said he was a Jew, and they foreclosed the mortgage on my mother's farm. Why, there wasn't anything they didn't do to try to defeat me that year. And that's why when 1948 came along, nothing surprised me. I'd already won in 1940 against the worst campaign I can ever rightly remember. . . . But I can't get into any of that now because the Boss will skin me alive if I'm any later."

3

John Anderson Truman

Harry Truman's father was born in Jackson County in 1851 and died there in 1914 at the age of sixty-three. He was at one time or another a mule trader, a farmer, a night watchman, a grain speculator, and a road supervisor. He was a small, feisty man, fastidious in dress and manner. Everybody called him Peanuts, and while, like his son, no one ever questioned his word, he was never a financial success. He dreamed always of the lucky break, of sudden wealth, but it didn't happen.

I asked Ethel Noland if she had ever heard him lament his fate. She said, "The Trumans have never been a lamenting people."

One day I said, *Mr. President, it's quite obvious that your mother was a great woman.*

"And don't overlook my father. He was just as great as she was and had every bit as much influence on me, although my mother was naturally the one that took care of the children in the home and saw to it that they grew up in the right way.

"But my father was a fighter, and if he didn't like what you did, he'd fight you. He was an Andrew Jackson descendant, you understand, and those people are all fighters. He was five foot six and weighed a hundred and forty pounds, and he'd whip anybody up to two hundred if they got in his way.

"I've told you about counterfeits. Well, there was an old fellow who was one of the greatest orators in this part of the country. We called him Colonel Crisp. His name was Crisp, and he was a colonel by agreement. He was a real counterfeit, though, and people never did trust him.

"I was with my father when he drove out to old Crisp's place, and I held the lines, and my father said, 'Colonel, I've come to collect for that nine cords of wood. Twenty-seven dollars. Three dollars a cord.' And old Crisp says, 'You oughter have better sense than to sell me anything like that, John. You know I never pay my bills.'

"The old man hopped out of the wagon and said, 'All right. I'll take it out of your hide then.'

"Crisp says, 'Wait a minute, John. I'll pay you,' and he did. . . . He made one of his great speeches down at Lone Jack where we went to picnic the other Sunday. He was telling all about how the Battle of Lone Jack took place, and there happened to be an old man there, Abe Koger was his name. He was a friend of my father's, and he said, 'Colonel, that didn't happen that way. I was there, and I know what took place. You've misrepresented the facts.'

"Old Crisp says, 'Goddamn an eyewitness anyway. He always spoils a good story.' And then he went right on with his speech. It didn't bother him a bit. He ran for Congress time after time, but he never made it. People knew he was a counterfeit, and they wouldn't vote for him."

Did your father ever take you to hear any political speeches when you were a boy?

"Oh, yes. He never liked to miss a political meeting, and he often took me along with him. There used to be some big political meetings in this county. Before they got these things (the microphone) and the radio and the television. I remember the first good political story I ever heard. My father took me, and it was a speech by a Congressman named William S. Cowherd, who was from Kansas City. The meeting was in the southern part of the county, and there must have been—oh, I guess there were two thousand people there, and that was a good many for that time.

"I remember Cowherd talked about how the Republicans had ruined this country with their tariff acts and one thing and another. Then he proceeded to tell a story. He said an old fellow from out in these parts went to New York for some purpose, and they took him to one of

those fancy restaurants, and then they brought him a
bowl of consommé, and he looked at it and then drank it.
And they brought him a couple stalks of celery, and he
ate that, and then they brought him a lobster, and he called
the waiter over and said, 'Look here, young feller, I
drank your dishwater, and I ate your bouquet, but I'll be
damned if I'll eat that bug.'

"And Cowherd said, 'That's what the Republicans
have had to eat all this time.' [Laughter.]"

_There weren't many Republicans in these parts when
you were a boy._

"Not very many, and the ones there were had the good
sense, most of them, to keep their mouths shut about it."

Were you always interested in politics?

"I was always interested. I didn't become old enough
to vote until about 1908 or '09, but I was always a clerk
of the election at the Grandview precinct in every election,
and the Republican judges always depended on what I
had to say about the situation because they knew I knew
all the people and what they were fitted for and things of
that kind. We had one old man in the neighborhood who
was a Socialist, and it was necessary to count those votes
the same as the others.

"But at one time there were two, and one of the judges
said to me, 'Harry, do you reckon that old man voted
twice?' And I said, 'No, his son's at home.' "

_I understand that you feel you learned a good deal
about politics from Plutarch's_ Lives _and that your father
read it aloud to you when you were a boy._

"He did. We saved our dimes, threw them into the
tray of an old trunk, and they accumulated faster than
you'd think even in those days, and then my father sent
away, or maybe it was my mother, but one of them sent
away, and we got the nicest set of Shakespeare you ever
did see and a book of Plutarch's _Lives._ It had a bright-red
cover, and you're right. My father used to read me out
loud from that. And I've read Plutarch through many
times since. I never have figured out how he knew so
much. I tell you. They just don't come any better than

old Plutarch. He knew more about politics than all the other writers I've read put together.

"When I was in politics, there would be times when I tried to figure somebody out, and I could always turn to Plutarch, and nine times out of ten I'd be able to find a parallel in there. In 1940, when I was running for re-election to the Senate, there was this big apple grower named Stark trying to beat me. I'd started him out in politics, but in 1940 he was out to lick me, and I couldn't figure it out.

"But the more I thought about him, the more he reminded me of what Plutarch said about Nero. I'd done a lot of thinking about Nero. What I was interested in was how having started as well as he did, he ended up in ruin. And Plutarch said the start of his troubles was when he began to take his friends for granted and started to buy his enemies.

"And I noticed some of those same traits in old Stark. That's how I decided I could lick him, and I did, of course. Nobody thought I could, but I did. I'll tell you about that campaign at another time. . . .

"But about Plutarch. It was the same with those old birds in Greece and Rome as it is now. I told you. The only thing new in the world is the history you don't know."

"I'll always be grateful to my father for introducing me to Plutarch. The things you happen on at an early age like that stay with you for the rest of your life."

Wasn't your father at one time an overseer of roads in Grandview?

"He was, and he was a good one. At the time every man in Missouri had to give two days' work or six dollars a year to keep up the roads. Now most of the overseers took the money, put it in their pockets, and let the roads go to hell.

"That sort of thing happens all through politics, the fellow who holds out his hand for a little money, a little bribe. And it always takes two, the briber and the bribee, and I don't know who is worse.

"It was the same when I got to be the chief presiding officer of the county. I came out of county government after ten years' service a damn sight worse off financially than when I got in, and it was the same in the Senate. There were bribes all over the place, and when I got into that committee work that I'll tell you about, during the war. Why, at one time or another I could have picked up a dozen fortunes. A lot of money was lying around loose in those days, billions of dollars, and the main people who weren't getting any of it were the kids who were off doing the fighting. They weren't getting rich; they were getting killed.

"I sent a few people to the penitentiary because of that, including two brigadier generals. I think the two of them are still over there at Leavenworth.

"But as I say it's the same in every branch of government. There are those who hold out their hand, and there are those who don't. My father never took a dishonest dollar in his life.

"And he was a determined cuss. One day, when he was road supervisor, there was a big boulder across the road, and he lifted it off all by himself. He wouldn't let his crew help him. That's the kind of man he was.

"Well, it hurt him, and when we finally got him to go to the doctor . . . the hospital, it was too late. I was with him when he died. I dozed off, and when I woke up, he was gone.

"I'll never forget him, though. He was quite a man."

Mr. President, I read some place that you had started to buy some Black Angus cattle for the farm at Grandview when your father died, but that you had to sell them to pay off the doctor's bills. Is that true?

"Yes, that's true. I had some Black Angus cattle, and I had to sell them, and I never owned any again. I've had a few setbacks in my life, but I never gave up. I went right ahead and did what was required of me. After my father died, somebody had to run the farm, and so I did it."

Were there other things you'd rather have done?

"Oh, there may have been, but I didn't give it any thought, because what would have been the use of it?"

Didn't you succeed your father as overseer of the roads?

"I did, and I didn't get any richer either. We just had good roads. In those days Grandview had the best roads in the county."

Would you say your father was a success?

"He was the father of a President of the United States, and I should think that that is success enough for any man."

Independence and the War
Between the States

As I've said, to understand Harry Truman it is necessary to understand Independence. One morning early on during our conversations I said that when I first came to Independence I'd expected that it would be rather like my hometown, Marshalltown, Iowa.

"Oh, no," said Mr. Truman. "Marshalltown is the Middle West, and Independence isn't like that at all. I've been in Marshalltown, though, several times. It's a fine town, and you've got that fine cemetery.

"I think it's hard for people in the Middle West to understand what the Civil War was really like in a place like Independence and how it divided people and left scars you might say both . . . it scarred up both the land and the people, too.* It left scars, and some of them it

* Historian Albert Castel has said of that war in American Heritage, "We like to think of the Civil War as the last romantic war—as a sort of gallant duel between gentlemen. There was a certain aura of 'swords and roses" in the East, but west of the Mississippi, that neglected area of Civil War history, quite a different atmosphere prevailed. Here the fighting was grim, relentless, and utterly savage—a 'battle to the knife, and the knife to the hilt.'

"Nowhere was this more true than in the bloody war-within-a-war that raged along the Kansas-Missouri border. There the people did not even wait for the bombardment of Fort Sumter. As early as 1855, armies of proslavery 'border ruffians' from Missouri and Anti-slavery Kansas 'jayhawkers' clashed in the fierce struggle which determined that Kansas would enter the Union as a free rather than as a slave state.

"This prelude to the Civil War engendered a mutual hatred and bitterness which, in 1861, flared into vicious reprisals and counterreprisals. As one Kansan later remarked, 'The Devil came to the border, liked it, and decided to stay awhile.' Led by Jim Lane, Charles Jennison, and Don Anthony, Kansas raiders swirled through western Missouri, looting, burning, and killing. Missouri 'bushwhackers' in turn made quick, devastating

72

took seventy-five years and longer to fade away, and in some cases I'm not at all sure they have to this day.

"Of course the people around Independence were very much involved on the Southern side of the thing, the Confederate side. The war here was a border war, what you might call a two-state war between Missouri and Kansas. The Federal troops, troops from Iowa and from Kansas, came in and wantonly destroyed houses, burned every house that they could get to and took everything out of it, furniture, fixtures, everything. My grandmother used to say, 'They stole everything loose that they could carry.' "

Mary Jane Truman: "When the Federal troops came to my Grandmother Young's house, they demanded food, and so my grandmother made biscuits. And I've heard her say that she made biscuits until her wrists were blistered from working with the dough and rolling the dough out. And then they killed hogs and just took the hams and the better part of it and left the rest.

"And I have a quilt. It was the first one that my grandmother pieced after she was married, around 1839 I think it was, and it's a beautiful old quilt, but the Federal troops took that out into the barn lot, and it was kind of wet, muddy weather, and they played cards on that quilt.

"It had to be washed so hard that it ruined the colors in the quilt, but the quilting. . . . You can still see . . . it's a star . . . what they called a star quilt, and it's a beautiful old thing. It's a keepsake but, of course, not what it would have been had it not been abused like that.

"I think I have heard my grandmother say that the place was raided at least two times during the war. And my Uncle Harrison, who was a boy of about thirteen at the time, was hanged because they thought he was telling a story about where his father was. His father was freight-

---

guerrilla forays into Kansas. Soon a border strip forty miles wide was a no man's land of desolate farmhouses, brush-grown fields, and prowling gangs of marauders."

ing across the plains and had started, I think, before the war was declared.

"So he was on his way out West, but they tried to make my uncle say that he was with the Southern Army. He told them the truth, but they wouldn't believe him. So they hanged him about three times, and he said the third time he thought he was a goner. But they finally let him down, and he lived to tell the story.

"The Federal troops tried the same thing with my Grandmother Young, tried to get her to say that my grandfather was in the Army. But she told them the same thing that my Uncle Harrison did. So they finally went away, but it was a very difficult time for all the members of our family who were alive at that time."

Harry Truman: "They tried to make my Uncle Harrison into an informer, but he wouldn't do it. He was only a boy, but he wouldn't turn informer. They tried to hang him, time and again they tried it, 'stretching his neck,' they called it, but he didn't say anything. I think he'd have died before he'd of said anything. He's the one I'm named after, and I'm happy to say that there were people . . . people around at the time who said I took after him."

Mrs. W. L. C. Palmer: "Everybody around here was very much involved in the War Between the States. My father was a native of Virginia. His name was Hopkins Hardin, and when the war came on, he joined up immediately with the Army of Northern Virginia, which was the army of Robert E. Lee, and my father was assigned to Pickett's Division [General George Edward Pickett]. My father went through many battles, all the famous battles before Gettysburg, and then at Gettysburg he was in Pickett's Charge.*

* Pickett's Charge is one of the bloodiest and most famous battles in American military history. Pickett's division was held in reserve at Gettysburg until July 3, 1863, when it led the attack on Cemetery Ridge. Three-quarters of Pickett's men were left dead or wounded in the field after the charge.

"I've heard him describe that charge so many times . . . until I can just see it. How they laid down in a wheatfield most of the morning until the order came to charge, and they did. They got up and charged. They had to go over a picket fence that they didn't know was there. I guess it was concealed by the wheat. And they were making for what was called Cemetery Ridge when my father was wounded. He'd been wounded twice, but the third time he fell on the battlefield, and he knew that General Lee's forces were defeated by the way the movement of the troops was going.

"He was on the battlefield for three days before he was found by the Sisters of Charity from Baltimore, who came out looking over the field. They took him to a hospital in Baltimore, where he recovered from a very severe wound in the hip.

"Federal officials, . . . officers from Washington, came out and asked him to take an oath of allegiance to the United States, but he refused to do it. Consequently he was kept in prison during the rest of the war, a dreadful prison down at Fort Pulaski in Georgia where there were six hundred men.

"He said he would have died if it hadn't been for my Aunt Lizzie McCurty, who had come out here to Independence in 1848. While he was in prison, Aunt Lizzie had sent him boxes of food. And when the war was over, in 1865, Aunt Lizzie wrote for him to come out here and not go back to his home in Virginia where everything was destroyed.

"So he came out here, and he met my mother, Susan Westmoreland, whose family had come from North Carolina. And they bought a farm south of town, the Pritchard Farm, and the old house is still standing there. I saw it a few days ago, and I was born on that farm, about five miles south of Independence in the year of 18 and 76.

"And of course, when I was a girl, everyone talked about the war and about the battle . . . the battles of Independence. Independence was captured three different times by the Federal troops and was recaptured each time.

The fighting . . . it was mostly guerrilla warfare, but in one battle . . . the Federal troops were very firmly entrenched in what is now the Christian Sawyer Bank downtown, and the Confederate troops were trying to take it. There were many shots fired on both sides. You can still see bullet holes in the bank where those troops fought, and then Quantrill, William Quantrill, came up, and he saw what was transpiring. And he said to whoever was in charge of the Confederate troops, he said, 'If you'll give me three hundred men, I'll get the Federal troops out of that building,' and he did. He got the three hundred men, and he drove out the Federal troops. Quite a number were taken prisoner, but the rest retreated to Kansas City. . . . But that is one of the reasons William Quantrill is a hero to many people in this part of the country."

William Clarke Quantrill was a dark, romantic-looking young man with hooded blue eyes who as a boy in Ohio was said to have enjoyed nailing snakes to trees and torturing dogs and cats; after he grew up, he emigrated to Kansas and then for unsavory reasons of his own crossed the border into Mr. Truman's Jackson County.

Among the many bloody exploits for which he was responsible was a raid on Lawrence, Kansas, during which almost the entire town was destroyed, including 150 men, most of them unarmed civilians.

As his men set fire to the town, Quantrill is alleged to have shouted, "Kill! Kill! Lawrence must be thoroughly cleansed, and the only way to cleanse it is to Kill, Kill."

That sounds like quite a mouthful to have been shouted from horseback at the beginning of a raid, but the evidence of Quantrill's bloodthirstiness is considerable. Historian Albert Castel has called him, "the bloodiest man in American history . . . in the company of Simon Girty and John Wilkes Booth as one of the great national villains."

On the other hand, the night before the Civil War conversation with Mr. Truman I was up until two drinking beer and sipping bourbon with an eighty-year-old admirer of both the President and Quantrill. The old man had a number of pictures of the President, one of them autographed, but an entire corner of his living room was devoted to a shrine to Quantrill. Among other items was a life-size photograph of him lighted the way some people light a statue of the Virgin Mary.

"If we'd had a few more like Quantrill, we'd of won the War Between the States," the old man said. "The history books are all written by Yankees. Why, Quantrill is one of the most misunderstood men in the War Between the States. I've known men who served with him, and they've said he wouldn't of hurt a fly if it wasn't that he was absolutely forced into it by the Yankees."

I asked Mr. Truman his opinion of Quantrill and his men, and he said, "I've told you that history is always written by the winners, and that's what happened in this case. In this whole border dispute the historians got only one side of it. As soon as the war was over, they had to justify what was done. Read up on the War of the Roses. It was the very same thing. It took hundreds of years before the real truth came out.

"There's a lot been written about what a terrible thing it was when Lawrence, Kansas, was destroyed, and it was a terrible thing. It never should have been allowed, but you hear very little about the towns that were destroyed here on the Missouri side, Osceola and Harrisonville and Independence. It's only now that the true facts are coming out, almost a hundred years, and it's a pity it took so long.

"But Quantrill and his men were no more bandits than the men on the other side. I've been to reunions of Quantrill's men two or three times. All they were trying to do was protect the property on the Missouri side of the line, and it was the same for the Red Legs. They were the Federal troops and were called Red Legs because they wore red leggings.

"And I've been to one or two of their reunions over in Kansas. I didn't let them know who I was, of course, but they were just the same as Quantrill's men. They set around telling lies to each other. Just like the reunions of

the soldiers in the First World War and, I suppose, of
every war there ever has been. The stories these fellas
tell, they get taller and taller with every passing year, and
after a time you can't believe a word any of them says.

"I remember one time when I came home from one of
those reunions in Kansas, and my mother said, she was
joking when she said, 'If you'd kept your eyes open, you'd
probably have seen your grandmother's silver and you
could have brought it home with you.'

". . . You can see that the War Between the States
or the Civil War, whatever you want to call it, has had
quite an impact on the people in these parts, and as I
say, some of them aren't over it yet.

"And you have to keep in mind another thing. The
Federal troops, after what happened over in Lawrence,
a . . . General Ewing issued something called Order
Number 11,* the order by which everybody in these parts
was moved into what they called posts.

"There was one in Kansas City where all my family
had to go.

"Everybody, almost the entire population of Jackson
County and Vernon and Cass and Bates counties, all of
them were depopulated, and the people had to stay in
posts.

"They called them posts, but what they were, they
were concentration camps. And most of the people had
. . . were moved in such a hurry that they had to leave
all their goods and their chattels in their houses. Then the
Federal soldiers came in and took everything that was left
and set fire to the houses.

"That didn't go down very well with the people in these
parts; putting people in concentration camps in particu-

---

* General Thomas Ewing issued Order Number 11 in August, 1863, and Mr. Truman's grandmother, Harriet Louisa
Gregg Young, loaded as many belongings as she could into an
oxcart and with six of her children, among them Harry Truman's mother, made the long journey to a "post" in Kansas
City. It was a journey that Martha Ellen Truman remembered
all her ninety-four years.

lar didn't. And the general who issued Order Number 11 never did live it down. He was from Ohio, and he went back there after the war. And he tried to run for governor and for the Senate, but he never did make it.

"The Red Legs made people . . . tried to make people sign loyalty oaths, too, and that was just a bunch of damn nonsense as it always has been and always will be. You can't *force* people to be loyal by making them sign a piece of paper, and it was the experience of my people . . . my family that made me be against loyalty oaths. And I have always been, was when I was President and before and am now.

". . . But the bad feeling that these things cause dies a very slow death. I had to overcome some of that hatred when I was president of the National Old Trails Association,* which has branches from Baltimore to Los Angeles, and I had to go over Kansas on many occasions and got to know the people over there. And I found out that they didn't have horns and tails. They were the same kind of people as we have over here. . . . I've always felt that people were pretty much the same everywhere, but isn't it a pity that we have to be *taught* that?"

Mr. President, in view of the extreme Southern sympathies of most of the members of your family and most people you grew up with in Independence, in retrospect your civil rights program of 1948 now seems even more remarkable than it did at the time.†

* In 1925, after Mr. Truman's defeat in his second race for county judge, he needed a job; he was forty-one years old and, as he has said, "completely broke and without much prospect of being any other way." He first got a job selling memberships in the Kansas City Automobile Club and later became president of the National Old Trails Association, which involved traveling all over the country to promote the idea of building highways over the famous trails that had been so important in the various historical moves West.

† In 1945 Truman, against the advice and protests of almost every admiral and general, as well as most of his civilian advisers on military affairs, ordered the integration of the armed

"As you know, in 1948 some of the Southern states walked out of the Democratic Party, but I won the election without the Solid South and without New York. Nobody'd ever done it before, and it hasn't happened since.

"There was one old woman in 1948, one of the Democratic committee ladies from one of the Southern states; I forget which one,* and she said she was just sure I hadn't meant what I said in my message to Congress, and she wanted to go back down wherever it was and tell them I hadn't meant a word I said.

"Well, the first thing I did, I read her the Bill of Rights; I doubt that she'd ever read it, probably hadn't even heard of it.

"Anyway, I read it to her, and I says to her, 'I said what I said because I meant it, and I have no intention in any way whatsoever in taking back one word, and you can go back down there and tell them what I said. Those . . . the Bill of Rights applies to everybody in this country, and don't you ever forget it.'

"I guess I lost her support for sure, but I could . . .

---

forces. In December, 1946, Truman named a Committee on Civil Rights. The report of that committee was called "To Secure These Rights," and most members of his Cabinet advised him to forget all about it, at least until after the 1948 elections.

But on February 2, 1948, Truman sent a ten-point civil rights message to Congress, asking, among other things, for a federal law against lynching, a strengthening of existing civil rights laws, a Federal Fair Employment Practices Committee, an end to Jim Crow in interstate transportation, and the protection of the right to vote.

While these demands seem mild in 1973, in 1948 they created an uproar in the South that was unprecedented in American history.

* Mrs. Leonard Thomas, a Democratic national committee-woman from Alabama. In reporting a slightly different version of the incident in *The Man from Missouri, Life and Times of Harry S. Truman,* Alfred Steinberg adds, "A Negro White House waiter got so excited listening to the argument that he accidentally knocked a cup of coffee out of Truman's hands."

you can always get along without the support of people
like that."

*Mr. President, I've often wondered whether your ex-
perience in seeing the bitterness between Kansas and Missouri after the Civil War, the things we've just been talking about, had anything to do with your sponsoring the
Marshall Plan after the Second World War.*

"Oh, yes. Very much so. I think I told you the other
day. You can't be vindictive after a war.

"After the Second World War, Europe had suffered in
the same way we had suffered after the War Between the
States, and that made me think that Europe had to be rehabilitated by the people who had destroyed it. And that's
what happened.

"But we'll get into that tomorrow. I've got a date with
the Boss in ten minutes, and she'll never let me hear the
last of it if I'm late."

The President paused at the door, and he started laughing. He said, "I was just thinking of that old woman's face
when I started reading her the Bill of Rights. It was quite
a sight. . . . But you know something? It's not a bad idea
to read those ten amendments every once in a while. Not
enough people do, and that's one of the reasons we're in
the trouble we're in."

5

Banking Days and Farming

Mr. President, in 1904 you went to work for the National Bank of Commerce in Kansas City, and in 1905 and 1906 you worked for the Union National Bank in Kansas City. Did you ever think of becoming a banker?

"No, I never did. I never liked it enough for that. I was good enough at it, I guess. I started out making thirty-five dollars a month and when I quit to go back to the farm, I was making fifty-five dollars a month, which was good money in those days. I still didn't like it much, though, and somehow it gave me a prejudice. Later I could never get myself to like very much people who make their living dealing with money. I don't like to say that, but I'm afraid it's true. We had this one old fellow, a vice-president I think he was, and he never did to my knowledge give anybody a raise. He kept a little book. I think it was a little book. Maybe it was all in his mind. But whatever it was, when anybody went to him for a raise, he could always remember something you'd done that he didn't like, and you never did get one. . . . Another thing I didn't like: I didn't have any responsibility. I just added up figures all day, and it didn't seem to me there was much of a future in it. . . .

"But that whole experience did cause me to realize that a lot of people in this world spend their time doing work they don't care much for, and that's a real pity."

I understand that you at one time lived in the same boardinghouse as General Eisenhower's brother Arthur.

"Yes, yes. We lived at a place called Mrs. Trow's boardinghouse, I believe it was called, and Arthur Eisenhower and I got along very well indeed. I'm sorry to report I can't say as much for his brother, the one you mention that went into the Army. It's too bad, too, what happened to him, because he had opportunities that no man I know had. But you take a man that has been educated in the professional military, especially if he

comes from a section of the country where all the folks
are plain folks the way that fellow did, it seems to go to
his head some way or other. I don't know what causes it,
but it's too bad. It oughtn't to happen.

"And then, when somebody like that gets into politics,
it's even worse. They never make a go of it. You'll find
that General Grant was in the same class exactly. Old
Zack Taylor was, too, and so was Benjamin Harrison.
As I say, I don't know how it happens, but when they get
into politics, those fellows, all hell breaks loose; it kicks
hell out of the country for a while, and it takes time to
get over it."

*Mr. President, several of your biographers have sug-
gested that you have great admiration for military men
and for the military. And one man whose name I won't
mention suggests that the fact that you wanted to go to
West Point proves it.*

"Well, that's a damn fool thing to say, and whoever
said it is a damn fool and I don't care how many degrees
he has or even if he's a professor at Ha-vud (an epithet)
College or some place like that. The only reason I wanted
to go to West Point was because I wanted a free education; my father'd lost his money, and that was the only
kind of education I could get. But because of my eyes,
I didn't get to go, of course. So there's no point in getting
into it. And even if I had gone, I'd have busted out in my
third year probably when they started getting into the
foreign languages. . . . The military man I liked best
you might say was General George Marshall, and he'd
have been a great man no matter what he was. It just
wouldn't have mattered at all what he was; he'd have been
the best there was at it."

*Dean Acheson wrote: "The moment General Marshall
entered a room, everyone in it felt his presence."*

"Yes, that's true. He was one of the most remarkable
men who ever lived, and one of these days I'm going to
tell you about him. I never knew anyone like him and
never will again."

Mr. President, didn't Theodore Roosevelt come to town while you were working at the bank in Kansas City?

"He did. It was in 1904 when he was President, and I went to hear him. I was working at the old National Bank of Commerce where the Commerce Trust Company is now, at Tenth and Walnut. Teddy made a trip to Kansas City and was scheduled to make a speech from the back end of a car at Tenth and Main, just a block down the street. When it came time for him to speak, half a dozen of us little clerks in 'the zoo' they called it, the cage where we worked, half a dozen of us left our desks and ran down the street to hear Teddy speak.

"He had a very high tenor voice, and it carried very well. He made a good speech, too, but nobody really wanted to hear him speak. They wanted to see him grin and show his teeth, which he did. He was a short man, only about five foot six. The Roosevelts were none of them very big people, and they all seemed to have a lot of teeth to show."

Did you like living in Kansas City?

"I liked some things about it. I went to every vaudeville show there was, and I saw some of the great ones, Weber and Fields and Eva Tanguay and Lillian Russell and 'The Four Cohans,' one of whom turned out to be the famous George M. Cohan himself. . . . I didn't have any too much spending money in those days. Arthur Eisenhower has been quoted as saying that after we'd paid all our expenses, we had a dollar left over. I don't remember how much, but I got a Saturday afternoon job either at the old Orpheum or the Grand as an usher, and I got to see the shows for free. I may have made a little bit extra, too. I don't remember. . . . I used to go to a lot of concerts in those days, too. People seemed to have more time to listen to music in those days."

Mr. President, speaking of music, I've read that when you were a boy taking piano lessons you got up at five every morning to practice. Is that true?

"Yes. When I was about seven or eight years old, we had a piano in the house, which wasn't usual at that time, although my mother played. We had a piano, and I wanted to learn how to play it. So I took a great many lessons on it and finally wound up with one of the great instructors in Kansas City. Her name was Mrs. E. C. White, and I took two lessons a week and got up every morning and practiced for two hours. . . . Mrs. White had studied with a man, one of the great teachers of the world, a man named Leschetizky, who was in Vienna and who was the teacher of Josef Lhévinne and Paderewski.

"Paderewski was in Kansas City when I was about twelve or thirteen and Mrs. White was giving me lessons on various things, and I was studying the Chopin waltzes. Chopin's A-Flat Opus 42 Waltz is one of the great pieces of music for the piano, maybe the greatest, and I played that, although never as well as I wished. . . . And I was studying the Minuet by Paderewski. And when he got through with his concert—which was a wonder—he played that Chopin A-Flat Waltz, Opus 42, which has always been a favorite of mine. And he played the waltz rendition of the 'Blue Danube,' and so on.

"When we went back behind the scenes, Mrs. White took me with her, and it almost scared me to death. She told him I didn't know how to make 'the turn' in his minuet, and he said, 'Sit down,' and he showed me how to do it. I played it at Potsdam for old Stalin. I think he was quite impressed."

What about Churchill?

"I don't think he was listening. Churchill was a man who didn't listen very often."

A few days later I said, *Sir, the other day, when you were talking about Churchill, you said he didn't listen very much. Could you tell me what you meant.*

"Well, he was more of a talker than a listener. He liked to talk, and he was one of the best. But he didn't care much for that kind of music.

"I was the only head of a state there at Potsdam. The others were Prime Ministers, and so I always sat next to the host. And the night Stalin was host I had some very nice conversations with him. I liked him. I didn't like what he did, of course, but I liked him. We talked about music. He was just like me about Chopin. He liked Chopin. Churchill didn't. He didn't care for that kind of music at all, and he told me that he wished I'd get up and go home because he couldn't do it until I did. But I stuck around there for a while because I was enjoying it, about an hour I guess. Stalin had some women from the Ukraine who sang and played the violin. It was quite a lengthy program."

Mr. President, did you ever think of being a concert pianist?

"Oh, I may have thought of it at one time or another, but that's as far as it ever went."

When did you give up the piano, studying the piano?

"About the time I was working at the bank I gave it up."

Why, Mr. President?

"Because I decided that playing the piano wasn't the thing for a man to do. It was a sissy thing to do. So I just stopped. And it was probably all for the best. I wouldn't ever have been really first-rate. A good music-hall piano player is about the best I'd have ever been. So I went into politics and became President of the United States.

"I guess it's too late to take it up now, playing the piano, although maybe I could become sort of the Grandma Moses of ex-Presidents."

Do you still listen to music?

"Oh, yes. I've got quite a collection of records. When I shipped them out of the White House, it took up most of the space in one whole truck. I guess what I've got most of is records by the great piano players of the world. Rubenstein, of course, and Horowitz. . . . And symphonies. Beethoven's First. I've got the Toscanini recording of that. And the Beethoven Concerto in D Major, the Francescatti recording with the Philadelphia orchestra."

Mr. President, do you ever regret giving up the piano?

"Young man, I've told you. I don't regret things like that. It's a waste of time."

When I'd recovered from that one, I said, *Mr. President, do you think Paul Hume knew much about music?*

"Not a damn thing. Not a goddamn thing. When he wrote what he wrote about Margaret in the Washington *Post,* he showed he didn't know a thing about music. He was just a smart aleck and a showoff. When she put on her singing program in Washington, it was a wonderful program. She was scared, of course, but she put on just the best program ever. And she had a nice young man for an accompanist who was a crackerjack. He played two or three pieces during the intermission.

"And then the next morning this Hume that you mentioned wrote the dirtiest, meanest critique you ever saw. And I wrote him a letter. I wrote him a letter saying that if I could get my hands on him I'd bust him in the jaw and kick his nuts out (chuckle). General Marshall thought that Margaret was his daughter; he was just crazy about Margaret. And when I told him what I'd done, he said, 'Well, I'm just as sorry as I can be that you couldn't get to him because that's what he deserved. He criticized everything but the varnish on the piano, and that's all that needed criticizing.' "

*Mr. President, could you tell me a little about how you got the letter off? ***

* It is generally forgotten that on the day of Margaret's concert, Charlie Ross, Mr. Truman's high school friend and his press secretary, died at his desk of a heart attack. Mr. Truman did not tell Margaret until after the concert.

Hume wrote, "She is flat a good deal of the time. . . . She cannot sing with anything approaching professional finish. . . . She communicates almost nothing of the music she presents."

As Bob Aurthur has written, "Now! You are Harry Truman, and you have a couple of problems: you'd surely like to destroy Douglas MacArthur, because on the front page of your newspaper the General, in the midst of a headlong retreat, is demanding the war be expanded into China; next, you want to lash out at a man you never heard of who, in the entertainment section of the same newspaper, is attacking your daugh-

"Why, I sent it by messenger, I guess, but I wrote it in long hand, and when he got to the *Post,* Hume—he didn't know much about *anything*—Hume couldn't believe it was from me, and he called in the music critic for the Washington *Star,* and they met in a coffee shop someplace, and Hume showed the letter to the man from the *Star.* He recognized my handwriting, but he told Hume he was sure I couldn't have written it, that it was written by somebody playing a joke.

"And then he went back to his office and wrote the whole story and scooped Hume [chuckle]. . . . I understand Hume's sold it. They tell me he's got several thousand dollars for it. . . . There was only one copy. I can't remember all that was in it, but it was pretty hot. When Margaret and Bess found out, they both wept and said that I'd ruined Margaret and I don't know what all. I said, 'Now you wait and see. Every man in this United

_____

ter. Given the fact that you can do only one thing at a time, which item do you deal with first? Remember, it's before breakfast, and your best friend has just died.

"What Harry Truman did was snatch up a pen and pad of White House notepaper and address the following to Mr. Hume:

" 'I have just read your lousy review buried in the back pages. You sound like a frustrated old man who never made a success, an eight-ulcer man on a four-ulcer job and all four ulcers working.

" 'I never met you, but if I do you'll need a new nose and a supporter below. Westbrook Pegler, a guttersnipe, is a gentleman compared to you. You can take that as more of an insult than a reflection on your ancestry.'

"Refusing the advantage of his franking privilege—the note after all, was personal—Mr. Truman affixed his own stamp ("We still had 3 cent stamps in my administration"), went on his morning walk, and dropped the envelope in the nearest mailbox. Mr. Truman's vengeful words have been quoted in full here as they appear in the books, but Merle Miller has an audio tape where the former President says what he really told Mr. Hume was he'd 'kick his balls in.' After the incident Margaret said she was positive her father wouldn't use language like that. Surely not."

States that's got a daughter will be on my side,' and it turned out they were."

Mr. President, tell me how you felt when you went back to Grandview in 1906. I won't ask you if you regretted going back to the farm.

"I'm glad you're cleared up about that. There's nothing much to tell. In the year 1906 they needed me back on the farm, and I went. There was some talk that I wouldn't stay, but I did. I don't give up on what I start. I'm a stubborn cuss. They all found that out when I was President. I was stubborn. . . . I stayed on the farm until the war came, and I had to go. I could have got an exemption, of course, being a farmer, but I never even thought of it."

The farm must have been lonely compared with Kansas City.

"No, it wasn't. You say you grew up on a farm. You ought to know better than that. A farmer's life is not a lonely life at all. You have the best time in the world on a farm like ours. You've always got the stock to take care of, and you've got people coming in to talk to you about whether you can help them out in harvesting the wheat or planting the corn or whatever else is necessary in the neighborhood. I was very active in the Farm Bureau out there and later in the 4-H and other organizations of that kind.

"We had six hundred acres at the time, finest land you'd ever find anywhere. We raised everything—corn, wheat, oats, clover—and we rotated them. I was very much interested in the creation of things that come out of the ground.

"I helped my brother and my father to sow oats, plow corn, and sow clover. And in the long run we improved the production of the farm nearly fifty percent. . . . I had a gangplow made by the Henderson Manufacturing Company, and I used that with four horses or two horses and two mules, whatever we had available. That was the way we plowed.

"Then the land had to be harrowed, and I enjoyed that. It gave me plenty of time to think. Farmers really all have time to think, and some of them do it, and those are the ones who have made it possible for us to have free government. That's what Jefferson was writing about. Farmers have more time to think than city people do."

Mary Jane Truman: "Harry was always very particular about how he laid off the corn rows. He laid it so that you could plow it every way, crossways and straight, every way. And it was the same with the wheat. When he sowed the wheat in the fall, you almost never saw a skipped place where he had missed sowing the wheat.

"He was really very particular. He kept books on everything that he did, and he raised fine hogs and some very good cattle. He was just a good all-around farmer and proud of it. I think perhaps he might have enjoyed other things more. I wouldn't say for sure, but while he was on the farm, he gave it everything that he had, just as he did in everything that he went into."

Mr. President, suppose in those years you were on the farm, from 1906 to 1917, somebody had told you that someday you would be President of the United States. What would you have done?

The President laughed, not unkindly; he was never unkind. He laughed because he was amused. He said, "That's a damn fool question if ever I heard one. Who in the world would have done such a thing? It just never would have occurred to anybody.

"Nobody ever thought I was going to amount to much,* and that's why when people are always asking about the records of when I was a boy and so on, the answer is no-

---

* Miss Zuba Chiles, a retired schoolteacher, put it this way: "When Harry was in school, well, we all liked Harry, and he always got his lessons but never much beyond that, and we never thought—people deny it now; they say they knew it all along, his becoming President—but nobody did. Nobody thought that he'd go far at all.

"Not that we didn't like him. Harry was always just as nice as he could be, but that's another thing."

body kept any records because nobody thought it was necessary.

"They say my grandfather, Anderson Shippe Truman, said I was going to be President someday, but since he died when I was only three years old, that doesn't seem to me very likely. You know how people sometimes are inclined to remember things after the fact."

And you yourself were never tortured by ambition to be head of the whole shebang?

"No, no, no. Those are the fellas that cause all the trouble. I wanted to make a living for my family and to do my job the best I could do it, and that's about the size of it."

6

On Battery D

One morning the President said that after lunch he was going to Kansas City.

"I've got to go in and see my haircutter at two thirty or something like that. My wife said it would be much better if I'd go to New York and get it done. She doesn't like my haircutter, but he's one of my boys. He's one of the Battery D boys, and so is my dentist and my tailor. You cain't quit them. You just cain't quit them.

"They're just like your family, your sisters and your cousins and your aunts. I had a hundred and eighty-eight men and a hundred and sixty-seven horses in Battery D, and my haircutter was one of my men, and I've stayed with him ever since. He's retired now, but he comes down a couple of days a week and takes care of the old-time customers, which I guess you might say I'm one of.

"Why, he cut my hair under a tree in the St.-Mihiel drive and the Meuse-Argonne drive, and he cut it under fire sometimes, and what are you going to do? You have to stick with them. What else is there to do?"

I guess what you do depends on the kind of man you are, Mr. President. Would you tell us a little about Battery D?

"Well, when I was still in Kansas City, I joined the old Battery B in Kansas City; it was a field artillery outfit, and we drilled once a week in the armory there."

I understand you had to pay twenty-five cents a week to drill there.

"We did. I believe that was for the upkeep, to keep it clean and so on, but I'm not sure why. I really don't remember.

"But I was a private in Battery B and finally became a sergeant and a corporal in that battery. And when the B Battery went to the border in Texas in 1916, chasing old Pancho Villa, well, I couldn't go because I was harvesting wheat and had a hundred and sixty acres that had to be cut, so they didn't require me to go to the border.

"But when the battery in Kansas City and Battery C here in Independence were expanded into a regiment, I helped to organize it. And it became the Hundred and Twenty-ninth Field Artillery, part of the Thirty-fifth Infantry Division, and I got a lot of those boys to join by promising them that if they'd join the artillery, they'd ride. But they never rode a mile. They walked every inch of the time.

"I'd expected to be a sergeant in F Battery when it was organized, but instead, they elected me to be a first lieutenant. In those days the enlisted men elected their officers.

"And after I got to be a first lieutenant, why, they sent me down to Camp Doniphan in Oklahoma. Near Fort Sill, the place where they kept that old Indian chief, Geronimo, in prison.

"They sent me to the school of fire down there, and they tried to give me . . . well, a college education in three months, and my head has never recovered from it since."

Mary Jane Truman: "When my brother Harry went off to enter the service during the First World War, he said I'd have to look after Mamma and the farm, and so I did. My brother Vivian was on another farm east of here.

"I ran the farm, but I did have one good man. He had a house down on the other part of the farm where he and his family lived. Our trouble was getting good help to help him. But we got through, and we raised wheat and oats and corn and came out very well with it."

Wasn't that pretty hard work for you?

"Well, not too hard. I didn't do any work in the field, of course, but I did help, and we cooked for the threshers and the hands that shocked the wheat and all that. Of course we didn't have the conveniences that you have today, you know, even in 1918, but it worked out just fine, and I got along."

Mr. President, didn't you meet Eddie Jacobson down at Camp Doniphan?

"Oh, no. I'd known Eddie long before that; I'd known him ever since I worked in the bank in Kansas City, and he was working in a clothing store, I believe, over at Eighth and Walnut streets. But we became very close friends when we opened the canteen down at Doniphan.

"Eddie was not in my battery. He was in Battery F. He was a sergeant in Battery F. And then the colonel gave me the job of canteen officer in addition to the other things I had to do, and I was dead sure he did it because he wanted to get rid of me. Because none of those canteens made money, and a lot of officers got in trouble with handling the money.

"But Eddie and I had the most successful canteen in the Thirty-fifth Division. We—Eddie and I went to Oklahoma City and got the merchandise we needed for the canteen, and every man in the regiment—there were eleven hundred men in the regiment—put in two dollars apiece, making a total of twenty-two hundred dollars. And within six months we returned their original investment and paid out fifteen thousand dollars in dividends.

"Then I had to go overseas, and Eddie ran the canteen from then on."

Eddie Jacobson's widow, Bluma Jacobson: "Before Harry went overseas . . . Well, Harry had been a farm boy, but I believe he always wanted to go into business, and before he went overseas, he said to my husband, Eddie, 'If we come back alive and in good shape, let's go into business together.' And they shook hands on it.

"There was never anything signed. In all their relationship there was never anything signed. They just felt that close to one another that they could trust each other, which they did all through their lives.

"Once in the canteen they had some sweaters that they

wanted to get rid of, and the two of them let it out that they'd be doing the men in the battery a favor by letting those sweaters go at six dollars apiece.

"I've been told that those men were like a bunch of women at a bargain basement sale. They just mobbed the canteen and bought up every sweater there was. And later one of the officers was going over the books, and it turned out Harry and Eddie had only paid three dollars apiece for those sweaters, and so the profit was exactly one hundred percent."

Harry Truman: "I got kidded a lot about those sweaters, but I always said, 'Well, that's the reason we made a profit, and we were there for that purpose.'

"Besides, those boys couldn't have bought those sweaters anyplace else for less than fifteen dollars. So I was doing them a favor."

When you went overseas, you went to France.

"We went to France. We landed at Brest, France, on April 13, 1918, and just twenty-seven years later on that same day you may remember I spent my first full day in the White House.

"I told you. I went to a French artillery school, and then I went to Camp Coëtquidan for some more instruction in French artillery, and then in July—the rest of the Hundred and Twenty-ninth had come over by that time—in July the colonel called me in and told me I was going to be the new captain in charge of Battery D, which was known as Dizzy D, and it had, to say the least, a very bad reputation indeed. They'd had four commanding officers before that, and none of them could control those Irish boys. They were most of them Irish boys from Kansas City, many of them college boys from Rockhurst College, which is a Jesuit school in Kansas City. They were very well educated, many of them, but they were wild.

"I told the colonel; I said he might just as well send me home right then and there. I was never so scared in my life, not even later when we were under fire, but I—well, it was one of the things I had to do, and I did it."

Judge Albert A. Ridge of the federal district court in Kansas City, a veteran of Battery D: "The first recollection I have of Harry Truman actually taking over the battery was the day he succeeded Captain Thatcher.

"Thatcher had been well loved by all the men in the battery, and there was a general feeling of unrest, of anger when he was relieved of duty. The men in the regiment . . . in the battery just didn't want to lose Captain Thatcher, and when it was learned that Captain Truman had been assigned to Battery D, there was a good deal of talk about mutiny, about causing trouble.

"I remember it was at retreat when he came before the battery, and I can visualize even now the emotion of that time. There was a stirring among the fellows in rank. Although they were standing at attention, you could feel the Irish blood boiling—as much as to say, why, if this guy thinks he's going to take us over, he's mistaken.

"I think perhaps Captain Truman could feel it, too.

"He looked the battery over, up and down the entire line, about three times, and the men were all waiting for the castigation that they really knew they were entitled to receive from a new commander. Because of their previous conduct.

"But Harry Truman . . . he just . . . continued to look at them, and then . . . his only command to the battery was—*Dismissed.*

"Well, of course, the dismissed battery went toward their barracks. But I think that that command to that Irish group was a sort of benediction. He had not castigated them. He had dismissed them as much as to say—like the Good Lord said to Mary Magdalene, 'Go and sin no more.'

"From that time on I knew that Harry Truman had captured the hearts of those Irishmen in Battery D, and he never lost it. He has never lost it to this day."

Eugene Donnelly, a veteran of Battery D and a Kansas City lawyer: "We were a pretty rough bunch of boys; anyway, we thought we were. We'd already got rid of four commanding officers when Harry came along. He looked like a sitting duck to us. He was sort of small and with four eyes.

"And then he called all the noncoms together, and he said, 'Now, look, I didn't come here to get along with you guys. You're going to have to get along with me, and if any of you thinks he can't, why, speak right up, and I'll give you a punch in the nose.'

"He was tough, but he was fair; he was a good officer.

"I remember once a bunch of us were going to Paris on a furlough, and we didn't have any money. Harry found out about it, and he lent us the money we needed. We'd have done anything for him then, and nobody that I know has changed his mind."

Mike Flynn, a Kansas City livestock dealer: "I first got acquainted with Harry Truman in 1917. I was transferred from Battery D to Battery E, but I saw a lot of him during the war. He was very much respected.

"He used to get a lot of letters from the old Irish mothers of the boys in the outfit, and most battery commanders, company commanders, wouldn't pay any attention, but not Harry. I don't think he ever went to bed at night before he answered every one of those letters.

"I used to come in, maybe late, maybe toward nearly dawn even, and I'd see him in his tent writing letters, answering the letters he'd got that day.

"And he never changed. Even after he got to be President.

"In 1948, in December, 1948, we had a bad accident. My only son . . . he had just been married two years, and we were driving down here when a . . . when an oil truck skidded in front of us, and my son . . . he was very badly hurt, and he lasted . . . lasted only five days.

"And during the time that we were praying for his

funeral [clears throat] I received a telegram of condolence from Harry Truman. I don't know how he was notified. I don't think he ever was. I think he saw it in the paper.

"He told me later that he kept in close touch with things [clears throat] while my son lived, and I thought it was very kind of him to remember us at that time, when he was President of the United States and had just won the election. And he must have . . . I always felt that he must have had many other things on his mind as well.

"I would say. If you were to ask me, I would say Harry Truman was the kindest and most thoughtful man I have ever known. Bar none."

Eddie Meisburger, a veteran of Battery D and a retired Kansas City newpaperman: "The men trusted him to get them through the war and to get them back home. And he went out of his way to help them.

"That was illustrated I think by something that happened when we were on the march in the Vosges Mountains on our way into the St.-Mihiel sector.

"The men would be walking all day and leading their horses, and the infantry would ride by in trucks and yell at us to join the infantry and ride.

"Anyway, they were riding, and we were walking. And we were pretty well fagged out. And the colonel of the regiment came by, and by the way, he had a fine mount. He came down the road one afternoon and started sounding off about how we were just straggling along and were a sight to behold and so on, and he wanted to know whose outfit it was.

"Captain Truman was walking at the time because he had put his own horse into the harness to help pull the guns. That's how bad things were. They had to have that horsepower. So he was walking with us, and when the colonel came up, Captain Truman said that this was his outfit, Battery D.

"And the colonel said it was a hell of a looking outfit and that he wanted the men to be called to attention and fall in and double-time up a hill about half a mile or half a kilometer, it being France, away.

"Captain Truman realized that the men were out on their feet, and instead of giving the men a double-time order, he took us off the road, gave us a right turn, and took us into a forest with instructions to put the horses on the picket line and to bed the men down.

"And he said that he would go down and see the colonel, which he did. And he risked a court-martial by his action. But he told the colonel that his men weren't going to go any farther. They were going to rest that night. And he said if the colonel wanted his job, why, to court-martial him.

"The result was, he came back with the orders that we'd stay right there that night, and the whole outfit bedded down.

"The next day word spread around that he'd gone to bat for us, and things of that nature happened all the time.

"And it has been the same way in civilian life. Men have gone to him; they still do. Men from Battery D. Only the other day a certain man from the outfit needed some help, and I went to Mr. Truman and told him, and he said that he always had a lot of people from his old outfit who came crying on his shoulder when they needed help, and he said that he had that shoulder ready to help them. And that in this case he would do what he could. And he did. He always does what he can."

Mr. Meisburger, I understand there's a bottle of 3-Star Hennessy somewhere. Could you tell me about that?

"It's customary in all outfits to . . . most of them have a 'last man's club,' and these clubs have something put away, generally a bottle of some refreshment for the last man to drink.

"In this case there's a bottle of 3-Star Hennessy which was purchased in France in 1919, when we held our first reunion after the Armistice. I don't know whether it was a contribution from the outfit or who purchased it. But we know that it is still in existence, and Harry Truman has vouchsafed us that it is in good hands. Locked up in a box in a vault. And we know that if it comes to a showdown, that bottle is there.

"We're sure that it is because Harry Truman told us that it is."

Edgar Hinde, a veteran of Battery D and the former postmaster of Independence: "He was a wonderful officer. I don't . . . I would never have described him as tough, but he was thoughtful. He always saw to it that his men were well taken care of. Where he was concerned, his men came before everything, and in the Army I've always felt that that's about ninety-five percent of what makes a good officer."

Mr. President, can you tell me about the Battle of Who Run?

"What they called . . . what the men called the Battle of Who Run. We were in the Vosges Mountains in position on a place called Mount Herrenberg, and the German artillery began to fire on us; it had been a very quiet sector up to then, but the Germans started firing, and one of the sergeants got panicked, you might say, and he started yelling about how the Germans had a bracket on us, and he said that everybody ought to run, and some did, including the sergeant.

"I stood right there, and I called them every name I could think of, which was plenty, and they came sneaking back and got the horses and the battery in a position of safety.

"Later they wanted me to court-martial the sergeant, but I wouldn't do it. I busted him to private, and later I got him transferred to another battery, where I understand he did very well for all the rest of the war.

"I tried never to get anybody court-martialed. When we had troubles, we handled them ourselves, and that's the way to do it. Why put a man through the disgrace of a court-martial, something that will follow him all the rest of his life, unless you absolutely have to? And ninety-nine times out of a hundred you don't.

"You have to have faith in a man—that if he makes a mistake, and if you treat him like a man, you'll find that he won't repeat that mistake. That's been my experience in any case, and it was the same in the Army and in politics."

You mean you have a basic trust in people.

"You have to. If you don't, what's the use of living? My goodness, if you don't have trust in your fellowman, how can you expect him to have trust in you?"

Those are very old-fashioned sentiments, Mr. President. A lot of people don't feel that way anymore.

"I know they don't, and it's a pity. That's the reason we're in the shape we're in."

Tell me about Father Tiernan [L. Curtis Tiernan].

"I used to walk at the head of my battery and lead my horses, and Father Tiernan, the Catholic chaplain, would walk with me. There were only five or six Protestants in my battery, and I was one of them. All the rest were Catholics.

"The father and I would walk along and discuss the history of the world and I don't know what all. And I'd corner him on the things that were done by the Jesuits in the Spanish Inquisition, and he always had an answer for me. Of course it was never the right answer as far as I was concerned [much laughter]."

I believe you saw him again at Potsdam.

"I did. He was chief of the Army chaplains in Europe during the Second World War.

"Well, when we landed in Antwerp on our way to Potsdam, General Jesus Christ Himself Lee was there to meet us. Do you remember him?"

I said, "Vividly."

Lieutenant General J. C. H. "Jesus Christ Himself" Lee was commanding general of the Communications Zone of the Supreme Headquarters of the American Expeditionary Forces during the Second World War. We were, you might say, both stationed in Paris at the same time.

I was editor of the Army weekly *Yank* in Paris, and the general threatened me with court-martial at least three times, largely because of material that appeared in the magazine, although we once had something of a disagreement over housing for the *Yank* staff. The general won the latter argument. As I say, he was a lieutenant general, and I was a master sergeant.

The general was a demanding martinet, and among other things that later got him into trouble—he retired in disgrace—was the fact that during the war and after he frequently sent an empty bomber from Paris to North Africa to bring back oranges for his breakfast mess.

I mentioned this to the President, who said, "Oh, yes. He was a regular son of a bitch and no two ways about it.

"But when I got to Antwerp on the way to Potsdam, he was appointed as my aide, and I said to him, 'There are two people I want to see.' I wanted to see a major general who'd been a private in my battery and finally retired a major general.

"I wanted to see him, and I said, 'And I want to see that damned priest that's the chief of chaplains down in Paris.'

"Old Lee said, 'Who?'

"And I said, 'Tiernan. That damn chief of chaplains that used to be in my battery.'

"He said, 'You mean *Monsignor* Tiernan?' I said, 'Yes. Go and get him.' And he did.

"And Tiernan came to Potsdam, and he brought along all his fancy vestments and one thing and another, and he and I had the best time you ever saw in your life. He sat up half the night with Charlie Ross [the President's press secretary], and the two of them drank a quart of cognac or whatever a bottle of cognac is in France.

"And the next morning he came to see me, and he said, 'Mr. President, I want to put on a high mass for you.'

"I said, 'All right. You can do it. But there's one thing you've got to do. You've got to get every Protestant in this outfit to be sure and be there at that mass because if they're not, they're going to be in trouble with me.'

"Well, they were all there, and it was just a wonderful service.

"That priest was a grand fella. Never was anybody like him. When I used to walk along with him in the First War, he'd talk about the religious history of the world and how the differences between the religions had caused all the trouble. He knew most of the answers, and I said, 'Padre, you know what? If all the damn priests were like you, there wouldn't be any Protestants.'

"And he said, 'I know that. And I ain't' [laughter].

"Oh, you know. Petty larceny things like religious differences and political differences never made any difference with me. And with people I like I don't care what they believe if they honestly believe it. It's up to them. . . . But I wish you could have known that priest. He was in a class by himself."

Judge Ridge: "Father Tiernan gave the best summing up of Harry Truman I have ever encountered. He said, 'Harry Truman had integrity and much more than normal intelligence, and there is no limit in a free society to what men with those attributes can attain.'

"Whenever the boys in Battery D would see Captain Truman, they would salute him, and that salute meant that they were saying to him—I'm with you. And he would salute back—I know you are. I'm with you also."

Harry Truman: "We finally worked up the battery to be one of the best batteries in the regiment. And we could always hit the target when the time came.

"I had quite a great time with those youngsters. We were in a great many engagements, fired eleven thousand rounds of seventy-five ammunition, came back here, and marched in a parade downtown, and even now there are about sixty or seventy of those men who are still alive and living in Kansas City, and we're still friends, and I'm just as proud of that as I am of having been President.

"It's quite a satisfaction to a fellow who's commanded men during a tour of duty on the front where there was a lot of shooting. It's not often that the men feel kindly toward the fellow who commanded them. Because he had to make them do things they didn't like.

"I've always felt that the best definition of a leader, and it doesn't matter where it is, in the military or in the White House. It doesn't matter. The best definition of a leader is a man who can make the people who served with or under him do what they don't want to do and like it."

That certainly can be said of you and the men of Battery D.

"Yes, I think it can be, and, hell, you know. They say I was ambitious, but I was never ambitious. If the only thing I'd ever done in my life was be the best damn battery commander I could be, I'd have settled for that.

"And now let's go to lunch. I told you we were going to the cheap place. Bess told me I ought to take you to lunch in New York, but I said to her, 'Why do that? I can do it a lot cheaper here.' "

As we went into the Howard Johnson's for lunch, several children standing outside recognized Mr. Truman and asked for his autograph, which he gave them.

As we walked away he said, "These kids and their autographs are just like a bunch of pups. One of them does it on a fire hydrant, and then they've all got to do it."

Harry Truman, Madge Gates Wallace, and the Haberdashery

On June 28, 1919, shortly after Harry Truman returned from France, he married Elizabeth Virginia Wallace.

I never asked Mr. Truman about his personal life; I felt that it would have been presumptuous to do so, and now, more than ten years later, I still think so.

I met Mrs. Truman several times, always briefly. She was a courteous woman with an enormous sense of personal dignity. A few days after Mr. Truman had told me that he liked to live up to his obligations Mrs. Truman agreed, I am sure with great reluctance, that for four hours the film crew—it seems to me its members numbered in the hundreds—could come inside the house at 219 North Delaware Street.

The house was built in 1867 by Bess Truman's grandfather, General Porterfield Gates, who made a fortune milling Queen of the Pantry flour, which in my youth was still popular throughout the Middle West.

The Gates family may not have been the richest family in Independence, but they were by far the fanciest, and Madge Gates Wallace, Bess' mother, certainly fancied herself as the grandest lady in town. David W. Wallace, Bess' father, was not, in the language of Independence, nearly as "well fixed" as the Gateses. He was a handsome man with long sideburns, a mustache that drooped over his wide mouth, and a charming manner that everybody in Independence remembered with affection.

But he was never quite able to make a living for his four children and his imperial wife, and again in the language of Independence, he "took to drink." And in 1908 he seated himself in a bathtub and shot himself in the head with a pistol.

After his death, Madge Gates Wallace, perhaps understandably, became not less imperious; she became more so. She was called "the queenliest woman Independence ever produced." I always felt that when Harry Truman talked, as he often did, never with affection, about "the high hats and the counterfeits" of Independence, he had the Gateses and the Wallaces in mind.

He had known Bess since they met at Sunday school in the First Presbyterian Church in 1890, but they were not married until twenty-nine years later. That may not have been the longest courtship in history, but it is certainly in the running.

Janey Chiles, a retired Independence schoolteacher: "I thought that they never would get married. I think Bess wanted to, although I'm not sure, but Mrs. Wallace. . . . Nobody was ever good enough for her, or so it seemed. She was a very, very difficult person, and there wasn't anybody in town she didn't look down on. And Harry Truman was not at that time I believe a very promising prospect."

Harry Truman was thirty-five years old; his only experience up to that time had been as a bank clerk, a farmer, and a soldier, and now he was proposing to go into the haberdashery business with, of all things, a Jew named Eddie Jacobson.

Bluma Jacobson: "Eddie and I were never at the Truman house. We went maybe two or three times on picnics and on the Fourth of July, but the Trumans never had us at their home. The Wallaces were aristocracy in these parts, and under the circumstances the Trumans couldn't afford to have Jews at their house."

Susan Chiles, another retired schoolteacher: "The Gateses, the whole Gates family, were all topnotchers here. If there was anybody in town that was high society, it was the Gates family."

Henry Chiles, a retired farmer: "I knew Bess long before I knew Harry. Bess lived over on Delaware Street, and it's just a block and a half away.

"Bess' brother Frank was just a little younger than I, but we played together. And her other brother George. It was altogether, the Wallaces were, one girl and three boys, and she straightened those boys out. Physically she could do whatever she wanted to do. She was just as good a ballplayer as they were, and they knew it.

"The Wallaces lived next door to the Paxtons, and the Paxtons were all boys and outweighed the Wallace boys just a little bit. But when the Wallaces were losing, Bess would come over, and she'd decide the battle right then and there. She was quite a tomboy, but she turned out to be a real Southern lady.

"Harry didn't play any of the rough games the way Bess did. He was wearing glasses, and he was afraid of breaking them. Vivian never paid much attention to the books. He was more like me in that."

Mary Jane Truman: I had taken over the farm when Harry went into the Army, and I had a hundred acres in wheat and sixty in oats, and the day of the wedding, I'll never forget, my mother and I cooked dinner for twelve threshers, and then we had to clean up and hurry to the wedding.

"It *couldn't* have come at a worse time. I remember the night before I went with Harry to pick some daisies in a field where they grew wild. I didn't have anything to do with decorating the church, but I certainly will never forget where the daisies on the altar came from."

After their marriage and brief honeymoon in Chicago and Detroit, Harry and Bess moved into the house on North Delaware Street with Mrs. Wallace, and the three of them lived together until her death in December, 1952. She was ninety years old, and in the thirty-two years between the marriage and Mrs. Wallace's death they lived not only in Independence but in Washington, D. C. At the time Harry Truman became President, she was sharing a bedroom with Margaret in the apartment on Connecticut Avenue, after which came Blair House and the White House.

But in all that time, I was told, she never quite reconciled herself to the marriage. In Mrs. Wallace's mind Bess had clearly married beneath herself. The Trumans were dirt farmers, and Mrs. Wallace said so, frequently in the presence of her son-in-law.

Henry Chiles: "I don't think Harry ever really *liked* Independence. Well, he liked it all right, I guess, but Grandview was always more like home to him, and Independence has always been more what you might call a *Wallace* town, and Mrs. Wallace never let him forget that for a minute."

Susan Chiles: "I probably shouldn't say this, but there just didn't seem to be any way in the world to get along with Mrs. Wallace. Bess put up with her, though, stuck with her through thick and thin, although I understand that even in the White House there was just not any way of satisfying her.

"But Harry was always as nice as he could be to her. It was just a most remarkable thing, and I think people around here respect him as much for that as anything else."

No matter what his job was, Harry Truman always took home a briefcase full of work, but the house on North Delaware never seemed to be quiet. Floors were forever being waxed, curtains hung, ceilings painted, and walls papered, particularly it seemed in exactly the places where Harry Truman was trying to concentrate. There were also Madge Gates Wallace's guests, frequently her sons and their wives, who also never seemed completely content with Bess' husband.

As I've said, even while she was living at the White House, Mrs. Wallace seldom failed to make it clear that Harry Truman was not what she had in mind as a son-in-

law. Or as a President. As late as 1948 she was often
heard to remark that she could not for the life of her understand why Harry was running against that nice man,
Thomas E. Dewey.

"And in all those years," said Mrs. W. L. C. Palmer,
"Harry Truman never once answered back. Never once.
You must remember Harry is a reticent man."

Mrs. Truman said that while she would allow the film
crew in the house, she would not take part in the filming
and would not be interviewed.

The house was immaculate. There are fourteen large
rooms with old-fashioned high ceilings, many with damask
wallpaper. There are seven bedrooms, three fireplaces
with marble mantels, and a dining room large enough to
seat thirty. I was pleased to see on one end table, a book,
undoubtedly Mrs. Truman's, called *The Corpse in the
Snow*. Otherwise, only history and biography, hundreds
of volumes of both.

We filmed the President reading the morning paper in
his study, then rising, going through one of the large living
rooms and into the hall, where he picked up his hat,
opened the front door, and went outside.

It might seem that this simple episode would take only
a few minutes to film, but it took the entire four hours,
and if there had been more time, it would have taken more
time.

At one point during the interminable waits between
takes a member of the crew whose job I never figured out
turned to Mrs. Truman and said, "I wonder if you'd mind
running out to the kitchen and getting me a glass of
water?"

Mrs. Truman, a woman of whom I believe it could be
said, does not run, went to the kitchen and got him a glass
of water.

I gave her a chance to recover, then asked her whether
she ever went to the door with the President when he
started on his morning walks. She said that sometimes she

did and sometimes she didn't. I asked whether she would
agree to accompany the President to the door and allow
us to film her doing that.

She hesitated a moment and looked with dismay at the
chaos around her, at the heavy cameras and the coiled
wires and the unshaven men and short-haired women.
She sighed, and then she said that she would. She said
it without joy.

I should have stopped then, but I didn't. I said, "And I
wonder if you'd mind saying whatever you might normally
say to the President and let us record that." And I added,
"We really ought to record it for posterity's sake."

Mrs. Truman gave me a look that Madge Gates Wallace might have envied, and she said, "I have no desire
to have my voice recorded for posterity."

Later that morning during another long delay and after,
I suspect, a few more "small libations," Mr. Truman
turned on the hi-fi and played excerpts of several pianists,
including, as I recall, Glenn Gould and, I think, Rubenstein playing Beethoven's *Appassionata*.

"I can play that," said the President, and he went to the
piano that he had bought for Margaret one Christmas
when she was a girl, sat down, and played a few halting
bars.

"Now, Harry," said Mrs. Truman, who was standing
near the piano, "we all know it's not the same."

She said it with kindness, though, and she smiled.

8

The Haberdashery

Not long before Harry Truman's marriage he met Eddie
Jacobson on the streets of Kansas City—"How the hell
are you, you baldheaded old son of a bitch?"—and they
decided that since they had both come back from the war
physically intact and since neither was overburdened with
attractive job offers, they would indeed go into business
together, the haberdashery business.

Mr. Truman told me, "We'd done so well in the canteen, we didn't see why we couldn't do just as well in
civilian life, and it looked like we were a pretty good
combination. I'd do the selling and keep the books, and
we had a clerk part of the time, and Eddie would do the
buying. Of course the way things turned out we both did
everything, a little of everything. We were open six days a
week at first, twelve hours or more a day, and the first
year we kept busy until late in the evening, and sometimes
I'd take the books home and Mrs. Truman would help me
with them."

Bluma Jacobson: "There were slack days as well as
good days, and if Harry wasn't around, you could always
look up in the balcony, and Harry would be up there
with a book, reading or studying. He studied law a good
deal in those days. Just picking it up, not going to law
school at that time. He later went to night school in Kansas City and studied law, but at that time you would always find him reading a book.

"The first year was a good year in the store. I believe
they sold as much as eighty thousand dollars' worth of
merchandise, because everybody coming back from the
war, all the men, needed new clothes, and they had very
good merchandise. Expensive shirts that were very good
. . . everything. Eddie had very good taste in men's fur-
nishings.

"Perhaps . . . it may be that they were overstocked; they had over thirty-five thousand dollars' worth of stock, or forty thousand dollars, and in the second year the price of the stock went down until it was worth only ten thousand dollars or less.

"When you speak of the depression these days, everybody thinks of the depression of the 1930's, but the depression in 1922 was just as bad, although it didn't last as long.

"The depression came, and there wasn't enough fuel. There was a coal shortage, and the store had to close at two or three in the afternoon. They couldn't stay open as they had the first year. I don't think Eddie ever worked as hard as he did that first year, or Harry either I guess."

Mary Jane Truman: "Harry and . . . and Mrs. Truman, they used to come out to the farm here at Grandview on a Sunday when Harry was in business. That was his only day off, and they'd drive out here to see Mother and me, and sometimes we, . . . Harry and I, would play duets on the piano, which my mother always very much enjoyed. She knew a great deal about music, and she liked to hear it.

"When Harry was in the haberdashery business, she very much wanted, we all did, for him to succeed, but when it did not work out that way, we knew it wasn't Harry's fault.

"Later, when Harry got into politics, the newspapers liked to make out that he had been a poor businessman, but that was not the case at all."

Judge Albert A. Ridge: "I believe I was working in a neighborhood grocery store at the time, and I didn't have much of a career in mind.

"But in the evenings I'd go over to the haberdashery, and there were always a lot of men from the battery hanging around, doing nothing much, but Harry was always busy. He was always being asked for advice of one kind or another. He was only thirty-five years old, but he

was an old man to us kids who were in our early twenties
at the time.

"And then I got a job in the courthouse in Kansas City,
as a clerk in one of the courts. And I got to thinking about
going to law school at night, and I talked to Harry Truman about that.

"He encouraged me to go to night school and study law,
but he said that just knowing the law wasn't enough. He
said that was the trouble with far too many lawyers, that
they knew the law but did not know much of anything
else. He said . . . he encouraged me to also study about
the nature of man and about the culture and heritage of
Western civilization in general.

"I was just a young . . . a not very serious young
man, and I'd never studied any of those things; I'd never
even thought of most of them, and they sounded a little
profound to me, a little difficult.

"But Harry Truman always said that I . . . that a
man could do anything he set his mind to, and that encouraged me. I once asked him. . . . No, I believe he
volunteered once to give me a list of about ten or so books
that I ought to read. I don't know what happened to that
list, although I treasured it greatly. But I can remember
that it included Plutarch's *Lives*. And Caesar's *Commentaries*. And Benjamin Franklin's *Autobiography*. He used
to say, 'Al, you'll find a good deal in there about how to
make use of every minute of your day and a lot of horse
sense about people.' And he was always talking about the
Roman lawgivers. He knew all about them. And he had
read all of Gibbon's *Decline and Fall of the Roman
Empire* several times. He was . . . himself he was always reading two or three books at a time and always
making notes in the margins, especially in history books.
Frequently . . . very often he knew much more than the
writer, the historian, and he would . . . his favorite word
was 'bunk,' and I guess it still is.

"He told me to read a book called *Bunker Bean* and
one called *Missouri's Struggle for Statehood*. The Bible.
I remember he said even back then that the King James

Version was the best and that he doubted it could be improved on. I believe he still thinks that. . . . Plato's *Republic*. Shakespeare. He said I'd have to read all of Shakespeare, but he recommended *Hamlet* and *Lear* and *Othello* in particular, and the sonnets. He insisted on the sonnets.

"He recommended to me the complete works of Robert Burns, which he was always reading himself. And Byron. All of Byron, too, I believe, although his favorite was *Childe Harold,* which is a poem most people who do not, did not, know Harry Truman would not have expected him to choose. It's a very . . . you might say it is not an easy poem.

"There was a book called *Fifteen Decisive Battles of the World.* Harry Truman felt that you had to understand war to understand mankind. Because man was always getting into wars, and if you didn't understand how wars happened, you couldn't be expected to understand how to prevent them.

"And I remember Charles Beard had just come out with a book on the history of the Constitutional Convention: *An Economic Interpretation of the Constitution.* I believe that book was a best seller at the time, and Harry and I each got a copy."

Bluma Jacobson: "Harry always kept in mind the other person's point of view. I remember not long after Harry got to be President, he came back here to Kansas City, and he and Eddie and some of the others were playing poker. Eddie lost. I don't know how much, but he lost, and the next morning Harry came into the store and bought eighteen or twenty pairs of socks. I don't think he actually needed that many pairs, size eleven, I think. It was just something he wanted to do for Eddie. Harry Truman has always been very, very aware of how other people feel about things."

Tom Murphy, a veteran of Battery D and a Kansas City salesman: "Our hang-around was the old haberdashery store. It's possible we scared out some customers by just hanging around like that.

"Harry was counselor for all the boys. In the war he was Captain Harry, not Captain Truman. And even after the war, if anybody was going to get married or go into business, they talked to old Captain Harry to ask his advice.

"Of course, now you know Battery D is the largest in the country. Since Harry became Senator and then Vice President and President, we got many more people in the battery. . . . Everybody claims they were in Harry Truman's battery.

"We were a rough outfit; we'd drink and get into fights, but we weren't mean. There wasn't much swearing, and we weren't brutal.

"Later we had occasion to see Harry at our reunions. The first reunion cost him some money. It was during Prohibition, and everybody came to the reunion with a jug of liquor. Not a bottle. A jug. And they got going and started throwing plates and saucers and things, and when it was all over, Harry paid for it. He just grinned and paid the bills. He never did drink.

"Like I said, we may have scared some customers away from the haberdashery, but Harry would never say a word, let a word be said against anybody who was in his outfit."

The store closed in 1922, and although Harry was advised to go into bankruptcy, he refused. It took him fifteen years to pay off his debts, but in 1937 he finally did it.

I once asked Mr. Truman what he felt he had learned from his experience in the haberdashery, and he said, "Well, I learned, although I'd never had much doubt about it, never to elect a Republican as President. [Warren G. Harding had been elected President in 1920.] Because he'll look out for the rich and squeeze out the farmer and the small businessman. And when you get a man like old Mellon as Secretary of the Treasury—Andrew Mellon was Secretary of the Treasury in the cabinets of Harding,

Calvin Coolidge, and Herbert Hoover from 1921 to 1931
—you've got somebody who'll do everything in his power
to make the rich richer and the poor poorer, and that's
exactly what happened. There just wasn't anybody in a
position of power in Washington at that time who gave a
good goddamn what happened to people. Except for the
very rich."

Mr. President, did you like being in the retail business?

"To tell the truth, I never had a chance to spend any
too much time thinking about things like that. What I did
was what I had to do or thought I had to do . . . to
make a living most of the time. I had a wife and later a
daughter to support, and I had to make a living for them.
And I always went ahead and did it as best I could without taking time out to worry about how it would have
been if it had worked out another way. Or to complain
about what happened.

"You'll notice if you read your history, that the work of
the world gets done by people who aren't bellyachers."

I had other questions, but somehow that didn't seem
the time to ask them.

9

Early Politics

Mr. President, what's the first Presidential election you can remember?

"In 1892. [He was eight years old.] Grover Cleveland was running for his second term." Cleveland, who had been President from 1885 to 1889 ran for a second term in 1892 and was elected.

"Cleveland was running for President, and Adlai Stevenson, not the one we've been talking about, his grandfather. He was running for Vice President on the Democratic ticket, and I had a white cap that said on it 'Cleveland' and 'Stevenson,' 'Grover Cleveland' and 'Adlai Stevenson' on the visor."

I gather you liked the first Adlai Stevenson better than you liked his grandson.

"Yes, I did. Old Adlai wasn't any reluctant debutante. They didn't have to beg him to make up his mind whether he wanted to run for office. You know if a man doesn't enjoy running for office and doesn't think he can do something good for people by doing it, I don't know what the hell he's in politics for in the first place.

"Anyway, Grover Cleveland ran against Benjamin Harrison in 1892, and when he was elected, my father climbed up on the roof of the old house out in Grandview. It had a tower on the corner with a rooster as a weather vane, and my father climbed up, after the election returns came in, and decorated it with red, white, and blue bunting. Then he rode a gray horse and carried a torch in a torchlight parade, and so did everybody else in town if he could get a gray horse. Everybody was very pleased that Cleveland had won the election.

"But in his second term Cleveland was a great disappointment. Between his first term and his second he'd worked for one of the big life insurance companies, as a lawyer. I believe it was the Prudential Life Insurance

Company that he worked for, and in his second term he was more interested in the big-money people than he was in the common people, and he accomplished very, very little. It's a shame when that happens to a man, but it sometimes does."

Why do you think some men are more—I guess susceptible to that kind of thing than others are?

"Some men are greedier than others, and they get to thinking they *are* the power rather than the instrument of power."

You were quite an admirer of William Jennings Bryan, I believe. Bryan was the Democratic Presidential nominee in 1896, 1900, and 1908; he was best known for being a proponent of the free coinage of silver, which he felt would help farmers and small businessmen.

"Old Bill Bryan was a great one, one of the greatest."

A good many people don't think as much of Bryan as they used to, largely, I believe, because of his opposition to the teaching of evolution in Tennessee. In 1925, wasn't it?

"Yes, yes. I think it was, around that period anyway, and he was an old man then. What he said then shouldn't be held against him because of . . . because of the things he said and stood for when he was at the height of his powers.

"My goodness, the things he stood for—he was one of the first to come out for the popular election of Senators, you know; Senators used to be elected by state legislatures, and you know how state legislatures are always, almost always controlled by the money people. And old Bill Bryan was one of the first supporters of an income tax, and he was for woman suffrage and I don't know what all.

"And in 1912 when the Democratic Party was split every which way—why, he held it together behind Woodrow Wilson. If it hadn't have been for Bill Bryan, there wouldn't be any liberal outfit in the country at all now. At least that's what I think. Old Bryan kept liberalism alive, kept it going.

"I don't know whether you ever heard him speak or not, but I used to drive a hundred miles to hear that old man speak; I didn't care what the subject was.

"I was at lunch with him one time in Kansas City, and he had a bowl of radishes and a plate of butter in front of him, and he'd butter the radishes and eat them. And that was his whole lunch.

"Nobody had a voice like old Bill. They didn't have any . . . things like this . . . like this microphone in those days. You didn't need them.

"And he made a statement here I'll never forget. You know what he said?

"It was just an ordinary luncheon. He just happened to be in town, and they invited him, and he came. And he said, 'I've been in this political game since 1896 when I got myself nominated for President, and I got licked, as I did twice after that.'

"But he said, 'You know, I've often thought of my first visit to a Democratic convention, which was in 1876' [Bryan was sixteen] and he said, 'They had to bring me up a side stair outside the building, and then they had to poke me in at a window, and you know, they've been trying to put me out over the transom ever since.' And then he went on and made a beautiful speech.

"And another time I heard him. In 1900 the Democratic convention was here in Kansas City, and I was a page. The hall there could hold . . . oh, thousands of people, maybe seventeen thousand people, and I was up in the roof garden. From where I was watching he didn't look more than a foot high, and as I told you he didn't have a microphone, but I could hear every word he said. I never will forget it."

Why do you think he never got elected?

"I don't know. I don't know. I've given it a great deal of thought, but I've never figured it out. I think . . . the best I've come up with is that he was just too far ahead of his time, and the people in the East, the big-money people, were against him and did everything they could to defeat him. Three different times they did it.

"And the first time, in 1896, we got McKinley. He got the Republican nomination, and he ran what they called a front-porch campaign. He didn't go anywhere. He just sat on his front porch in Canton, Ohio, and they brought people to meet him.

"He didn't *say* a damn thing, of course, which in a way reminds me of the fellow who ran against me in 1948. He talked a lot, but he didn't ever *say* anything.

"People said that old McKinley had his ears so close to the ground he got grasshoppers in them.

"The whole campaign was run by a man named Mark Hanna, who was a rich old man whose only interest was in getting richer, and that is what happened when McKinley got elected. He was another one of those who was good for the rich and bad for the poor.

"They say he was a nice man, and I'm sorry he got shot. But he was still a damn poor President.

"And then we had—for almost two terms we had Teddy Roosevelt, and he was just one of our best Presidents."

How did a man like Teddy Roosevelt get to be President, elected President on a Republican ticket?

"Well, in 1898 he got back from Cuba, and he and his Rough Riders, his soldiers, had just won some great victories in the Spanish-American War, and he was a great hero. About the most popular hero since Andy Jackson won the Battle of New Orleans against the British in the War of 1812.

"He got back, and the old Republicans, the Republican bosses, couldn't stop him; he practically got unanimously elected governor of New York in 1899. And he made just a wonderful record in favor of the common people, the same kind of record that Franklin Roosevelt made later. And the bosses were scared of him. They didn't want him to be reelected, which is what he had in mind. And that old boss in New York, whatever his name was, was scared of what Teddy might do in a second term."

Actually, there were two political bosses in New York who were opposed to Roosevelt's renomination and re-election as governor of New York. They were Richard Croker of Tammany Hall and Tom Platt, a reactionary Republican leader. Roosevelt's ideas and programs terri-fied both of them. Platt wrote of him that he had "various altruistic ideas and was . . . a little loose on the relations of capital and labor, on trusts and combinations and the right of a man to run his own business in his own way." Another boss, one "Tim" Campbell, appealed to Roose-velt not to "let the Constitution stand between friends." He couldn't understand why Roosevelt first was angry and then laughed.

In any case, as Mr. Truman said, the bosses of New York were willing to go to any lengths to prevent Teddy Roosevelt from being governor for a second term.

Mr. Truman continued: "And so they arranged for him to get the Vice Presidential nomination. They figured he couldn't do any harm there.

"Then, of course, we know what happened. McKinley and Roosevelt were elected in November and inaugurated in March, and in the fall, September 4, McKinley was up in Buffalo at the Pan American Exposition, and he got shot, and Roosevelt wound up being President.

"I'll bet those old birds were plenty scared when that happened, and they should have been. . . . That's one of the things you have to keep in mind in picking a Vice Presidential candidate . . . It's a place . . . well, as you know I've had some experience in that line."

Whoever it is may end up being President.

"That's right, and some have made good, and some haven't. Someday I'll tell you which is which. But Teddy . . . he was just a crackerjack. He didn't do all he had in mind doing, of course. You never can do that, but there've just been very few Presidents who've done as much for the country as he did. . . . The biggest mistake he made was picking William Howard Taft to succeed him. He picked Taft, and Taft beat Bill Bryan in 1908.

"Taft was the father of the man [Robert A. Taft, Republican Senator from Ohio] I had so much trouble with when I was in the Senate and in the White House. And as Vice President, too. There wasn't anybody who was more against what I stood for as Taft was.

"And his father, the fat old man who was President. Roosevelt handpicked him to be his successor in the White House, and he was no damn good at all. He didn't have the slightest idea of what being President meant. At least that's my opinion.

"And the minute Teddy Roosevelt got out of the White House, the moneybags took over again, as they always do if you don't keep your eyes and ears open. Taft wasn't even *in* Washington most of the time, and he didn't have any understanding at all of the office."

I understand he wanted to be a judge.

"Maybe so, and he might have been a good one, but I'm talking about the Presidency of the United States. And the fact that during the four years Taft was in the White House the country started going to hell."

I gather you think the system can take a bad President now and again and still survive.

"Oh, yes. That's the . . . beauty of what those men who wrote the Constitution did. You can have a bad President. Why, I'll tell you— There was a time when we had five bad Presidents in a row, and it . . . we might not have had a Civil War if it hadn't been for those five fellas, but the government survived. It's just a miracle is all, what this government is."

Getting back to William Jennings Bryan, Mr. President. Do you think he understood the system?

"I haven't the slightest doubt of it, and he understood the people, too, and in my opinion he knew what the people wanted, needed.

"And I told you. He was a real honest-to-goodness orator. I've got a book on him here with all his principal speeches, and it was a wonder what he knew, the things he knew. He was a Congressman, but he didn't like Congress because he felt . . . he thought he didn't have any power in Congress and couldn't get his ideas across.

"He ran for the Senate and was beat. Maybe if he'd been elected to the Senate, he'd have become President the way I did. He'd have been a good one.

"Of course most of the things that he was for were what eventually happened anyway, even though he was never elected.

"My father was a violent Bryan man, but my old Uncle Harrison Young, he thought that the country would be ruined if we had free and unlimited coinage of silver.

"But you know what happened. In the Wilson administration they set up the Federal Reserve Board, the Federal Reserve System, which obtained the authority, and they still have it of issuing money against the commodities. And that's exactly what Bryan had been fighting for in 1896 and all along. That's the whole background of the Federal Reserve Bank.

"So you see even though he was never elected President, he still did the country a lot of good, and that's what you have to remember about him. That thing about his being against the teaching of evolution, that was when he was an old man. And I don't think . . . what an old man said should be held against him as long as his record was good when he had the power."

Mr. President, I understand you were very interested in the Presidential election of 1912 when Woodrow Wilson was elected for the first time.

"I was, and so was my father, and we were both also interested in the Democratic convention that year.

"My father was for old Champ Clark, who was the Speaker of the House and was quite a man. . . . The blood in the family was running quite a little thinner when his son, . . . the one that nominated me for Vice President, came along. Besides, he was drunk half the time and more. . . . Still, after he got defeated for reelection to the Senate and I got to be President . . . well, he had a law firm in Washington that wasn't doing at all well; I could have told him why it wasn't, but I didn't. I appointed him to be an associate justice of the circuit court of appeals. He was no damn good, though."

Mr. President, why—I hope you won't think me impertinent, but under the circumstances and considering the way you felt about him—why did you do that?

"I . . . felt I owed him a favor; that's why, and I thought as a judge he couldn't do too much harm, and he didn't. That . . . he wasn't the worst court appointment I ever made. By no means the worst. But we'll talk about that at another time. I'm none too proud of it. I'll tell you that."

We were talking about 1912. I gather Bennett Clark's father, Champ Clark, was a better man.

"Much better. My father was for him, as I say, for the Democratic nomination in 1912. And during the convention, which was in Baltimore, Maryland, I believe, I was binding wheat, driving a binder. Binding a hundred and sixty acres of wheat where that business proposition, . . . where what they call Truman Corners, is now.

"The little railroad station was just about a quarter mile from the corner where I had to turn the team to go back to the other end of the half-mile field, and in the afternoon I tied up the horses, and I ran over to the station to find out what had happened at the station."

How did they know?

"There wasn't any radio in those days, of course, and those old birds, those old stationmasters had teletype machines in every station, and when the machines weren't being used to send over railroad information, they'd send news over them.

"Out at Grandview we didn't get the Kansas City papers until the next morning, and so if you wanted to find out what was going on, that was the only way you could do it."

How did your father feel about the fact that Wilson won the nomination?

"Well, of course, when Wilson got the nomination, my father was all for him. He was always for the Democratic candidate, didn't matter who it was, and so was my mother, and I've been pretty much a Democrat, you might say, for most of my life [much laughter]."

Mr. President, it seems almost incredible that with your having such a deep interest in politics, you never really . . . well, yearned to run for office yourself.

"Well, I never did. Oh, I might have thought about it, wondered how it would be to run for office, but that's about all.

"But then as I have said I went broke trying to run a haberdashery, and I had to have a job, and when it was suggested that I might . . . run for county judge [an administrative job in Missouri, similar to a county commissioner in most other states] of the eastern district of Jackson County, I decided to do it. I had a lot of good friends in that part of the county and was kin to most of the rest. So I ran. There were five; I was one of five candidates. I licked all the rest of them because I knew more people in the county than they did. That's all.

"And after that, why things just happened. That's about the size of it. Things just happened, and I wound up being President of the United States, which was the last thing in the world I had in mind."

Did you know Tom Pendergast when you first ran for office, Mr. President?

"No. I'd known his nephew Jim, of course; he was a lieutenant in the war with me in the 129th, but I did not know Tom at that time. It was Jim, and it was Tom's brother Mike who agreed that I might be a good candidate.

"And I had an old Dodge roadster, and I drove all over the county and went to each of the seven townships in the district and met people, and I spoke wherever I could find anybody to listen to me, you might say."

Could you tell me about your first speech?

"My first speech was out at the town of Lee's Summit, as I recall, and I was so scared I couldn't say a word. So I just got off the platform. It was good for me because I began to learn how to make an appearance before a crowd. It took time, but I learned.

"And in 1948, in the campaign of 1948 I made quite a few speeches, you may recall, and when I . . . well, just talked to people without anything being written down, just stood there and talked, people seemed to understand what I was getting at, and the result was the same as it was here in Jackson County in 1922."

Edgar Hinde: "Harry learned how to make a speech, but it was slow going, and in that first campaign, the first time I heard him speak, it was . . . I think it was the most painful thirty minutes of my life. I just couldn't wait for him to finish."

Mr. Hinde, I understand you tried to persuade Mr. Truman not to run in that first campaign.

"I did. He came to see me; I believe he came to see most of his old buddies of Battery D, of which I was one. And he told me he was planning to run for county judge. I said to him, 'What do you want to do a thing like that for, Harry?' And he said, 'I've got to eat, don't I?'

"I still tried to discourage him, though; to me . . . he just wasn't the politician type. The kind who would slap somebody on the back; he was just not that sort of man, and it seemed to me he should . . . stay out of politics.

"He paid no attention to me, of course, and I suppose you might say he didn't do too bad a job of it."

Tom Evans, an old friend of Mr. Truman's, owner of a chain of drugstores and radio and television stations: "The first time I met Harry . . . I was a soda jerk, not a soda squirt, a soda jerk at the drug store at Twenty-Sixth and Prospect streets in Kansas City. And that was where the headquarters of the Tenth Ward Democratic Club was. It was headed by Mike Pendergast, brother of Tom

Pendergast, and it was a good thing to belong to that club if you were in the neighborhood, and everybody did belong.

"Harry came, this was at a time when he was in the haberdashery business, he came to the club, and he was different from most of the others. They were most of them out for a good time. But Harry wasn't that type at all.

'I remember that at first I thought he was a school-teacher. He struck me as a schoolteacher type, and then when the rest would go out on the town for drinks and things like that, Harry never joined in. He always went home. He was a very sturdy type of young man.

"So when I heard that he was running for office, I wasn't too surprised, and I wasn't surprised when he got elected. There was something about him that you . . . that you wanted to trust and knew you could."

Did you ever think he would wind up being President?

"A thing like that never occurred to me, but Harry . . . Harry Truman was always the type of man you felt could do whatever he set out to do, and one other thing about him: He never got discouraged. He never showed it anyway if he did. He kept his feelings to himself, and he was always very, very cheerful when you met him, and he was always interested in you and in your . . . wel-fare."

Tom Murphy, a veteran of Battery D and a Kansas City salesman: "I used to box in France, and I lost one big match there with a guy who was fifteen or twenty pounds heavier than I was. Harry bet money on me, and he lost it all.

"After the armistice he had a furlough to go to Paris, and he did, and while he was gone, some of the men found some bottles of green cognac, and we all got very drunk and disorderly.

"When Harry first came back, he didn't say a word, and I had . . . well, I had started oversleeping and missing reveille, and he called me in. I was a sergeant, and he called me in and said, 'Sergeant, that business with the cognac was pretty disgusting, and I understand you've been missing reveille. I'm going to bust you.'

"I said, 'Well, sir. I certainly do deserve it.' He looked at me in the eye and paused for a minute, and then he said, 'Okay. You go back and behave yourself now.'

"I'm sure if I'd pleaded to keep my rank, he'd have busted me. But he appreciated the fact that I didn't do it, and after that . . . I'd, . . . like most of the rest of Battery D, would do whatever we possibly could for Harry Truman.

"I fought in Boston in 1920 and won the national AAU boxing championship. And in 1922, when Harry first ran for office, I was still boxing, and I helped him open his campaign out at Lee's Summit. I went out there with a boxing partner and gave an exhibition to help draw a crowd.

"A lot of men in the outfit helped him in the campaign. They'd go out in cars and tack up campaign posters for him, and we'd go to the rallies and cheer and applaud.

"We'd do whatever was necessary to help Harry. We were that loyal to him."

Harry Truman: "If you're going to be in politics, you have to learn to explain to people what you stand for, and learning to stand up in front of a crowd and talk was just something I had to do; so I went ahead and did it.

"You might say I never got in a class with old Bill Bryan, but . . . well, by the last meeting of that campaign in 1922 there was a meeting up in front of the courthouse here on the square in Independence. I guess there must have been five thousand people there, and they had to listen to all five candidates, all of them supposedly more qualified than I was, but I maneuvered it . . . I was friendly with the chairman and the secretary of the county committee, and I maneuvered the thing so that I was the last one on the program, and I got the ovation and won the election. I won by about five hundred votes over all the other four, and from then on I had no difficulty in getting along before an audience."

Mr. President, in the theater the star always maneuvers to have the last act in the show. Did you know that when you arranged to be last?

"Of course not. How would I know a thing like that? I was just using common sense, which if you've got it helps in getting what you want."

What if you haven't got it?

"If you haven't got it, the best thing to do is not get out of bed in the morning."

10

The Only Defeat—and
Then Victory

*Mr. President, in 1924 when you ran for reelection as
county judge, you were defeated. Why was that?*

"The two factions of the Democratic Party in this
county [the Rabbits under a boss named Joe Shannon and
the Goats under Pendergast] were more interested in fighting each other than they were in winning the election.
That was the biggest reason. I was defeated by an old
Republican, an old harnessmaker named Henry Rummel.
That was a great time for Republicans. Calvin Coolidge
was in the White House, and a lot of people thought the
prosperity was going to last forever. I knew better than
that, but it didn't do any good . . . not that year."

*Wasn't another reason for your defeat the fact that the
Ku Klux Klan was against you?*

"The Klan was against me. That's true."

*I've read that the members of the Klan in Jackson
County weren't only one hundred percent Americans.
They thought of themselves as two hundred percent Americans, and they didn't just hate Catholics, Jews, and Negroes. They hated everybody.*

Mr. Truman laughed. "That's what they were all right.
They claimed . . . later it was claimed that I was a member, but I never was. I've told you; most of the boys in
Battery D were Catholics, so how could I be a member of
something like the Klan? I told them to go to hell. They
were a bunch of damn cowards hiding behind bedsheets.

"Here in Jackson County the Klan was a Republican
adjunct, just like it was after the Civil War. And it was
used politically to cause a great many good people in
Missouri, Democrats, to be defeated. And they had several
meetings in Jackson County when I was running for
county judge and also when I was running for presiding
judge and the Senate.

"And in 1924 I went to one of their meetings; it was in

the daytime down in the eastern part of the county. I guess there must have been a thousand people there, and I knew every durned one of them."

They weren't wearing their sheets?

"Oh, no. This was in the daytime. And I got up and told them exactly what I thought of them. Got down off the platform, walked right down through the center of them, and started home.

"And I got about halfway home, and I met two carloads of my Democratic boys coming out from Independence with shotguns and baseball bats, and I made them turn around and go back. I said, 'You don't need to use guns. Those guys are scared when they don't have their sheets on.' And that's all there was to it."

Did you have any thoughts before you went that you were risking a thousand votes?

"No, no. I went down there to tell them what I thought of them, and I did, and half of them voted for me."

How do you explain that?

"Because they knew what they were doing wasn't right. I told them that anybody that had to work behind a sheet was off the beam and that my partner in the haberdashery business, Eddie Jacobson, had told me that the fellow that was organizing the Ku Klux had to be a Jew because nobody but a Jew could sell a dollar ninety-five-cent nightgown for sixteen dollars. That's what it cost them to get in."

Mr. President, under the circumstances mightn't it have been wiser not to go out and tell off those Klanners?

"It might have been, yes, but once a man starts thinking that way, about what it's wise to say and what isn't, why, he might just as well cash in his chips and curl up his toes and die.

"I tried never to act that way, and for the most part I think you can say I succeeded. Sometimes I was advised to hold my fire on this and that because they said telling the truth would *offend* people. But whenever I took such advice I never thought much of myself.

"If you keep your mouth shut about things you think

are important, hell, I don't see how you can expect the democratic system to work at all.

"I wouldn't want you to say this . . . not as long as the boy [John F. Kennedy] is in the White House, but in 1952 I was out campaigning for the fellow we've talked about [Adlai Stevenson] and I made some speeches up in Massachusetts. The Kennedy people got the word to me that they'd very much appreciate it if I'd hold my fire on Joe McCarthy. I believe . . . I was told that they were afraid I might say something against old Joe that would cost the ticket some votes up there, but I didn't pay any attention to that. I went right ahead and said what I had on my mind, and I believe you'll find that in the long run it did more good than it did harm.*

* "The shadow of Joe McCarthy hangs like a great pall over the Democrats of Massachusetts. At Joe's lightest breath they button their coats to the chin and shiver. John Kennedy, the Massachusetts' Democrats' great hope for the Senate, never mentions Joe's name.

"It is Kennedy's view that the Irish core of his party likes Joe McCarthy and will grievously punish any man who traduces him.

"The Democrats of Massachusetts sent that message to Harry Truman just before he went into New England week before last. Take it a little easy with McCarthy, they said; talk about Hoover. The people up here don't have to be told why they hate Hoover.

"A few weeks ago the Republican National Committee gave Eisenhower the lay-off McCarthy warning for Wisconsin. Eisenhower took their orders like a soldier.

"But Harry Truman marched into Boston's Symphony Hall last Friday with his lips tight and his eyes hot. Just before he got there, Jack Kennedy had completed a nice, alliterative, inoffensive assault on the 'Capeharts and the Cains, the Brickers, and the Butlers.' . . .

"Mr. Truman looked Boston in the face and read it a lecture about McCarthy. He could speak without shame, he said, of his administration's record against Communism.

"He told them what McCarthy had done in pillorying the innocent. He spoke of 'those moral pygmies, Senators Jenner and McCarthy,' and he fairly spat their names. He reminded

"I cussed out old McCarthy every chance I got. He was nothing but a damn coward, and he was afraid of me. The only thing he ever did that I approved of was when he knocked down Drew Pearson.

"And when Eisenhower let McCarthy get away with calling General Marshall a traitor. Why that was one of the most shocking things in the history of this country.

---

them that in a choice between McCarthy's favor and his debt to General Marshall, Eisenhower had gone with McCarthy.

" 'I stand by my friends,' said the President, and suddenly Boston's cheers came pounding back at him. He spat out McCarthy's name again, and they were booing it. Mr. Truman had taken his chances on Boston, and Boston had come through.

"For Harry Truman, wherever he goes, is campaigning unafraid against the McCarthys and the Jenners. He is telling his party to meet them beard to beard. He singed the Connecticut Republicans for coddling them. In New Jersey, last Tuesday, he singled out that ancient fraud, Senator Smith, for 'his sad lack of backbone' in caving in before McCarthy.

"Not even for campaign purposes would Harry Truman blanch or quail. Yesterday in Cumberland, Maryland, where McCarthy is generally credited with deciding the 1950 Senate election, the President called Joe 'a political gangster,' a denizen of the 'political underworld,' a dealer in 'the big lie.' His audience listened open-mouthed and then applauded.

"The President of the United States, a man nobody writes off as a political scientist, is gambling that McCarthy is an overrated punk. And, even if he isn't, Mr. Truman will not bow before him, and none of the faint-hearted can tell him to.

"You cannot write about this little man with thick glasses in the language of politics. The words are the sparse words of a military citation—the citation, for example, of a soldier named Charles Kelly, who stood off a German battalion in Italy. The sergeant who wrote it remembered leaving Corporal Kelly with his machinegun burned out and rifle useless.

" 'When last seen,' the sergeant said, 'Corporal Kelly was observed loading and firing a rocket launcher at the advancing enemy.' A soldier like Harry Truman fights the enemy on the ground of the enemy's choosing. He'll run on your own terms —any track, anywhere, any time and distance and who in the hell are you?"

—Murray Kempton, Washington, D.C.,
October 15, 1952

The trouble with Eisenhower . . . he's just a coward. He hasn't got any backbone at all, and he ought to be ashamed for what he did, but I don't think there's any shame in him."

Mr. President, I believe that in 1926 when you ran for presiding judge of the county, you were elected.

"Yes. In 1926 they got together, the two factions of the Democratic Party got together, and I ran for presiding judge, which is the chief executive officer of the county, and I held that position for eight years.

"The county was in debt when I got in because the previous occupants of the job were the kind who were always standing with their hands out when contracts were let for buildings or roads or anything at all.

"I put a stop to it, and I came out of the county courts after ten years of service a damn sight worse off than when I went into it. No man can get rich in politics unless he's a crook."

Edgar Hinde: "I have had the President tell me many, many times that Tom Pendergast never asked him to do anything that wasn't absolutely all right. And I think he gave the President a free hand while he was in county politics, and he ran his job as he saw fit. There was never any hint of graft or skulduggery all the time he was in office in Jackson County. . . .

"In 1931 I believe it was they voted a bond issue. They voted seven million dollars to build a road system in Jackson County, and every one of those contracts, with I believe the exception of one, was let to out-of-state contractors. There was only one contractor in the state of Missouri that got a job here. That was because Harry never let politics enter into a thing of that kind. He gave the bid to the lowest bidder, didn't matter who he was as long as he could do the job.

"And when they finished they had about twenty-five miles more of road than they had contracted for and about two hundred and thirty thousand dollars left in money. So I don't think you could say there was any graft in that deal.

"In fact, when Harry started that bond issue, he appointed a bipartisan board of supervisors to oversee things under his supervision, and there was not a bit of graft in this expenditure of ten million dollars."

Mrs. W. L. C. Palmer: "My husband, who was principal of the high school, was one of the few people who thought Harry was going to be President someday. I have to admit I didn't. I was just too young and flighty at that time, so that I didn't think anybody was going to be President would be going to school with me.

"But my husband did. That was when Harry was presiding judge of the county, and he built—oh, I think ten million dollars' worth of roads. Up to that time the roads in Jackson County were in dreadful condition. You couldn't get anywhere except through mud.

"But Harry got a bond issue approved, and he built those roads. I've heard it said those were the finest roads of any county in the country except Westchester County in New York.

"I remember Harry came to see us one afternoon, and he got out a book showing different parts of the county and what he had done. He gave my husband one of the books and wrote in it, 'To my good friend and preceptor, Professor W. L. C. Palmer, whose ideals were impressed upon me at the right time. Harry S. Truman.'

"I wanted a book, too, of course, and Harry had another one, and he wrote in it, 'To Mrs. W. L. C. Palmer, who tried to teach me to do what I ought. Harry S. Truman.'

"After Harry had gone, Mr. Palmer said to me, 'That boy is going to be President of the United States someday.' So I'm very proud to tell you that while I didn't predict Harry would be President, my husband did."

Harry Truman: "Mrs. Palmer, Miss Hardin her maiden name was, Ardelia Hardin, used to quote that proverb from the Bible, 'Seest thou a man diligent in his business? He shall stand before kings.' I was always diligent enough, I guess. Maybe that's why I've stood before a few kings. I've even sat down with one or two.

"About this getting rich in politics. Like I said, you just can't do it unless you're a crook. After being in politics in the county here, I went to the Senate and stayed there for ten years, and the same thing was true. There were fellas that had their hands out for crooked money. So you could do the same thing in the Senate. You could do the same thing as President of the United States. But I didn't believe in it."

Mr. President, have we ever had a President who was financially dishonest?

"No, no. We've had Presidents who've had crooked men around them. Grant and Harding and perhaps some others who don't come to mind at the moment. But so far as I know, we have never had one who was himself dishonest. And we have never had one who tried to be a man on horseback. We've been very lucky in that regard, and I just hope our luck holds out."

Mr. Truman continued: "When I took office I found the county with two million three hundred thousand dollars in protested warrants, which would bring six percent. And so I went to Chicago. I went to the Harris Trust Company and the First National Bank of Chicago and got them to refinance those warrants on a three percent basis, and that was accomplished. Then I succeeded in getting the court to agree with me to raise the tax enough to meet the county income, and on that basis eventually the county was no longer in debt.

"And when I quit the county, we had a road system that was one of the best in the United States at that time. . . . The protested warrants had all been paid; the county was out of debt, and I was, . . . a fella doesn't like to say this about himself, but I was pleased with what I had done

"Then I got fooled into running for the United States Senate, and you know what happened after that."

I understand Tom Pendergast once asked you to come into Kansas City to meet some contractors who were unhappy that they weren't getting awarded contracts while you were in office.

"He did, and I went, and here were all these birds in his office, local contractors, and they said they *deserved* to get the bids for building the roads because they were local people and local taxpayers and that sort of thing.

"And I said I didn't give a damn who they were or where they were from. I said I was going to give the bids to the lowest bidders who could do the job, and I didn't care if they were from California or China or where.

"And old Tom Pendergast told them, he said he'd warned them that I was the contrariest goddamn mule in the world. And they left. They were sore as hell and were mumbling and carrying on, but they left, and afterwards Tom Pendergast said to me that I was to go ahead and carry out my commitments as best I saw fit, and that is what I did."

And you never had any more trouble with Mr. Pendergast on that score?

"No, nor on any other. I've said many times that he never asked me to do a dishonest deed, and that's the God's truth. I did my job in the way I thought it ought to be done. And he never interfered, not even when he was in deep trouble himself."

Mr. President, I understand you built a courthouse while you were presiding judge.

"I did. I built a courthouse in Kansas City, and I remodeled the courthouse here in Independence. It was in 1931, and I was in my second term, and it was in the depth of the Depression. Nobody thought I could do it, but I wanted . . . I proposed a bond issue of close on to eight million dollars to build more roads and a new courthouse and make other improvements in the county. And to provide jobs, of course; a lot of people were out of work.

"As I say, nobody thought the voters would approve, but I simply told them what I had in mind, and I told them that not a penny would be wasted, and they understood, and the bond issue was approved."

I understand you've always been interested in architecture.

"Yes, I always have been. I might even have studied architecture if I'd gone off to college, which, as you know, didn't happen. But I've always felt that architecture was most important. You can tell a lot about a country by the kind of building it has.

"And so when we were about to build the courthouse in Kansas City I wanted the best-looking one you could get for the money, built by the best architect. So I got in a car, and I traveled a good distance before I ended up in Shreveport, Louisiana, in Caddo Parish down there, and that was the courthouse I liked. It had been designed by a man named Edward F. Neild, and I hired him to come to Kansas City and build the courthouse there, and it's twenty-two stories high, and it's a beauty.

"And after I became President and we had to rehabilitate the White House because it was falling apart, Neild was in charge of that, too. And he did a crackerjack job."

Who paid for that trip to Shreveport?

"I did. There wasn't anything in the budget to take care of a thing like that, but I felt it was necessary, and so I went ahead and did it. I must have traveled—oh, twenty-five thousand to thirty thousand miles. I went down to Texas and up to New York and out to Denver and Wisconsin. Wherever I heard there was a good courthouse, I went to look at it."

I hear there wasn't a stone that went into the courthouse in Kansas City that you didn't watch being put into place.

"There were some. I had a few other things to do, but there were very few working days when I wasn't there.

That courthouse was costing the people of Jackson County a lot of money, and I didn't want anybody, the workers or the contractors or anybody, to lay down on the job. When you're spending the taxpayers' money, you've got to have a sense of responsibility."

That was pretty much the same thing that motivated you when you started the Truman Committee in the Senate, wouldn't you say?

"It was. And I've said this so often people get sick of hearing it, but the only way free government works is if the men in charge of it have got the welfare of the people in mind at all times. If a man loses sight of that even for a minute, you don't have free government anymore.

"That's why I was never any too happy about the fellow that succeeded me in the White House. He didn't give a damn about the welfare of the people."

How about the Vice President?

"Now let's not get into that. I've told you, all the time I've been in politics there's only two people I hate, and he's one. He not only doesn't give a damn about the people; he doesn't know how to tell the truth. I don't think the son of a bitch knows the difference between telling the truth and lying."

Mr. President, I understand you also took considerable pains to find a sculptor to design the statue of Andrew Jackson in front of the Kansas City courthouse.

"I did. We had a little . . . some money left over from building the courthouse, and I wanted it to go into a statue of old Andy. And I wanted it to be a statue of a real man on a real horse. The one of Andrew Jackson on the horse in Lafayette Square is a ridiculous man on an impossible horse. Every time I looked out of the window in the White House and saw it over there it made me angry. I don't know what got into them, allowing a statue like that across the street from the White House.

"And . . . so to get the right statue, when I was on my trip about the courthouse, I went to see a man named Charles Keck. He'd done a statue of Stonewall Jackson that's down in Charlottesville, Virginia, which is one of the best equestrian statues in this country and maybe the world.

"I went to see him, and I got him to do the Andrew Jackson statue that's in Kansas City. I also went to Andy Jackson's old place, the Hermitage down near Nashville. They've got some of old Andy's uniforms there, and I measured them and gave the measurements to Keck so they'd be just right. And I got the War Department to send him the information on what a general like old Andy would be wearing. They did, and Keck made use of that information."

Mr. President, did you have to do any of those things?

"Of course I didn't, but I wanted to. I wanted that courthouse and that statue to be the best they could be. . . . When I was a boy, that was the way everybody went about things. Or so it seems to me. Nowadays in politics and just about everywhere else all anybody seems to be interested in is . . . not how much he can do but how much he can get away with. And I don't like to see it. I don't know what's going to become of us if everybody starts thinking and acting that way."

Since we were talking about architecture, I asked about the balcony.

In January, 1948, President Truman announced that he was going to build a balcony off his second-floor study in the White House. Those were days when nothing he did went without criticism, and in this instance the outcry was immediate. The New York *Herald Tribune* angrily said that Mr. Truman was only a part-time President of the White House and that he had "a lamentable penchant for meddling with an historic structure which the nation prefers as it is."

I said, *Mr. President, how did you feel when there was so much criticism of your putting that balcony on the White House?*

"It didn't surprise me a bit. That was an election year if you recall. And anyway people get in an uproar whenever any change is suggested in the White House. My goodness, when Mrs. Fillmore wanted to put in bathtubs, the way people screamed and carried on you'd have thought it was the end of the world, but, of course, eventually everybody calmed down."

And the Fillmores were a lot cleaner.

"That's right. They were, and I knew the furor over the balcony would calm down, too. If you read Jefferson's idea of the White House, that balcony ought to have been there in the first place. And that's where I got the idea, from old Tom Jefferson."

I pointed out that now the balcony seemed to be widely admired.

"Well, of course, and that's the way it ought to be. And I never spent any time on that balcony. They claimed I built it so I could sit on it, but I never did. I never had time. I put it there because I thought that it belonged there."

Mr. President, I've read that Chester Arthur sold a lot of White House furniture when he was President.

"He had an auction sale right in the front yard of the White House, and I believe he sold twenty-four or more wagonloads of furniture. He sold a pair of Lincoln's pants and some of Jackson's furniture, and I don't know what all he sold. The whole thing only brought in about four or five thousand dollars, and there were some things that were just invaluable.

"I don't know why he did it. But then he was a President I couldn't ever figure out. They say he kept a whore in the White House, but I don't suppose I ought to say that. He's got some relatives still living out in San Francisco, and they wouldn't like it a bit."

Mr. President, could you tell me about the cheese some of Andrew Jackson's admirers sent him from New York? While he was in the White House, wasn't it?

"It was some people up in Herkimer County, New York, which used to be, maybe still is, cheese country. And some people there wanted to show old Andy how much they liked him, and so they decided to send him the biggest cheese in the world. It weighed about two thousand pounds and was round and as big as a silo, and they brought it down to Washington in a wagon, and naturally, it got a little riper every day.

"And then on the day of old Andy's last reception in the White House. He didn't invite people. He just opened up the doors and let people pour in, and they did, and they started cutting into that cheese, and when they were finished, there was hardly any left over for old Andy. Just about enough to go with a piece of pie, I believe.

"And then what happened? People trampled that cheese all over the White House, into the drapes and the rugs and everything, and when old Van Buren moved into the White House, he wasn't a man of the people like Jackson, and they had to spend I don't know several thousand dollars cleaning up the mess left by that cheese."

I said, still thinking of architecture, that I had recently built a house near Brewster, New York, that was half glass and half brick.

"Like one of those damn things Lloyd Wright used to put up?" asked the President, his lips drawn in a thin line.

Mr. Truman said, "I don't understand fellows like Lloyd Wright. I don't understand what gets into people like that. He started this whole business of chicken-coop and hen-house architecture, and I don't know why in the world he did it.

"I think what the building people do shows what they are thinking for that period, and that's why I hope that one of these days we'll get back to some real architecture."

So much for modern architecture.

On the way back to Kansas City that afternoon my associates were making fun of Mr. Truman's architectural taste, and I went along with the crowd. But that night I walked over to the courthouse and stood there for quite a long while, looking at it and at the statue of Andrew Jackson. And I thought of a man pushing fifty with no money except a salary of $6,000 a year getting into his car and at his own expense driving 25,000 to 30,000 miles so that he could build a courthouse and have a statue that were the best that in his mind they possibly could be. And paying not a cent more than they were worth because he had some old-fashioned idea about his *duty* as a public servant. Duty. Obligations. And what was it Dean Acheson had said of him, that he was a man of rectitude?

And I thought, those things are more important than his opinions of Frank Lloyd Wright. I haven't changed my mind either.

11

The First Race for the Senate

Mr. President, in 1934 you went from being presiding judge of Jackson County to being a candidate and a successful candidate for the U.S. Senate. How did that happen?

"In 19 and 34 I was finished with the county; I'd done my job, and there wasn't any more reason for my staying on around here than there was for me to stay in the White House in 1952 after I'd finished what I set out to accomplish. Besides which, I felt somebody else deserved a chance. . . . But as you know, I was very much disappointed in the Democratic campaign and in the way the candidate ran it. And I was also very disappointed in the way the election turned out that year.

"But in 1934 there was a new Congressional district . . . a couple of years before the state legislature had redistricted the state, and one of the districts included my old stamping ground, the eastern part of Jackson County. I had intended to run for that seat, but that just didn't happen. And so I went down and filed for the Senate, running against two fine Congressmen who later became friends of mine, Tuck [Jacob L. Milligan] and Jack [John J. Cochran].

"And, oh, the newspapers made quite a bit of fun of me, especially the St. Louis *Post-Dispatch* and the Kansas City *Star* and the St. Joseph *News-Press* and the Springfield *Leader-Press*—they made quite a big to-do about a little country judge who wasn't even a lawyer running for the U.S. Senate. Especially the Kansas City *Star,* which never has liked me and doesn't to this day. The *Star* has always supported the big-business interests of this community . . . , this area and no doubt will continue to do so.

"But when the time came for the campaign to start, I went into sixty counties, and I talked in all kinds of places

. . . any place there was any kind of audience at all, in the little towns and in the country stores, and I shook people's hands, and sometimes, why, sometimes there weren't more than two or three people, but I'd go in, and I'd shake hands, and I'd tell people that I was a farmer and a failed businessman and that I understood the problems that the common people were facing because I was one myself, and they could see that despite what the newspapers were saying, I didn't have horns and a tail. And Roosevelt . . . the Roosevelt New Deal was just getting under way at that time, and I told the people that I was a supporter of Roosevelt and his policies, and I told them why.

"I told them that . . . I said that it was the first time since Woodrow Wilson had been in the White House . . . the first time in more than ten years that there was a President who had the people's welfare at heart. I must have made . . . oh . . . sometimes as many as fifteen or twenty speeches a day. And it was the same kind of deal as I had in 1940 when I ran for reelection to the Senate and there wasn't a person who thought I had a chance to get back to Washington in any way whatever. And in 1948, when as you may recall I ran for reelection as President, and my prospects were not considered any too . . . very likely.

"I just stood there, and I didn't have to make any fancy speeches or put on any powder or paint. I just told people the facts, and the people believed me and didn't pay any attention to what some of the newspapers said about me. They could see for themselves that I was telling the truth as I saw it.

"And I spent time seeing the county courts like the one here in Jackson County, and I saw the clerks who make the appointments for the judges, and there wasn't a precinct in the whole of Missouri where I didn't have a friend, where there wasn't somebody to see to it that I got the votes that had been voted for me. They didn't have to cheat; that wasn't necessary. The votes were there. All they had to do was see to it that they got added up properly. And I came out ahead. I had a plurality of forty thousand votes in the primary, and after that I went ahead and won the election.

"We didn't have a lot of money to spend. But I never stopped talking to people and explaining the issues. I even had a car accident and sprained some ribs. I didn't stop campaigning, though, and, as I say, I got myself elected to the U.S. Senate.

"And so . . . eventually we moved to Washington. Margaret wasn't any too happy about it, and neither, I believe, was Mrs. Truman, but that was how it had to be."

Tom Evans: "I don't think Harry was looking forward to going to Washington that first time . . . or moving to Washington, but in 1940 he certainly wanted to go back, to be reelected, and nobody except maybe Harry himself thought he had a chance to do it."

Mrs. W. L. C. Palmer: "I believe he was somewhat nervous about going to Washington the first time. I remember he talked about the Senate and what an important body of lawmakers it was, and he talked about the Roman Senate and some of the Roman Senators and how grateful he was that I had taught him Latin and something of Roman history.

"He was not the quickest to learn; I believe Charlie Ross was quicker than he, and I believe you could say Bess was, too. But what Harry did learn it seemed he never did forget.

"Even after he became President, he was having a discussion with Chief Justice Vinson about some bill that was being debated in Congress, and Chief Justice Vinson quoted Marcus Porcius Cato about that Carthage must be destroyed. Except he said it in Latin. I forget how he said it, but I remember Harry said, 'That's the idea, but you didn't say it right. You should have said, 'Ceterum censeo Carthaginem esse delendum.' And Harry was right, of course.

"The newspapermen who wrote the story up wondered how Harry Truman knew anything about Latin. So they went to the encyclopedia and took it out and found that it was exactly as Harry Truman had said it was. So when I read that, I wrote to him, and I said, 'I want to congratulate you on your Latin. I don't suppose I taught it to you. You probably got it out of the *Encyclopaedia Britannica.*'

"He answered my letter and set me a photograph, and on it was inscribed 'To Mrs. W. L. C. Palmer, from her old Latin publicity man.' "

The last time I saw Mrs. Palmer the autographed photograph was hanging on the wall of the living room, slightly to the right of the horsehair sofa.

When I mentioned what Mrs. Palmer had said about Cato and the quotation from Cato, Mr. Truman said, "Mrs. Palmer—she was Miss Ardelia Hardin when I was in school—was a crackerjack of a teacher. She was so interested in what she was teaching that you just couldn't think of letting her down.

"I don't remember what Fred Vinson and I were talking about, what bill, but it was probably something to do with that damn Eightieth Congress. The majority of those fellows were just as bad as Cato was. He was against just about every progressive idea that came up in his whole lifetime, and they called him 'The Censor' because he was opposed to new ideas and tried to suppress them. And he was jealous of Carthage because it was more prosperous than Rome. That's why for years he ended every speech by saying, '*Ceterum censeo Carthaginem esse delendum.*'

"But I'll tell you one good thing about him, Cato. He wrote one of the best books about farming in Rome and farming anywhere else that I've ever come across. *De Agricultura* it's called. I read it in Latin before the war, when I was on the farm out at Grandview. I think I've got a copy in the library here someplace.

"I've told you. The only thing new in the world is the history you don't know. And that's true because human nature doesn't change. I sometimes wish it did, but I'm afraid it just isn't possible. At least that's what I've learned from studying history.

"And it's the same with farming. It hasn't changed from Roman times until now. We've got a few more machines now, but that's about the only difference."

Returning to the time Harry Truman went to Washington as a freshman Senator from Missouri, Mrs. Palmer said, "Mr. Palmer said to him, 'Harry, of course, this is just the first step for you. You have just started on your way, and I remember Harry said, 'Oh, no,' he said. 'The Senate is going further than I have any right to expect.'

"Harry Truman was a very modest boy and a modest man, and I believe that that is why he has been so successful in whatever he has done. People always felt they could count on him, and he has never disappointed them. At least if he has, I have never heard of it, and neither has anyone else in Independence.

"I don't believe that it is true, about a prophet being without honor in his own land. I think Harry Truman has always been very much honored by the people of Independence. There is not a man of his time who in this town has been so much revered."

Harry Truman: "Before we moved to Washington and after we got there, I studied up on the lives of each Senator, and by the time the session started I knew pretty much the history of every man. So I felt sure that when I got there, got to Washington, I'd understand all those men and why they acted the way they did."

Is that what happened?

"Oh, no. Oh, my, no. I guess you might say that is . . . . was really the first time I realized that there is often a considerable difference between what people write about themselves and what is written about them . . . even when the writer has set out to tell the truth . . . and the way things really are.

"There were some very good men in the Senate; most of them were, but there were some who were not so good, who were lazy, who never did any work but who got the headlines every time they made a speech, and some of them got sent back to the Senate time after time."

In other words, you can fool some of the people some of the time.

"Yes. Old Abe was right about that. As he was about most other things. But most of the Senators were very good men and worked very hard at their jobs."

Were you happy in the Senate?

"At first I wasn't. At first I was not very comfortable at all. And one day old Ham Lewis [J. Hamilton Lewis of Illinois, then the Democratic whip of the Senate] came over to me, and he said, 'Harry, the first six months you're here you'll wonder why . . . you'll wonder how the hell you got here, and after that you'll wonder how the hell the rest of us got here.' And that's pretty much the way it turned out. Old Ham pretty much hit the nail on the head."

Mr. President, is it true that when you were in the Senate your mother used to write you letters telling you how she felt you ought to vote on certain legislation?

"She very often did that. She read the *Congressional Record* every day, and she understood what was going on a lot better than some Senators I could mention. And she was one of my constituents, in addition to being my mother, and she had every right to write to me."

Did you always agree with her and follow her suggestions?

"Most of the time, yes; she was very strong for Roosevelt, and so was I, and so we agreed most of the time, but when she thought I'd voted wrong, you can bet I heard from her in no uncertain terms. She was a woman who knew her own mind."

Did you ever have the feeling that some people in Washington are convinced that people in the western part of the country can't read at all? And don't think?

"I did. Oh, my, yes. That's why when there was some talk that Washington might be bombed, while I was President, I wanted to move the capital out to Colorado so the people in the Senate, in the government, many of whom had never been west of the Appalachians would have to come across the country—they'd have to drive; I wouldn't let them fly—would come across and see the country and get to meet people who aren't suffering from what I call Potomac Fever."

What's Potomac Fever?

"It was Woodrow Wilson who coined the phrase. He said that some people came to Washington and grew with their jobs, but he said a lot of other people came, and all they did was swell up. Those that swell up are the ones that have Potomac Fever. They're the people who forget who they are and who sent them there."

Does that happen very often?

"I'm afraid so. Washington is a very easy city for you to forget where you came from and why you got there in the first place."

Did you ever feel you were in any danger of doing that?

"No, no. I always came back to Independence every chance I got because the people in Independence, the people in Missouri had been responsible for sending me to Washington. And that's why when I ended up at the White House, after I had finished the job, I came back here. This is where I belong."

Mr. President, I understand that during your first term in the Senate, you met Justice Brandeis.

Justice Louis D. Brandeis was appointed to the Supreme Court by Woodrow Wilson and was the first Jew to serve. He was a man of awesome intellect, a graduate of the Harvard Law School, and along with Justice Oliver Wendell Holmes one of the great and most consistent liberal dissenters on the Court until the New Deal came along. Until his retirement in 1939 he was an almost equally consistent supporter of New Deal legislation.

"I did know Justice Brandeis, and he was a great old man. I went to his place very often, and we seemed to have no trouble in hitting it off. We had many a long talk. I had read many of his decisions and his books, two of them. I believe there were two. One was called *Other People's*

Money, and I've forgot, don't remember, the name of the other. But he was very pleased that I had read his books."

I said, "Writers often are," and the President laughed.

Did you in general agree with Justice Brandeis' philosophy?

"Oh, yes. Very largely yes. He was one of the great Justices. He and Oliver Wendell Holmes were my favorites. And Justice Brandeis and I were certainly in agreement on the dangers of bigness, and my goodness . . . I cannot . . . I have often wondered what Justice Brandeis would think of these great combines of business now. He wouldn't have liked it. Of that I am sure, and neither do I."

I'm not sure the word "conglomerate" was in general circulation in 1961; it certainly was not in Harry Truman's vocabulary, and he would have despised it, both the word and the idea. We will come to what Mr. Truman thought about the Pentagon.

Mr. President, I've been told that you made a largely forgotten speech on the floor of the Senate during your first term in which you blasted big business.

"There were . . . I've got them. There were two speeches, and they are in one of the books here."

The speeches were in a collection of Mr. Truman's speeches. One was delivered in June, 1937, and it said in part:

"Some of the country's greatest railroads have been deliberately looted by their financial agents. . . . Speaking of Rock Island reminds me that the first railroad robbery was committed on the Rock Island in 1873 just east of Council Bluffs, Iowa. The man who committed that robbery used a gun and a horse, and he got up early in the morning. He and his gang took a chance of being killed, and eventually most of them were killed. The loot was $3,000. That railroad robber's name was Jesse James. The same Jesse James held up the Missouri Pacific in 1876 and took the paltry sum of $17,000 from the express car.

"About thirty years after the Council Bluffs holdup, the Rock Island went through a looting by some gentlemen known as the 'Tin Plate Millionaires.' They used no guns, but they ruined the railroad and got away with seventy million dollars or more. They did it by means of holding companies. Senators can see what 'pikers' Mr. James and his men were alongside of some real artists."

In the speech Senator Truman delivered on the floor of the Senate in December, 1937, he said in part:

"One of the difficulties as I see it is that we worship money instead of honor. A billionaire in our estimation is much greater in the eyes of the people than the public servant who works for the public interest.

". . . It makes no difference if the billionaire rode to wealth on the sweat of little children and the blood of underpaid labor. . . . No one ever considers the Carnegie libraries steeped in the blood of the Homestead steel workers, but they are. We do not remember that the Rockefeller Foundation is founded on the dead miners of the Colorado Fuel Company and a dozen other performances. We worship Mammon. Until we get back to the . . . fundamentals and return to the Giver of the Tables of the Law and His teachings, these conditions are going to remain with us.

"It is a pity that Wall Street with its ability to control all the wealth of the nation and to hire the best brains of the country has not produced some statesmen, some men who could see the dangers of bigness and of the concentration of the control of wealth. Instead of working to meet the situation, they are still employing the best law brains to serve greed and selfish interest.

"People can only stand so much, and one of these days there will be a settlement. We shall have one receivership too many, one unnecessary depression out of which we will not come with the power still in the same old hands.

"I believe this country would be better off if we did not have sixty per cent of the assets of all insurance companies concentrated in four companies. I believe that a thousand insurance companies with $4,000,000 each in assets would be just a thousand times better for the country than the

Metropolitan Life with $4,000,000,000 in assets. The average brain is not built to deal with such astronomical figures.

". . . a thousand county seats of 7,000 each are a thousand times more important to this Republic than one city of 7,000,000. Our unemployment and our unrest are the result of the concentration of wealth, the concentration of population in industrial centers, mass production, and a lot of other so-called modern improvements.

"We are building a tower of Babel."

After reading the two speeches, I said, *Mr. President, you said some pretty strong things in those speeches. You sound like a Populist.*

The President had been rereading the speeches with, I felt, considerable pleasure. He said, "Maybe I do. I don't like giving names to things if I can help it, but that's the way I felt at the time and still do.

"That's one of the things I try to tell these youngsters when I talk to them. That people have to keep their eyes and ears open at all times or they'll be robbed blind by the Mugwumps in politics and by the big-business interests.

"Every generation seems to have to learn that all over again, and it's a shame. I've wondered and I've wondered and I've wondered why. It's a human trait, I guess. Every youngster as he grows up knows he was a darned sight smarter than his daddy was, and he has to get to be about forty before he finds out the old man was smart enough to raise him.

"But as I say, I don't know why it is. Why the next generation can't learn from the one before until they get knocked in the head by experience.

"I'll tell you one thing for sure. The only things worth learning are the things you learn after you know it all."

During your first term in the Senate you served on a committee under Senator Wheeler [Burton K. Wheeler of Montana] to investigate the railroads.

"Senator Wheeler set up a subcommittee to look into railroad finances. They were in bad shape and going bankrupt because the more money that was poured into them, mostly by the government, the more 'the tin-plate millionaires' that I mentioned in that speech, the more they and the rest of the big-money boys and their lawyers stole.

"Wheeler wanted me to look into that. At first I wasn't a member of the committee, but I was allowed to sit in on the hearings, which I did every day."

I understand that you did a lot of reading, too, and at one time you took fifty books on railroads and railroad history out of the Congressional Library so that you could bone up on the subject.

"I don't remember that I did, but I wouldn't doubt it a bit. As I've told you, I like to be thorough, to have a thorough knowledge of whatever I'm involved in."

You spent a lot of time in the Congressional Library?

"I used it a great deal, and the people there were just as nice, as helpful, as they possibly could be. My goodness the trouble they'd go to if you asked them a question, to look something up.

"What surprised, what disappointed me about the Congressional Library was how few members of Congress ever seemed to use it; I used to go in there, and there sometimes wouldn't be anybody else there except a few young people and the librarians. Seldom any . . . very seldom any members of Congress.

"I couldn't understand it then, and I still can't."

Eventually you were appointed to the Wheeler committee, weren't you?

"Yes, eventually when there was a vacancy on the committee, Wheeler appointed me, and . . . I believe a year or so later, when he was out of Washington a good deal of the time, making speeches against what was called the Roosevelt court-packing plan, I became vice-chairman of the committee."

You liked Senator Wheeler, didn't you?

"I did. Later, of course; we always disagreed on many things, and we were in almost total disagreement on the

THE FIRST RACE FOR THE SENATE

Second World War. He was an isolationist, and as you know, I was not.

"But on other issues he was just as valuable as he could be, and he was honest as the day is long. When I first came to Washington, he was one of the first Senators to be . . . who took the trouble to be kind to me, and I never forgot a thing like that."

You presided over a good many meetings of that committee.

"I did, and it was very good training for what came later when I presided over what people called for whatever reason the Truman Committee.

"I presided, and one of the first investigations I conducted was into the affairs of the Missouri-Pacific Railroad, and my goodness, the telegrams I got, and the phone calls and letters. And visitors, quite a number of visiting firemen who asked me to call off my dogs. I was threatened with political ruination of every kind you can imagine if I didn't call off the investigation, but, of course, I didn't do it."

Max Lowenthal, who was counsel to the committee, has said that there were very few if any other Senators out of all the ninety-six who could or would have withstood the pressure you withstood.

"That may be, but it didn't make any difference. I had undertaken to do a job, and I was not about to give up without finishing it no matter what was said. So we went ahead with the hearings, and my, the lies I listened to from all those lawyers with their Ha-vud accents. It just seemed they didn't make any bones about telling lies, and a lot of people believed them. You dress a man up in a fancy suit and give him a fancy accent, and a lot of people seem to think he has to be telling the truth, but I never did.

"I went right ahead and found out the truth, and the result was that I was able to present to the Senate a new law regulating railroad finances, and oh, my, the shouting and screaming that went on from the big corporations and the holding companies.

"I was called every name in the book that they could

think of, including that I was a Socialist and a Communist and an anarchist and I don't know what all. And every Senator and every Congressman got a number of telephone calls and telegrams.

"But we went right ahead, and after some time . . . it took some time to do it, but after a while we got the law passed. It was called the Transportation Act of 1940, and at that time it represented a very good piece of legislation that had the interests of the people at heart, and I was happy to have had some part in getting it . . . enacting it into law."

Mr. President, I'm an occasional victim of the New York Central Railroad. Do you feel that railroad management perhaps needs looking into again perhaps?

"Yes, yes, of course. Those lawyers with their Ha-vud accents are always thinking up new ways to take advantage of people, and you need a new investigation every five, every ten years or so."

And now it's been more than twenty years since there was one.

"It has, and it's a great pity."

As of this writing it has been more than thirty years since such an investigation was held, and the corrupt New York Central has become the even more corrupt and bankrupt Penn Central, but there is no Harry Truman to conduct an investigation. To care even.

It *is* a great pity.

Another major achievement of Harry Truman's first term in the Senate was his fight for the Wheeler-Rayburn bill in 1935; that bill, also known as the Public Utility Holding Company Act, had at its heart what was called the Death Sentence clause, which proposed dissolving all public utility holding companies on the grounds that they drained off the profits from the utility companies themselves, thus causing consumers to be charged higher rates.

In opposing the bill as a whole and that clause in particular the utility companies put on what was said to be the most extensive and expensive lobbying campaign in history up to then.

I said, *Mr. President, I understand that you got as many as thirty thousand letters from people in Missouri asking that you vote against the Public Utility Holding Company Act.*

"I did. Twenty-five to thirty thousand, something like that, and I had them burned."

You had them burned?

"I most certainly did. Those letters and telegrams . . . were caused by the lobbyists who'd been sent out to Missouri to tell people lies. You have to watch out for the people's interest in that kind of thing, and the people's interest, for the vast majority of the poor and middle-class people, it was in their interest to get that bill passed into law. So I didn't pay any attention to all those letters.

"And they sent a . . . the utility people sent a lot of high-powered people down to Washington to stir up things. One of them was a fella by the name of John Foster Dulles who later wound up in the Cabinet of the fella that succeeded me. And Mr. Wendell Willkie was another. So when in a year or so in 1940, when he ran for President against Roosevelt and told the people how he was out to protect their interests, I wasn't much impressed."

I believe Harold Ickes [Roosevelt's Secretary of the Interior] called Willkie "the barefoot boy from Wall Street," because he'd, . . . Willkie, had made so much of being from Indiana, although he'd lived in New York for twenty years or so and he was head of a big utility company [Commonwealth and Southern].

"Did he? I'd forgot that. . . . Sometimes Harold Ickes got off a good one. Not too often, though. He was mad too much of the time."

The controversial Death Sentence section of the utility bill was passed by the Senate 45-44, and the complete bill was passed by a vote of 56–32. Truman was paired in favor of the bill.

Mr. President, in 1940 did you want to return to the Senate?

"No question about it at all. For one thing there were too many people around who didn't want me to run.

"I knew it was going to be a hell of a fight, but I've never backed away from a fight. Roosevelt got word to me that I could be on the Interstate Commerce Commission if I'd get out of the race and support Lloyd Stark." Stark was then the Democratic governor of Missouri.*

"Well, I wouldn't. I wouldn't at all, and I got word back to Roosevelt that if the only vote I got was my own, I'd still run. Roosevelt was a fine man and a great President, but he sometimes made mistakes, just like the rest of us."

Mr. President, would you describe yourself as a stubborn man?

The President smiled, and he said, "What I am . . . I don't know if I'm stubborn or not, although I've been called that from time to time, but when I make up my mind to do something, I believe you'll find I usually carry through on it.

"Lloyd Stark is a no good son of a bitch, and I don't care what anybody says. He's the president of Stark Orchards, which is the biggest in the country. He and his cousins and his brother run it, and they're all fine people. But Lloyd's a nut. He couldn't make up his mind what he wanted to be, and then he tried to run for everything at the

---

* During his first term in the Senate Mr. Truman was often referred to as "The Senator from Pendergast." It was thought that he had been elected by a corrupt machine and must, therefore, be corrupt himself. Thus, many Senators ignored him, and so for a very long time did the White House. Lloyd C. Stark, the nurseryman who was to be Truman's opponent in his 1940 race for the Senate, was often a guest on the Roosevelt yacht on the Potomac; Truman never was. Stark, of course, was a graduate of Annapolis and a man of polish and sophistication. Harry Truman was not, and Roosevelt, despite his political programs for the common man, was a considerable snob socially.

Truman liked to remember being closer to Roosevelt than he ever was.

same time.* He's sort of like that fellow we were talking about downstairs [Adlai Stevenson]. Couldn't make up his mind what he wanted to do.

"I had more to do with making him governor than anybody else in the state, and then he turned around and ran against me for the Senate.†

"He'd come to my office in Washington. He was always dropping in to ask some favor or other. I don't think he ever once visited me without wanting a handout of some kind, and in those days if I could give it to him, I did.

"One day long before the primary [the Democratic primary to choose a nominee for the Senate which in Missouri at that time was tantamount to election] he came into my office. I forget what he wanted on that occasion, but he said some people in Missouri wanted him to run against me for the Senate.

"But he said [imitating Stark's voice], 'I'm not a gonna do it, Harry.' He says, 'You know I'm a friend of yours, Harry, and I wouldn't do anything in the world to hurt your feelings.'

"When he left my office I said to my secretary [Victor

---

* In 1940, at the same time that Stark was threatening to run for the Senate, he showed up at the Democratic convention in Chicago with a number of Stark Delicious apples to hand out to the delegates and an announcement that he was *available* for the Vice Presidential nomination on the ticket with Roosevelt. He withdrew before the balloting for that office began, but a good many potential supporters from Missouri felt that he had made a fool of himself and of them by running for two offices at the same time.

† In the summer of 1935 Harry Truman and Senator Bennett Clark, the senior Senator from Missouri, at his request took Stark to New York to introduce him to Tom Pendergast, who was about to sail for Europe. Stark begged for Pendergast's support in his race for governor. Truman has reported that Pendergast said of Stark, "He won't do, Harry. I don't like the so-and-so. He's a no-good."

Nevertheless, with the urging of Truman and Clark, Pendergast did support Stark, and he was elected.

Messall], I said, 'That son of a bitch is gonna run against me,' and sure enough I was right. That's exactly what happened.

"I believe I mentioned that Lloyd Stark is one of the two people I have ever held a grudge against."

12

The 1940 Campaign

The historic triumph was in 1948, of course, the year
Mr. Truman astounded everybody, friends and enemies
alike, and he did it with the whole world looking on and
a good part of it delighted with the miracle he had somehow managed.

But in 1940 when he ran for reelection to the Senate,
with nobody much watching and everybody who mattered
against him, he was even more of an underdog, and he
won that time, too.

That looked like a bad year for a man turned fifty-six
years old who, if he didn't get reelected, would be out of
a job, permanently it looked like. His old friend Tom Pendergast was in jail, convicted of income-tax evasion. He
had failed to report almost half a million dollars, a bribe
given him by various insurance companies.

They had tried to dig up dirt on Harry, but there just
wasn't any. Still, he suffered from old Tom's downfall.
Birds of a feather, the newspapers said. And, anyway, if
Harry wasn't involved, why didn't he denounce Pendergast? That would clear the air.

"No," said Harry. "I wouldn't kick a friend who was
in trouble no matter what it might do to win me votes."

And Harry was broke, as usual. His mother was eighty-
eight years old, and they were threatening to foreclose the
mortgage on her farm, which later, as you'll see, did happen. But Harry couldn't give her any financial help. Hell,
at the beginning of the campaign he couldn't even afford
stamps to write to people, old friends, asking for money.
Later, he did manage to borrow $1,000 from a St. Louis
contractor, which was repaid after the Democratic primary.

Harry had two opponents in the primary, Maurice Milligan, the prosecutor who had earned a name for himself
by sending Pendergast to jail, and Lloyd Stark.

Both Milligan and Stark vigorously campaigned against Tom Pendergast, and they indicated that Harry Truman was no more than his crooked errand boy. If the truth be known, they said Harry ought to be in jail himself, and when the whole truth came out, he no doubt would be.

All the important papers of the state were against him. The St. Louis *Post-Dispatch* just never let up on the man, and one cartoon showed two heavy trucks, one named Milligan, the other named Stark, with Harry in a toy car between them. The caption was: "No Place for a Kiddy-car."

After he got to be President, the cartoonist sent Mr. Truman the original of that cartoon, and it is in the library at Independence now.

The campaign began at Sedalia, Missouri, a town of 20,000 people in the center of the state, and Mr. Truman and his supporters had trouble getting enough money to pay for the posters advertising the meeting. Quite a few people turned out, though, and that proud Rebel Martha Ellen Truman sat in the front row. And it was there, on the courthouse steps in Sedalia, of all places and all times, that Harry Truman made a speech on civil rights. By 1973 standards it may not seem like much, but by 1940 standards it was quite something.

I wondered why, why then, why there. Of course the record of his administration on civil rights was clear enough. Clinton Rossiter has written that of two major accomplishments of Mr. Truman as President: "One was domestic in character: the first real beginnings of a many-sided program toward eliminating discrimination and second-class citizenship in American life." True. And we remember that at the 1953 inaugural blacks were invited to all the social events for the first time in American history. But that was public, that was *politics;* people were watching, and the black vote was getting to be important.

But in 1940 in Sedalia, Missouri, before an audience mostly of farmers, many of them ex-Ku Kluxers, and not a black face anywhere, Harry Truman spoke out on civil rights. While the words were not eloquent, the man's words were never eloquent, they were unequivocal, and they had a simple beauty of their own:

"I believe in the brotherhood of man, not merely the brotherhood of white men but the brotherhood of all men before law.

"I believe in the Constitution and the Declaration of Independence. In giving Negroes the rights which are theirs we are only acting in accord with our own ideals of a true democracy.

"If any class or race can be permanently set apart from, or pushed down below the rest in political and civil rights, so may any other class or race when it shall incur the displeasure of its more powerful associates, and we may say farewell to the principles on which we count our safety.

"In the years past, lynching and mob violence, lack of schools, and countless other unfair conditions hastened the progress of the Negro from the country to the city. In these centers the Negroes never had much chance in regard to work or anything else. By and large they went to work mainly as unskilled laborers and domestic servants.

"They have been forced to live in segregated slums, neglected by the authorities. Negroes have been preyed upon by all types of exploiters from the installment salesmen of clothing, pianos, and furniture to the vendors of vice.

"The majority of our Negro people find cold comfort in shanties and tenements. Surely, as freemen, they are entitled to something better than this. . . . It is our duty to see that Negroes in our locality have increased opportunity to exercise their privilege as freemen . . ."

Mr. President, when I came across that speech in Jonathan Daniels' book last night, I found it surprising. It seems to me to have been very courageous.

"I don't know why. That sort of thing, whether what I was saying was courageous or not, never did occur to me. And you have to understand what I said out there at Sedalia wasn't anything *new* for me to say. All those Southern fellas were very much surprised by my program for civil rights in 1948. What they didn't understand was that I'd been for things like that all the time I was in politics. I believe in the Constitution, and if you do that, then everybody's got to have their rights, and that means *everybody*, doesn't matter a damn who they are or what color they are.

"The minute you start making exceptions, you might as well not have a Constitution. So that's the reason I felt the way I did, and if a lot of folks were surprised to find out where I stood on the colored question, well, that's because they didn't know me."

On the same page in the Daniels book that quotes your speech there's something Lincoln said about the Know-Nothings that I guess you'd agree with.

"If Lincoln said it, the chances are ninety-nine out of a hundred that I'd agree with it. What's that? Read it to me."

Well, he said, "As a nation we began by declaring that 'all men are created equal.' We now practically read it 'all men are created equal except negroes.' When the Know-nothings get control, it will read 'all men are created equal except negroes and foreigners and Catholics.' When it comes to this, I shall prefer emigrating to some country where they make no pretense of loving liberty,—to Russia, for instance, where despotism can be taken pure, and without the base alloy of hypocrisy."

"Well, that's just as true these days as it was in Lincoln's time, both about this country and Russia, too. I've always known it and always said it. That's what they never seemed to get right when they were writing me up in the newspapers. I always meant what I said, especially about the Constitution. You'll never find me playing fast and loose with that. Never."

Getting back to the 1940 campaign, tell me about that.

"Well, what we've been talking about. The first meeting was at . . . in the town of Sedalia, and Lew Schwellenbach [U.S. Senator from Washington] made a pitch for me, and there was quite a good crowd, friendly, but that was just the first step. I realized that if I was going to win, I had to go out and beat the bushes, which I did. Missouri's got a hundred and fourteen counties, and I got into seventy-five of them and finally won by a very close shave when you take into consideration that nearly four hundred thousand votes were cast in the primary and I won by about eight thousand. Altogether it was one of the toughest, maybe *the* toughest campaign I ever went through."

I understand your mother was at the meeting at Sedalia.

"She was. I couldn't have kept her away if I'd tried."

I've read that when people were taken up to meet her, she could always tell who was your friend and who wasn't.

"She was a very good judge of people, and although she was eighty-eight years old, her eyes were just as sharp as ever they had been, and she never had any trouble sizing up who was going the right way and who was going the wrong way as far as I was concerned. And she did not like Lloyd Stark. She said she'd just like to get her hands on Lloyd, and there were times when I wouldn't have minded if she could have.

"I've been called a lot of things in my life, but some of the things Lloyd said about me—(imitating Stark) 'I'm your friend, Harry, and I wouldn't do anything to hurt you'—some of those things I never will forget. Never in a hundred years."

Mr. President, is it true that at the same time that Stark was attacking you for accepting Pendergast support you had a letter signed by him, thanking you for introducing him to Tom Pendergast so that he could get such support?

"Oh, yes, I did."

But you didn't use that letter in the campaign—despite Stark's vicious attacks on you. Why?

"I didn't think it would be right to do a thing like that."

Rufus Burrus, Mr. Truman's Independence lawyer and longtime friend: "I campaigned for him when he was running for reelection to the Senate in 1940. Things were very, very difficult; it was like 1948, when he was running for reelection to the Presidency. Nobody around here, including me, thought he had a chance.

"The two candidates running against him were talking about their virtues and waving their names in front of the people. And all Harry talked about was Roosevelt and the New Deal and how it ought to be supported. And I said, 'Mr. Truman, don't you think it's about time you said something for Harry Truman? Or if you don't, let me say something for you.'

" 'No,' he says. 'I'm talking about the Democratic achievements in Congress and the Democratic program, and people will catch on and know I've had some part of it. Those other fellows are doing enough blowing their own horns.' "

Mr. Burrus, I understand there wasn't much money to toss around in that campaign.

"No, no, there wasn't. Mr. Truman . . . part of the time I believe he didn't have enough money for a hotel room, and I believe he slept in the car. A United States Senator . . . sleeping in his car. And they were . . . his opponents were accusing him of being dishonest and of having a slush fund and I don't know what all.

"But the people he met . . . they could see just by looking at him that what was said about him was a bunch of lies. There wasn't anybody who saw him or listened to him talk who ever thought there was a dishonest bone in Harry Truman's body. He was . . . was just about the worst speaker ever, but people never doubted he was telling them the truth.

"But that campaign in 1940 was very, very difficult. He never complained, though. He went right ahead and did it, and of course he won."

Mr. Burrus, how has your relationship been with Mr. Truman as his attorney all these years?

"Mr. Truman is just the best kind of client there is or ever could be. He never tells you what to do or how to do it the way so many people do. He just says, 'Would you please see about getting this taken care of?' And of course I do, and that's how our relationship works.

"Mr. Truman and I never talk about money. I'm always glad to do Mr. Truman's legal chores and errands for him without discussing money. He's endeavored to make me take some money at times, but I don't see fit to do that.

"That would be like taking money from my own family members that I do things for. And I've always considered my relationship with Mr. Truman as being a family relationship rather than as attorney and client. And here in Missouri we don't charge our kinfolks with fees like we would do if they were strangers."

Mr. President, I understand they foreclosed the mortgage on your mother's farm during that campaign.

"Yes, they did. They did foreclose it. Had an old squint-eyed guy that was head of the county government, and he thought that would be a good way to help in my defeat, but nearly everybody in Missouri had a mortgage, so it didn't do me a bit of harm.

"But it was a sad thing to see. We had to move my mother and the furniture and everything else off the old farm, and not long after she moved, she fell and broke her leg, which I don't think would have happened in the old place.

"It wasn't a pretty thing to see . . . to have to move an old lady of eighty-eight out of her home place, but they went ahead and did it. Some people will do anything to win an election, and it's a sorry thing to see. If you have to do something . . . pull a thing like that, I've never seen the use of winning."

You don't think the end justifies the means then?

"No and never have. Never."

How much money do you think you spent in that campaign, Mr. President?

"I didn't have any of what you'd call real money, didn't have any at all. I finally raised about eight or nine thousand dollars. We sent out some letters saying that if people wanted to see me go back to the Senate, they ought to send one dollar each, and we got a good deal in small contributions like that.

"But that's about all. I think we had one fifteen-minute radio broadcast in St. Louis a few days before the election, but the St. Louis organization paid for that.

"The whole thing made me convinced that it isn't money that wins elections, although in some instances I know it has."

Like in the last Presidential campaign, for instance. (I meant the 1960 campaign when John F. Kennedy was said to have spent a fortune in the primary campaigns in particular.)

"You said that; I didn't. But it's a very bad thing spending hundreds of thousands of dollars . . . trying to buy the votes of the people.

"I was always very particular about where my money came from. Very few people are going to give you large sums of money if they don't expect to get something from it, and you've got to keep that in mind.

"At least that's the way I've always felt."

Did you make your last campaign appearance in Independence that year?

"Oh, yes, same as usual. It didn't matter what I was running for; I always ended up the campaign back here in Independence, and we had a rally out at the football field of the high school, and there were some stands selling hot dogs and the like and quite a good crowd of people. And I ended up the program by telling the people what I stood for, and that was that.

"I came back home, and I started getting calls. Everybody thought for sure I was beat, and I wasn't too sure myself how it would turn out that time. And when I went to bed, Stark was eleven thousand votes ahead, so I thought for sure I was a goner."

But you went to bed anyway, and I suppose went to sleep.

"Yes, I did. Of course I did. But along about three o'clock in the morning an old man called me from St. Louis. And he had a Dutch accent I think it was, and he said [imitating the accent], 'I want to congratulate you.' And I said, 'Quit kidding. What are you congratulating me about?'

" 'Well,' he said. 'You're five thousand votes ahead, and the St. Louis *Post-Dispatch* says you're elected.' And that's what happened."

Truman carried St. Louis by 8,411 votes, which put him ahead of Stark by about 8,000 votes in the state and won him the primary. The Truman victory in St. Louis was made possible by a young Irishman named Bob Hannegan, who four years later as chairman of the Democratic national committee played an important part in getting the Vice Presidential nomination for Harry Truman.

Mr. President, I understand that being a Mason helped you win the election over your Republican opponent that November.

"I was . . . I had just been made Grand Master for the whole state of Missouri, and the Republican candidate for the Senate [Manvelle Davis] was cussing me out every time he opened his mouth. He said I was guilty of every crime in the book, and then one day at a meeting down at Wellsville a friend of mine was down there, and so was the fella running for governor on that ticket. His name was Forrest Donnell, and he was a Mason, as I was.

"So my friend said to Donnell that if I was as bad as Davis was saying, how was it possible that I could be Grand Master of the Masons? And Donnell said, 'He couldn't be.'

"Well, that word got around the state, and it did me no harm at all at the polls."

Mr. President, I understand that when you got back to the Senate the next year, following that election, you got a standing ovation from the Senators of both parties.

Mr. Truman was a sentimental man; his eyes misted over, and it was a moment before he could speak. Then he said, "It was one of the . . . it impressed me very much indeed, and that's one of the reasons when they mentioned that other job to me [the Vice Presidency], I didn't want to take it. Because the Senate of the United States is one of the greatest, maybe *the* greatest legislative body in the history of the world.

"It takes a long time for a person to reach a position of influence in the Senate. Eight or ten Senators really run the whole thing. And you have to have their confidence to get anything done, and I think it can be said that eventually I did have. Just to . . . as an example, the Senate was considering the approval of one of those admirals, Admiral Land [Emory S.] as chairman of the Maritime Commission I think it was.

"And when I came into the Senate, I'd been over to the House, and I came in the door and stopped by Vandenberg's desk [Arthur H. Vandenberg, Republican of Michigan], and he turned to me and said, 'Harry, what do you think of Admiral Land?'

"I said, 'Senator, I think he's all right. I think he'll do a good job.' And I went around to my seat, and Vandenberg got up and said, 'When the junior Senator from Missouri makes a statement like that, it's worth agreeing to.' And they did. The Senate approved of Land for the job.

"But that's what I mean. That shows you that if you have a fundamentally honest background with the Senators, you can get things accomplished. The whole thing, our whole government works on trust. If you can't trust a fellow Senator or anybody else in our government, the whole thing breaks down.

"And of course there are always those on the other side of the fence, the ones whose word you know isn't worth a good goddamn. Like Huey Long [Senator from Louisiana] who was later assassinated. He was a liar, and he was nothing but a damn demagogue.

"It didn't surprise me when they shot him. These demagogues, the ones that live by demagoguery. They all end up the same way.

"One day I was sitting in the chair. I was the only one there because the minute he started talking the other Senators started leaving. But I had to stay in the chair. And he was carrying on. And he had a big stack of books, you know. He always read the newspapers and books and everything else he could lay his hands on when he was carrying on a filibuster.

"I adjourned the Senate when he closed his book, and we walked across the street from the Senate, and he said, 'What did you think of my speech, Harry?'

"I said, 'Hell, Huey, I had to sit there and listen to it.' And he never spoke to me after that. Not that I was missing much."

As I said the other day, the extraordinary thing to me is the amount of homework you did while you were in the Senate.

"Well, as I told you, I did that just like I did everything else. Whenever I had to have information on a subject that was to come up before any of the four or five committees that I belonged to, I made it a point to find out exactly what I needed to know to vote the right way. The way that would benefit the most people."

13

The Truman Committee

Mr. President, tell me about the Truman Committee.

"That wasn't the name of it. It was called the Committee to Investigate the National Defense Program. Of course later they gave it that shorter name, and I didn't like it at all, but I couldn't put a stop to it.

". . . the way the committee started . . . I've said before. My Jackson County experience gave me an idea of how contractors and people who are dealing with government funds, whether they are local, state, or national, have very little respect for them. I had made some investigations of county government and state government before I went to the Senate. And so when the first draft act was passed and all the construction of those camps got under way, I felt that we would be in serious trouble if the matter wasn't investigated. At that time nobody seemed to care much, so I decided I'd have to do it.

"It's an amazing thing. Every ten cents that was spent for those work relief projects, the WPA and the PWA and those, every dime was looked into, and somebody was always against spending a nickel that would help poor people and give jobs . . . to the men that didn't have any.

"But the minute we started spending all that defense money, the sky was the limit and no questions asked. The 'economy boys' never opened their mouths about that, and I don't understand it. I don't now, and I didn't then.

"I do know from my experience that all . . . that no military man knows anything at all about money. All they know how to do is to spend it, and they don't give a damn whether they're getting their money's worth or not. There are some of them . . . I've known a good many who feel that the more money they spend, the more important they are.

"That's because of the education they get. I told you.

172

It's like putting blinders on a man. He can't see on either side of him, and he can't see ahead of him beyond the end of his nose.

"So somebody has to keep tabs on the military and all the time, too. That's the reason our government is set up the way it is."

Mr. President, there are those who think, and I must say I'm one of them, that since there's much more profit in spending money for arms and Army installations and bombs than there is in feeding the hungry or giving jobs to the unemployed, that's why the military usually has first priority on spending.

Harry Truman didn't speak for quite a time. I'm not sure why. It was certainly not that such a simple idea had never occurred to him before. After all, he understood the system very well. See the speeches he made on the Senate floor about 'the tin-plate millionaires' and the railroads. Maybe it was just that nobody had ever said it in quite that way to him.

In any case after a moment he said, "Of course that's true, and we shouldn't ever forget it. All through history it's the nations that have given the most to the generals and the least to the people that have been the first to fall."

Getting back to the committee, Mr. Truman said: ". . . Around that time Gene Cox [Congressman Eugene Cox, a Georgia Democrat who was a rabid Roosevelt hater] wanted to set up an investigating committee in the House, but that never happened. And anyway all he wanted to do was embarrass Roosevelt.

"Like the Committee on the Conduct of the War. That was the committee that was set up during the Civil War, and it wasn't so much interested in finding out what was going wrong as they . . . its members wanted to cause trouble for Lincoln, which they succeeded in doing. Lee [General Robert E. Lee, commander of the Confederate Army] later said that committee was worth at least two divisions to the Confederate cause, and I think he was right. Except I wouldn't doubt the committee did more harm than that.

"I'd read the hearings those birds had, every damn one of them. They only had one copy in the Library of Congress, and I guess it must have been . . . all those books must have been about so long (indicating a five-foot shelf), but I read them all to learn what *not* to do.

"And I am happy to say that so far as I know our committee did not make any of those mistakes. We were never an embarrassment to Roosevelt, not at any time.

"The chairman of that Civil War committee [Benjamin Franklin Wade, U.S. Senator from Ohio] was a mean old man, a real son of a bitch, one of those radical Republicans that was more interested in his own career than he was in anything else. And he interfered with Lincoln and his conduct of the war in every way you can possibly imagine.

"Once he told Lincoln he had to get rid of General McClellan, and Lincoln asked him who he'd get in McClellan's place. Wade says, 'Anybody.'

"And Lincoln says to him, 'Well, Senator, anybody may be all right with you, but I've got to have somebody.'

"Later Wade was one of those who was in the lead to convict Andrew Johnson of impeachment, and the reason he was so hot for it was that he was President pro tem of the Senate, and if Johnson had been convicted, Wade would have been President of the United States. . . . I don't like to think what would have happened to the country. Because Wade was a man . . . he was just a no-good son of a bitch."

So you weren't going to set up a committee like that.

"No, no, I wasn't. And I knew that after the First World War there'd been a hundred and sixteen investigating committees *after* the fact, and I felt that one committee *before* the fact would prevent a lot of waste and maybe even save some lives, and that's the way it worked out."

I understand that prior to setting up the committee, you got some letters from people in Missouri saying that there was a lot of waste at Fort Leonard Wood.

"I did, and so I decided . . . just the way I'd done in

Jackson County, I decided to take a look for myself, and I got in an old broken-down Dodge and drove down there and saw for myself. There were buildings—this was all cost plus, you understand—being built, barracks, mess halls, all kinds of building, and they were costing three to four times what they should have. I've told you before. Contractors and people who deal with government funds have very little respect for them.

"And at Fort Leonard Wood in Pulaski County there were . . . was material of all kind that was out in the snow and the rain, getting ruined, things that could never be used, would never be used. Some of them had been bought because somebody knew somebody who. . . . Well, you know what I mean.

"And there were men, hundreds of men, just standing around and collecting their pay, doing nothing. And I made notes on everything that I saw . . . and what people said, and after that I drove twenty-five thousand to thirty thousand miles or so, all over the country, looking at what money was being spent for, and it was the same everywhere. Millions of dollars were being wasted.

"And then I went back to the Senate, and I saw to it that the committee you were speaking of was set up, and you know what happened after that. It got me into all kinds of trouble."

I speak here in ignorance, Mr. President, but how do you go about setting up a Senatorial committee? How do you get approval?

"In the first place I made a speech [on February 10, 1941] telling the Senate what I had seen, and then I introduced a resolution calling for a committee to be set up. And after that was passed, it is customary for the author of the resolution to be made chairman of the committee, and that was done.

". . . Eventually the committee was authorized to spend fifteen thousand dollars and we took it from there.

"As soon as I was made chairman, I called up Jackson, who was Attorney General [Robert H. Jackson, later chief counsel of the War Crimes Trials at Nuremberg], and I said to him, 'I want the best investigator that you have on your payroll, and I'd like to interview him if you'll send him to see me down here at the Senate Office Building.

"So Jackson picked out the fella who had sent a couple of federal judges to jail for misuse of their positions. His name was Hugh Fulton. He was a great big, fat, nice-looking fella. Wore a derby hat. And he had kind of a high-pitched voice, and at first I didn't know what to think, but I looked him over, and finally I decided to take Jackson's recommendation. So I said to Fulton, 'I want you to make an investigation for me on the expenditures in the national defense program. What salary are you getting?'

"He said, 'I'm getting eight thousand dollars a year.'

"I said, 'All right. I'll give you eighty-five hundred.'

"And he said, 'Are you . . . is your committee just interested in getting headlines or is this going to be a real investigation?'

"I said, 'It's going to be real, and all you have to do is get the facts and nothing else. Don't worry about another thing. We haven't got any sacred cows around here. If you do your job, I'll do mine. You've got my word on that.'

"So he said, 'Okay. I'll take the job,' and we shook hands on it, and he did a very good job all the time he worked for me. But later . . . later he got too big for his breeches, which as I've told you happens time and again around Washington.

"Eventually we had about a dozen or so investigators, and the committee went from five members to nine, and we went ahead and did our job.

"After we ran out of money they gave us another sixty thousand dollars, and the next appropriation that was made was for three hundred thousand dollars. Those were the only appropriations that were ever made, and I guess you could say it was money well spent because it was said . . . I believe it was established that we saved the taxpayers about fifteen billion dollars. And the lives of some kids. I don't know how many. It was said . . . some reporters estimated we may have saved the lives of a few thousand kids.

"I can tell you the story of the airport between Fort Worth and Dallas. Myself and a couple of Senators went down there because the payrolls were outrageous.

"But they heard we were coming, and so they straightened things out, and everything looked perfectly fine. But under a great big hangar was a kind of basement which was above ground.

"And I said, 'What's under there?' And they said, 'Oh, that's just a basement for storage.'

"So I said, 'Fine. Raise up the trapdoor and let's see.' And I counted over six hundred men come out of there. They were hiding. They were on the payroll, but they weren't doing a day's work.

"And that's what you run into. Of course that contractor had to restore the overpayments which he had received, and he didn't get any more contracts.

"But dozens, hundreds of things like that and worse happened. They . . . Glenn Martin was making B-26 bombers, and they were crashing and killing kids right and left. So I said to Martin, 'What's wrong with these planes?'

"He said, 'The wingspread isn't wide enough.'

"So I said, 'Then why aren't you making it wider?'

"And he said, 'I don't have to. The plans are too far along, and besides, I've got a contract.'

"So I said, 'All right. If that's the way you feel, I'll see to it that your contract is canceled and you won't get another.'

" 'Oh,' he says, 'if that's the way it's going to be, we'll fix it,' and he did.

"I just don't understand people like that. He was killing kids, murdering kids, and he didn't give a damn. I never will understand people who can do a thing like that."

Well, greed is one of the seven deadly sins.

"And I guess maybe it's the worst. Down at Curtiss-Wright at the airplane plant in Ohio, they were putting defective motors in planes, and the generals couldn't seem to find anything wrong. So we went down, myself and a couple other Senators, and we condemned more than four or five hundred of those engines. And I sent a couple of generals who'd been approving, who'd okayed those engines to Leavenworth, and I believe they are still there. I certainly hope so."

Did you put many people in jail?

"We only had to jail about three or four people. The whole time only about three or four people went to jail.

"Just the fact that there was such a committee, that there was an investigation going on caused a lot of people to be more honest than they'd had in mind being. I wish it didn't have to be that way, but I'm afraid that's the way it is."

How did the President, did Roosevelt, feel about the committee?

"At first Roosevelt hadn't been any too fond of the idea, but as things went along, he saw that we were out to help him and not hinder the war effort, and he'd call me in from time to time, and he'd tell me there was something I ought to look into.

"He'd say, 'I can't do a thing with the sonsabitches. See what you can do.' And I would, and I . . . we were very often quite effective in clearing up whatever it was. And the Secretary of War and General Marshall would call me in. That's the first time I got to know General Marshall really well, and I got to know that you could depend on every word that he said, that he just never would lie to you, and that he always knew what he was talking about.

"Eventually, as I've told you, we saved the taxpayers fifteen billion dollars. And what frightens me . . . what I often think about: What if somebody hadn't been there looking after the interest of the taxpayers who were putting up all the money?

"And another thing I'm proud of. We didn't give a hoot in hell about publicity. My goodness, if I'd got into that committee to make headlines, I could have made enough to cover the whole of this room, but I didn't do it. We didn't give anything to the reporters unless the case was closed down tight. Nobody got his case before the public until we had the goods on him, and that's what I'm proudest of.

"And also the fact that we never issued a report that wasn't unanimously approved by every single member of the committee, and we had five members at one time and then seven and then nine."

Mr. Truman was succeeded as chairman of the committee by Senator James Mead, a New York Democrat. But nothing much happened, ever again.

Mr. President, why do you suppose it is that after you left the committee, it was more or less allowed to die?

"I'm afraid that's true. As soon as a war's over, nobody gives a good goddamn anymore. Of course the war went on for a time after I got that job I didn't want, but the fellow that took my place as chairman, well, he was as nice a fella as he possibly could be, but he just didn't have much get-up-and-go.

"And when the war ended . . . as I say, nobody gave a damn anymore. And all the Mommies wanted to get their little boys home. During a war they're men, but the minute it's over they're all of a sudden babies, and their Mommies want to get them home. I suppose it's . . . I suppose it's understandable, but it's a shame.

"Once there's an armistice, *everybody* gets selfish all of a sudden."

William James said that there ought to be a way to find the moral equivalent of war in peacetime.

"There ought to be, but I'd be greatly surprised to see it come about."

You don't think man is perfectible then?

"No, no. He can be improved on, but that's about it."

Mr. President, how do you feel about all the money that's being spent now by the military, without a Truman Committee to keep an eye on what's being done with it?

"It's a crime and disgrace. I'll bet you . . . I'll bet billions of dollars are being wasted over there at the Pentagon. Billions of dollars lining somebody's pocket.

"The thing I've always felt about the Pentagon is that while it was probably necessary . . . it's not right to have all those people in one building without a single watchdog. There ought to be somebody looking into every penny that's spent, but there isn't. And we're all in trouble when that goes on, when the generals get that much power."

Mr. President, you'll pardon my mentioning it, but earlier this year the fellow that succeeded you in the White House warned people against what I believe he called the military-industrial complex and its growing power in peacetime, what we've just been talking about. I believe he said that if we weren't careful that complex would engulf democracy and the people as well. Something like that.

Mr. Truman paused for a long time, very long. Finally, and with difficulty (it was not easy for him to say anything good about Dwight D. Eisenhower), he said, "Yes, I believe he did say something like that. I think somebody must have written it for him, and I'm not sure he understood what he was saying, but it's true. And I don't know why people aren't more concerned. Why the Congress isn't, but they aren't . . . don't seem to be anyway."

Mr. President, you once said you might run for reelection to the Senate when you were ninety. If you did and if you were reelected, as I'm sure you would be. . . .

The President laughed. He said, "That's one of the first damn things I'd look into. They'd probably try to stop me, but at ninety I'm still going to be a contrary goddamn cuss."

Unhappily, Mr. Truman died before he was able to run for reelection to the Senate. And the military-industrial complex continues to grow unchecked.

14

The Convention and the Campaign
of 1944

In the summer of 1944 I was a sergeant in the Army and was in the United States between an assignment in the Pacific and another in Europe. I wrote in my journal of the Democratic convention that year—I seem to have expressed myself more dramatically in those days—"President Roosevelt has betrayed all of us who are fighting for freedom by endorsing a little machine politician, his name is Harry Truman, for the Vice-Presidential nomination.

"Naturally, with Roosevelt's backing Truman was forced down the throats of the delegates . . . and he got the nomination. Under the circumstances I thought Vice President Wallace took it very gallantly. But if anything should happen to President Roosevelt during his fourth term, I fear the direst consequences. We shall have as our leader a political hack when we could have had a great man."

Well.

Years later Henry A. Wallace had a farm not too far from the place I'd moved to in Brewster, New York, and we had several conversations. I decided, I think rightly, that he would have been a disaster as President of the United States. More on that later.

Franklin Roosevelt was not at his best in the summer of 1944. For one thing he was tired; he had, after all, been President since 1933, most of three four-year terms, and the strain was beginning to show. I had dinner at the White House that summer, a guest of Eleanor Roosevelt, and I was dismayed at the President's appearance. I hadn't seen him for two years, but it seemed to me that he looked twenty years older. His eyes were sunken and tired; he seemed to have shrunk in size, and his hands trembled as he ate.

181

The dinner was not a joyous one, although I was *on* a satisfactory amount of the time. Mr. Roosevelt wanted to know about the morale of the troops in the Pacific, and I told him. It was not an optimistic report, but he listened. A few weeks later, when I said some of the same things before a group of officers at the Special Services School in Lexington, Virginia, I almost got court-martialed.

Although it was generally agreed that Roosevelt knew all along that he was going to run for a fourth term, that indeed since there was a war going on he *had* to run for a fourth term, he did not announce his candidacy until a few days before the Democratic convention in Chicago, which began on July 19.

As for his running mate he not only allowed total confusion to reign; he seemed to insist on it. Henry Wallace, his former Secretary of Agriculture and by his own choice Vice President since 1940, went to Chicago convinced that it was to be the same ticket again. And somehow James F. Byrnes, the small, feisty South Carolinian, a former Senator who was then head of the Office of War Mobilization, got the idea that he was Roosevelt's first choice, and so did Harold Ickes, who was Secretary of the Interior, and Alben Barkley, who was then majority leader of the Senate.

After Roosevelt's death Harry Hopkins told Robert E. Sherwood, "I'm pretty sure that Jimmy Byrnes and Henry Wallace and Harold Ickes are saying right now that they'd be President if it weren't for me. But this time I didn't have anything to do with it. I'm certain that the President had made up his mind on Truman long before I got back to the White House last year. I think he would have preferred Bill Douglas, because he knew him better, and he always liked Bill's toughness. But nobody really influential was pushing for Douglas. I think he'd gone off fishing out in Oregon or someplace. And Bob Hannegan [then chairman of the Democratic National Committee] was certainly pushing for Harry Truman, and the President believed he could put him over at the Convention. So the President told him to go ahead and even put it in writing when Bob asked him to. People seemed to think that Truman was just suddenly pulled out of a hat—but that wasn't true. The President had had his eye on him for a long time. The Truman Committee record was good—he'd got himself known and liked around the country—and above all he was very popular in the Senate. The President wanted somebody that would help him when he went up there and asked them to ratify the peace." *

Recently some historians have said that Harry Truman really lusted after that Vice Presidential nomination. If that is so, he certainly kept it a secret from everyone, and he said the opposite to everyone, including his mother, and Harry Truman was not a man who lied to his mother.†

Sue Gentry, the reporter for the Independence *Examiner* who covered the Trumans for so many years, told me the last time I was in Independence, "Mr. Truman was never ambitious for power. He never went after it in that sense, but when he got it, he certainly knew how to use it."

Mrs. Ralph Truman, the wife of Harry Truman's first cousin Brigadier General Ralph Truman, remembered that July this way:

"We had been getting reports from all over the country that Harry Truman was going to be the choice for Vice President. And the day he was leaving for the 1944 convention, a niece of the general was visiting us here in Kansas City, and I took the niece, and we went out to

---

* See Robert E. Sherwood's *Roosevelt and Hopkins*.
† At lunch one day at the Carlyle, I forget in what context, too many slight libations, Mr. Truman said, I remember the tone being one of complete incredulity, "What kind of a man would lie to his mother?"

Later at that same lunch he returned to the subject of Adlai Stevenson; Stevenson had said what Mr. Truman considered some damn fool thing at the United Nations the day before.

"The real trouble with Stevenson is that he's no better than a regular sissy," said Mr. Truman.

Grandview to have lunch with Harry and Mary Jane and Aunt Mat [Harry Truman's mother].

"And during the course of our conversation at lunch, I said to Harry, 'Well, when you come back, the next time we see you, you'll be the nominee for Vice President.'

"And he said, 'God forbid.' He said, 'I don't want the job.' And he says, 'In fact I have a speech right here in my pocket. I'm going to nominate Jim Byrnes for Vice President.'

"And I said, 'Well, nevertheless, when you come back you'll be Vice President—the nominee for Vice President. And Aunt Mat said that she knew Harry didn't want that. But she says, 'Harry, if they nominate you, I know you'll do a good job because you've always been a good boy.' And that was the way she always talked. . . . She always talked about Harry that way, that he'd always been a good boy.

"Of course as I found, after I was in the Truman family for a number of years, they were a very close-knit family. And they all looked to Aunt Mat for advice and counsel because she kept a firm hand on the family, always."

It's one thing to be firm and another to be just. Generally, would you say she was pretty just?

"She was very just. She was one of the most broad-minded women I ever knew. And even up to the date of her death, when she was ninety-four years old, she had a very clear mind and she was very much interested in everything—in world affairs and everything. And even though she'd got where she couldn't see to read herself, she insisted that newspapers and the *Congressional Record* and things of that kind be read to her every day so she could keep up with what was going on because she didn't want to be left out."

General Ralph Truman: "Harry said he didn't want the nomination, and I have known Harry since 1891 when he was seven years old, and I knew one thing. I knew that Harry had never told me a lie, and I have never told him one."

Do you remember, sir, anything about the first time you met Mr. Truman?

General Truman: "No, I can't say I formed much of an impression of him at that age. As I say, he was only seven years old, but I do remember one thing about that day. Aunt Mat served biscuits. That was very unusual. In those days, in my family at any rate, the only time we had biscuits was when the preacher came, about once a month. The rest of the time we were accustomed to eating corn bread. And we liked it. I still do. . . . But I remember Aunt Mat made biscuits that day."

Sir, do you remember anything about the summer of 1944, before Harry Truman got the Vice Presidential nomination?

General Truman: "I remember Harry said he was happy right where he was in the Senate, and he said he was doing his best for the country right there, and he didn't want to change. And I said to him, I remember I said to him, I says, 'Harry, whoever gets that Vice Presidential nomination is going to be President because there is no man alive who can be in that job for sixteen years.' And Harry said, says, 'I know. I know, and that is why I do not want the nomination.' He says, 'The responsibility is just too great.'

"And so the night when President Roosevelt passed on, I had great emotion. I thought, 'The responsibility. The awful responsibility,' and I am afraid that I shed tears."

Mary Jane Truman: "Harry said, he said, 'I'll bet you can't name the names of half a dozen Vice Presidents,' and I had to admit that I couldn't, and he said, 'No,' he said. 'The Vice Presidency is simply not a place I wish to be.' And Harry was always very serious about things like that. I remember once he said, I'm not sure when it was, he said, 'Being President is not a job a man should go after. There is too much involved for one man to do.'

"And I believe he still felt that way after he became President, but then it was too late, of course, and he had to do what he could. Whatever he did, he always did well, and he was conscientious and worked hard, and I believe that can be said of what he did as President."

Mr. President, in 1860, before the Republican convention in Chicago, Lincoln said that he did not want the nomination, but when he was pressed, he said, "The taste is in my mouth a little." Was the taste for the Vice Presidency ever in your mouth a little in 1944?

"No, no, not a bit, not at all.

"I was home here in Independence getting ready to go to Chicago, and the phone rang, and it was Jimmy Byrnes, and he said, 'Harry, the old man is backing me; I'm going to be the Vice Presidential nominee. Will you make the nominating speech?' I said that I'd be happy to.

"And a little later Alben Barkley called and wanted me to nominate him. I said, 'I'd be glad to, Alben, but I've already promised Jimmy Byrnes.' "

Had Roosevelt really backed Byrnes?

"No, he hadn't, and I never did know how Jimmy got that idea, but he did. Maybe Roosevelt just had never said he *wouldn't* back him. Jimmy was a man who sometimes heard things that hadn't been said at all. I found that out later when he was my Secretary of State. He sometimes claimed I said things I hadn't said, and I don't think he was lying, didn't know he was lying anyway."

What would you say he was doing?

"He was fooling himself."

How is that different from lying?

The President smiled. "I'll tell you. Some men when they *taste* wanting to be President, they can fool themselves without much trouble. There's something about the Presidency that causes that to happen to some men.

"After I got to be President, I knew every time Jimmy and I talked that he thought it ought to be the other way around. He ought to be sitting where I was sitting. That happens, and in a way you can understand it."

Would Byrnes have made a good President?

"He was a good Senator. I didn't agree with him on a lot of things, but he was a damn good Senator.

"But you never can tell what being President will do to a man. It's made some, and it's broken some. There's no way to tell unless you know a lot more about a man than the people ever have a chance to know."

We just have to leave it to chance—and maybe pray a little?

"That's about right. Of course you have to find out as much as you can about a man, and we have been very lucky in this country up to now. We have had some damn poor Presidents, I've told you about them, but we have never had a man who was totally dishonest in the White House."

What about Henry Wallace? Would he have made a good President?

"I don't know about being President, but he was a damn poor Vice President. Why, hell, he'd been there presiding over the Senate for almost four years, and I'll bet there weren't half a dozen Senators who'd call him by his first name. He didn't have any friends in the Senate, and that's the way things get done in the Senate . . . in politics. You may not like it, but that's the way it is.

"If you don't like people, you hadn't ought to be in politics at all, and Henry talked a lot about the common people, but I don't think he liked them, couldn't get along with them anyway.

"The fellow we were talking about from Illinois [Adlai Stevenson] could never understand that either, how you have to get along with people and be equal with them. That fellow was too busy making up his mind whether he had to go to the bathroom or not [much laughter]."

I was never much impressed by Wallace's speeches. Most of the time I couldn't decide what he was getting at.

"I'm not sure he could either, and long-winded. . . . Those long-winded birds. They're all the same. The less they have to say, the longer it takes them to say it."

I understand that you had a little experience in that line in 1940 with the man who was running for the Democratic nomination for governor.

"That's true. In 1940 when I was running for reelection, going around the state and meeting people, shaking their hands, I never talked more than twenty minutes, twenty-five.

"A fellow named Larry McDaniel was running for governor, to get the governor nomination as you say, and he couldn't stop talking. I guess his speeches must have got up to two hours long and more, and people were walking out on him in droves, but you couldn't stop him. I told him he was losing votes, but he just couldn't stop.

"And that November, although he got the nomination, he lost the election. I knew he would. . . . It's the same way out there in California now. With Pat Brown."

Edmund "Pat" Brown, then governor of California, was running for reelection; his opponent was Richard Nixon.

"I talked to Pat on the phone the other day, and I told him every time he makes a speech he loses ten thousand votes.

"If you're running against Nixon you don't have to say *anything.* You don't even have to get out of bed in the morning to beat him. My goodness, if I'd ever had a chance to run against *him,* it would have been the easiest campaign I ever had." *

Bob Aurthur once described the President as chuckling dryly, and I guess that is as good a description as any of what Mr. Truman did then. He chuckled dryly.

"I could have stayed right in Washington and licked him," he said, still chuckling.

How do you explain that, Mr. President?

"Because Nixon is a shifty-eyed, goddamn liar, and people know it. I can't figure out how he came so close to getting elected President in 1960. They say young Kennedy deserves a lot of credit for licking him, but I just can't see it. I can't see how the son of a bitch even carried one state."

Mr. President, would it be fair to say that you dislike Richard Nixon?

* Pat Brown must have stopped talking because he won the election; after his defeat his opponent told the press that it wouldn't have Dick Nixon to kick around anymore.

More dry chuckling. "Yes, I guess you could say that. . . . Now I never carried personal grudges. Only two, only two. There are only two men in the whole history of the country that I can't stand. And . . . I've told you . . . one of them was the former governor of Missouri, Lloyd C. Stark, who followed me around like a poodle dog to get the support of the organization of which I was a member so that he could be governor of the state.

"Then he forgot where he got that support, and he did everything he possibly could to beat me for the Senate the second time I ran.

"And Nixon is in that same class exactly. He went down to Texarkana, Arkansas, and he called General Marshall and me traitors. And I knew it, and the big fat Leonard Hall, when he was chairman of the Republican National Committee, he said he'd give a thousand dollars to any charity I wanted if I could prove it, prove Nixon said that.

"Well, I sent down there and got the reports verbatim from the Texarkana paper and sent them to Hall, and I said, 'Now you can send that one thousand dollars to the Korean Red Cross.' But I never heard from him."

Do you know whether he ever sent it?

"He didn't, of course. He didn't think I could find it.

"But those are the only two, Nixon and Stark. I've often said around the country that if General Marshall and the former President of the United States are traitors, then the country's in one hell of a fix.

"You can't very well forget things of that kind, and that's why I don't trust Nixon and never will." *

---

* According to an Associated Press dispatch from Texarkana on October 2, 1952, Nixon said that Truman, Acheson, and Stevenson were all three "traitors of the high principles in which many of the nation's Democrats believe." These "real Democrats," he was quoted as saying, were "outraged by the Truman-Acheson-Stevenson's gang's toleration of and defense of Communism in high places."

But what he really said may remain as forever disputed as what his friend Senator Joseph R. McCarthy really said that

I gather you don't think he's much of a campaigner either.

"He's one of the few in the history of this country to run for high office talking out of both sides of his mouth at the same time and lying out of both sides."

Do you think he talks too long?

"Any talk at all from him is too damn long."

Some people think Senator Humphrey talks too much sometimes.

"Hubert has that same difficulty, but I wouldn't want to

---

dark afternoon in February, 1950, when he made a Lincoln Day address before the Republican women of Wheeling, West Virginia.

The climax of the speech came when McCarthy waved a sheaf of papers in his hand and said, "I have here in my hand a list of. . . ."

After that, confusion. Either he said a list of 205 members of the Communist Party who were working for the State Department and whose names were known to the Secretary of State. Or else he said he had in his hand a list of 57 people who *probably* were or *appeared to be* card-carrying members of a party they *seemed* to be *loyal to*. Or else he said he had in his hand a list of 110 Communist sympathizers or anti-anti-Communists, which was pretty much the same thing.

In any case, the speech in Wheeling was delivered on February 9. On February 20 when it or something like it was placed in the *Congressional Record*, there was no list of any kind. The speech McCarthy read into the *Record* said, "The reason why we find ourselves in a position of impotency . . . is the traitorous actions of whose who have been treated so well by this nation. It is not the less fortunate or members of minority groups who have been selling this nation out but rather those who have had all the benefits the wealthiest nation on earth has had to offer—the finest homes, the finest college educations, the finest jobs of the government that we can give. This is glaringly true of the State Department. There the brightest young men who were born with silver spoon in their mouth [sic] are the ones who have been worse [sic]."

Quite a different speech, and so in Texarkana Nixon may have said Truman and Marshall or Truman and Acheson and Stevenson were *traitors* to their party or to their country. No matter, really. *Traitors* was the operative word.

say it in public. . . . You can't win many votes if people are either asleep or walking out on you."

How did you learn that? Did you know that in your first campaign?

"I had to learn it the hard way like everything else. I learned it in a lot of campaigns, and I learned it by keeping my eyes and ears open. That's the only way you learn anything. But some men just never do it. I can't figure out why."

Anyway, you don't think Henry Wallace would have made a good campaign in 1944?

"No, he would not have, and what campaigning he did do he was no good at.

"Roosevelt didn't want him to have the nomination, but he couldn't tell Wallace to his face. Roosevelt wasn't much good at telling things like that to people's faces. He told somebody, I forget who it was, 'I'm afraid Henry just hasn't got it,' and he was right, of course.

"As I say, Henry's speeches ran on and on; he didn't say anything, but you couldn't get him to stop talking."

Tell me about the 1944 Democratic convention.

"I went there to nominate Jimmy Byrnes, and as I told you, I had no thought at all of accepting the job and no idea it would be offered me. If it'd been an *offer,* I'd have turned it down."

Truman with Bess and Margaret drove to Chicago from Independence; they got there on Friday, July 14; the convention was to open the following Wednesday at noon.

The day the Trumans left Independence Roosevelt got on a special railroad car that would take him from Washington to San Diego. There he would board the U.S.S. *Baltimore* and go to Pearl Harbor for conferences with Admiral Chester Nimitz and General Douglas MacArthur to discuss the future strategy of the war in the Pacific.

The President agreed, apparently with reluctance, to stop off in Chicago and have a conference in the railroad yard there with Bob Hannegan and Ed Pauley, a California oilman and Democratic kingmaker. I have read at least a dozen different versions of what happened during that conference, but it is certain that Pauley and Hannegan emerged with a note from Roosevelt saying:

July 19 1944

DEAR BOB:

You have written me about Harry Truman and Bill Douglas. I should, of course, be very glad to run with either of them and believe that either of them would bring real strength to the ticket.

Always sincerely
FDR.

Since Douglas had no apparent support at the convention and since Wallace had been conveniently ignored by the President, with Byrnes never taken seriously by anyone much except himself, it was clear that the nominee would be Truman. It was, on the second ballot.

Mr. President, did you know that there was a lot of activity on your behalf going on behind the scenes?

". . . The only thing I knew: I had breakfast on Sunday with Sidney Hillman." Hillman had been co-chairman of the wartime Office of Production Management and was in Chicago as head of what was then the CIO's new Political Action Committee. "I had breakfast with Sidney Hillman, and I told him I was going to nominate Jimmy, and he said, 'Harry, that's a mistake. Labor will never support Byrnes. He's against labor. His whole record proves it.'

"And I said, 'Who the hell do you want then?'

"He said, 'We're supporting Wallace, but we have a second choice, and I'm looking right at him.'

"I had breakfast with Phil Murray [head of the CIO] the next morning, and he said pretty much the same thing. And I talked . . . I saw every political leader and every labor leader. I knew them all, and not a single one of them would be for Jimmy Byrnes. They said—there'd only be two people they'd be for: 'That's you and Henry Wallace.'

"And I said, 'You needn't be for me. I'm not going to be a candidate.'

"Well, on the afternoon of the day the President was nominated, would be renominated for the fourth term, they had a meeting up at the Blackstone Hotel. Suite 560 or 570 or wherever it was. If you're ever up there some time, I'll show you where it took place.

"And Bob Hannegan was there. He was an Irishman from St. Louis and a particular friend of mine. I made him Postmaster General before he died.

"The room was crowded. Every damn political boss in the country was there, any of them you would want to name, and half a dozen governors.

"And they all said, 'Harry, we want you to be Vice President.' I said, 'I'm not gonna do it.'

"Well, Bob Hannegan had put in a call to Roosevelt who was . . . down at San Diego. They finally got him on the phone. And with Roosevelt you didn't need a phone. All you had to do was raise the window and you could hear him.

"I was sitting on one twin bed, and Bob was on the other in this room, and Roosevelt said [Mr. Truman gave a near-perfect imitation of Roosevelt, Harvard accent and all], Roosevelt said, 'Bob, have you got that guy lined up yet on that Vice Presidency?'

"Bob said, 'No. He's the contrariest goddamn mule from Missouri I ever saw.'

" 'Well,' Roosevelt said, 'you tell him if he wants to break up the Democratic Party in the middle of the war and maybe lose that war that's up to him.' Bang."

Did Roosevelt know that you could hear him?

"No, no, he didn't. But hell, he'd been through Chicago a couple or so days before that, and I made my call on him, and he never said a word to me about the situation. And I said to Bob, 'Why in hell didn't he tell me that when he was here or before I left Washington? He knew I was coming here.'

"Bob said, 'I don't know, but there it is.'

"Well, I walked around there for about five minutes, and

you should have seen the faces of those birds. They were just worried to beat hell.

"Finally, I said, 'All right, Bob, if that's the way the old man feels, I'll do it, but who in hell's gonna nominate me now? I've told everybody here that I'm not a candidate, and every member of my committee and everybody else is committed to somebody else.'

" 'Well,' Bob says, 'maybe your colleague will do it.' *

"I said, 'All right, Bob, but where is he?'

"He said, 'Damned if I know. We'll have to find him.' So I spent the afternoon and half the night trying to find Bennett Clark. At about five o'clock in the morning I found him in the penthouse of the Sherman Hotel, which was Democratic headquarters, and he wasn't—well, he had a lot of whiskey in him. And I got a pot of coffee, and I put it on the table next to the empty whiskey bottle, and I said, 'Bennett, they want you to nominate me for Vice President. Will you do it?'

Mr. Truman then imitated a drunken Senator Clark. "He said, 'Yeah, Harry. I'll do it.' So I called Bob and said, 'I found your boy. He's cockeyed. I don't know whether you can get him ready or not, and I hope to Christ you can't.'

"Well, Bob did get him ready, and he was ten minutes late, but he nominated me, and then half a dozen fellas around over the country did it, too. And that was the worst time I ever spent in my life."

I read some place that after you were nominated the crowds started pressing in on you and trying to reach you, and you got in the street and there were more crowds, and Mrs. Truman turned to you and said, "Harry, are we going to have to go through this all the rest of our lives?"

"Yes, she did say that, something like that. It's an awful thing, crowds and the way they want to grab hold of you and all of that, and it's frightening. I did my best to keep the Boss and Margaret out of it as much as I could, but

* Bennett Clark, then senior Senator from Missouri.

that didn't always happen, and that's why we were glad to get back here to Independence."

Where people leave you alone?

"They don't leave us alone exactly. A fella like me who's been notorious and who's been what I've been and been *through* what I've been through, well, there are always curiosity seekers waiting out there, and you sometimes can't even go out to get the papers. You have to send the old nigger cook out to do it for you." *

What happened after the 1944 convention in Chicago?

"I went to see Roosevelt in August after . . . after he got back from Hawaii, and we had lunch in the backyard of the White House—there's a picture of that in that stack somewhere—and he said, 'I want you to do some campaigning. I don't feel like going everywhere.' I said, 'All right. I'll make some plane reservations to go around over the country anywhere you want me to go.' He says, 'Don't fly. Ride the trains. Can't both of us afford to take chances.' "

I understand you had trouble sometimes raising money for that train ride.

"Yes, yes, we did. We ran out of money a few times, but Tom Evans, who was chairman of the finance committee, he and Eddie Jacobson always managed."

Tom Evans: "Eddie was really a whiz at raising money. I don't know how he did it, but he'd pick up the phone and call somebody, and while we never got great amounts, we always got enough money to get the train moving again. That was the trouble. We'd be in some town, and we

---

* Privately Mr. Truman always said "nigger"; at least he always did when I talked to him. That's what people in Independence said when he was growing up. Of course, Independence was a Southern town, a border town, one of whose more prominent organizations has been the United Daughters of the Confederacy.

Considering his use of the word his civil rights program is even more remarkable.

wouldn't have enough money to pay to get the train to the next town. But with Eddie—we managed to have enough to make the full journey."

Mrs. Eddie Jacobson: "I don't think there was anything in the world that Eddie wouldn't have done for Harry, and raising money in that campaign—he was, I think he was only sorry he couldn't do *more*. . . . He and Harry never quarreled. Even when the haberdashery, even when business was bad, when it was going to go broke, they never quarreled. The newspapers always said that Harry had a very quick temper, but we never saw it around here."

Tom Evans: "Harry wouldn't take money from just anybody. He always told me, any contribution, to clear it with him. Harry was particular about where the money came from.

"One of the things we had to try to do, we had to get him to bed early at night because he had always been an early riser, and he had a lot of work to do, but one night in the hotel in Boston—we had a suite, a living room here, a bedroom over there, which was Senator Truman's room, and another bedroom off from that, which was Mrs. Evans and I.

"And we got him to bed, and we frankly thought he was sound asleep, and Matt Connelly, who'd worked with the Senator on the committee, and Ed McKim, one of his overseas buddies in Battery D, and Mrs. Evans and I were in the living room having a few drinks.

"And the door opened, and here was the Senator in his bathrobe, and he said, 'Can I please come in and have a little fun, too?' We said no. We said he had to go get some sleep, but he came in for a few minutes, and then he said that he'd go and let us have a good time. He said he had to wash his socks, and Mrs. Evans jumped up and said, 'You're a candidate for Vice President of the United States, and you won't wash your socks,' and she did it for him."

Mrs. Tom Evans: "He always said that that was one thing everybody had to do himself, wash his own socks and his own underwear, and I believe he always did. Even after he became President I believe he still did."

Tom Evans: "My biggest job in the campaign. We had a special car, the 'Henry Stanley,' it was a club car and a sleeping car, and it was attached to a regular train. And of course everybody knew when the train was coming through and that the candidate for Vice President would be on the train.

"We couldn't stop in the smaller towns, of course, and Senator Truman gave me the job of standing outside, on the back of the platform and waving at the people as we went through. Of course I'm much taller than President Truman, but I do have gray hair, and I wear glasses, and I can wave. And we went through so fast that people never knew the difference.

"But that was the big job I had in the campaign of 1944."

Harry Truman: "That day Roosevelt and I had lunch under old Jackson's magnolia tree, he looked very sick and tired. I knew he was a sick man. And what he said about both of us not being able to take chances, why, what more did you need?"

I understand that you and Ed McKim went to a movie at the White House that September. Tell me about that.

"It wasn't a movie. It was a reception for the actors that were in a movie about Woodrow Wilson, early in September this was, and Eddie and I went, and afterwards, when we went outside, Eddie said he'd been looking at the President, and he said something like I was going to be living in the White House before long. And I said, 'Eddie, I'm afraid I am, and it scares the hell out of me.'

"But after that lunch with Roosevelt, that's when the real train ride began, and we went just everywhere. New Orleans, Los Angeles, San Francisco, Seattle.

"And when we were in Uvalde, Texas, we saw old Jack Garner (Roosevelt's first Vice President), and he came down to see me, and we talked a little about this and that;

he'd been out in the cornfields that day I remember, and he said, 'Harry, do you think there's any chance you'd find the time to strike a blow for liberty? Somewhere in the world it must be twelve o'clock.'

"So I knew what he wanted. He wanted a slight libation, and I took him on the train, and we both had one. . . .

"But that campaign. That was the meanest campaign I ever can remember. I think it was even meaner than the campaign in 1948—the things they said about me. Most of the newspapers didn't hesitate to lie, and there was a whispering campaign—I've always thought it was organized—that Roosevelt—well, that his mind was gone and he was senile and I don't know what all.

"That about his mind was a damn lie. He wasn't well, but his mind—his mind was just as sharp as ever it had been, and that was the case whenever I saw him right up to the end.

"And Mrs. Luce—well, she said things about Mrs. Truman that I never will forgive her for, and that's another reason I never had the Luces to the White House. I don't care what they say about me, but when you get into saying things about Mrs. Truman and Margaret, you're bound to have some trouble on your hands.

"And before the campaign was over, the Hearst papers said I'd been a member of the Ku Klux Klan, which was a damn lie as I told you. But as I say, that was the worst campaign I ever can remember. They even claimed I was Jewish because I had a grandfather named Solomon."

What kind of audiences did you have?

"I had every kind of audience there was from those big auditoriums in places like Boston and Madison Square Garden to . . . one time in a little town in Idaho there were just three people showed up, three schoolteachers as I recall it."

Did you give them a speech anyway?

"Of course I did. It wasn't their fault that only three people were there, and they deserved the same consideration as the audience at Madison Square Garden, and I believe I can safely say that I gave it to them.

". . . As I say, we went just everywhere, Los Angeles and San Francisco and then up the coast, stopping at various places as we went along, and we stopped in Seattle and in St. Paul and Minneapolis and in Chicago, and we were in Boston.

"And when we were in Boston, Bob Hannegan was in a suite at the Ritz-Carlton Hotel, and who should be in his suite but old man Kennedy, the father of the boy that's in the White House now?

"Old man Kennedy started throwing rocks at Roosevelt, saying he'd caused the war and so on. And then he said, 'Harry, what the hell are you doing campaigning for that crippled son of a bitch that killed my son Joe?'

"I'd stood it just as long as I could, and I said, 'If you say another word about Roosevelt, I'm going to throw you out that window.'

"And Bob grabbed me by the arm and said, 'Come out here. I'm gonna get ten thousand dollars out of the old son of a bitch for the Democratic Party.' And he did.

"That is absolutely correct and the way it happened. I haven't seen him since. . . . When they asked me down in Richmond, I was down in Richmond, Virginia, delivering a lecture on the Constitution to the law school down there, and one of the smart-aleck kids got up—this was before the 1960 election—got up and said, 'What's going to happen when the Pope moves into the White House?' I says, 'It's not the Pope I'm afraid of, it's the Pop.' And that's still true. Old Joe Kennedy is as big a crook as we've got anywhere in this country, and I don't like it that he bought his son the nomination for the Presidency."

He really did buy it?

"Of course he did. He bought West Virginia. I don't know how much it cost him; he's a tightfisted old son of a bitch, so he didn't pay any more than he had to, but he bought West Virginia, and that's how his boy won the primary over Humphrey.

"And it wasn't only there. All over the country old man Kennedy spent what he had to to buy the nomination. . . . Of course, he didn't buy the Presidency itself. He didn't

have to. I told you. When you're running against a man
like Nixon. . . . Oh, my, I do regret I never had the
chance to run against him." *

* Mr. Truman and I never got back to the subject of Joe
Kennedy buying the Democratic nomination for his son in
1960, but Robert Alan Aurthur recalls a conversation among
Truman and two advisers, David Noyes, and William Hillman.
The conversation took place at about the same time as the
above during a ride between Independence and Kansas City,
as dreary a stretch of road as there is anywhere in the world:

". . . Mr. Truman reiterated his disappointment when Kennedy had taken the nomination from Lyndon Johnson in 1960.
In response to my question as to what specifically had set him
against Kennedy, Mr. Truman answered abruptly, 'I felt he
was too immature.'

" 'The Boss doesn't like wealthy Northeast elitists,' Hillman
told me, sotto voce, to which I commented that Franklin
Roosevelt had been exactly that.

" 'But one of the greatest politicians that ever lived,' Mr.
Truman said, putting the art of politics above anything else.' "

Noyes observed that at least Jack Kennedy was willing to
listen, and he seemed to be maturing fast. Mr. Truman
laughed.

" 'The Presidency will make a man out of any boy,' he said."

Hillman wondered if anyone could fault the Kennedys as
practical politicians, citing their extraordinary gift for organization, and Mr. Truman mumbled something half under his
breath to the effect that ". . . if you have enough money you
can buy almost anything.

"With Mr. Truman no more than two feet from us, Hillman
whispered loudly to me, 'He hates the idea that Joe Kennedy
bought the nomination for his son Jack.'

". . . Mr. Truman stared straight ahead, thin lips pressed
tightly together to indicate his residual disapproval of Joe
Kennedy. It was quiet for a moment, and then the participant
[Aurthur] asked hesitantly how one would go about buying the
Presidency.

"Not the Presidency," Mr. Truman said. "The nomination.
You can't buy the office itself . . . at least, not yet."

". . . One has to know where the local power is, Hillman
said, then be prepared to use leverage as ruthlessly as necessary. Like in West Virginia, the muscle is in the counties, exercised by the individual sheriffs. With tight, tough organization,

More sustained laughter and dry chuckling here and something about "as easy as shooting fish in a barrel."

Did you think you and Roosevelt would win in 1944, Mr. President?

"Never doubted it for a moment. I knew he'd win because the country wouldn't want to change Presidents while there was a war on. Besides, there was something about that other fellow [Thomas E. Dewey, the Republican candidate for President, then governor of New York] that people just never did trust. He had a mustache, for one thing, and since in those days, during the war, people were aware of Hitler, that mustache didn't do him any good.

"I also made use of that mustache during the 1948 campaign. I never mentioned him by name, but I kept

and a maximum of a thousand dollars a sheriff in the key counties, a wealthy man could bag the primary for his son.

"Money, Mr. Truman mused; just knowing there's an unlimited money available is often enough to cause the opposition to cut and run.

"And a Midwestern politician, not a Kennedy man to begin with, and with the power to control his delegation, who was also running for governor of his state. One phone call, just one phone call from old Joe with the threat to throw a million and a half dollars into this man's opponent's campaign, was enough to swing his support into the camp of the future leader of the New Frontier.

"(". . . ask not what your country can do for you. . . .")

"Oh, said Noyes, Whatsisname—another local politico who held sway over his delegation—had sold out for a measly $14,-500, just enough to pay off his house mortgage. The marvelous acumen of old Joe, finding each man's price, never spending more than he had to.

"Wide-eyed and slack-jawed, your hang-about, a self-admitted cynic, had never conceived of such political opportunities in the Presidential arena, but Mr. Truman reacted with contempt for that local nabob's cheap price. The damn fool could have held out and got at least a hundred thousand, Mr. Truman said.

"Maybe more, Noyes said, and Mr. Truman nodded. Probably. The state was worth a hundred and fifty to the Kennedys."

mentioning that I had a feeling I was being followed, and I'd make a motion of stroking a mustache. People got the idea. And I said, 'There's one place he's not going to follow me, and that's into the White House.' That got a considerable round of applause."

In your 1944 speech at Madison Square Garden, I understand there was some feeling that, since it was New York, Wallace might get more applause than you did.

"There was some talk like that, yes, and it was finally decided . . . that Henry and I ought to walk in together so that nobody would know who was getting the most applause.

"Well, we waited, and we waited, and I think maybe Henry had found out what we planned because he didn't come and he didn't come until about five minutes before we were supposed to go in, but we waited him out, and the two of us went in together. There was plenty of applause to go around for everybody that night, but Henry was not any too friendly.

"I tell you. I always thought Henry was more interested in the pe—he kept talking about the pee-pul—the pee-pul this and the pee-pul that. I always thought he was more interested in the pee-pul's applause than he was in the people themselves.

"You take a fella that carries on too much about the pee-pul—it's like what I told you about folks that pray too loud. You better get home and lock the smokehouse, and that's the way I always felt about Henry Wallace. I didn't trust him."

You came back to Independence on election day.

"Oh, yes. No matter where I was I always came back to Independence on election day, and we had . . . we had some of the fellows from Battery D and some others up in the penthouse of the Muehlebach (a hotel in Kansas City), and we were waiting for the returns, and they were worried to beat hell.

"I understand Roosevelt was, too. Old man Leahy [Admiral William D. Leahy, Chief of Staff both to Roosevelt and Truman] told me. He was staying with Roosevelt up at Hyde Park on the night of the election. And he told me he came downstairs about four in the morning to raid the icebox or something, and Roosevelt was still up, sitting there in front of the radio, and Roosevelt says to Leahy, 'I've been waiting for two hours for the son of a bitch to concede.'

"He didn't concede until three forty-five in the morning, you know, and it was the same in 1948. I have never understood why that fellow was such a slow conceder."

I understand you played the piano while waiting for the returns.

"I did. I wasn't scared, but everybody else was, and so I said, 'I guess what we need is a little piano music,' and I played a little while we were waiting."

Do you remember what you played?

"No. I don't remember. A little Mozart, I guess, and maybe some Chopin. I always played Chopin every chance I got."

Mr. President, when you knew the election was won, did you think about the fact that now you were almost surely going to be President?

"Oh, yes. I was scared. Ever since that interview with him in the garden, in the backyard of the White House . . . I was worried about it all the time, and when it finally happened, it was a terrible thing to have to take over after a three-term President who had been so nearly unanimously elected every time. It was something to worry about, and I did worry about it.

"Maybe that was just as well. Maybe that made me work harder."

15

The End and the Beginning

Harry Truman became Vice President of the United States on January 20, 1945, and he became President less than three months later, on April 12.

After the January inaugural Harry went back to the Capitol and called his mother in Grandview. Had she heard it on the radio, he asked, heard old Henry Wallace administering the oath of office to him and heard Chief Justice Harlan F. Stone swear in Franklin Roosevelt?

She said she had; she'd heard it all. "Now you behave yourself up there, Harry," she said. "You behave yourself."

"I will, Mamma," said the Vice President of the United States.

In his last years, as I've said, Harry liked to remember that he and Franklin Roosevelt were closer than they were; Roosevelt hadn't been close to any of his Vice Presidents. Truman liked to believe that Roosevelt had prepared him to take over, but that really hadn't happened. Not at all.

The truth is Roosevelt knew very little about Mr. Truman. Apparently he felt he didn't need to know much. Truman had done a good job as head of that investigating committee in the Senate; he was popular up there on the Hill, as poor Henry, "poor Henry just doesn't have it," had not been. When the time came to call on the Senate to ratify the kind of peace agreement that he in his wisdom had made or to get the Senators to agree to the setting up of the United Nations, Harry Truman could manage it for him.

It never seemed to occur to Franklin Roosevelt that he wouldn't be running things. Like most of the rest of us at the time, Franklin Roosevelt couldn't imagine anybody else as President. He began to think of himself as immortal.

The Trumans hadn't even been invited to the White House to break bread with the Roosevelts, not that that was any treat. The Roosevelts didn't set much of a table. Frances Perkins, who was Secretary of Labor, remembered that Mr. Roosevelt could and did carve seventeen to eighteen helpings from *one* side of a *small* turkey. See below what the Roosevelt boys have to say about meals at the White House in those days.

Well, as I say, we were lucky. Harry Truman was better prepared for the job than anybody, including, perhaps, Mr. Truman himself, would have guessed.

There are a few things that all of us of a certain age remember, and chief among them, I think, is where we were the night, the day Franklin Roosevelt died, what we did, what we said, what we thought. I was in Paris in the shabby office on the rue de Berri, where the European edition of *Yank* was, always haphazardly, put together. We were playing poker, with the radio turned low.

Suddenly the music—was it "Don't Sit Under the Apple Tree"?—was interrupted, and the sorrowing voice of a sergeant on the Armed Forces Network said, "President Franklin D. Roosevelt died this afternoon at. . . ."

As I wrote sometime back, "We put down the cards and, wrapped in our separate silences, went our separate ways. I walked up the Champs Elysées to the Arc de Triomphe. It was one of those bleak hours before dawn, and even the whores had retired for the night. I stood for a time in front of the light of the Unknown and, it seems, Eternal Soldier, and in the grim and ghostly dawn I prayed. I do not believe in God or gods, but I prayed to the promising sunrise.

"For nearly three years, first in the Pacific and then in Europe, I had seen killing and destruction, suffering and starvation that even in my darkest melancholy I could not imagine. I did not think that we had made the world safe for anything at all, none of us did, but we had bought ourselves a little peace, had we not, a time of quiet?

"In the twenty-five years since that April dawn a new war has broken out in the world every five months."

So much for what I thought that dawn or what in my better moments I like to think I thought. By noon chow that day I was feeling somewhat less melancholy and more realistic—but frightened. I remember saying, again like millions of others, "My God, now we're left with Harry Truman. Are we in trouble?"

That was one of the biggest things wrong with Harry Truman, that he wasn't Franklin Roosevelt. With Roosevelt you'd have known he was President even if you hadn't been told. You'd have known he was head of whatever he wanted to be head of. He looked imperial, and he acted that way, and he talked that way.

Harry Truman, for God's sake, looked and acted and talked like—well, like a failed haberdasher. He *certainly* wasn't any Roosevelt, and another trouble with him, for people like me anyway, was that he wasn't Henry Wallace.

And that first day, naturally, it was Friday the thirteenth, after Harry went up to the Capitol for lunch with some of his former colleagues ("cronies" was soon to become the word to describe any associate of Truman's), he said to the newspapermen, "Boys, if you ever pray, pray for me now. I don't know whether you fellows ever had a load of hay fall on you, but when they told me yesterday what had happened, I felt like the moon, the stars, and all the planets had fallen on me."

My God. Pure cornball. I had left Marshalltown, Iowa, at the earliest possible age to get away from people who talked like that, thought like that, and now we had one of them in the White House.

Where had all the poetry gone?

Mrs. Ralph Truman: "After the election, I decided that I would like to go to the inauguration. The general was busy and couldn't go. So I went to Washington to attend the inauguration ceremonies.

"It was during the war, and it was very short because of the war, and Mr. Roosevelt took the oath of office on the south porch of the White House. The weather was bad, and they didn't want to have too much display. And so on January 20 Mr. Roosevelt came out to take the oath of office. Everybody, myself included, was horribly shocked. You could tell he was a very sick man. I was close enough to him so that I could see how sick he was.

"And after the inauguration I came back to Kansas City, and I told the general, I said, 'President Roosevelt cannot possibly live more than three months because,' I said, 'he's terribly ill.' And I said, 'It's going to mean that Harry is going to be President,' and, of course, I missed it by eight days. He died on the twelfth of April, and if it had been the twentieth, it would have been three months.

"Of course it was a tragic thing for the world and the country, and it put a tremendous burden on Harry Truman to have to take over then.

"I couldn't help thinking what a responsibility it was—what an awful responsibility."

Mary Jane Truman: "After my brother Harry got nominated as Vice President, Mother and I talked about what would happen after he got elected. We never doubted that Mr. Roosevelt would be reelected, and we realized that he was not well, but I don't think we really thought about his passing away. And I know we didn't think it would come as soon as it did.

"When it did happen, when we realized that Harry had become President we felt—oh, sorry that Mr. Roosevelt was dead, but we also felt sorry for Harry.

". . . At the time Mr. Roosevelt died I had been at Joplin, Missouri, at an Eastern Star meeting, and I had to come home to get some things so that I could go back to Joplin that same evening.

"While I was getting ready to go, my mother was at my brother Vivian's, and my sister-in-law, Mrs. Vivian Truman, called me and asked me if I had the radio on, and I told her no. And she said, well, it had just come over that Mr. Roosevelt had passed away.

"And it was really, oh, it was really quite a shock. But then, just as quickly as I could, I went down to my brother's and brought my mother home. And shortly after that —why, of course the callers began to come.

"I shall never forget what my mother said later on. Someone asked her if she wasn't proud of the fact that her son had become President. I believe she stated she was not happy about it. 'Well,' she said, 'I can't say that I'm happy because I wouldn't want Mr. Roosevelt to die for him to be President, but if he is ever elected President, I'm going to get out and wave a flag.'

"She never did do that, of course, because by . . . in 1948 when Harry was elected President, she had passed away."

Mr. President, I have read that even though it was short, President Roosevelt had worked very hard over his fourth inaugural address. Do you remember anything about that day? And what Roosevelt said?

"Never will forget any part of it. I got sworn in by Henry Wallace, and then Roosevelt was sworn in by Chief Justice Stone, and he stood there on the south portico. He stood there. You remember later, when he made that speech before Congress on Yalta, he sat in the wheelchair the whole time, but at the inauguration he stood. He had on his braces, and you could see from his face that it was hard on him. He was in pain, I think, considerable pain, but he stood there, and he took the oath. He wasn't wearing an overcoat or a hat, nothing but a thin suit, and it was a cold day. It may even have snowed a little that day. I don't remember. But it was cold, and he said. . . . It's right here. Read it."

The President handed me a book with, as I recall, various inaugural addresses. Roosevelt's address was very short; it lasted only about five minutes and, among other things, said, "We have learned to be citizens of the world, members of the human community. We have learned the simple truth, as Emerson said, that 'the only way to have a friend is to be one.' "

Mr. Truman continued, "He stood there in the cold, very, and his hands shook, and his voice was not steady. I remember Frances Perkins [Secretary of Labor in Roosevelt's Cabinet] was crying, I think. But she was careful not to let Roosevelt see her.

"It was a very sad sight to see, especially if you remembered how he had sounded in former days."

He was about to go off to Yalta?

"He was. In a few days. And, of course, later I learned all about Yalta, and there's very little in our history that's been lied about as much. They said Roosevelt sold out the United States, which was a damn lie, of course; if the Russians'd lived up to their agreements that they made at Yalta, there wouldn't have been any trouble at all, but they didn't; they never lived up to an agreement they made ever, and that's what caused the trouble, and we all know what happened as a result."

I understand one of the things you did during the eighty-two days you were Vice President was to convince the Senate to agree to Wallace's confirmation as Secretary of Commerce.

"Yes, Roosevelt wanted to get rid of old—he called him Jesus H. Jones." [Jesse H. Jones was Secretary of Commerce and Federal Loan Administrator; he was a Texas financier and became a firm enemy of the New Deal.] "Jesus H. Jones, and he wanted to get Henry in both jobs, but I knew the Senate would never sit still for that, and . . . we had to concentrate on the Secretary of Commerce situation, and that was hard enough to do. I told you. Henry was not at all liked in the Senate. And I had to break two ties to get the son of a bitch confirmed. I didn't want to do it, but if that's what the old man wanted, I did it."

It was about that time that Tom Pendergast died, wasn't it?

"Tom Pendergast died on January 26, and everybody . . . everybody said I shouldn't go to the funeral. They said I should send a note or something, but I couldn't do that. Tom Pendergast was a good and loyal friend, and he never asked me to do a dishonest deed, and so I went to his funeral. I've said that time and again, and I say it now.

"I got into an Army plane, and I went to the Catholic church in Kansas City, and I attended his funeral.

"You should have heard the squawks. Headlines in the newspapers and editorials and I don't know what all. And they said some very mean things, but I didn't care. I couldn't have done anything else. What kind of man would it be . . . wouldn't go to his friend's funeral because he'd be criticized for it?"

After a while I said, *Mr. President, how many times did you see Mr. Roosevelt between the inauguration and his death? I've read that there's a record of only two such meetings: March 8 and March 19.*

"There were more meetings than that. Those were *scheduled* meetings, but there were other times . . . several other times when I wouldn't go in the front way at the White House, but I went. And there were Cabinet meetings. I attended the Cabinet meetings, not that Roosevelt ever did much at his Cabinet meetings. He did it, tried to do it all himself, which was one of his troubles.

"But when I saw Roosevelt, it was usually about something that was coming up in the Senate."

Mr. President, some historians feel that you might have been better prepared for the Presidency and some of the enormous problems that you inherited if Roosevelt had told you more about them, had been more frank.

Mr. Truman's mouth became a very thin line, and he said, "He did all he could. I've explained all about that, and I told you that's all there is to it, and it is."

I had learned by then that there were times when it was useless to pursue a subject. This was clearly one of them, and so I adjourned the session for the day and went back to Kansas City. Evenings are longer in Kansas

City than in any other city in the United States, with the possible exception of Los Angeles.

A few days later I said, *Mr. President, can you tell me about the day Franklin Roosevelt died?*

"It is a day . . . it's a time I can even now not think about without feeling very deep emotion.

"It was an ordinary day in the Senate, and I presided. I usually presided most of the time when I was Vice President. Senator Wiley [Alexander Wiley, a right-wing Republican from Wisconsin] was making a speech about something. I forget what it was about; it didn't make any difference with Wiley. He could go on forever about nothing. And so I wrote a letter to Mamma. . . .

Dear Mamma and Mary:

I am trying to write you a letter from the desk of the President of the Senate while a windy Senator is making a speech on a subject with which he is in no way familiar. . . .

. . . Turn on your radio tomorrow night at 9:30 your time, and you'll hear Harry make a Jefferson Day address to the nation. . . . It will be followed by the President, whom I'll introduce.

"Along about, oh I guess it was probably half past four or a quarter of five, Sam Rayburn called. He'd been in Texas, and he called and said there was a meeting of the Board of Education."

The Board of Education was the name of a group of legislators who dropped into Rayburn's private office from time to time after a legislative session to share stories and drink a little bourbon and tap water. Rayburn, a bachelor from Texas, was Speaker of the House.

". . . the Board of Education, and so I went over, and before I could sit down, Sam told me. Before I could even begin a conversation with the half a dozen fellows that were there, Sam told me that Steve Early (Roosevelt's press secretary) had called and wanted me to call right back. I did, and Early said to come right over to the White House and to come to the front entrance, and he said to come up to Mrs. Roosevelt's suite on the second floor. I didn't think much about it. I just supposed that the President had come back from Georgia [Roosevelt died at Warm Springs, Georgia] and was going to be at Bishop Atwood's funeral. [Julius W. Atwood, the former Episcopal Bishop of Arizona, was a friend of Roosevelt's.] Roosevelt was an honorary pallbearer, and I just supposed that was what had happened.

"And so I went over to the White House, and Mrs. Roosevelt . . . Mrs. Roosevelt . . . she told me that . . . the President . . . was dead."

For a moment Mr. Truman was unable to continue.

When he could, he said, "I was able . . . I told Steve Early to call the Cabinet, and they started phoning for the Chief Justice [Harlan F. Stone] and members of Congress.

"I went over to the office of the President in the West End of the White House and tried to call my wife and daughter. I had a hard time getting them, but I finally did, and they came, and the Chief Justice was there, and all the others, including the Cabinet, and everybody was crying.

"They had just an awful time finding a Bible. I'm sure there were plenty of them in the family living quarters of the White House, but down in the executive wing they had a terrible time finding one, and the Chief Justice was waiting to swear me in.

"Finally, they found one in the office I believe it was of Bill Hassett, who was Roosevelt's secretary.

"It had a red cover I remember. It looked sort of like a Gideon Bible, but I don't think it was. . . . Anyway, that's the one I was sworn in on, and there were half a dozen people that were sworn in on it. Dean Acheson and two or three other Cabinet members, and the flyleaf is covered with the signatures of Chief Justices, Chief Justice Stone, Chief Justice Vinson, and so on. . . .

"I gave it to Margaret, and she kept it for two or three

days, and then she insured it and sent it back and said, 'Put this in the safe in the library; I'm afraid to keep it.' And it's now . . . now on display in the library.

"I was sworn in—there was a clock on the mantel— and I was sworn in at 7:09. Exactly at 7:09 on April 12, 1945, and that's all the time it took for me to become President of the United States.

What happened next?

"Well, Margaret and Mrs. Truman went back to our apartment; they were both crying, and all the members of the Cabinet were there, I believe, except the Postmaster General, Frank Walker; I forget where he was. And we all sat down around the Cabinet table, and then Steve Early or Jonathan Daniels [another Presidential press secretary] came in and said the newspapermen were outside, and they all wanted to know if there was going to be the United Nations meeting in San Francisco in April as had been planned, and I said it most certainly was. I said it was what Roosevelt had wanted, and it had to take place if we were going to keep the peace. And that's the first decision I made as President of the United States.

"And we sat there for a little while. I told them . . . I told the Cabinet that I wanted them all to stay on as long as they could. Harry Hopkins later told me that was a mistake. He didn't call it a mistake. He didn't really advise me to do anything in particular, but he said that it would be difficult for some of the members of the Cabinet to understand a change in policy and administration, and I believe he did say that some of them might be comparing me to Roosevelt, but I said, well, I said, 'Harry, I am not gonna fire anybody. Those fellows have been working their heads off. There's a war going on, and I'm going to keep the same outfit. I'll keep the press secretaries and the other people on as long as they want to stay. Whenever they want to quit, why, they can,' and that's the way it worked."

Nobody talked about quitting that night?

"No, no, they were all so broken up and upset that they didn't . . . none of them did much talking. I did say, did emphasize that the decisions to be made . . . I was President, and they could . . . tell me if they thought I was wrong, but in the long run, I said . . . I told them I'd make the final decisions, and I'd expect them to support me. And that was about all that happened."

Didn't you have a conversation with Secretary Stimson?

Henry Stimson, then seventy-seven, had been Roosevelt's Secretary of War.

"Yes, Secretary Stimson stayed behind, and he said that the most destructive weapon in history was being built, and that is about all he said that night.

"I already knew something was going on. The committee . . . what they called the Truman Committee sometime before had learned that a good deal of money was being spent on what I thought then was two projects, one in the state of Washington and the other in Tennessee. I had sent some people out to look into the projects, to investigate what was going on. And Stimson came to see me. He said that one of the biggest, most significant projects in the history of the world was going on, and he asked me not to investigate. He said that the whole thing could be ruined if it was made public in any way.

"And I said, 'Mr. Secretary, if you tell me that, the dogs are called off.' And that is exactly what I said and what I did. And I was never sorry for it because Stimson was a man you could trust. One hundred percent.

"When I got to be Vice President, Jimmy Byrnes told me something was going on that was a tremendous explosive that would surely end the war, which is exactly what it did."

And that was the first you knew of the atom bomb.

"I didn't know, had no idea from what Byrnes said or Stimson told me that it was a bomb of any kind, and the night we're talking about I must confess I had some other matters on my mind as well."

Did you go back to your apartment after that?

"I went to the apartment at 4701 Connecticut Avenue, and Margaret and Bess were at the apartment of General Davis [General Jeff Davis, a retired brigadier general], and I had a sandwich with them there. And they were all very upset about Roosevelt's death.

"They were also concerned about what would happen in the apartment house while we were still there, living next door to a President.

"And I said, 'Well, it'll cause you plenty of trouble. Don't worry about that.' But I said, 'As soon as we can, we'll move out. So you won't be disturbed.'

"And I'd say within a week, maybe less than that, we moved to Blair House and stayed there three weeks until Mrs. Roosevelt had time to move her things out of the White House.

"After I finished the sandwich, I went back to our apartment and called Grandview. My mother, of course, knew what had happened. I told her, I said, 'Mamma, everything is all right,' and I told her not to worry. I said I was busy, and I said she probably wouldn't hear from me for a little while. And after I talked to her, I went to bed."

Did you sleep?

"Of course."

Right away?

"Of course. I knew I had a big day coming up. I had to sleep."

Mr. President, I've read—I find it almost impossible to believe—that General Marshall went right to sleep at the usual time the night before D Day.

"Knowing General Marshall, I wouldn't doubt it a bit. If you've done the best you can—if you have done what you have to do—there is no use worrying about it because nothing can change it, and to be in a position of leadership . . . you have to give thought to what's going to happen the next day and you have to be fresh for . . . what you have to do the next day. What you're *going* to do is more important than what you have done."

If you've done the best you can.

"That's right. That's the main thing. A man can't do anything more than that. You can't think about how it would be . . . if you had done another thing. You have to decide."

Mr. President, how do you think Hamlet would have been as President?

"He'd have made a damn . . . a poor President, and old Lear. That's a good play, great play, but old Lear couldn't even handle his daughters, let alone the country."

Mr. President, now that you've been out of the White House for a number of years, do you ever look back, have you ever looked back and wished you had done something different when you were President?

"No. Never. Not one time that I can recall. What would be the use of it?" *

Mr. President, when you put it that way, there wouldn't have been any use of it at all. . . . Could you tell me what happened, if you'd be good enough, on the first full day when you were President, April 13, 1945?

"I got up a little later than usual, around six thirty, and I didn't take my morning walk. I had breakfast with . . . I'd just as soon not mention the gentleman's name.†

"The car was setting out there waiting for me, and as

---

* For an exception see Chapter 19, "My Biggest Mistake."

† That morning Mr. Truman had breakfast with Hugh Fulton, who had been chief investigator for the Truman Committee. Fulton went into private practice in Washington and had sent out announcements advertising that fact, which Mr. Truman felt was unethical.

Mr. Truman had strong feelings about using one's official position, past or present, for gain. He was extremely fond of General Omar Bradley, the fellow Missourian who at one time during Mr. Truman's administration was Chief of Staff. After Bradley returned, he took a job as chairman of the board of the Bulova Watch Company, and one day in discussing General Bradley, Mr. Truman said, "I hold it against him, taking that job. They weren't hiring him; what they thought they were doing was buying some influence in the Pentagon, and I don't care at all for that sort of thing, and I can't understand how General Bradley could bring himself to do it."

Being an admirer of General Bradley, I said, no doubt apologetically, "He probably felt he needed the money."

And Mr. Truman said, "Nobody ever needs money that bad."

we drove down Connecticut Avenue past Chesapeake Street, which is on the east side of 4701, there was Tony Vaccaro [an Associated Press reporter] leaning against a telephone pole, and he was the saddest-looking kid you ever saw. He'd been assigned to me by the Associated Press when I was Vice President.

"And I said, 'Stop the car. Come on. Get in, Tony. I'm on my way to the White House. What are you so sad about?'

"And he said, 'Mr. President, I've lost my job, and I'll probably get fired. There's nobody for me to cover anymore.'

"I said, 'I wouldn't worry.' I said I doubted very much if he would lose his job, and sure enough he got assigned to the White House, and the next week he got a thirty-five-dollar raise in salary.

"But that morning Tony and I rode to the White House, and he got out of the car, and I believe he wished me luck.

"I went in, and then the business began.

"I saw more people that day than anybody in the history of the Presidency up to then. The first person I saw was the Secretary of State [Edward R. Stettinius], and he told me and later gave me a memo saying that Churchill was very upset. The Russians weren't living up to their agreements. And they hadn't been since Yalta.

"He [Stettinius] said that before his death Roosevelt had been upset, too. Later a lot of people said that before Roosevelt died, everything was going along just fine with the Russians and that I was to blame for the whole thing that happened, but that is a damn lie. All they have to do is read their history to know that's a damn lie.

"They weren't living up to their promises, especially in Poland, as I've said."

At Yalta Roosevelt, Churchill, and Stalin had agreed to a compromise government in Poland that would include all the anti-Fascist parties in Poland, as well as Polish diplomatic leaders living abroad, to be followed by a free election based on a secret ballot and with universal suffrage. But the Russians were sabotaging that agreement in every way possible.

"That same morning I saw the Secretary of the Navy and Secretary Stimson, and old man Leahy, Admiral Leahy. He was Chief of Staff to the President, and I saw the other Chiefs of Staff."

They were . . . I know because I read about it at the hotel last night. They were Admiral Ernest J. King of the Navy, Lieutenant General Barney M. Giles of the Air Force, and General George C. Marshall of the Army. That wasn't the first time you ever saw General Marshall, was it?

"Oh, no. No. I believe I'd seen them all before in one way or another when I was working with the committee and when I was Vice President. But General Marshall, I've told you, I knew him in France in the First World War. I didn't know him well, of course, because he was a colonel, and I was only a captain.

"He was General Pershing's aide [General John J. Pershing, head of the American Expeditionary Force in France during the First World War]. But I met him. He made the inspections around the AEF, and he came to the school where I was going when I went over there to study French artillery."

Where was that?

"At Chatillon-sur-Seine and at Coëtquidan, which was Napoleon's artillery headquarters in his time. I went down there and worked as an instructor part of the time, and that's where I met General Marshall for the first time. And everybody knew that he was just about the best of the young officers in France at the time. And I believe that even then he was a man who knew exactly what he wanted to do at all times.

"And when he got to be Chief of Staff at the beginning of that other war I knew that things were in good hands. When Marshall said, 'This is it,' that was it. I had some dealing with him in the Senate when I was . . . head of that committee, and he'd listen to whatever it was I told him. He'd listen until you got through. And then I'd say, 'What about it?'

"He'd say, 'Go ahead. You're on the right track.' He never wasted words. Never argued with me at all. Although in the middle of the conversation if he thought of something that would add to the efficiency of the program, in it went.

"And later, as you know, I made him Secretary of State and Secretary of Defense. There never was a man like him."

Mr. President, I understand that when you were still in the Senate, you went to see General Marshall and told him that you wanted to be in the Army. Could you tell us about that?

"That's right. I did. I went to him, and I said, 'General, I'm a colonel in the field artillery, and I've kept it up, and I've trained a lot of these youngsters since the First World War, and I'd like to command a group, or a regiment, or whatever a colonel has in this war.'

"And he looked at me—he could look right through you if he wanted to, although he was the kindest man that ever was—he looked at me, and he said, 'Senator, how old are you?' I said, 'I'm fifty-six.' He says, 'You're too damn old.'

"I said, 'I'm four years younger than you are.' And he said, 'Yes, but I'm already in.'

"Well, I went back and started on this other thing [the Truman Committee] which was as helpful to him I guess maybe as if I'd been a colonel in the field artillery.

"And one day he came to see me after I got to be President, and some visiting fireman was in the Oval Room with me, and he sat outside for a while and talked to Matt Connelly [the President's appointments secretary], and Matt said, 'General, what about the fact that you wouldn't let the old man be a colonel of field artillery in this war? Don't you wish you'd a done it?'

"Marshall kinda grinned at him, and he says, 'All of us make mistakes, but I don't think that was one.'"

I said, *Getting back to that first morning you were President. Wasn't it Friday the thirteenth?*

"Yes, it was, Friday the thirteenth, 1945, and I keep going off . . . getting off the subject."

Mr. President, that's not possible. Whatever you say is very much on the subject.

"No, no, it's not, and when I do it, you've got to stop me. I said, was saying that I had a meeting with the Chiefs of Staff of each of the services, the four of them, and they said that the war . . . the war in Europe was going to last another six months and the war in Japan, they said would go on for another year and a half."

Germany surrendered unconditionally only twenty-five days later, Japan four months later. I said, *Were the Chiefs of Staff always so wrong?*

"You always have to remember when you're dealing with generals and admirals, most of them, they're wrong a good deal of the time. Even Washington knew that; he kept warning the people, and Jefferson, too, warning the people against letting the generals give you too much advice. I told you. They're most of them just like horses with blinders on. They can't see beyond the ends of their noses, most of them."

Would you say that General Marshall was an exception to the rule?

"General Marshall was wrong about when the war would end; at least if he didn't agree with the others, he didn't let on. Not the day we're talking about here, but General Marshall was an exception to every rule there ever was."

What were some of the other things that happened that day, the first full day you were President?

"Well, I went up to the Senate, and I had lunch there, and I asked them to support me. I wanted to make a speech to a joint session of Congress just as soon after the Roosevelt funeral as I possibly could. And I did, on the following Monday.

"I wanted Congress to . . . well, to see the new President and to hear him, and I wanted the people to hear him, too. I thought it was important. People were very, very confused, and some of them . . . well, they were frightened, and I wanted to tell them that the Roosevelt policies would go on.

"Later, that afternoon, of course, I saw Byrnes. He'd been to Yalta, and he'd made a good many notes, and I wanted him to tell me what he remembered and later to transcribe the notes he'd made, which he did. And I told him I was going to ask him to be Secretary of State. And at that time he seemed to be very pleased. Of course later he changed his mind, and as I say, I always felt sure that he thought he ought to be President and that he'd have done . . . possibly a better job of it, and maybe he would have. . . . If I'd have died while he was Secretary of State, of course he would have been President. When there is no Vice President, the Secretary of State is next in line for succession."

Did you think that first day would never end?

"Yes, yes, I did, but of course, even when it did, even when I went home, I had a lot of reading still to do.

"And there was all that fuss, of course, with the Secret Service, and before anybody could get into the apartment house, they had to present their identification, and we felt, Mrs. Truman and I felt that the sooner we could move, the less trouble our neighbors would be put to."

Mr. President, a great many people will find it difficult to believe that at a time like that with everything else you had on your mind after your first full day as President of the United States, you were thinking about the convenience of your neighbors.

"I don't know about that, but that is what happened. I told Mrs. Roosevelt that she should take all the time she needed to move out of the White House and that we would move into Blair House across the street, and that is what we did."

Did you work after you got back to 4701 Connecticut Avenue, to your apartment that night?

"Oh, yes. I had quite a good deal to do that same night. I always thought . . . all the time I was President I thought it would let up, but it never did. It never got any easier.

"On the fourteenth [Saturday, April 14, 1945, Mr. Truman's second full day as President] I got up a little earlier than usual, around five in the morning I think it was, and I worked on my speech that I was going to give to Congress, and later that morning we had to go up to Union Station to bring . . . to escort Roosevelt's body back to the White House, and I asked Byrnes and Wallace to go with me, which they did do."

Why was that?

"Because I knew, as I told you, that they both thought they ought to be sitting where I was. A lot of people in the country also thought so, and so I thought asking them was the proper thing to do, and I did it.

"We went up to Union Station to meet the body, and when we started back to the White House, the streets were just jammed. People on both sides of the streets when we brought the body back, people were crowded together, and people were crying. I saw one old nigger woman sitting down on the curb with her apron up to her eyes just crying her eyes out.

"It was a very sad occasion. I'll tell you that, and before . . . as soon as we got back to the White House, I had to slip away, and I went to my . . . to the President's office in the west wing of the White House.

"I knew Harry Hopkins [Roosevelt's top adviser during the whole of his White House career] had been out at the Mayo—no, it wasn't the Mayo Clinic. It was a hospital in Rochester, Minnesota, but it wasn't the Mayo Clinic. I don't remember which hospital it was.

"Anyway, I went to my office in the west wing of the White House, and I called him in. He looked just like a ghost, pale and thin. Like a ghost."

I believe you'd known Harry Hopkins before.

"Oh, yes. I first met him back in 1933, when I was presiding judge of the county and I was also head of the federal relief program for the state. I believe I got a dollar a year for that, but I don't believe I ever did collect it.

"Harry came out to Kansas City to see me, and we couldn't have got along better."

I've read that the two of you had a good deal in common, that you both came from families that weren't rich, that you were both Midwesterners, and that no matter what happened to you, how much power you got, you never forgot your origins.

"I don't . . . I wouldn't care to comment on myself, but I believe Harry Hopkins was from Grinnell, Iowa, and his father was . . . I believe was a harnessmaker.

"We agreed that when we first met . . . a lot of people were out of work, and our job . . . my job in Missouri was to see to it that they got work . . . and enough to eat. Some people said and the newspapers said that that relief money was wasted, but it wasn't. Some of the finest buildings in the state of Missouri were built with that money.

"The only people who objected were the damn rich, and I didn't pay any attention to them, and neither did Harry Hopkins.

"We stayed friends through the years. When I was operating the committee, he was one of the men in Washington that I knew I could go to, and he'd tell me the truth. He always told the truth. Never tried to fool you.

"After I was sworn in as Vice President, one of the first people that came to see me was Hopkins. He said, 'I'm going to tell you something. I've been around the old man for a long time, and I'll tell you exactly the approaches that he likes,' and he gave me a steer that was exceedingly useful in the dealings that I had with the White House.

"He was just as fine a man as I've ever met, and his word was perfectly good. Better than most bankers' bonds."

What did you talk about that first day, the day of Roosevelt's funeral?

"Well, I asked him to come in. I told you how bad he looked, and I apologized for calling him in, but I said I wanted as best he could tell me about our relations with Russia. He'd been to all those conferences with Roosevelt, to Yalta and the ones at Casablanca and Teheran and I believe Cairo, and he filled me in. He told me everything that he could, and it was very helpful indeed.

"He said he was going to resign; he didn't have a cent to his name. After all those years in the government, in the service for Roosevelt he never made any money, and he said he had to make some. I'm sorry to say that I don't think he ever did. I think he died before he ever had a chance, and it's a pity.

"But he really understood Stalin. He told me that first afternoon that Stalin . . . he said you could talk to him, and I knew *he* could, and so in May, when we were having trouble with Stalin, Molotov [Vyacheslav Molotov, Russian Foreign Minister] was threatening not to sign the United Nations Charter. I called Hopkins in again, and I said, 'Harry, are you physically able to go to Moscow? If you are, I want you to go over there and tell Stalin to make Molotov sign this Charter.'

"And he got in a plane and went. He had a three-hour conference with Stalin, and about an hour and a half after that Molotov signed the Charter."

Why do you think Hopkins was so successful in talking to the Russians?

"I don't know. I don't know, but he knew exactly how to do it. He talked tough to them all the time. I don't know how he did it, but he got it done. That was the main thing. He always did whatever he promised to do.

"And when he got back from Russia, he made a report to me, and he said, 'Old Stalin seemed to be very happy to see me, and he said to give his best regards to the President of the United States.'

" 'Well,' I said, 'I'm exceedingly obliged to you for what you did, and I want to thank you for it.'

"Harry Hopkins, as he went out, said to Steve Early or whoever was out there, he said, 'You know, I've had something happen to me that never happened before in my life.'

"Steve Early or whoever it was looked at him and said, 'What's that?'

" 'Why,' he said. 'The President just said, "Thank you" to me.' "

You mean in all those years he'd worked for Roosevelt he'd never been thanked for all he did?

"Now I told you what he said. And that's all I told you."

A few minutes later I said, *But on the afternoon of Roosevelt's funeral, Hopkins mostly filled you in on the . . . on what had happened at the various conferences and told you the kind of man Stalin was.*

"That's right. He answered all my questions just as fully and completely as he could, and I was very grateful to him for it. But I felt very, very sorry for him because he had worked a very long time and contributed to the victory as much as any man, and, well, he hadn't got much out of it."

Except historically, perhaps. I mean his place in history seems very firm.

"Yes, yes. I suppose, but you can't read what they say about you in the history books if you're not around to read it."

I believe you went on the funeral train to Hyde Park.

"Yes, yes, we went, on Saturday night, and every place we stopped there'd be a crowd just as if . . . well, you'd think the world had come to an end, and I thought so, too. So there you are.

"On the way back I heard old Harold Ickes [Secretary

of the Interior] carrying on about how the country would go to hell now that Roosevelt was gone. He said there wasn't any leadership anymore, something like that. He went on and on. He was a man who carried on a good deal."

Did he know that you could hear him?

"I think yes, I think that is what he had in mind, that I'd hear him."

You didn't fire him when you heard him talk like that?

"No, no. I didn't have to. I knew he'd talk himself out of a job sooner or later. I knew the kind of man he was. He was a resigner. He reminded me of old Salmon P. Chase, who was Secretary of the Treasury in Lincoln's Cabinet, and he thought he ought to be President, that he'd be a better President than Lincoln, and he was always resigning. He must have resigned a dozen times, and he caused Lincoln more trouble than all the generals put together, and that was not an easy thing to do.

"Lincoln said some place that old Chase wasn't happy unless he was unhappy, and that was just about the case with Ickes. I knew he'd turned in his resignation a few times while Roosevelt was President. So I knew I could wait.

"The trouble with Ickes was . . . well, he was no better than a common scold. I don't like saying that about a man, but it's true, and he wanted to be President the worst way. That's about the size of it. Lincoln said about Chase that he thought he was indispensable to the country, and he didn't understand why the country didn't realize it."

Did Ickes think he was indispensable?

"I don't think he ever doubted it for a minute.

"About a year after I became President I was going to appoint Ed Pauley [a California oilman and Democratic Party leader] Undersecretary of the Navy, which was exactly what Roosevelt had intended to do before he died.

"Well, old Ickes—'Honest Harold' they called him— he went up to the Senate, and he called Pauley every name he could think of, including some things that were not facts and he knew it.

"Pauley asked me to withdraw his nomination, and that is what happened. But I said at a press conference that I was still behind Pauley, and Ickes fired off a letter saying he was resigning. As I say, it wasn't the first time. Roosevelt had just never accepted those letters of resignation, but I did. I told him he could go right away. He wanted to stay on for another couple months I think it was, but I got word to him that he could leave the next day.

"The whole thing . . . it was a great pity because he'd been a good man in his day."

What happened to him?

"He got to thinking he was more important than he was. I told you. I've seen that happen time and again in Washington.

"I think when old Honest Harold left, he thought the government couldn't run without him."

But you managed.

"Yes, we managed."

Mr. President, can you remember anything else about coming back on the train from Hyde Park, after Roosevelt was buried?

"Well, we came back on the special train, and Mrs. Roosevelt and two of the boys, Franklin, Jr., I think it was, and Elliott, they came in to see us, and they said to Mrs. Truman with their mother sitting right there, they said, 'The first thing we want you to do. We want you to fire the housekeeper at the White House. She's starved us to death. She wouldn't give us anything at all to eat.'

"And Mrs. Roosevelt said, 'Why, you boys had enough to eat, and you know you did.'

" 'Well,' the boys said to Mrs. Truman, 'she's no good as you'll find out.'

"Well, that woman. Her name I believe was . . . I can't for the life of me remember her name."

I believe it was Mrs. Nesbitt.

"Mrs. Nesbitt. I believe that she several times said to Mrs. Truman that Mrs. Roosevelt had done it, whatever it was, had done it in a different manner, and after a time

Mrs. Nesbitt left. I believe she decided, suddenly, to resign."

Did the food improve after she left?

"When Mrs. Truman took charge, the food was always good."

Mr. President, last night I was reading a book by Alonzo Fields, who for twenty-one years was a butler at the White House.

"He was. He was a fine old fellow. He had wanted to be a singer, but it hadn't worked out, and he worked at the White House, and he was just as nice, just as dependable as he could be. We were always good friends."

He says in his book, My Twenty-one Years in the White House, *that of all the Presidents he served under, from Herbert Hoover to your successor in the White House, you were the only one who took the trouble to understand him as a person.*

"I know he did. I know he did. He sent me a copy of the book; it's in there somewhere, and he was just as generous as he possibly could be.

"But I've never understood how to do anything else except try to understand the other fellow, and most of the time I've succeeded to some degree, I believe.

"But as Fields says, whenever I'm in Boston—he's retired and living in Boston now—whenever I'm there, he comes up to my hotel, and we have a long talk.

"You see the thing you have to remember. When you get to be President, there are all those things, the honors, the twenty-one-gun salutes, all those things, you have to remember it isn't for you. It's for the Presidency, and you've got to keep yourself separate from that in your mind.

"If you can't keep the two separate, yourself and the Presidency, you're in all kinds of trouble."

Jonathan Daniels says in one of his books that—I hope you'll forgive me—he was very upset when he was a boy, and he and a friend were passing the White House, and his friend reminded him that the President—I believe

*it was Coolidge at the time—the President had to go to
the bathroom just like everybody else.*

"That's right. We've had a few Presidents who've not
remembered a thing like that, and the minute it happens,
you can't possibly do the job.

"I've told you before. The fella that succeeded me, it
got so he didn't see anybody but millionaires and more.
He forgot all about the common people, and it had very
bad results for the country.

"But we go through those periods, and it always comes
out all right in the end."

Israel

Mr. Truman was speaking of April 20, 1945, the eighth day of his Presidency. He said, "I remember that day very well. I was still having trouble with the boys in the Secret Service; they wanted to drive me from Blair House to the White House in one of those damn limousines. Can you imagine being *driven* across the street?

"Of course I wouldn't allow it, and so that morning at a little after seven—I was *late*—I walked across the street, and I think I had three briefcases full of papers. Two or three. I forget which, but that wasn't anything new, of course. It seems to me all the time I was in Washington and a good part of the time when I was an old country judge back in Independence I always had papers to work on at night, always had a briefcase. Mrs. Truman once told me that a briefcase was as much a part of my outfit as my suit and hat.

"I had a long list of appointments that day, and one of them, you were asking earlier about Palestine, one of them was with Rabbi Wise [Dr. Stephen S. Wise, chairman of the American Zionist Emergency Council]. I saw him late that morning, and I was looking forward to it because I knew he wanted to talk about Palestine, and that is one part of the world that has always interested me, partly because of its Biblical background, of course.

"I told you. I've always done considerable reading of the Bible. I'd read it at least twice before I went to school. . . . I liked the stories in it. I never cared much for fairy stories or Mother Goose, not that I'm sure we had any Mother Goose at our house, but I just didn't care for that *kind* of thing.

"The stories in the Bible, though, were to me stories about real people, and I felt I knew some of them better than *actual* people I knew.

"I liked the New Testament stories best, especially the

Gospels. And when I was older, I was very much interested in the way those fellas saw the same things in a different manner. A very different manner, and they were all telling the truth. I think that's the first time I realized that no two people ever see the same thing in quite the same way, and when they tell it the way they saw it, they aren't necessarily lying if it's different.

"I think I told you, in school we usually had only one man's point of view of the history of something, and I'd go to the library and read three or four, sometimes as many as half a dozen, versions of the same thing, the same incident, and it was always the *differences* that interested me. And you had to keep in the mind that they were all telling what for them was the truth.

"And that is one of the reasons that when I got into a position of power I always tried to keep in mind that just because I saw something in a certain way didn't mean that others didn't see it in a different manner. That's why I always hesitated to call a man a liar unless I had the absolute goods on him."

There was a brief interruption while the President left the room; I later learned that sometimes when he left, he refreshed himself with a small "libation" or two, and I think that is what happened this morning because the President, when he returned, was more loquacious than he was in any other conversation.

Of course it may simply be that he was, as he says, vitally interested in the area and in the subject of Israel.

In any case he said, "We were talking about the Bible, and I always read the King James Version, not one of those damn new translations that they've got out lately.*

"I don't know why it is when you've got a good thing, you've got to monkey around changing it. The King James Version of the Bible is the best there is or ever has been

---

* The first edition of the New Testament of the New English Bible had just been published, and I believe Oxford University Press, the publishers, had sent him a copy asking for a quote.

or will be, and you get a bunch of college professors spending *years* working on it, and all they do is take the poetry out of it.

"The next thing they'll do, they'll probably appoint some committee of college professors to rewrite Shakespeare.

"But as I started to say . . . it wasn't just the Biblical part about Palestine that interested me. The whole history of that area of the world is just about the most complicated and most interesting of any area anywhere, and I have always made a very careful study of it. There has always been trouble there, always been wars from the time of Darius the Great and Rameses on, and the pity of it is that the whole area is just waiting to be developed. And the Arabs have just never seemed to take any interest in developing it. I have always thought that the Jews would, and of course, they have. But what has happened is only the beginning of what could happen, because potentially that is the richest area in the world.

"But getting back to what you were asking about, that morning I saw Rabbi Wise. It was late in the morning, and I remember he said, 'Mr. President, I'm not sure if you're aware of the reasons underlying the wish of the Jewish people for a homeland.'

"He was just as polite as he possibly could be, but I've told you in those days nobody seemed to think I was *aware* of anything. I said I knew all about the history of the Jews, and I told the rabbi I'd read all of Roosevelt's statements on Palestine, and I'd read the Balfour Declaration [Britain's statement in favor of a Jewish homeland, issued in 1917], and of course, I knew the Arab point of view.

"I also said that I knew the things that had happened to the Jews in Germany, not that I . . . at that time I didn't really know what had happened. At that time I couldn't even have *imagined* the kind of things they found out later.

"But I said as far as I was concerned, the United States would do all that it could to help the Jews set up a homeland. I *didn't* tell him that I'd already had a communica-

tion from some of the 'striped pants' boys warning me
. . . in effect telling me to watch my step, that I didn't
really understand what was going on over there and that
I ought to leave it to the *experts.* *

"The rabbi—he was just about the most courteous man
I've ever seen—said he believed me, but he said he was
sure a great many people, including some State Department
people, wouldn't go along with me. The *experts* on
the Middle East, he said.

"I told him I knew all about *experts.* I said that an
expert was a fella who was afraid to learn anything new
because then he wouldn't be an *expert* anymore.

"And I said that some of the *experts,* the career fellas
in the State Department, thought that they ought to make
policy but that as long as I was President, I'd see to it that
I made policy. Their job was to carry it out, and if there
were some who didn't like it, they could resign anytime
they felt like it.

"The rabbi thanked me very much for my time and my
assurances, but I knew that wasn't the . . . I knew it
would be a very, very long time before matters in that area
got themselves sorted out, and that proved to be the case."

---

* As reproduced in the *Memoirs,* the State Department
communication read: "It is very likely that efforts will be made
by some of the Zionist leaders to obtain from you at an early
date some commitments in favor of the Zionist program which
is pressing for unlimited Jewish immigration into Palestine and
the establishment there of a Jewish state. As you are aware,
the Government and people of the United States have every
sympathy for the persecuted Jews of Europe and are doing all
in their power to relieve their suffering. The question of Palestine
is, however, a highly complex one and involves questions
which go far beyond the plight of the Jews in Europe.

". . . There is continual tenseness in the situation in the
Near East, largely as a result of the Palestine question, and as
we have interests in that area which are vital to the United
States, we feel that this whole subject is one that should be
handled with the greatest care and with a view to the long-range
interests of the country."

Mr. Truman is perfectly right; the tone is that of a wise and
wealthy uncle writing to a nephew who is none too bright.

Mr. Truman had masterfully understated the case. Almost three years later, in March, 1948, not only were matters in the Middle East not yet sorted out, but it looked very much as if open warfare between the Arabs and the Jews might break out at any minute, and Israel was not yet a state.

As Mr. Truman says in the *Memoirs*, ". . . the matter had been placed in the United Nations and, true to my conviction that the United Nations had to be made to work, I had confidence that a solution would be found there." But pressure on the White House from American Zionists was, as Mr. Truman told me, so great that: "Well, there'd never been anything like it before, and there wasn't after. Not even when I fired MacArthur, there wasn't. And I said, I issued orders that I wasn't going to see anyone who was an extremist for the Zionist cause, and I didn't care who it was. There were . . . I had to keep in mind that much as I favored a homeland for the Jews, there were simply other matters awaiting . . . that I had to worry about."

And then late on the morning of March 13 Mr. Truman got a telephone call from the Statler, where his old friend and business partner Eddie Jacobson was staying. Eddie wanted to come to the White House to see the President.

"I said to him, 'Eddie, I'm always glad to see old friends, but there's one thing you've got to promise me. I don't want you to say a *word* about what's going on over there in the Middle East. Do you promise?' And he did."

A little later Eddie was ushered into the Oval Room, and this is the way Harry Truman described what followed:

"Great tears were running down his cheeks, and I took one look at him, and I said, 'Eddie, you son of a bitch, you promised me you wouldn't say a word about what's going on over there.' And he said, 'Mr. President, I haven't said a word, but every time I think of the homeless Jews, homeless for thousands of years, and I think about Dr.

Weizmann [Chaim Weizmann, head of the World Zionists and the first President of Israel], I start crying. I can't help it. He's an old man, and he's spent his whole life working for a homeland for the Jews, and now he's sick, and he's in New York and wants to see you. And every time I think about it I can't help crying.'

"I said, 'Eddie, that's enough. That's the last word.'

"And so we talked about this and that, but every once in a while a big tear would roll down his cheek. At one point he said something about how I felt about old Andy Jackson, and he was crying again. He said he knew he wasn't supposed to, but that's how he felt about Weizmann.

"I said, 'Eddie, you son of a bitch, I ought to have you thrown right out of here for breaking your promise; you knew damn good and well I couldn't stand seeing you cry.'

"And he kind of smiled at me, still crying, though, and he said, 'Thank you, Mr. President,' and he left.

"After he was gone, I picked up the phone and called the State Department, and I told them I was going to see Weizmann. Well, you should have heard the carrying-on. The first thing they said—they said Israel wasn't even a country yet and didn't have a flag or anything. They said if Weizmann comes to the White House, what are we going to use for a flag?

"And I said, 'Look here; he's staying at the Waldorf-Astoria hotel in New York, and every time some foreign dignitary is staying there, they put something out. You find out what it is, and we'll use it. And I want you to call me right back.'"

On March 18 Chaim Weizmann came to the White House, but no flag was necessary. He came in through the east gate, and the fact of his visit was not known until later.

In any case, only eleven minutes after Israel became a state in May, its existence was officially recognized by the United States.

A year later the Chief Rabbi of Israel came to see the

President, and he told him, "God put you in your mother's womb so that you could be the instrument to bring about the rebirth of Israel after two thousand years."

At that, great tears started rolling down Harry Truman's cheeks.

17

On Herbert Hoover

One day I said, *Mr. President, I think one of the reasons
that so many people have such a special feeling for you is
that after you left the White House you didn't go to the
Waldorf Towers* [the home of former President Herbert
Hoover]. *And you didn't go to Gettysburg* [the home of
former President Eisenhower].

"Leave the Waldorf Towers out of it; you're making a
reflection there. You can use Gettysburg."

Tell me about your relations with Mr. Hoover.

"Well, not long after I got the job as President I read
in the morning paper [May 28, 1945], that he was in
Washington, and was staying at the Shoreham Hotel, and
so I picked up the phone—I told you a lot of times I didn't
bother to go through the switchboard—I picked up the
phone and called the Shoreham and got through to him.

"And I said, 'Mr. President, this is Harry Truman.'

"Well, Hoover was just flabbergasted. He said, 'Mr.
President, I don't know what to say.'

"And I said, 'Mr. President, I want to talk to you. If I
may, I'll come right up there and see you.'

"He said, 'I couldn't let you do that, Mr. President. I'll
come to see you.' *

* From Alfred Steinberg's *The Man from Missouri, The
Life and Times of Harry S. Truman*: "On May 10, 1945, Truman felt lonely in his position and sought advice in an eight-
page longhand letter to Eleanor Roosevelt. In her reply, Mrs.
Roosevelt scolded him for wasting time writing longhand letters. Her advice was that he should quickly get on a personal
footing with Churchill. 'If you talk to him about books and
let him quote to you from his marvelous memory, everything
on earth from Barbara Frietchie to the Nonsense Rhymes and
Greek Tragedy, you will find him easier to deal with on political subjects. He is a gentleman to whom the personal element
means a great deal.'

"The tone of her reply made it clear to Truman that he had
to depend solely on himself for answers to the problems he

"So I said, 'That's what I figured you'd say, and I've got a limousine on the way to pick you up."

"A few minutes later they brought him into the Oval Room, and I said to him, 'Mr. President, there are a lot of hungry people in the world, and if there's anybody who knows about hungry people, it's you. Now there's plenty of food, but it's not in the right places. Now I want you to—' *

"Well, I looked at him. He was sitting there, just as close to me as you are, and I saw that great big tears were running down his cheeks. I knew what was the matter with him. It was the first time in thirteen years [since Hoover left the Presidency in 1933] that anybody had paid any attention to him.

"He said, 'Excuse me a minute, Mr. President,' and he went in the other room there for a few minutes, and when he came back, everything was all right, and we went on

---

faced. Indeed, his self-assurance grew with practice, though it took time. On May 28, for instance, when Herbert Hoover called on him to discuss the devastation and hunger in Europe, Truman kept addressing Hoover as 'Mr. President,' to the former President's embarrassment."

* Shortly after the outbreak of the First World War, with Belgium and northern France occupied by the Germans, almost 10,000,000 Belgians and Frenchmen faced starvation. Hoover arranged a Commission for Relief in Belgium and in four years of war got a billion dollars' worth of food to those people.

After the United States entered the war Hoover was appointed Food Administrator by Woodrow Wilson and, once again, got great quantities of much-needed food to the Allies. After the Armistice he continued to head both governmental and private organizations that fed and clothed millions of cold and hungry Europeans in twenty-three countries, including millions of children.

It was those widely publicized humane activities in Europe that caused Hoover to be so powerful a candidate in the 1928 Republican convention and strongly influenced his getting nominated and elected. When the Depression began while he was President, many people felt that Hoover was less understanding of the hungry in his own country.

from there. I wanted him to find out how our European relief program was going and how to get the food from the places where there was more than enough to the places where there wasn't any, and he agreed to do that.

"But don't you ever cast any aspersions on Mr. Hoover because he's done some very important things for this country and the world."

Early in 1946, when large parts of both Europe and Asia were threatened with a famine, Truman made Hoover honorary chairman of a Famine Emergency Committee, and in that capacity Hoover traveled 35,000 miles to twenty-two countries threatened with famine. As a result of his recommendations, the United States in five months shipped more than 6,000,000 tons of bread grains to the people of the hungry nations.

Hoover's friendship with Truman continued until the end of his life in 1964.

Did you and he ever talk politics?
"No, no, we never did. Because we never could have agreed, and besides, there were always plenty of other things to talk about."
Could you give me an example?
"Well, of course, we'd had one great experience in common. We'd both been President of the United States, and we talked a good deal about that experience. We talked about what it was like being President."

Mr. Truman stopped there, and I wanted to say, "What *was* it like, for God's sake?" Because how can any of us who has not been President possibly understand what it was like? Come even close to understanding?

But I didn't ask that question; I couldn't somehow; it didn't seem proper.

18

Los Niños Heroes

In March, 1947, at the invitation of President Miguel
Alemán, President Harry S. Truman visited Mexico, and
while in Washington there had been considerable concern
about a possible "incident," there was none. To the contrary, everywhere Truman went, mingling with crowds of
cheering people, he seemed to diminish whatever resent-
ment of "gringos" there might have been.

And in the afternoon he made an entirely unexpected
appearance at Chapultepec Castle, where a hundred years
before General Winfield "Old Fuss 'n' Feathers" Scott's
troops stormed the heights and captured the castle. The
only survivors in the castle, which was the West Point of
Mexico, were six cadets, and they committed suicide rather
than surrender.

Truman went to the monument to "Los Niños Heroes,"
placed a wreath on it, and bowed his head in tribute. The
cadets in the color guard burst into tears. Later it was said
that in the history of the two countries, nothing has ever
been done that was so helpful in cementing their relationship. Even now in Mexico City if you mention Harry
Truman's name, taxi drivers of a certain age will weep.

I asked Mr. Truman about the incident at Chapultepec
Castle, and he said, 'Well, when I first suggested it, everybody, *everybody* said I couldn't do it. They trotted out all
the so-called protocol experts, and they all said no. Those
birds, all they know how to say is, 'You can't do this, and
you can't do that.' And if you ask them *why* you can't, all
it ever adds up to is, 'It's never been done before.'

"And then they went on to say that if I did it, it would
remind the Mexicans of the war with the United States,
and they'd resent that. And some others said that if I paid
tribute to those Mexicans' boys, it was going to alienate
the Texans.

"I said, 'What the hell. Any Texan that's damn fool

enough to be put out when a President of the United States pays tribute to a bunch of brave kids, I don't need their support.'

"So I went out there, and I put a wreath on that monument, and it seemed to work out all right."

19.

My Biggest Mistake

What do you consider the biggest mistake you made as President?

"Tom Clark was my biggest mistake. No question about it."

I'm sorry, sir. I'm not sure I understand.

"That damn fool from Texas that I first made Attorney General and then put on the Supreme Court [Thomas C. Clark, Attorney General, 1945–1949, Justice U.S. Supreme Court, 1949–1967]. I don't know what got into me. He was no damn good as Attorney General, and on the Supreme Court . . . it doesn't seem possible, but he's been even worse. He hasn't made one right decision that I can think of. And so when you ask me what was my biggest mistake, that's it. Putting Tom Clark on the Supreme Court of the United States.

"I thought maybe when he got on the Court he'd improve, but of course, that isn't what's happened. I told you when we were discussing that other fellow [Nixon]. After a certain age it's hopeless to think people are going to change much."

How do you explain the fact that he's been such a bad Justice?

"The main thing is . . . well, it isn't so much that he's a *bad* man. It's just that he's such a dumb son of a bitch. He's about the dumbest man I think I've ever run across. And lots of times that's the case. Being dumb's just about the worst thing there is when it comes to holding high office, and that's especially true when it's on the Supreme Court of the United States.

"As I say, I never will know what got into me when I made that appointment, and I'm as sorry as I can be for doing it."

I had hoped that when Mr. Truman began considering the biggest mistake he had made as President he might

242

have something new to say about dropping the Bomb, perhaps some second thoughts on the Berlin Airlift, the Marshall Plan, the creation of NATO. But no, it was Tom Clark and the Supreme Court.

And to be sure, Clark's career on the Court was, to be charitable, lacking in distinction. It was characterized by its illiberality, by the Justice's apparent inability to figure out what was going on most of the time, and the fact that he wore outrageous bow ties under his judicial robes.

Tom Clark was at one time described as the oldest Eagle Scout in America, which is a pretty fair summation.

His son, Ramsey Clark, was Lyndon Johnson's Attorney General, a job which, despite perhaps some blemishes in the field of civil liberties, he held with honor.

20

The Bomb

There had to be a program on the Bomb, the Bombs
really, the one that was dropped on Hiroshima on the
morning of August 6, 1945, and the one that was dropped
on Nagasaki on August 9. I had written a book about the
latter, deploring it. I don't know whether Mr. Truman had
read that book; I doubt it. To my almost certain knowledge nobody had after the proofreader had finished with
it.

But if there was one subject on which Mr. Truman was
not going to have any second thoughts, it was the Bomb.
If he'd said it once, he'd said it a hundred times, almost
always in the same words. The Bomb had ended the war.
If we had had to invade Japan, half a million soldiers on
both sides would have been killed and a million more
"would have been maimed for life." It was as simple as
that. That was all there was to it, and Mr. Truman had
never lost any sleep over *that* decision.

Well, yes, and since Mr. Truman had made the decision to drop the Bomb all by himself, no one else was
around when he made up his mind, it wouldn't be possible
to bring other people into the program as we did with the
Korean decision. Besides which, except for Brigadier General Leslie R. Groves, who had been head of the Man-
hattan Project that produced the Bomb,* most of the peo-

* I have elsewhere described my single encounter with General Groves, an experience I had, as you will see, no wish to
repeat:

"In 1945, shortly after my Army discharge, I was for rea-
sons I prefer to forget in the Grand Ballroom of the Waldorf-
Astoria listening to a speech by Brig. Gen. Leslie R. Groves.
. . . The general stood a little way from where the fillet of
beef had been, and he said, the words loud and clear, that the
United States didn't need to worry about the Russians ever

ple who had had anything to do with it were dead. Or
they were in one way or another unacceptable to the
President. J. Robert Oppenheimer, for instance, a man
who had had as much as any other to do with making the
Bomb, had, in Mr. Truman's mind, ". . . turned into a
crybaby. I don't want anything to do with people like
that."

No further questions.

The film on Mr. Truman as a man of Independence
and/or independence was still being assembled in a cutting
room on Broadway, a process that took months and, as
I recall, the services of hundreds. David Susskind had,
however, *described* the program to the officials of all the
networks, and they had scarcely been able to stay awake.
"Who cares? That old man?"

So for the second program we needed something dramatic, and what was more dramatic than the Bomb? We'd
bomb the bastards awake.

All right, but we needed a format for the program, and
that was what I was being paid for. Not only was I being
paid, but I was already more or less responsible for the

---

making a bomb. 'Why,' he said, smiling, 'those people can't
even make a jeep.'

"You should have heard the applause; thunderous is the only
way to describe it; a great many people stood and cheered.

". . . I hesitate to think how many months of my life,
maybe years, I've spent in the Grand Ballroom of the Waldorf,
how many overdone fillets of beef I've eaten, how many Cher-
ries Jubilee, how many idiot statements I've listened to, sometimes, too often, applauded.

"As I left the Waldorf that night a woman with blue hair
and the face of a parakeet in distress looked at me with a
snarl; she was wearing mink; they always wear mink; it's
wrong about tennis shoes. You don't have to kill anything to
make tennis shoes. The woman, her voice that of a finger on
a blackboard, said, 'Now that we've got the Bomb let's hope
we use it again and the sooner the better, and we could start
out with some of the Commies right here at home.' "

spending of at least $100,000 of David's money, the money of his company, Talent Associates, anyway. I never knew which was which, a problem I'm sure David never had.

In any case, on September 27, 1961, I wrote a long and diplomatic memorandum to David, one that would, I was sure, end up in the hands of Mr. Truman; hence, the diplomacy:

"I have given deep and serious thought to the A-bomb program or programs, and it seems to me that there is only one way to deal with the subject tastefully and dramatically. As I said yesterday, Mr. Truman should himself go to Hiroshima, and he should speak in the museum there, preferably to a group of local schoolchildren. Essentially he would have to say only one thing, that the bomb must never be used again. There is no need for him to justify his decision to drop it. It was a simple, necessary military decision. Thus, to justify it or in any way to apologize for it would be repugnant.

"I think we might open the program by seeing the President enter Hiroshima, and as he does so, he might recall the events leading up to the decision to drop the bomb. We would see film of the explosion at Alamogordo, New Mexico, then film of the President at Potsdam, then of the notes that were sent to Japan asking them to surrender, then the unsatisfactory Japanese reply, then the city of Hiroshima itself, then the explosion, and the President's explanation of how and why he felt the decision was necessary. Then we go back to the President entering the city as it is today; then we talk with some Japanese people, a military man, perhaps, explaining that regrettable as the bombing was, the military of any other country would probably have decided the same thing, a Japanese intellectual saying that the Japanese now feel no bitterness toward the United States or toward the President, another intellectual who is still bitter over the A-bomb and still resents Mr. Truman because of his role in its use, a Japanese child talking about what the bomb means to him. And so on.

"Finally, the President arrives at the museum; we go through it with him, and he goes to the auditorium and speaks to the children gathered there.

"MERLE MILLER"

Of course, Mr. Truman never went to Hiroshima. I'm not sure whether he ever saw the diplomatic, duplicitous if you will, memorandum. If he did, he never mentioned it.

But when Bob Aurthur joined the project in November, taking David Susskind's place as producer, having Mr. Truman go to Hiroshima was one of the two suggestions he made for a program to follow the one that was on the cutting-room floor. The other was for a film on the Korean decision.

Bob writes of his first meeting with the President: "When I went into my outline of the Korean film, he stared at me, unblinking, his face, deeply lined, set in Rushmore-like granite, and all at once the participant realized whom he was conning, what this man was and what he had been, and the words sounded trivial, the idea infantile. But when I finished, Mr. Truman nodded sharply once, saying, 'All right, sounds pretty good,' and I knew Noyes and Hillman had already briefed him and gotten his approval.

" 'Just one thing,' Mr. Truman warned, 'don't try to make a playactor out of me.'

"Swearing this was the last intention possible, the participant needed only to flee, but Hillman held me back. 'Tell the President your idea for the atom-bomb film,' he said.

"Mr. Truman looked at me with quick suspicion; this was something he hadn't been told. No way out for me; I explained my desire to film the basic framework for the hour in Hiroshima.

"It was the only time I ever saw him blink. He was silent for a moment as Noyes studied the rug pattern and Hillman shuffled some papers, and then he said something surprising to me, if not to Noyes and Hillman.

" 'I'll go to Japan if that's what you want,' he said. 'But I won't kiss their ass.'

"Unhappily, we never got a chance to find out what he meant."

I expect what Mr. Truman meant was that while he was perfectly willing to explain why he had decided to drop the Bomb, he wasn't going to apologize for it, wasn't going to say that he had been wrong. And for all I know he wasn't wrong. Maybe it did save lives, ours and theirs.

My only insight into Mr. Truman's feeling about the Bomb and its dropping, and it isn't much, came one day in his private library at the Truman Memorial Library. In one corner was every book ever published on the Bomb, and at the end of one was Horatio's speech in the last scene of *Hamlet*. Mr. Truman had underlined these words:

> . . . let me speak to the yet unknowing world
> How these things came about: So shall you hear
> Of carnal, bloody, and unnatural acts,
> Of accidental judgements, casual slaughters,
> Of deaths put on by cunning and forced cause,
> And, in this upshot, purposes mistook
> Fall'n on the inventors' heads. . . .
> But let this same be presently perform'd,
> Even while men's minds are wild; lest more mischance,
> On plots and errors, happen.

Mr. Truman had underlined the last line twice. Which would indicate, I guess, that while he may not have lost any sleep over his decision, he had certainly given it a good deal of thought.

21

General Marshall and the Marshall Plan

. . . not the discovery of atomic energy but the solicitude of the world's most privileged people for its less privileged as vested in Truman's Point 4 and the Marshall Plan . . . this will be remembered as the signal achievement of our age.

—ARNOLD TOYNBEE

. . . it [the Marshall Plan] was the most unsordid act in history.

—WINSTON CHURCHILL

Mr. President, today if we may I'd like to talk again about General Marshall and your relationship with him and then get into the Marshall Plan itself. In his new book, Sketches from Life, *which I'm sure you've read Dean Acheson says that the general always insisted on complete frankness from his subordinates. He quotes him as saying, "I have no feelings except those I reserve for Mrs. Marshall."*

And Mr. Acheson says that's the way it always worked out with him. I wonder, sir, if that's the way it worked out with you, too, his Commander in Chief?

"It didn't matter what you were as far as General Marshall was concerned, didn't matter a damn. I've told you. I knew him long before I got that job in the White House, knew him in France when he was a young colonel . . . and kept track of him as best I could from then on, and he was always outstanding in every way.

"General Pershing wrote a book I read some time ago, and in it he said that General Marshall, Colonel Marshall then he was, did one of the most remarkable jobs on the entire western front when he was responsible for moving about a million men and God knows how many horses and mules and ammunition from the battlefield at St.-Mihiel to the Meuse-Argonne for the offensive there.

"And as you know I was around there at the time. The Germans were caught completely by surprise, and the man responsible for planning and executing that whole thing was Marshall. Pershing said it was one of the most remarkable things of the war.

"So Marshall always was the man everybody knew was going to have a wonderful future. No one who worked with him ever doubted it.

"So it wasn't any surprise at all when in 1939 Roosevelt made him Chief of Staff of the Army. He was only a brigadier general, wasn't even near the top of the list of brigadiers eligible for promotion, but Roosevelt reached right down there and brought him up, one of the smartest things Roosevelt ever did. Because General Marshall, more than any other man, was responsible for winning that war. At least that's my opinion.

"Of course he wanted a field command, and he'd have been wonderful at it, but Roosevelt convinced him his job was in Washington as Chief of Staff, and so that's what he did, and he did it without a single complaint.

"A lot of them had big parades after the war, a lot of the generals, but there was never a parade for General Marshall, and he deserved it more than all the rest put together.

"I gave him a decoration or two, but there wasn't a decoration anywhere that would have been big enough for General Marshall.

"But what you started to ask me, about him wanting to be told the truth. He was the kind of man who always insisted that he be told exactly what was on your mind, and he never failed to tell you exactly what was on his. Always, when I was a Senator and again when I was President. He was one of the men you could count on to be truthful in every way, and when you find somebody like that, you have to hang onto them. You have to hang onto them.

"When I first got that job in the White House, General Marshall was Chief of Staff of the Army, of course, and I saw him several times a week, which was always a pleasure because he never said much, but what he said was always exactly to the point. He never made any speeches at you. He told you what you wanted to know, and that was all he told you.

"And when you're in the kind of position I was in at the time, you appreciate that.

"And then he . . . he had no more than announced his retirement, and he and Mrs. Marshall had moved down to a new home in Virginia when I had to call on him to undertake another job."

In November, 1945, Major General Patrick J. Hurley, a reactionary, mean-spirited man from Oklahoma who was then ambassador to China, returned to the United States for conferences with various State Department officials and with President Truman. While he was in Washington, it became clear that relations between the Chinese Communists and the forces of Chiang Kai-shek were developing into a full-scale civil war. The alternatives open to the United States seemed to be either to pour further huge sums of money, weapons, and possibly soldiers into China to support Chiang or to try to convince Chiang and the Communists to work out some kind of compromise agreement. Mr. Truman favored the latter course and so instructed General Hurley, who said he agreed with him.

As Mr. Truman described it, "Old Hurley came to see me one morning [November 27, 1945], and he said he was sure everything would work out all right over there, and I said, 'Will you go back and finish the job?'

"He said that he would, and that was about eleven thirty or so in the morning, and then, I'd say it must have been somewhere between twelve thirty and one, why, Tony Vaccaro [Associated Press White House correspondent] called me up from the press club, and he said, 'Hurley's down here abusing you in every way he can think of.'

"I said, 'He just told me he was going back to China.'

"And Tony said, 'Well, he just told these people that he *won't* go back.'

" 'Well,' I said, 'all right. He won't.'

"And then I called up General Marshall, and I said, 'General, Hurley's conked out on me. And I want you to go to China. Will you go?'

"He said, 'Yes, Mr. President.' And bang went the phone. I thought he'd argue with me because I'd told him that since he'd retired, I wasn't going to bother him, that he was going to have a chance to rest.

"When he came in the next morning, I said, 'General, what did you cut me off so short for? I thought you'd argue with me.'

" 'Well,' he said, 'Mrs. Marshall and I were just unpacking and getting things ready to live in that house down there, and I thought I'd break the news gently. But before I could get to Mrs. Marshall, the radio was on and blared out, "Marshall goes to China." '

"He said, 'I was in the grease sure enough then.' "

Marshall served in China until January, 1947; then he was called back to Washington and shortly thereafter became Secretary of State. He retired two years later, after a series of operations. He was then seventy, but in September, 1950, President Truman called on him once again.

As Mr. Truman remembered it, "I had the same kind of experience with him when I wanted to make him Secretary of Defense. He had to have a kidney stone taken out, and of course, after that he didn't come back.

"But I needed him. I was having a terrible time with this Secretary of Defense thing.* And I knew he was the only man in the country who could handle the job, getting everybody together, and I knew if I asked him, explained to him how necessary it was, he'd say yes because he was

* The Secretary of Defense had been Louis Johnson, a man of many limitations, who, before Truman sacked him, had publicly criticized the State Department's China policy and was said to have been giving material critical of Dean Acheson to at least two of Acheson's Senate enemies. With the war in Korea only recently under way Truman had to have a man of Marshall's stature to succeed Johnson.

a man who never turned down a job that needed to be done.

"So I called up Mrs. Marshall, and I said, 'Where's the general?'

"She says, 'He's fishing up in Michigan. I guess you want to get him in trouble.'

"I said, 'Yes, I do.'

" 'Well,' she said, 'go ahead. He'll go anyhow.'

"So I called him up, took me a long time to get him. He was about five or six miles from a telephone, maybe further. He finally returned the call, and I said, 'General, I want you to be Secretary of Defense. Will you do it?'

"He said, 'Yes, Mr. President.' And he did the same thing to me, banged down the receiver.

"When he came back, he said, 'I want to tell you why I had to hang up in such a hurry. I was . . . it was a general store, and all the cracker-barrel experts were sitting around there waiting to see what I was going to get from the President.' "

At the time of his appointment as Secretary of Defense Marshall was attacked by, among others, Senator Robert A. Taft of Ohio, who accused him of having "encouraged" the Chinese Reds. Senator William Jenner, an Indiana Republican, went considerably further. He said, "General Marshall is not only willing, he is eager to play the role of a front man, for traitors.

"The truth is this is no new role for him, for Gen. George C. Marshall is a living lie.

". . . [As a result], this government of ours has been turned into a military dictatorship, run by a Communist-appeasing, Communist-protecting betrayer of America, Secretary of State Dean Acheson. . . .

"Unless he, himself [General Marshall], were desperate, he could not possibly agree to continue as an errand boy, a front man, a stooge, or a co-conspirator for this administration's crazy assortment of collectivist cutthroat crackpots and Communist fellow-traveling appeasers. . . .

"It is tragic, Mr. President, that General Marshall is not enough of a patriot to tell the American people the truth of what has happened, and the terrifying story of what lies in store for us, instead of joining hands once more with this criminal crowd of traitors and Communist appeasers who, under the continuing influence and direction of Mr. Truman and Mr. Acheson, are still selling America down the river."

As Dean Acheson writes in that admirable book *Present at the Creation,* "Immediately, an honorable gentleman from Massachusetts, Senator Saltonstall, followed by Senator Lucas, rose to rebuke such words as being as contemptible as any ever uttered in that place of easy standards."

Mr. President, how do you explain a man like Jenner?

"There's no explaining him. Birds like that are just part of the dirt that comes up when we're in for a run of hysteria in this country.

"He's just one of the dirty sonsabitches that gets elected to the Senate and elsewhere when we're going through one of those periods.

"But I told you. I don't worry so much about them as I do about the ones that kiss their ass and let them get away with it. Eisenhower got his picture taken with him, sitting right next to him on the same platform. Kissing the ass of a man who said things like that about General Marshall when General Marshall had made Eisenhower, helped him at every point in his career.

"The whole thing was something I just never will forget. There are some things people do that you have to forgive them for, but there are some . . . a few that you just can't. I can't anyway."

Mr. President, do you feel that despite attacks like Jenner's, do you think history always catches up, that the true facts always eventually emerge? As in the case as we've discussed of Andrew Johnson and some others?

"No question about it. It always does, and in my opinion General Marshall will go down in history as one of the great men of his time. And of course, people like Jenner, they aren't even a footnote in history.

"And I am sure that General Marshall knew that. We never did discuss it, but he knew that. I'm sure it still hurt some, though. When they stand up and call you names, it always hurts some, and I don't care how old or how young you are, what age you are."

Mr. President, did you ever see General Marshall ruffled, lose his temper?

"No, no. He was a man you couldn't ruffle. And I never saw him lose his temper. When they were cussing him out in Congress, like Jenner, calling him every name in the book that they could think of, he never lost his temper, and he never answered back.* He wouldn't take the time. He performed . . . I'd say he performed more important jobs for this country than any other man I can think of, and I don't know where we'd be if we hadn't had him."

Mr. President, how do you explain the fact that you and General Marshall and Dean Acheson, who are so widely different in background, formed one of the most remarkable and to me awesome trios in all our history?

"I don't know about that. I don't know about that, and I don't like to talk about myself in terms like that, in that way. But I'll tell you this. Dean Acheson and General Marshall were men who went ahead and did what had to be done. And they both realized that if you are going to keep the government running, you have to make decisions, and you have to meet the deadlines, whatever they are.

---

* In *Sketches from Life* Dean Acheson has written: "General Marshall never answered his critics. It would have been wholly out of character for him to have done so. But more than this, he had a sort of sympathy with them. His decisions, he said more than once, were adopted and were largely successful. Why should he now try to prove that his critics' views would not have succeeded? If they wished to justify their views, it was their privilege. This tolerance of criticism, this willingness to let the record speak for itself with interpretation by him, is supremely typical of him."

"That's what some of these fellas that sit on the sidelines and criticize never do seem to realize, that you have got to do your best to keep things moving. And you hope you're moving in the right direction, moving forward. Because the minute things start slipping in the other direction, the country is in trouble. And so is the world."

And it would be true, I think, that you three men had something else in common. You were all unselfish.

"You said that. I didn't."

I'll tell you something else they had in common, the members of that remarkable trio. Dean Acheson expressed it more eloquently than either Mr. Truman or General Marshall could have managed, but I am certain they totally agreed with what he said in a speech to the Associated Harvard Clubs of Boston when he was Undersecretary of State in 1946:

"For a long time we have gone along with some well-tested principles of conduct: That it was better to tell the truth than falsehoods; that a half-truth was no truth at all; that duties were older than and as fundamental as rights; that, as Justice Holmes put it, the mode by which the inevitable came to pass was effort; that to perpetuate a harm was always wrong, no matter how many joined in it, but to perpetuate it on a weaker person was particularly detestable. . . . Our institutions are founded on the assumption that most people will follow these principles most of the time because they want to, and the institutions work pretty well when this assumption is true.

"It seems to me the path of hope is toward the concrete, the manageable. . . . But it is a long and tough job, and one for which we as a people are not particularly suited. We believe that any problem can be solved with a little ingenuity and without inconvenience to the folks at large. . . .

"And our name for problems is significant. We call them headaches. You take a powder and they are gone. These pains about which we have been talking are not like that. They are like the pain of earning a living. They will stay with us until death. We have got to understand that all our lives the danger, the uncertainty, the need for alertness, for effort, for discipline will be upon us.

"This is new to us. It will be hard for us. But we are in for it, and the only question is whether we shall know it soon enough."

That is what we have got to get back to or move forward to, those well-tested principles of conduct. As the dean says, it will be hard for us. No other way to get the institutions working again, though.

Mr. President, why was the Marshall Plan called the Marshall Plan?

"It was called that because I realized that it was going down in history as a very great, very important thing, and I wanted General Marshall to get credit for it, which he did. I said to him, 'General, I want the plan to go down in history with your name on it. And don't give me any argument. I've made up my mind, and, remember, I'm your Commander in Chief.' "

How would you describe the plan to those who don't know what it was?

"It was a plan after the Second World War to prevent the kind of thing we had happen in this part of the country after the War Between the States. I think I told you the other day you can't be vindictive after a war. You have to be generous. You have to help people get back on their feet.

"After the Second World War, Europe had suffered the same way we had, and that made me think that we had to help rehabilitate Europe. It had to be rehabilitated by the people who had helped destroy it.

"The reports from Europe that I got in the winter and spring of 19 and 47 . . . it's easy to forget, but I doubt if things in Europe had ever been worse, in the Middle Ages maybe but not in modern times. People were starving, and they were cold because there wasn't enough coal, and tuberculosis was breaking out. There had been food riots in France and Italy, everywhere. And as if that wasn't bad enough, that winter turned out to have been the coldest in history almost.

"And something had to be done. The British were broke; they were pulling out of Greece and Turkey, and they couldn't put up money to help the people on the Continent. The United States had to do it, had to do it all, and the people and the Congress had to be persuaded that it was necessary.

"I had a chance to make a speech in Mississippi—in the spring of 1947, May, I think it was, and I couldn't do it. So Dean Acheson made it for me, and that was one of the first places we started laying out what the facts were and what had to be done.

"We had several conferences on what he was going to say."

The President had promised to make a speech to a gathering of several thousand farmers and their families at the annual meeting of the Delta Council in Cleveland, Mississippi, on May 8. But for a number of reasons, partly political, partly personal, the continued illness of his ninety-four-year-old mother, who had broken a hip in February, he was unable to go.

Dean Acheson went in his stead.

Dean Acheson: "It was quite clear that in the President's mind the speech was to be a major statement on foreign policy, and we had several meetings on its contents.

"I was to say, as I did say, that Europe and Asia were totally exhausted after a terrible war and after two horrible winters. It was necessary for the United States to help them recover, and to do that, huge sums of money would have to be appropriated. And it must all be done soon.

"That was the way the President saw it, and that was the way it was. As Mr. Truman has very often said of very many things, that was all there was to it.

"I have never known a man who kept so clearly in mind what were first things. Mr. Truman was unable to make the simple complex in the way so many men in public life tend to do. For very understandable reasons, of course. If one makes something complex out of something simple, then one is able to delay making up one's mind. And that was something that never troubled Mr. Truman.

"The speech I was to make was only one of several dozen, no doubt several hundred matters with which the President was concerned at that time. In many ways it was surely one of his lesser concerns, and yet every time we went back to the speech he seemed to remember every word.

"Now having a precise memory may not be one of the major virtues, but it is, I submit, in every way preferable to having an imprecise memory.

"And Mr. Truman was never troubled by hindsight, feeling, as I do, that it is a waste of time. Hindsight only tells you what did happen. It never tells you what did not happen and what might have occurred if you had taken action you did not take."

Mr. Secretary, speaking of memory, in Joe Jones' book on the Marshall Plan, The Fifteen Weeks, *he writes about a time in 1949 when Mr. Truman's knowledge of the history of the Dardanelles and that whole area astonished both you and Mrs. Acheson, especially Mrs. Acheson. Could you tell me about that?*

"We had been in New York for the dedication of the United Nations Building, and on the train going back to Washington, Mr. Truman for reasons I don't remember began talking about Central Asia and the Middle East. We had just finished dinner, and I remember that as he talked, he drew outline maps with a spoon to demonstrate what he was saying.

"It was one of the most lucid presentations I have ever heard, beginning with the travels of Marco Polo up through the conquests of Genghis Khan, the rise and fall of the Ottoman Empire, and in modern times the increasing Russian ambitions in the area, including control of the Dardanelles.

"Of course I was quite familiar with the President's wealth of historical knowledge and his ability to apply it to the problem at hand, but Mrs. Acheson was very much impressed with his profound knowledge of what to most people is a puzzling and obscure part of the world.

"He told her that it wasn't surprising at all, that he had spent a good part of his life reading history and that for reasons he really could not explain Central Asia and the Middle East had always held a very special interest for him.

"But there were very few subjects on which Mr. Truman did not have a detailed and accurate knowledge and which he could not explain with complete lucidity."

There's another episode in Joe Jones' book about a meeting in August, 1946, a meeting with some people from the State Department and from the armed services, including you as Undersecretary of State and General Eisenhower, who was Chief of Staff of the Army. The Russians had recently made demands on the Turkish government which would, I gather, have meant the virtual abandonment of its independence.

I believe that at that meeting there was an exchange between the President and General Eisenhower.

"No, I wouldn't describe what happened as an exchange. The President conducted that meeting as he conducted all such meetings. He elicited the point of view of everyone present at the meeting, and then he said it would, of course, be necessary to take a firm stand against the Russian demands and that to make sure that everyone realized we were serious in our support of the Turks, we were sending a considerable naval force to rejoin the USS *Missouri,* which was already in Istanbul. That had been the recommendation, and he approved it and directed that it be carried out, fully realizing that such action could lead to armed conflict.

"General Eisenhower, who was seated next to me,

leaned over and in a stage whisper asked whether I thought the President realized the implications of what he had done.

"With as benign a smile as I could under the circumstances manage I suggested that the general ask the President that question, which he did do.

"The President reached in a drawer, took out a large and clearly much-studied map of the area, and proceeded for the next fifteen or twenty minutes once again to give a detailed account of the history of the area up to the present day. It was once again a masterful performance, and when it was over, Mr. Truman turned to the general and asked whether or not he was satisfied that the President understood the implications of what he was saying.

"I believe the general did have the grace to join in the laughter that followed, although I would not say that in general he was burdened with a sense of humor."

Mr. Secretary, I gather you don't have too high a regard for General Eisenhower.

Mr. Acheson smiled, no doubt as benignly as he could manage, and we went on to other matters, but in *Present at the Creation* he says that during the 1952 Presidential campaign:

General Eisenhower began discussing foreign policy in terms surprising for him. The great chain of events begun under his benefactor, General Marshall, he called a 'purgatory of improvisation.' In the same speech, relating what he termed some 'plain facts' about the period leading up to the attack on South Korea, the General grossly distorted my Press Club speech, and, when I publicly set the record straight, severed all relations with me. It appears to be true that one who unjustly injures another must in justification become his enemy. During the eight years of his Presidency I was never invited into the White House or to the State Department or consulted in any way. However, this involved no invidious discrimination, since my chief, President Truman, was treated the same way.

Mr. Secretary, what was the reaction to your speech in Mississippi?

"The reaction was quite favorable and widespread, particularly in the foreign press.

"What I was doing, of course, was really no more than preparing the way for what General Marshall was to say at Harvard the following month. The President always called my remarks at Cleveland 'the prologue to the Marshall Plan.' "

Mr. President, why was it that General Marshall announced the Marshall Plan at Harvard?

"General Marshall told me about a month before, maybe more, that he was going up there. They were going to give him an honorary degree, and he said to me, 'I've got to make this damn speech, and you know how I hate to make speeches. And I don't know what to talk about.'

"I said, 'I want you to spell out the details of this plan that's being worked out over in the State Department to save Europe from going under.' And I said, 'This plan is going down in history as the Marshall Plan, and that's the way I want it.'

"He blushed. He was just about the most modest man I ever did know, and he said, 'I can't allow a thing like that to happen, Mr. President.'

"And I says to him, 'You won't have anything to do with it, but that's what will happen, and that's what I want to happen.' And I was right. It did." *

* General Marshall made his speech on June 5, 1947, at the 296th Harvard commencement. In presenting him with an honorary degree President James B. Conant compared Marshall to that other general who was also a George, Washington, "An American to whom freedom owes an enduring debt of gratitude, a soldier and statesman whose ability and character brook only one comparison in the history of this nation."

In his short speech Marshall described the horrors of the winter in Europe that had just passed and, further, what would surely happen in the months ahead—the increasing shortages

Winston Churchill has called the Marshall Plan "the most unsordid act in history."

"Well, there wasn't anything selfish about it. We weren't trying to put anything over on people. We were in a

of food and fuel and money, the physical wreckage, the dislocated economies.

Then he said, "The truth of the matter is that Europe's requirements for the next three or four years of foreign food and other essential producers—principally from America—are so much greater than her present ability to pay that she must have substantial additional help or face economic, social, and political deterioration of a very grave character. The remedy lies in breaking the vicious circle and restoring the confidence of the European people in the economic future of their own countries and of Europe as a whole. The manufacturer and the farmer throughout wide areas must be able and willing to exchange their products for currencies the continuing value of which is not open to question. . . .

"It is logical that the United States should do whatever it is able to assist in the return of normal economic health in the world, without which there can be no political stability or secured peace. Our policy is directed not against any country or doctrine but against hunger, poverty, desperation, and chaos. Its purpose should be the revival of a working economy in the world so as to permit the emergence of political and social conditions in which free institutions can exist. Such assistance, I am convinced, must not be on a piece-meal basis as various crises develop. Any assistance that this government may render should provide a cure rather than a palliative. Any government that is willing to assist in the task of recovery will find full cooperation, I am sure, on the part of the United States government. Any government which maneuvers to block recovery of other countries cannot expect help from us. Furthermore, governments, political parties, or groups which seek to perpetuate human misery in order to profit therefrom politically will encounter the opposition of the United States. . . .

"An essential part of any successful action on the part of the United States is an understanding of the character of the problem and the remedies to be applied. Political passion and prejudice should have no part. With foresight, and a willingness on the part of our people to face up to the vast responsibility which history has clearly placed upon our country, the difficulties I have outlined can and will be overcome."

General Marshall did not mention the Soviet Union or

position to keep people from starving and help them preserve their freedom and build up their countries, and that's what we did."

Mr. President, the plan called for expenditures of sixteen billion dollars. Didn't that cause a lot of concern in Congress?

"Yes, it did, but it had to be done, and so I called in all the favors I was owed, and we got it through. I called in Sam Rayburn and when I told him what we had in mind, he just wouldn't believe it. His first reaction was just like everybody else's. He said we couldn't afford it. He said, 'Mr. President, it will bust this country.'

"And I said to him, 'Sam, if we don't do it, Europe will have the worst depression in its history, and I don't know how many hundreds of thousands of people will starve to death, and we don't want to have a thing like that on our consciences, not if it's something we can prevent, we don't.

"And I said, 'If we let Europe go down the drain, then we're going to have a bad depression in this country. And you and I have both lived through one depression, and we don't want to have to live through another one, do we, Sam?'

"He says, no, we didn't. And then he kind of swallowed hard, and he says, 'Harry, how much do you figure this thing is going to cost?'

"And I looked him right in the eye. I never told Sam anything less than the whole truth at all times. That's the kind of relationship we had. I looked him right in the

---

Communism in his speech; the only enemies he enumerated by name were the abovementioned "hunger, poverty, desperation, and chaos."

It could not have occurred to the general that some years later revisionist historians would see that speech as a bomb-rattling threat to the peace by a dedicated cold warrior. Nor did it occur to me when talking to Mr. Truman and Mr. Acheson about General Marshall and the Marshall Plan in 1961 and 1962.

eye, and I said, 'It's going to cost about fifteen, sixteen billion dollars, Sam.'

"Well, his face got as white as a sheet, but I said to him, 'Now, Sam, I figure I saved the people of the United States about fifteen, sixteen billion dollars with that committee of mine, and you know that better than anyone else.

" 'Now we're going to need that money, and we can save the world with it.'

"And he says to me, 'Harry, I'll do my damnedest. It won't be easy, but you can count on me to help all I can.' And he did, too, and so did a lot of others in both parties. There wasn't anything partisan about any part of this or anything else where foreign policy was concerned. Not when I was in the White House there wasn't.

"We always went ahead and did what had to be done, and the Marshall Plan saved Europe, and that's something I am glad I had some part in helping accomplish."

22

The 1948 Victory

Mr. President, you said the other day that you decided you were going to run for reelection the first day you were President, in April, 1945, but you didn't go into any detail about that. What were some of the reasons you decided so soon?

"I always knew that from April, 1945, until January, 1949, what I would really be doing was filling out the fourth term of Roosevelt, who was a great President, but I had some ideas of my own, and in order to carry them out I had to run for reelection and be reelected, and that is exactly what happened.

"Of course I didn't say I was going to run for quite some time. It didn't do any harm that I could see to keep people guessing for a while. I knew I'd be able to win, though: I knew that all along."

You knew?

"Of course I knew. I knew the Republicans would come up with somebody like Taft or Dewey, and I knew that the people of this country weren't ready to turn back the clock—not if they were told the truth, they weren't.

"The only thing we . . . I had to figure out was how to tell them the truth, in what way, and I decided that, the way I'd always campaigned before was by going around talking to people, shaking their hands when I could, and running for President was no different. The only difference was instead of driving to the various communities where people were, I went by train. But otherwise, it was exactly the same experience. I just got on a train and started across the country to tell people what was going on. I wanted to talk to them face to face. I knew that they knew that when you get on the television, you're wearing a lot of powder and paint that somebody else has put on your face, and you haven't even combed your own hair.

"But when you're standing right there in front of them

and talking to them and shaking their hands if it's possible, the people can tell whether you're telling them the facts or not.

"I spoke I believe altogether to between fifteen and twenty million people. I met them face to face, and I convinced them, and they voted for me."

Did you think it would be a three-way race, that Henry Wallace would run against you?

"Never had the slightest doubt of it. All through 1947 Henry went around the country making speeches saying that I was trying to get this country into war with Russia, which, of course, was the opposite of what I was doing. I was doing everything in the world to prevent a war, and I succeeded.

"But Henry said I was trying to start a war, and he also kept saying that he was still a loyal Democrat, and the more he said it, the more I was sure he was going to run against me on a third-party ticket."

Why?

"Because Henry was like Lloyd Stark, the fella that ran against me for the Senate. What he said he wasn't going to do was exactly what I knew he was going to do. I don't know, in Henry's case, if you'd say he was a liar as much as that he didn't know the difference between the truth and a lie.

"And anyway the way he . . . the way Henry talked to you, you had to listen very hard to understand what he was getting at, and half the time I was never sure if Henry knew. He was a very difficult man to follow what he meant." *

* As I said earlier, some years after the 1948 election I moved to Brewster, New York, not far from Mr. Wallace's large farm at South Salem. At one time I thought of writing something about him, maybe a biography, although I felt his campaign in 1948 had been a shambles and a shame.

In any case, I made several trips to South Salem and had several conversations with him. I have never been more disappointed in a public figure. He was a muddled, totally irrational man, almost incapable of uttering a coherent sentence. He was also the bitterest man I have ever encountered.

Mr. President, you have quite a reputation as a poker player. Would you say there's any resemblance in politics and poker in that in both you seem to have to size up your opponent pretty well if you want to win?

"I was never much of a poker player. Roosevelt was more of a poker player than I was. But they never wrote anything in the papers about it. But they were always writing about me playing poker.

"Newspapermen, and they're all a bunch of lazy cusses, once one of them writes something, the others rewrite it and rewrite it, and they keep right on doing it without ever stopping to find out if the first fellow was telling the truth or not.*

"But it is true that you have to size up the other fella, in politics, too. And I'd sized up Henry as a fella that would say one thing and do another. So it didn't surprise me a bit when he came out with a third party.

"And I knew another thing. He was like the other fella that ran against me that year. I knew the more he talked, the more votes he'd lose."

Do you mean he was dishonest?

"It wasn't so much that. It was that half the time and more he just didn't seem to make sense."

---

* Dr. Wallace Graham, the President's personal physician in the White House and until the time of his death, said, "When Mr. Truman was in the White House, we would play poker sometimes in the evening. I don't think he really enjoyed it much. He played more to find out about people. Often he'd play with someone he was considering for some office or other, some appointment. He'd ply him with champagne, and then General Vaughan [Colonel Harry Vaughan, a veteran of Battery D who followed Harry Truman right into the White House and was his most-criticized associate] would rib whoever it was, and the President would watch to see what the reaction would be. If the guy got flustered, if he couldn't take the ribbing or got too tight, Mr. Truman would feel, I believe, that he shouldn't be given whatever the appointment was.

"But I don't think he ever played much for his own enjoyment. He'd never give up, though. The way we'd play you couldn't lose more than eighty dollars or so, but Mr. Truman would stay in every hand, always."

Were you surprised when the Dixiecrats walked out of the convention and Strom Thurmond, who I believe then was governor of South Carolina, became another third-party candidate?

"No. When 1948 was coming along, they said that if I didn't let up with my asking for a Fair Employment Practice Commission and asking for a permanent commission on civil rights and things of that kind, why, some of the Southerners would walk out.

"I said if that happened, it would be a pity, but I had no intention of running on a watered-down platform that said one thing and meant another. And the platform I did run on and was elected on went straight down the line on civil rights.

"And that's the beautiful thing about it. Thirty-five votes walked out of that convention and split up the Solid South, and because of Wallace, Dewey was able to carry New York State by sixty thousand votes.

"So I always take a great deal of pleasure in saying I won without the Solid South and without New York, which wasn't supposed to be able to be done. It was never done before, and it hasn't been done since.

"People said I ought to pussyfoot around, that I shouldn't say anything that would lose the Wallace vote and nothing that would lose the Southern vote.

"But I didn't pay any attention to that. I said what I thought had to be said. You can't divide the country up into sections and have one rule for one section and one rule for another, and you can't encourage people's prejudices. You have to appeal to people's best instincts, not their worst ones. You may win an election or so by doing the other, but it does a lot of harm to the country.

"Another thing about that election. I won it not because of any special oratorical effects or because I had any help from what you call 'the Madison Avenue fellas' but by a statement of fact of what had happened in the past and what would happen in the future if the fella that was running against me was elected.

"I made three hundred and fifty-two speeches that were

on the record and about the same number that were not.
I traveled altogether thirty-one thousand seven hundred
miles I believe, and it was the last campaign in which that
kind of approach was made, and now, of course, everything is television, and the candidates travel from one
place to another by jet airplane, and I don't like that.

"You get a real feeling of this country and the people
in it when you're on a train, speaking from the back of a
train, and the further you get away from that, the worse
off you are, the worse off the country is. The easier it gets
for the stuffed shirts and the counterfeits and the fellas
from Madison Avenue to put it over on the people. Those
people are more interested in selling the people something
than they are in informing them about the issues."

*You didn't have any Madison Avenue people on the
campaign train with you?*

"No, no. We couldn't afford their services to speak of.
In Detroit the day when I was going to make the Labor
Day address from Cadillac Square they had quite a time
raising the money for a radio broadcast, fifty thousand I
think it was, and we were always running short of money
throughout the campaign just paying to keep the train
going from station to station.

"But we didn't have any advertising men along. I never
felt the need for any."

*Mr. President, speaking of money, in Jack Redding's
book,* which I know you've read because some of your
marginal comments were printed in the book, he says that
Senator Howard McGrath said in 1948 that if you had
just invited some potential contributors to take a cruise
aboard the Presidential yacht, the* Williamsburg, *the
Democratic National Committee would have had no trouble at all raising a lot of money but that you wouldn't*

---

* Jack Redding was director of public relations for the
Democratic National Committee in 1948; his book, published
in 1958, was called *Inside the Democratic Party.* Howard Mc-
Grath was a Senator from Rhode Island, as well as chairman
of the Democratic National Committee in 1948.

agree to that, to inviting them. Although, as you say, the party was nearly broke during the entire campaign.

"That's true. I wouldn't."

Why?

"Because it's the Presidential yacht. It belongs to the President."

That was another time when I waited for more, knowing there would be no more.

I gather you have no faith in advertising men in politics.

"None at all. I'm sure they're very good at what they're trained to do, but in politics what you're doing, and I've said this a few times before, what you're doing or ought to be doing is discussing ideas with people so they can decide which is better, yours or the other fellow's.

"And as I say, you don't have to have any oratory to put it over. You just have to set down the facts, which is what I always did.

"The thing I never could understand about the fella that ran on the Democratic ticket in 1952 [Stevenson], he always spent a lot more time worrying about *how* he was going to say something than he did on *what* he was going to say. I told him once, I said, 'Adlai, if you're telling people the truth, you don't have to worry about your prose. People will get the idea.'

"He never did learn that, though. He was a very smart fella, but there were some things he just never got through his head, and one of them was how to talk to people."

That's not uncommon in politics, would you say?

"No, and it's a pity. It seems to get more that way all the time. The more time goes on, it seems people running for public office just don't tell what they have on their minds. There was a lot of that in the last campaign [1960]. The candidates for President didn't talk any less, but they said a lot less."

Mr. President, early in 1948, long before the convention there was a lot of talk among some Democrats about

trying to nominate or draft the fellow who in 1952 suc-
ceeded you in the White House. Did that bother you?

"Not a bit. It didn't make any sense at all. They didn't
know what party he belonged to even or how he stood on
any issue at all."

There are those, myself among them, who would say
that after eight years in the White House you still didn't
know, the country didn't know, where he stood on almost
any issue at all.

The President laughed, and then he said, "All that
carrying-on before the convention in 1948, I knew nothing
much would come of it, and it didn't."

What did you think of the Democrats who did it, the
two Roosevelt boys, among others, James and Elliott, I
believe?

"Well, their father was a great politician, but none of
his sons seem to have inherited his abilities in that line.
They just never seem to have what it takes to get people
to vote for them. I told one of them, James I think it was,
and I was out in California making a speech. I told him
he was a goddam fool for trying to get rid of somebody
who was just carrying out his father's policies. Trying to
anyway.

"Of course, later, after the convention, he came around
and supported me, but I never did forget what went on
earlier.

"I never did anything about it, but the old man never
forgets."

Weren't you a little bitter?

"No, no. I didn't have time for that. Being bitter . . .
that's for people who aren't busy with other matters."

Mr. President, didn't you make what you called a "non-
political tour" across the country before the Democratic
national convention?

"I did. I had to dedicate some things. I think I dedicated
the Grand Coulee Dam two or three times. I forget which,
and it was, as you say, 'nonpolitical.' But on the way I
made a few stops and told the people what was going on

in Washington, and they showed up in large numbers and listened and seemed to appreciate what I had to say. About a million people were lined up on the streets of Los Angeles alone, but they never took any pictures of that. They took pictures to prove . . . at times when there weren't big crowds."

Could you tell me how the phrase "whistle-stop" originated?

"Robert Taft [Republican Senator from Ohio] started it, and he wished he hadn't. Somebody asked him what was happening on my tour, and he said that I was lambasting Congress at all kinds of 'whistle-stops across the country.'

"Of course some of the boys at the national committee picked that right up and got word out to towns all across the country about what Taft had said, and the mayors of those towns didn't like it a bit. It did us no harm at all at the polls in November, of course."

What he was saying was, "Well, where the President is going is just to all these tiny towns that are of no importance."

"That's right, and some of those towns had populations of a hundred thousand people and more, including Los Angeles, of course, and, after that, the whole campaign became what was called a whistle-stop campaign, and I saw to it in my speeches that people remembered what Taft had said about their towns."

Why is it do you suppose that Republicans so often make mistakes like that? Or seem to. Is it stupidity?

"No. Most of them are smart enough. It's just—this is only my opinion, of course—it's just that they don't seem to know or care anything about people. Not all of them but a lot of them don't.

"The fella they nominated to run against me was a good example of that. People could tell he wasn't open and above board, and the more he talked, the more he showed that he didn't have any program at all in mind if he got elected. Except to set things back a few dozen years or more. So he didn't get elected. It was as simple as that."

Mr. President, you said the other day you hadn't given much or any thought to what you were going to say at the convention, but it says in the Memoirs that I believe you had made some informal notes.

"Yes, I'd written down some notes when Margaret and the Boss and I were coming from Washington to Philadelphia, and they were in a big black notebook that I carried to the podium with me when I made my acceptance speech. There were two things I was sure of that I was going to say. I was going to tell them that Alben Barkley [Truman's Vice Presidential running mate] and I were going to win the election, and I'd made up my mind that after I lambasted into the do-nothing Eightieth Congress that I was going to call them back into a special session, which is what I did do.*

* "On the twenty-sixth of July, which out in Missouri we call 'Turnip Day,' I am going to call Congress back and ask them to pass laws to halt rising prices, to meet the housing crisis—which they are saying they are for in their platform.

"At the same time I shall ask them to act upon other vitally needed measures, such as aid to education, which they say they are for; a national health program; civil rights legislation, which they say they are for; an increase in the minimum wage, which I doubt very much they are for; extension of the Social Security coverage and increased benefits, which they say they are for; funds for projects needed in our program to provide public power and cheap electricity. By indirection, the Eightieth Congress has tried to sabotage the power policies the United States has pursued for fourteen years. The power lobby is as bad as the real-estate lobby, which is sitting on the housing bill.

"I shall ask for adequate and decent laws for displaced persons in place of this anti-Semitic, anti-Catholic law which the Eightieth Congress passed.

"Now, my friends, if there is any reality behind the Republican platform we ought to get some action from a short session of the Eightieth Congress. They can do this job in fifteen days, if they want to do it. They will still have time to go out and run for office.

"They are going to try to dodge their responsibility. They are going to drag all the red herrings they can across this campaign, but I am here to say that Senator Barkley and I are not going to let them get away with it."

"That really stirred things up. It was in the middle of my speech, and I said, 'The Republicans have agreed on a platform. Now I'm gonna call a special session of the Congress and give them a chance to put their platform into effect.

"And of course they didn't do a damn thing. If they had been smart and even passed one measure along the lines they'd promised in their platform, I'd have been up a creek, but I knew damn well they wouldn't do it, and of course, they didn't."

Mr. President, you said you were calling that special session for Turnip Day. What's Turnip Day?

"The twenty-sixth of July, wet or dry, always sow turnips. Along in September they'll be four, five, maybe six inches in diameter, and they're good to eat—raw. I don't like them cooked."

Turnip greens are pretty good.

"Well, yes, but the only way to get turnip greens is in the spring. You take out the turnips that you've kept in the cellar all winter and set them out in the garden, and then they come up. You grow them, and the greens that have come up when they're both, oh, about four or five inches long you mix them with dandelions and mustard, and they make the finest greens in the world. Spinach isn't in it.

"That's what the country people used to have in the spring. Turnip greens with dandelions and mustard and things of that kind.

"But you have to know which is which with plants like that. Plenty of those things are violent poison. You take poke berries, pokeroots. When they're so long, they're good to go into greens, but you wait a little longer, and you might as well order your coffin. Because you're done. They're as poisonous as cyanide."

How do you find out when to pick them?

"Your grandmother has to tell you."

Mr. President, during the campaign, how did you decide where to go, where to speak? For instance, you spoke at

*a plowing contest I think it was in Dexter, Iowa. I'm from
Iowa, and I don't even know where Dexter is. How did
you happen to decide to go there?*

"Well, there were ninety-six thousand farmers at Dexter, Iowa [I-uh-way], and somebody had to go there and
talk to 'em, and I went."

How do you know there were ninety-six thousand?

"There was a lot of disagreement in the papers and
the newsmagazines about how many people were there.
Nobody asked me, but I could have told 'em. Some said
fifty thousand, some said seventy-five thousand, and some
said ninety thousand.

"But there were ninety-six thousand people there. There
was ten acres, and the place was jammed full. Now figure
two to the square yard and you'll see how many there
were. Figure it out yourself."

*How do you think those farmers felt about what you
said?*

"I don't know, but they voted for me. I've told you
time and again. You've got to know how to talk to people.
That's the whole thing, and you've got to convince them
that you know what you're talking about. They don't go
for high hats, and they can spot a phony a mile off.

"I stopped one time in a place in either Montana or
Idaho. And I guess there must have been two or three
hundred people there, and I got off the train, and some
smart aleck on a horse rode up and said, 'Mr. President,
how old is this horse?' I said, 'Which end do you want me
to look at, his tail or his mouth?' I looked at his mouth,
and I said, 'He's so old.' The fella said, 'Jesus Christ, he
knows, doesn't he?'

"If you don't think I had that vote committed.

"Some of these smart alecks are always saying that to
tell how old a horse is you can look either at his tail or his
mouth, but that isn't true. You have to look at his teeth,
and this horse had teeth that long. I said, 'This old son of
a bitch must be fifteen or twenty years old, and he ought
to be taken out to pasture.' The fella turned and rode him
off."

I read someplace that when you were in Dexter, you talked at some length about the differences between mules and machines.

"I did. I don't remember what I said, but all those speeches were recorded. They're in a book in there. But what I probably said is that there's a hell of a lot of difference between riding behind a mule and riding behind a tractor.

"The most peaceful thing in the world is riding behind a mule, plowing a field. It's the calmest and most peaceful thing in the world, and while there's some danger that you may, like the fella said, get kicked in the head by a mule and end up believing everything you read in the papers, the chances are you'll do your best thinking that way. And that's why I've always thought and said that farmers are the smartest people in the world.

"My father used to trade mules, and he knew a lot about them. He didn't have to look at a mule's teeth to tell how old he was. All he had to do was look at him, and he was never wrong.

"A tractor will never be as . . . satisfactory as a mule. It makes a noise, for one thing, and noise interferes with a man's thoughts.

"But plowing a field with a mule is the most satisfying thing a man can do. And at the end of the day, looking over what you've done, you can feel a real sense of accomplishment, and that's a very rare thing."

Mr. President, I see by Jack Redding's book that not all your speeches in 1948 were for votes, that when you were in Dallas, you stopped at an orphanage and talked to the children there.

"Yes, I did. Yes, I did. I just told them to stop the cars, and I went inside and talked to those children."

Why?

"I thought that, well, being spoken to by the President of the United States was something they'd remember all their lives. It's a very lonely thing being a child. It was for me, and I had a family, including, as I think I told you, thirty-nine first cousins, and I was the only one they all spoke to.

"So I was very lucky when I was a child, and I had a happy childhood, but sometimes . . . well, I was lonesome, and I felt that it must be twice as bad for boys and girls who are orphans. So I went inside and talked to them.

"I was glad I did it, and I guess they were, too."

And when you were in Dallas, Texas, you had the first integrated rally in the history of the state.

"Oh, yes, and there was quite a to-do over that. They said I'd lose votes, and they said there'd be race riots, and I don't know what all they said.

"But that rally was just as peaceful as any of the others. If you just give people a chance to be decent, they will be. If the fella that succeeded me had just given people a little leadership, there wouldn't have been all that difficulty over desegregating the schools, but he didn't do it. He didn't use the powers of the office of the President to uphold a ruling of the Supreme Court of the United States, and I never did understand that.

"If he'd got out in front and told people that they had to uphold the law of the land, it's my opinion that they'd have done it. But he didn't; he shillyshallied around, and that's the reason we're in the fix we're in now."

Mr. President, didn't your train run out of money in Oklahoma someplace?

"In Oklahoma City. We ran out of money, and some of them got in a panic again and said we'd have to call off the campaign and go back to Washington, but we raised it. We never had much, but we raised enough to finish the trip. And then we got up enough money for a second trip."

It sounds as if it was always nip and tuck as far as money was concerned, though.

"It was, but that's the way it ought to be. I think I've told you. When people are anxious to give you a lot of money in a political campaign, you always have to ask yourself what the reason for it is. People just don't give money away for no reason."

What are some of the other highlights of that remarkable campaign that you remember?

"Well, in an auditorium in Seattle that holds seven thousand people, they had eight thousand or more crowded in, and some bird way up in the balcony shouted, 'Give 'em hell, Harry. We'll take 'em.' And that's where that whole thing started. After that a lot of people started shouting it."

Was that spontaneous?

"Oh, yes. None of those things was ever worked up. I didn't believe in that. The minute you start planning things, why, the next step is powder and paint, and they want you to become a playactor, and I believe I've told you a time or two how I feel about that."

Yes, sir, I remember. . . . Could we try a typical day on the campaign train? What would happen? What time would you get up in the morning?

"Five o'clock."

And would you take a walk?

"The first time where there, was a stop I'd get off and take a walk. And of course, they had to hold the train as long as I wanted it held. I was President."

And after the walk? What happened next?

"We'd go on, and whenever the train got to a spot where there were enough people on the platform to be talked to, we'd stop, and I'd talk to them."

What did you consider enough people?

"Ten to a thousand."

Did you ever actually speak to an audience as small as ten people in 1948?

"Many a time, many a time. They'd come out to hear me, and I talked to them."

And did you lambaste the Republicans at every stop?

"Most of the time, but there were some exceptions, and they got me into trouble with some of the local politicians. When I was in Michigan, they wanted me to light into

Senator Vandenberg [Arthur Vandenberg, Republican Senator from Michigan]. But I wouldn't do it. He'd supported the Marshall Plan; if it hadn't been for him, it might never have been approved in the Senate, and I wasn't about to forget that and start attacking him, and I didn't. It made a lot of those birds in Michigan unhappy, but I wouldn't do it.

"And in California I wouldn't say anything against Governor Warren [Earl Warren, Republican candidate for Vice President] because he was a friend of mine.

"If you can't win an election without attacking people who've helped you and who're friends of yours, it's not worth winning. I think I've told you. You can't pay too high a price to win an election."

Didn't Mr. Dewey have a little trouble with the engineer of his train out in Illinois?

"He said something about how maybe he ought to have the engineer shot at sunrise because he backed up the train too far. We managed to get that news around the country, and it didn't help him much with the working people. The trouble was he'd forgot what it was like to have to work for a living, and it showed on him, which is why he lost the election." *

Someplace I read that Lester Biffle [Secretary of the Senate] went around during the campaign disguised as a chicken peddler and made a poll that was the only poll that showed you were going to win.

---

* In his illuminating book on 1948 *The Loneliest Campaign,* Irwin Ross writes of that incident, which took place in Beaucoup, Illinois, on October 12: "As Dewey began to speak from the rear platform, the train suddenly moved backward into the crowd. It stopped after a few feet and no one was hurt. Dewey momentarily lost his poise. 'That's the first lunatic I've had for an engineer,' he told the crowd. 'He probably ought to be shot at sunrise but I guess we can let him off because no one was hurt.' The flash of temper was forgivable under the circumstances, but it was to cost Dewey dearly. Before the campaign was over, the Democrats inflated the remark to the dimensions of a cause célèbre, charging that it proved that Dewey was unfeeling and hostile to the workingman."

"That's right. He went around in a spring wagon and dressed in overalls, and he got more information for me than anybody else in the business. He said, 'Now listen, Harry, you don't have to worry. The common people are for ya.' And they were."

What's a chicken peddler?

"Well, in every neighborhood in the country where they raise chickens there was always a fella who drove around either in a truck or an old spring wagon with a team of mules who bought the surplus chickens and eggs.

"That's what a chicken peddler is, and in the old days there were a tremendous number of them. There used to be an old man with whiskers who'd come out to our farm, and my mother would sell him eggs and butter, and with the money she got she'd buy all the coffee and sugar and everything else we needed.

"They called him Old Folks, and he was always honest with my mother. He'd give her a fair price for the chickens by weight and eggs by the dozen, and he was always welcome because people knew he was honest.

"But I don't think they have them anymore. I think they're gone. I think they're gone."

So Mr. Biffle's poll was the only one that had it right?

"The only one. The rest of them, what they were doing was polling each other, and I didn't let it worry me. What I did was keep on giving the facts to the people."

Weren't you worn out at the end of the campaign?

"I felt better at the end of the campaign than I had at the beginning, and I'll tell you why. I got the feeling . . . a real feeling of the kind of country we've got here and the kind of people, and it sort of you might say renewed my faith."

Especially since you won the election.

"No, no, no. Even if I'd lost the election, my feeling for the common people of this country wouldn't have changed. You know what Lincoln said. 'The Lord must have loved the common people he made so many of them.' Well, the feeling I got in that campaign was that most of the people in this country are not only, like I said, decent people, they want to do the right thing, and what you have to do is tell them straight out what the right thing is.

"And feeling . . . like that, I didn't get tired."

Mr. President, I guess everybody in the United States who was alive at the time remembers what he did on election day, November 2, 1948. For one thing, the radio networks had sent out word to expect Mr. Dewey's victory announcement around nine in the evening. So we all planned to listen to that and then go to bed and get a good night's sleep. Instead of which, we stayed up all night, and, as you may recall, Mr. Dewey didn't concede until almost noon the next day. I wonder, sir, could you tell me what you did that day?

"Nothing very special. I got up at the usual time and took my morning walk, and then later, of course, we voted, and I had a nice, long lunch at the country club. Mayor Sermon [Roger T. Sermon, mayor of Independence] gave a little party out there, and we all had a good time. Just a few old friends was all it was, but we had a good time."

Rufus Burrus, Harry Truman's personal attorney: "We had lunch . . . and Mr. Truman said, 'Now, fellows, don't worry. I'm going to get elected. You can depend on it. But you'd better go out in the precincts and do a little work, see that the vote gets out.

"None of us believed it, believed that he was going to win, but he did. He was as sincere in his belief that he was going to be reelected President as he was at any time when he was running for judge of the county or the Senate of the United States.

"And before that lunch was over, speaking only for myself, of course, he'd brought me around to thinking that way, too."

Tom Evans, an old friend of Harry Truman's: "He called me from the country club, and he said he was having dinner there but that he was going to escape out the back door and go down to Excelsior Springs [about thirty miles north of Independence]. Which is what he did."

Mr. Truman: "We drove down to Excelsior Springs, and I had a bath in the hot springs and a little something to eat and went to bed, about six o'clock in the evening I think it was."

And you went to sleep, of course.

"Oh, yes, and about midnight I tuned in the little radio there, and old H. V. Kaltenborn was carrying on about how while I was ahead, he didn't see how I could win."

Tom Evans: "I called him about midnight. He had just lost New York State to Dewey, and I knew he had to carry Ohio, Illinois, and California. And when I called him to tell him that he said, 'Tom, I'm going back to sleep. Now don't call me any more. I'm going to carry all three of those states.' Which he did." *

Mr. Truman: "The Secret Service, one of the Secret Service men woke me up the next morning around four thirty, and I was elected. So I got up and got dressed, and we drove over to the Muehlebach Hotel to celebrate."

---

* Truman carried Ohio by 7,107 votes, California by 17,-865, and Illinois by 33,612.

23

The Korean Decision

Dean Acheson was understandably proud of a hand-written note from Mr. Truman. It was, in Mr. Acheson's words, "written on scratch-pad, with *The White House* at the top of it . . . dated the 19th of July 1950, when the first phase of the Korean operation was over. . . . I think it throws some light on the type of man that I worked for and the kind of relationship we had:

"Memorandum to Dean Acheson. Regarding June 24 and June 25. Your initiative in immediately calling the Security Council of the United Nations on Saturday night and notifying me was the key to what developed afterward. Had you not acted promptly in that direction we would have had to go into Korea alone. The meeting, Sunday night, at the Blair House, was a result of your action Saturday night. The results thereafter attained show that you are a great Secretary of State, and a diplomat. Your handling of the situation, since, has been superb. I am sending you this for your records. Harry S. Truman."

Bob Aurthur and I tried to persuade Mr. Truman to read that note on camera, but he refused. It was the old business of trying to make a playactor out of him. "I'm not putting on a show. I'll tell you the facts *as they occurred*. I'm not gonna try to put on any show. If I have to put on a show . . . it'll be a failure."

The President asked Mr. Acheson to read the note, which he did. He added, "I should have preferred to have President Truman read this note rather than to have to read it myself. The problem, of course, is who is more embarrassed by it. Is it more embarrassing for me to read a note praising me, or is it more embarrassing for him to read a note that shows what a great man he is? He chose that I should be embarrassed—and I am happy to abide by his orders once again."

That note sums up how the United Nations and not just the United States got into the Korean War or "police action," they are hard to tell apart, about as well as is possible. Largely but not wholly because of Dean Acheson's quick thinking and action, we did not have to go it alone in Korea. That happened in Vietnam. We went it alone, and it was perhaps the costliest disaster in our history.

But in Korea, in Mr. Truman's words, "For the first time in history, an aggressor was opposed by an international police force, and it worked. It saved the free world."

I guess all but a handful of revisionist historians would agree that it worked, but as you will see in following the way it all began, it wasn't just what Mr. Acheson and the President did. A lot of it was pure luck. *If* Jacob Malik, the Soviet delegate, had come to the meeting of the United Nations Security Council and exercised his veto power. . . . And *if* Dean Acheson hadn't been at his farmhouse in Maryland that Saturday night. And *if* Harry Truman out in Independence hadn't said, "Dean, we've got to stop the sons of bitches no matter what. . . ."

But all that is hypothesis, idle speculation, and as I believe I've explained Harry Truman thought all such exercises were "a damn waste of time."

He was probably right, too. Besides, what did occur that June weekend and on the Monday and Tuesday that followed reads like an exercise in high adventure. A cliffhanger. An eerie whodunit involving the fate of the world. All you have to keep in mind is that it all really happened and no so long ago either.

What's more, the story has a happy ending, and that all by itself is rare enough these days to make it worth telling.

As Mr. Acheson told Bob Aurthur and me in the winter of 1962, "Fate never selected a more unlikely place to plant the seeds of great events than in Korea as it appeared in the late 1940's and the beginning of the 1950's."

Korea, which in English means "the land of the morning calm," has had a tempestuous history, and Harry Truman knew it as well as he knew the history of the Dardanelles. One afternoon at the Carlyle Hotel in New York Mr. Truman spent more than an hour tracing the history of that never-calm peninsula from about 57 B.C. when it was known as the kingdom of Silla until the present day. It was depressing but fascinating, and for our purposes I think we can safely begin with the end of the Second World War. Later that month, January, 1962, in Washington Dean Acheson said, "When the Japanese indicated that they were ready to surrender, the question arose as to whom they should surrender.

"On about the twelfth of August, 1945, the Pentagon sent over to us in the State Department—I was then an Assistant Secretary of State—a memorandum dealing with many affairs, but among them it said that the Japanese troops north of the thirty-eighth parallel in Korea should surrender to the Russians and those south should surrender to a representative of General MacArthur.

"This was exactly what it purported to be. It did not intend to be a boundary. It did not intend to be zones of occupation. It was merely that for convenience troops north of this dividing line should surrender to one commander, those south of it to another. And this was done.

"Immediately afterward we discovered in Korea, as we discovered in Germany, that when one dealt with the Russians any sort of dividing line meant much more than one had supposed it was going to mean. It meant that an Iron Curtain descended at that point and that everything north of the thirty-eighth parallel became completely Russian and everything south under Allied or American control."

And that is the way things nervously remained until the weekend we're coming to. True, in 1947 Mr. Truman ordered General Eisenhower, Admiral Leahy, Admiral Nimitz, and General Spaatz to study the military value of Korea, and their report, issued in September of that year, said, "The Joint Chiefs of Staff consider that, from the standpoint of military security, the United States has little strategic interest in maintaining the present troops and bases in Korea."

General MacArthur agreed. Moreover, he said that anyone who advocated a land war on the Asian continent had clearly gone bonkers.

For the way the general changed his mind, changed it several times and in several different ways, read on.

In January, 1950, Dean Acheson, then Secretary of State, made a speech at the National Press Club in which, as he put it almost exactly twelve years later, "I pointed out that we had established our own troops in what I called a defense perimeter and that this perimeter, beginning in Alaska, running along the Aleutian Islands, then touched Japan, where we had a garrison, went from there to the Ryukyu Islands, where we had both a military garrison and an Air Force base—from there to the Philippines. And I said that in this way we had established ourselves in the Western Pacific rather than in the Central and Eastern Pacific as we had before the war.

"I said, 'So far as the military security in the other areas of the Pacific is concerned, it must be clear that no person can guarantee those areas against military attack. . . . But should such an attack occur, the initial reliance must be on the people attacked to resist it and then upon the commitments of the entire civilized world under the Charter of the United Nations.' "

It all *seems* clear enough, and indeed it all was clear enough until the Presidential campaign of 1952, when the Republican right, the China Lobby idolators, and the superhawks who are always among us dug up that speech to *prove* that Mr. Acheson by its words had *invited* the North Koreans to invade South Korea.

At one point a bill was introduced in Congress to cut off his salary.

Mr. Acheson, like General Marshall, never answered his attackers. He maintained throughout his remarkable calm. I once asked him how he managed, and he said,

"I am something of a stoic both by nature and by inheritance. And I learned from the example of my father that the manner in which one endures what must be endured is more important than the thing that must be endured. I am inclined to agree with Sir Francis Bacon that: 'The good things which belong to prosperity are to be wished, but the good things that belong to adversity are to be admired.' "

We come now to Saturday, June 25, 1950.

Dean Acheson: ". . . I had gone from the State Department around noontime, expecting to have a relaxed and quiet weekend at my farm, in a quiet old Maryland farm house about twenty miles north of the capital. The house was built in the nineteenth century and is very simple, very small, very quiet, and very secluded.

"I was sitting there reading with my wife when about ten o'clock I received a telephone call on what we called the white telephone. I had in my office and also in my house a white telephone which was connected directly with the switchboard of the White House. If one lifted the receiver, one got the switchboard in the White House and could be directly connected with the President or through that switchboard with any other department or Cabinet officer in Washington.

"The telephone rang, as I say, about ten o'clock, and I answered it to find on the wire Assistant Secretary of State Jack Hickerson, who had charge of international organization affairs, including the United Nations. He said he was in the State Department with Assistant Secretary Dean Rusk, who is now Secretary of State, and that they had just received an alarming message from Ambassador [John Joseph] Muccio in Seoul. This message was to the effect that there was a serious attack along the whole northern border of South Korea. They were not sure whether this was a determined effort of the North Koreans to penetrate South Korea or whether it was a larger than usual border incident.

"But the military mission was alarmed. The Korean

forces were alarmed, and the ambassador was standing by to confer with the head of our military mission and let us know more details during the course of the night.

"I asked him what recommendations they had, and he said that it was their view that we should call for a meeting of the Security Council of the United Nations for the following afternoon, Sunday, and obtain a resolution requesting or ordering all parties to return within their borders, to cease any aggression, and calling upon all members of the UN to assist in this endeavor.

"I said that they were to get in touch with our representatives to the United Nations, have them available in New York the next day, and that in the meantime I would call the President, who was then at his home in Independence. And if the President approved this action, they would already have started on it. If he disapproved it, they could stop it at once. But I thought that time was so pressing that we should not even delay while I spoke to the President.

"I told them that I would call them back, but immediately to get in touch with people in the Pentagon to set up a working force which would be there all night . . . so that we could find out more about this situation and be prepared to take further action in the morning.

"I then called the President. I gave him this message and told him what I had done, saying that I had done it entirely subject to his approval and that I wished further orders or instructions from him. The President said he approved this action entirely and that I was to proceed with it with the utmost vigor."

Mr. Truman: "It was about ten thirty on Saturday night, and I was sitting in the living room reading. The phone rang, and it was Dean Acheson calling from his home in Maryland. He said, 'Mr. President, I have serious news. The North Koreans are attacking across the thirty-eighth parallel.'

"I wanted to get on the plane and fly to Washington right that night, but he said that I shouldn't, that a night flight wasn't necessary. He said that I should stand by for another call from him when he'd have more details. And I agreed.

"I also gave my approval to his suggestion to call an emergency session of the United Nations Security Council to consider a declaration that active aggression had been committed against the Republic of Korea.

"I went to bed, and that was one night I didn't get much sleep."

John Hickerson, Assistant Secretary of State for United Nations Affairs: "I knew that Ambassador Warren Austin, our permanent representative to the United Nations, was in Rutland, Vermont, for the weekend. So . . . after talking to Secretary Acheson, I called Ambassador Ernest Gross, who was our deputy representative to the United Nations. I called him at his house and was told that he was out to dinner somewhere on Long Island and they did not have the telephone number. I asked that he call me urgently at the State Department as soon as he came in. . . .

"At twelve o'clock, not having heard from Ambassador Gross, it seemed to me it would be a good idea to call the Secretary-General of the United Nations, Trygve Lie, and alert him. . . . I got him on the phone at five minutes past twelve. He had been listening to the midnight news, and there was something I had not heard about disturbances on the Korean border. He had some inkling of it but no idea of whether it was simply a minor clash or what. I told him that it was an all-out massive attack from the North Koreans against South Korea.

"I shall never forget his words. He listened. And then— Trygve Lie speaks perfect English but with a Norwegian accent—and he said, 'My God, Jack, that's war against the United Nations!'

"I regret to say that I couldn't think of anything more original to reply than, 'Trygve, you're telling me!'

"We ended the conversation. He said he would alert his boys—find out where every member of the Security Council was—and would wait further word from Ambassador Gross."

Ernest A. Gross, who was acting chief of the U.S. delegation to the United Nations: "Jack Hickerson called me at a friend's house where a dinner party was just breaking up. He told me that it seemed quite certain that the forces of North Korea had suddenly mounted an offense across the thirty-eighth parallel, and he instructed me to return immediately to my home on Long Island to wait further word.

"He also said that because of some slight difficulty in tracing me, he had called Trygve Lie and told him what had happened.

"He said that I would be expected to take it from there and would be in communication with Trygve Lie during the night.

"I went back to my home, and my teen-age daughter was having what was then called in the adolescent vocabulary a slumber party. A dozen or so of her teen-aged friends were sprawled all over the living room, and I had to stagger over the recumbent bodies to get to the telephone.

"And they clustered around the phone and began to get very excited. I imagine for them it was a memorable night, but they didn't get any more sleep than I did.

"I talked with Trygve Lie I think four times between midnight and five A.M. And in the meantime I telephoned virtually all the members, at least seven or eight of the members of the Security Council at their homes.

"I called them all in the middle of the night and got them out of bed, and I can say . . . that they were all profoundly shocked by what had happened. They felt that the United Nations had to do something about it, that this was an attack on the UN itself. There was no question about that.

"And they were ready to act even though many of them would not . . . there would not be time to get instructions from their governments.

"We did not know whether the Soviet Union would show up for the emergency meeting on Sunday. It may be recalled that the Soviet delegation had walked out of the Security Council in early January on the ground that the Council was illegally composed because the Chinese Communist regime did not occupy the seat of the Republic of China. The Soviet delegate had not attended any Security Council sessions between that time and the moments of our impending meeting on Sunday, June 25. It was obvious that if the Soviet delegate were to attend the meeting, any resolution would be vetoed, and the Security Council would be precluded from action, as had happened so many other times by the abuse of the Soviet veto.

"But we went ahead and did what we had to do, and I was instructed by Mr. Hickerson to notify the other members of the Security Council . . . to communicate a formal request to Secretary General Trygve Lie to convene a meeting on that day . . . an emergency meeting for two o'clock that Sunday afternoon."

Dean Acheson: "On Sunday morning I drove immediately to the State Department and found that my colleagues there had been working throughout the night with representatives in the Department of Defense. And they had brought together all the information available and necessary for decisions as to what should be done.

"In the first place, it was clear that this was not an isolated border incident. This was a general attack which extended all across the border and therefore was a matter of the utmost seriousness. And in the second place, it was established that it was an attack in very considerable force. The South Korean forces were falling back. They had not yet lost contact with one another. The retreat was orderly, but it was precipitant, and it seemed fairly clear that before long the capital of South Korea would be overrun. Therefore, we knew that we had a critical military situation to handle. We then had reports on enemy strength insofar as our intelligence was able to gather them. They indicated that these forces were well trained. Many of them had been within the Soviet Union for some time. They were well equipped, and this was a dangerous attack.

"We then had an up-to-date report on our own forces. The nearest available, of course, were in Japan. These, for the most part, were untried divisions. The veterans had all been mustered out. A few of the soldiers had had battle experience but not many. The Navy was in the Philippines at Cavite. There were Air Force planes available. So we knew that much. We knew what we had available.

"We knew that the United Nations was convening at two o'clock, and that was about all the information that we had. We then began to get to work on recommendations to the President, and I called him on the telephone in Independence."

Mr. Truman: "I'd been out to my brother Vivian's farm, and when I got back, a little while after I got back, the telephone rang, and Margaret went to answer it. She came back and said, 'Daddy, it's Dean Acheson, and he says it's important.'

"I went to the phone and said, 'What is it, Dean?' And he said, 'Mr. President, the news is bad. The attack is in force all along the parallel.' And I said, 'Dean, we've got to stop the sons of bitches no matter what.'

"He said he agreed with me, and he told me that an emergency meeting of the Security Council was all set for two o'clock that afternoon.

"I said fine, and I said I was returning to Washington immediately, and we were on our way back in less than an hour. In fact we left in such a hurry that two of my aides were left behind.

"The flight took about three hours, and on the way I thought over the fact that what the Communists, the North Koreans, were doing was nothing new at all. I've told you. The only thing new in the world is the history you don't know.

"And it was always the same, always had the same results. Hitler and Mussolini and the Japanese were doing exactly the same thing in the 1930's. And the League of

Nations had let them get away with it. Nobody had stood up to them. And that is what led to the Second World War. The strong got away with attacking the weak, and I wasn't going to let this attack on the Republic of Korea, which had been set up by the United Nations, go forward. Because if it wasn't stopped, it would lead to a third world war, and I wasn't going to let that happen. Not while I was President.

"That's what a lot of people never understood, including the general we had over there at the time. This was a police action, a limited war, whatever you want to call it to stop aggression and to prevent a big war. And that's all it ever was. I don't know why some people could never get that through their heads.

"When my plane, the *Independence,* landed in Washington, the Secretaries of State and Defense were there to meet me, and we rushed to the Blair House for the conference. We had a quick dinner. We were living at Blair House at the time, and this dinner was in the dining room in the Lee House, which joins the Blair House. After it was over and the dishes were cleared away, I asked Dean Acheson to give me the joint recommendations of the State and Defense departments." *

Dean Acheson: "This I did. The recommendations were three. They were, first of all, that Americans should be evacuated from the Seoul area. Those Americans consisted of most of the people attached to the political mission there, the military mission—that is, the wives and children, all the people who were not required to be there.

* According to Dean Acheson those present at the meeting, "Aside from the President and myself . . . were the Undersecretary of State James Webb, Assistant Secretary Dean Rusk . . . , Ambassador Philip Jessup, Assistant Secretary of State John Hickerson, Secretary of Defense Louis Johnson, Secretary of the Army Frank Pace, Secretary of the Air Force Thomas K. Finletter, Secretary of the Navy Matthews, General Vandenberg, Chief of Staff of the Air Force, General Collins, Chief of Staff of the Army, Admiral Sherman, Chief of Naval Operations, and General Bradley, who was Chairman of the Joint Chiefs of Staff."

"And in order to do this and to allow any other people who wished to leave to go, General MacArthur was asked to give air protection to the airport to prevent any North Korean troops or soldiers or air forces from interfering with it.

"The second recommendation was that General Mac-Arthur should be instructed to air-drop supplies—food, ammunition, weapons, whatever he could to the Korean forces to strengthen them.

"The third recommendation was that the fleet should be ordered to move north from Cavite at once and to take up a position between Formosa and the mainland. And we added along with that the recommendation that the President should announce that we would not permit any attack, either upon Formosa or from Formosa upon the mainland. The idea being that we wanted strictly to limit the sphere of military operations and did not want to have several wars on our hands at the same time.

"The President, when I had finished making these recommendations, asked each person in the room to make his own statement of how the situation appeared to him and his own view as to these recommendations. Each person did so. They all agreed with the recommendations made and the President, therefore, who had been considering all of this while the discussion was going on, said that he would adopt the three recommendations which I made and the orders should be prepared immediately for his signature with the proviso that he would not that night make any statement as to what the fleet would do until the fleet was in a position to do it.

"This was rather typical of President Truman. It is extremely unwise to say what is going to happen when one is not in a precise position to do it. I realized at once that he was right and that our recommendation was wrong.

"The fleet did a remarkable job. It was a time of peace. Men were ashore in Cavite Harbor. They had no expectation of leaving on any kind of a mission at all. But steam was gotten up, or whatever is the equivalent of steam today in the Navy, and by the time the orders to sail came every man was aboard. Battle stations were maintained, and the fleet was moving northward. This was an extremely praiseworthy operation.

"That concluded our operations for Sunday night. The President told us to stand ready to meet again on Monday night, when the situation became clearer. I told all my people to go home and get some sleep, which they needed very badly, having missed one night entirely."

That afternoon, as the President was flying to Washington, the Security Council, as planned, held an emergency meeting. Calling the session to order, Trygve Lie said, "The present situation is a serious one and is a threat to international peace. . . . I consider it the clear duty of the Security Council to take the steps necessary to reestablish peace. . . ."

Mr. Gross then spoke, saying that the attack on South Korea was "of grave concern to the governments of all peace-loving and freedom-loving nations" and that it "openly defies the interest and authority of the United Nations." The hastily written resolution he introduced asked the Security Council to accuse North Korea of the "armed invasion" of South Korea, asked that it order an immediate cease-fire and withdraw all its troops south of the thirty-eighth parallel. Finally, it asked every member of the UN "to render every possible assistance to the United Nations in the execution of this resolution."

The resolution that was passed at the end of the afternoon, by a vote of 9 to 0, with Yugoslavia abstaining, was somewhat weaker. The words "armed invasion" were changed to "armed attack," and both North and South Korea were called on to order a cease-fire.

Jacob Malik had not been at the meeting, but how long could his absence be counted on? Already in Washington a much-stronger resolution was being drawn up, to be presented at another meeting of the Security Council, it was hoped, on Tuesday, June 27. Suppose Malik showed up for that and exercised the Soviet veto? The United States would then face two extraordinarily difficult decisions. It could take the matter to the General Assembly and ask that the veto be overridden, but that could only be done by a two-thirds majority, a most unlikely prospect at that moment, not to mention the considerable time such an action might take.

Or the United States could unilaterally enter the Korean conflict. But that might easily deal a death blow to the UN. Would Harry Truman risk that? * After all, minutes after he took the oath of office as President back in 1945 his first order of business was to announce that the United Nations Charter Conference would go forward in San Francisco just thirteen days later. And on Monday, June 26, the fifth anniversary of the signing of the Charter would be observed.

Was the possibility of unilateral action discussed by the men in Washington making those monumental decisions that weekend?

Dean Acheson: "I've been asked several times whether in these critical meetings we considered what would be done in the event that the United Nations refused to take any action. . . . I think in asking these questions, those who do so have not participated in decisions of this sort. This business of making decisions is a continuous process. One does not say, 'We will do this,' then someone else says, 'Suppose this doesn't work, what do you do?'

"This is not the way it is done if the action is as vague and general as proceeding through the United Nations as against proceeding unilaterally.

"For instance, it was perfectly clear that the United Nations would and must denounce an aggression. It could not do otherwise. The Charter prohibited an aggression, and this was clearly one. Moreover, there was a report from the United Nations Commission itself in Korea branding this as an aggression from the north.

* Mr. Acheson's answer to that question is coming up. I once asked Mr. Truman if the United States was prepared to go it alone, and his answer, as usual, was short and to the point. He said, "No question about it."

"Therefore, it was certain that the United Nations, in some form or other, would denounce this action, would state that opposing it was a good thing and that continuing it was bad. This we knew would occur.

"It was doubtful that it would go further, that it would call on its members to fight. However, it would have gone far enough so that those who wanted to fight would be fighting with its blessing and not against it.

"But one says, suppose Mr. Malik appeared and interposed a veto? He might have appeared. It was extremely unlikely. The very fact that it was unlikely underlined the importance of immediate action. One thing that one can be fairly sure about in the Soviet system is that they are not capable of making instantaneous decisions. There has to be even more palaver in the Soviet system than there does in the democratic system. They can make decisions over a long period of time, so that action appears to be peremptory—but it really isn't. . . . And here was something that they had undoubtedly inspired. And undoubtedly they had not expected us to take the action that we did.

". . . To have reversed their boycott of the UN would have taken a major decision of the Politburo. So the betting was all in favor of Malik's not returning, *if* we acted fast. If we didn't act fast, why, anything could have happened.

"Therefore, I think to all of us it would have been a waste of time to spend the precious minutes that we have saying what we'll do if Malik appears.

"The answer is, 'Let's wait and see. Chances are seventy-five out of a hundred that he won't. We haven't got time to fool with the twenty-five percent chance. Let's get forward with the job.'

"If he had appeared, we would immediately have adjusted ourselves to that and taken some other action, either through the General Assembly or unilaterally. I think Mr. Truman was quite right that the interest of the United States and its allies and of the free world was so great in defeating this aggression . . . that it had to be done. And if through some sort of legal mechanism one operation was blocked, then another operation would have to be found to do it.

"My own view was not to worry about things that were *not* likely to happen. And therefore, I was in favor of Admiral Farragut's advice, 'Full steam ahead and damn the torpedoes.' "

Do you wonder that I never felt more inarticulate than in the days I spent with Mr. Acheson?

To continue. Monday, June 26:

Dean Acheson: ". . . We prepared a new resolution to lay before the Security Council, feeling that the earlier one did not go far enough in branding the North Korean invasion as an aggression and declaring that it was a violation of the Charter and calling upon its members to stop it."

On Monday, June 26, the news from Korea was very bad indeed. The South Korean forces were in headlong retreat. North Korean tanks were near Seoul, and the government had retreated to Taegu, 150 miles to the south.

John Hickerson: "By Monday it was apparent that massive United States assistance would be necessary if Korea was to be saved. And on Monday night we had another meeting at Blair House, at about nine o'clock. Again the President heard reports from Secretary Acheson, from the diplomatic front, and from the military representatives on the military situation.

"It was at this meeting that a decision was reached for us to give all-out air and naval support, under the United Nations, to Korea. The necessary directions were given by the President.

"Again let me emphasize the fact that he went around the table and asked everybody present to state his views. There was unanimity of opinion, but the President took the action. He was the only one who could do it, and he unhesitatingly did it.

"I never shall forget at the end of the meeting Secretary

Acheson and I left together to go back to the State Department, and I had to check with the President and Secretary on one or two points of phraseology on the draft resolution which we had prepared to be introduced to the Security Council on Tuesday.

"We very quickly disposed of those minor things, and the President said to Secretary Acheson and me, with great earnestness, in effect, these words, 'I've been President a little over five years, and I've spent five years trying to avoid making a decision like the one I've had to make tonight. What I want you to know is that this is not a decision just for Korea. It's a decision for the United Nations itself.'

"I went back to the State Department and put the necessary steps in motion to get ready for the Security Council meeting the following afternoon."

Ernest A. Gross: "Prior to the session of June 27 when the American resolution was passed, it happened that a luncheon had been arranged by the Soviet delegation, arranged about a month before Korea, to say good-bye to Malik, who was going back to the Soviet Union, either permanently or for a rest cure. You never knew.

"This was to be a farewell luncheon at the Stockholm Restaurant in Syosset, Long Island. Trygve Lie had been invited, and a number of other delegates were there.

"I was seated between Trygve Lie and Jacob Malik, and, naturally, I tried to discuss with Malik what was happening, what was behind this whole business in Korea. He, of course, as was to be expected, was noncommittal. He said nothing.

"But Trygve Lie felt it expedient to urge Malik to drive back to Lake Success with us and take his seat in the Security Council. I think that Trygve felt this would be a great thing for the organization and might be a step toward a resumption of peace. I don't know what was in his mind, but it made me very unhappy, and I kept glaring at Trygve and urging him to stop inviting Malik back.

"Fortunately, of course, Malik didn't come back, and

Trygve Lie and I got into his car and drove back to Lake Success. I rather sternly reprimanded him, as an old friend, for what he had done. And I expressed my relief that he'd been such a poor advocate that he hadn't persuaded Malik to return. I said, 'Trygve, can you imagine what would have happened if he *had* accepted your invitation?' "

As a result, I told you luck was with us that week, at ten forty-five that night the Security Council passed a resolution recommending that "members of the United Nations furnish such assistance to the Republic of Korea as may be necessary to repel the armed attack and to restore international peace and security in the area."

For the first time in recorded history a world organization had voted to use armed force to stop armed force. Lucky or not, it was a considerable victory for Harry Truman.

Dean Acheson: "On Tuesday morning, before the Security Council meeting, the President called in the Congressional leaders and informed them of the decisions we had made the night before.

"We had supposed the resolution we had drawn up was to be laid before the Security Council in the morning. But the Indians had asked for a postponement until the afternoon.

"We were unaware of this when we were meeting with the Congressional leaders. But we had no doubt that in the absence of the Russian delegate, it would pass.

"Therefore, as the Congressional leaders were leaving, knowing that there would soon be in the press as many different views of what was said as there were Congressional leaders, it seemed to us desirable that an exact statement be made as to what the President had decided the previous night and what he had said to the Congressional leaders.

"Such a statement was made public. However, the United Nations had not passed the resolution, and the Russians had a good deal of fun with this, saying that we had decided to use military force before the United Nations had called on us to do it. This was a debating point to which they were entitled but no more than that because the previous resolution had done practically the same thing, and, as I say, there was no doubt that the stiffer resolution would also pass.

"Also on Tuesday we sent a note . . . to the Soviet government asking them to use their good offices with the North Korean government to bring this aggression to an end. It seemed to us that it might be possible that they would do it, but in any event they should be asked to do it. The Russians replied on Thursday. This reply said that the real aggressor was South Korea; therefore, there were no good offices for them to use, but we must use *our* good offices to prevent the South Koreans from continuing their aggression.

"Since the South Koreans had already lost their capital, this seemed to be slightly an ironic thing to do. We noted, however, that the Russian note was not vitriolic, and it seemed to us a good sign that they intended to disengage from this operation and at least not be caught publicly having anything to do with it.

"Meantime, the situation in Korea was deteriorating very rapidly. It was clear that the retreat had become a rout. The Korean Army was throwing away its weapons and was moving fast . . . as fast as it could go.

"On Wednesday Washington time General MacArthur flew over the battlefields, saw what was going on, talked to President Syngman Rhee, talked to the American military mission, and on the night of the twenty-ninth and thirtieth, between Thursday and Friday, General MacArthur put in what is known as a telecon. This is a form of communication which is highly secure and consists of two typewriters and two screens. In one place a message is typed out which appears immediately thousands of miles away in typewritten form on the screen before the audience receiving it. They consider this message; then they type out and send back the reply. This appears on your own screen and on the recipient's screen. So the whole conversation remains constantly before you and is not subject to any of the difficulties which come from oral talk and can so easily be misunderstood.

"General MacArthur got General Collins on the telecon and told him that it was a disaster in Korea, a complete rout. The Korean Army had ceased to exist. That if there was to be any resistance on the ground, it had to be by American troops. And he requested permission to bring over from Japan a regimental combat team as the initial point of a twelve-division buildup to try and hold the area around Pusan, until stronger measures could be taken to defend South Korea.

"General Collins suggested that this would be put up to the President when he was awakened a little bit later. But General MacArthur said there was not time to do that. And therefore, General Collins called General Bradley [Chairman of the Joint Chiefs of Staff] and the President at five o'clock in the morning to discover that Mr. Truman was already up, dressed, and at work. They put this to him, and the President gave his approval at once. Therefore, before the rest of us were awake, the regimental combat team was on its way to Korea.

"Friday morning . . . at the Friday morning Cabinet meeting the President reported to us what had occurred. He had thought what he did was the right thing to do. But he asked us if we had any comments to make about it. There was no doubt in any of our minds that this was the correct step.

"We all voiced our strong endorsement and approval of it, and I haven't the slightest doubt that every member of the Cabinet would have done that if he had been asked in advance. This is one of the situations in which the course of events really determines action. And having decided that we were going to meet this aggression, we could not flinch even though the course of the aggression turned out to be much more serious than it had first appeared to be.

"About this same time we were offered by Generalissimo Chiang Kai-shek thirty thousand Chinese troops for use in Korea. The President asked for a recommendation in regard to this from the Defense and State departments. And after conferring about it, we agreed that the offer should not be accepted. It seemed to us that these troops were not reliable, were not very good troops, were not well armed, and would perhaps cause more trouble than they would be helpful. They were not too sure of their loyalty, and we did not want to get into that difficulty."

Mr. President, Dean Acheson has said that there was some consideration of using Chiang Kai-shek's troops in Korea. How serious was that consideration, on your part, I mean?

"Not very damn serious. What would have been the use of it? They weren't any damn good, never had been. We sent them about three billion five hundred million dollars' worth of matériel, sent that to the so-called free Chinese, and then about five million of Chiang's men between Peking and Nanking surrendered to three hundred thousand Communists, and the Communists used that matériel to run Chiang and his men out of China. I told you. He never was any damn good.

"They wanted me to send in about five million Americans to rescue him, but I wouldn't do it. There wasn't *anything* that could be done to save him, and he was as corrupt as they come. I wasn't going to waste one single American life to save him, and I didn't care what they said. They hooted and hollered and carried on and said I was soft on Communism and I don't know what all. But I never gave in on that, and I never changed my mind about Chiang and his gang. Every damn one of them ought to be in jail, and I'd like to live to see the day they are." *

Dean Acheson: "Another reason for not using Chiang's troops. . . . If one had to use other than European and American troops, the troops required were Koreans. This was their country. They had been defending it. And it seemed to us that we could far better get the equivalent of

---

* For more of Mr. Truman's observations on Chiang and his Madame and others in their crew, see the next chapter.

thirty thousand troops from reorganizing the Korean Army and using them.

"And finally, we did not wish to raise the political complications which would have been raised, if we had introduced the Nationalist–Red Chinese controversy into the battle in Korea. We were going to ask many of our European allies to take part in this battle. Some recognized Chiang Kai-shek; some recognized the Red Chinese. And it would have been a divisive and not a unifying action, if we took it.

"Therefore, we thought it wise to decline, and the President did decline."

Sir, the other day you mentioned, when you were discussing the Tuesday meeting between Mr. Truman and the Congressional leaders you mentioned that there was some talk about asking for a Congressional resolution.

"Toward the end of our meeting on Tuesday with the Congressional leaders, Senator Alexander Smith of New Jersey, who was a member of the Senate Committee on Foreign Relations, asked the President whether or not he thought it would be a good idea if the Congress would pass a resolution approving what the President was doing in Korea or what the United States was doing in Korea. The President said he would take that under advisement.

"After the meeting broke up, he asked me to consider it and meet with him later and discuss it. I gave it a good deal of thought and then gave the President this advice, which he followed. It seemed to me that this should not be done. At the moment the troops of the United States were engaged in a desperate struggle in and around Pusan. Hundreds, thousands of them were being killed. The outcome of the battle was not at all clear. It seemed to me if, at this time, action was pending before the Congress, by which hearings might be held, and long inquiries were being entered into as to whether or not this was the right thing to do, or whether the President had the authority to do it, or whether he needed Congressional authority for matters of that sort—we would be doing about the worst thing we could possibly do for the support of our troops and for their morale.

"I felt that we were in this fight—and it was a desperate fight—and we had better concentrate all our energies in fighting it and not in trying to get people to formally approve what was going on.

"The President accepted this advice. This is what was done. In other words we did not follow up Senator Smith's suggestion. This may well, in the light of events, have been a wrong decision. I don't think so myself. But it can be argued that it was wrong. If the Congress had promptly and without debate passed a resolution endorsing vigorously what had happened, this, of course, would have been fine, and it would have nipped in the bud all the statements about the Korean War being Mr. Truman's war and so on.

"But that is hindsight, and I have said that I think hindsight is nonsense. It proves nothing."

Mr. Secretary, as you know, Mr. Truman has said that the Korean decision was his most important decision. Do you agree with that?

"Yes. In this I think he is wholly right. It was a critically important decision, and I think it was important for this reason. This was an occasion upon which a perfectly clear alternative was presented to the United States, an alternative between withdrawing, retreating in front of Russian pressure brought through a satellite, or standing up and fighting and taking the consequences, and Mr. Truman did not shrink from that decision. The United States, under his leadership, decided to fight and did fight. And I think that this has changed the whole history of events since then.

"I think that if we had continued to negotiate, discuss, to take measures which were not the ultimate measures of physical resistance, if we had gone before the United Nations, gotten resolutions condemning the North Koreans . . . if, after the event was over, we'd had all kinds of commissions appointed for the relief of Korea, this would have been a disaster. But when the Russians, to their great surprise, found that they had started something which the

United States met absolutely squarely and hit with the ut-most vigor, I think they stopped, looked, and listened. And the whole history of the world has since changed. . . . We have not had to fight a third world war, which, as Mr. Truman has often said, would destroy us all. What we did in Korea, fighting a limited war for limited objectives, was not an easy thing for many people to understand. Never-theless, it was what had to be done and what was done."

That is the way it began in Korea, or the way in 1961 and 1962 the men responsible for that beginning remem-bered it. Now, the revisionist historians are saying we should never have gone into Korea. Myself, I go along with Mr. Acheson. Hindsight is nonsensical, and as nearly as I can make out revisionist history is all hindsight.

Mr. Truman was fond of the work of Horace, that most civilized of Romans, who wrote "The man who is just and firm of purpose can be shaken from his stern resolve neither by the rage of the people who urge him to crime nor by the countenance of the threatening tyrant."

Both Mr. Truman and Mr. Acheson had to endure the rage of those who urged them to crime as well as the countenances of an extraordinary number of threatening tyrants, at home and abroad, and they were never shaken from their stern resolve.

24

Firing the General

What happened in 1948 was wonderful to behold, but in this summer of Watergate with its reports of secret bombings and the generals' falsified communiqués, something else old Harry did seems even more miraculous—when he gave the biggest general of all, Douglas MacArthur—his comeuppance.

Mr. President, I know why you fired General MacArthur, but if you don't mind, I'd like to hear it in your own words.

"I fired him because he wouldn't respect the authority of the President. That's the answer to that. I didn't fire him because he was a dumb son of a bitch, although he was, but that's not against the law for generals. If it was, half to three-quarters of them would be in jail. That's why when a good one comes along like General Marshall . . . why, you've got to hang onto them, and I did.

"But MacArthur . . . well, to understand what happened and what I think most people don't understand is that the so-called China Lobby was very strong in this country when I was in the White House. They had a great many Congressmen and Senators lined up to do pretty much what they were told, and they had billions of dollars to spend, and they spent it. They even had some newspapers lined up, some big ones at that.* I'm not saying that they bought anybody out, but there was a lot of money floating around, and a lot of people in Washington were following what I call the China Lobby Line.

"You used to hear a lot about the Communist Party

---

* Unfortunately, we never did get to the Congressmen, the Senators, and the newspapermen the China Lobby had lined up, but, as Harry would say, if you want to find out, all you have to do is read your history.

Line, but the China Lobby Line was a lot . . . had a lot more people going along, powerful people, too. And what they wanted, they wanted to put old Chiang back in power. And the first step in that direction was getting . . . was trying to get Chiang's army into the war in Korea, which I was not about to let happen in any way.

"It wasn't only that I didn't want . . . had no intention whatsoever of starting a third world war. I knew Chiang's forces wouldn't be any damn good.

"Whatever they did, they'd be more trouble than they were worth, and any money we spent to support them would end up . . . a good deal of it would end up in the pockets of Chiang and the Madame and the Soong and Kung families.

"They're all thieves, every damn one of them."

Mr. President, did you ever meet Chiang Kai-shek?

"No, I never met him. I met the Madame. She came to the United States for some more handouts when I was President [in 1948]. I wouldn't let her stay at the White House like Roosevelt did. I don't think she liked it very much, but I didn't care one way or the other about what she liked and what she didn't like."

I've read in Alonzo Fields' book [a White House butler; his book was called My Twenty-one Years in the White House] *that she brought her own silk sheets and they had to be changed from top to bottom as many as four or five times a day. They had to be changed even if she took a ten-minute nap. And he says she was very mean to the help in the White House. He says, "Any opinion of the Great Lady of China . . . depended on what status of life the observer might happen to belong to."*

"If Fields says it, it's true, because he doesn't lie. I didn't know that . . . what he says, but I knew that the Madame is a very difficult lady. She just didn't make much of an impression on me, but I never met him. He never was in this country, and I was never in China.

"But ole 'Vinegar Joe' Stilwell [General Joseph W. Stilwell, commander of U.S. troops in the China-Burma-India theater during the Second World War; he was recalled

in 1944 because of his inability to get along wtih Chiang],
he came to see me. He was stationed over there, and he
made that famous march down . . . along the Burma
Road. He came to see me, and he said, 'You know, Mr.
President, that Chiang Kai-shek is nothing but a damn
son of a bitch, and he's gonna lose that war just as sure
as you're sitting here. Because his head's made out of
iron, and you can't tell him a goddamn thing.'

"Chiang wouldn't do what ole Joe wanted him to, which
if he had, he'd of been out of trouble."

*In the Army they used to call him, the GI's who were
over in China called Chiang Chancre Jack. And in England
during the war they had a radio program; I believe it
was a radio program with a character named Cash-my-
Check. A Chinese general.*

"That's exactly the way it was, and that kind of put
me off the whole works. I discovered after some time that
Chiang Kai-shek and the Madame and their families, the
Soong family and the Kungs, were all thieves, every last
one of them, the Madame and him included. And they
stole seven hundred and fifty million dollars out of the
thirty-five billion that we sent to Chiang. They stole it,
and it's invested in real estate down in São Paulo and
some right here in New York. [This conversation was
held at the Carlyle Hotel.] And that's the money that was
used and is still being used for the so-called China Lobby.
I don't like that. I don't like that at all. And I don't want
anything to do with people like that."

Because of the way Truman and for that matter all
his advisers, including the Joint Chiefs of Staff, felt about
Chiang and his army, only a little more than a month after
hostilities in Korea began, MacArthur was sent to Formosa to tell Chiang that the use of his troops "would be
inappropriate."

Only God, MacArthur, and Chiang know what happened at that meeting, but it is assumed that MacArthur
delivered the message. Nevertheless, no sooner had he left
the island than Chiang's spokesmen were on the radio
telling the world that he and MacArthur were in total

agreement. Formosa should not be neutralized, as Mr. Truman had insisted. Not only that. MacArthur felt that Chiang's troops should be "unleashed," but they shouldn't bother with Korea at all. They should immediately go to the mainland.

I said, *Mr. President, what did you think when that happened?*

"I didn't know what to think. One of them was lying, but since I wouldn't have trusted either of them as far as I could throw them, I decided to wait and see. Sometimes that's the best policy. I sent Averell Harriman to Tokyo to see MacArthur and get him cleared up on anything he maybe didn't understand."

You called on Mr. Harriman a good many times to undertake delicate missions.

"Yes, I did, because he was completely trustworthy. He'd do what you asked him to do, and you could depend on him to tell you the complete truth about what had happened. As you know I wanted him to be the Democratic nominee for President in 1956 and I still think he'd have done a hell of a lot better than the fella that got it.

"So I sent the right man to see MacArthur, but, Christ, you couldn't depend on a word MacArthur said, and when he got back, Harriman warned me about that."

After a series of conferences with MacArthur Harriman wrote a long memorandum to Truman saying that MacArthur had told him he had no doubts at all about the wisdom of the Korean decision. He quoted MacArthur as saying, ". . . It was an historic decision which would save the world from communist domination and would be so recorded in history."

Moreover, MacArthur said he had no intention of letting Chiang drag the United States into a war with the Chinese Communists. According to Harriman he said that ". . . he would, as soldier, obey any orders that he received from the President. . . .

"I pointed out to him the basic conflict of interest between the U.S. and the Generalissimo's position as to the future of Formosa. . . . Chiang had only the burning ambition to use Formosa as a stepping-stone for his re-entry to the mainland. MacArthur recognized that this ambition could not be fulfilled, and yet thought it might be a good idea to let him land and get rid of him that way."

So much for Douglas MacArthur's devotion to Chiang Kai-shek.

"I thought it was all worked out with him," said Mr. Truman, "but I should have known that he was a man you couldn't depend on. Roosevelt had all kinds of trouble with him in that other war. He was just a man who couldn't sleep easy at night without thinking up ways and means of getting himself and everybody else into trouble."

He certainly seemed to do just that. In late August the general sent a message to the annual encampment of that farsighted patriotic group the Veterans of Foreign Wars outlining his very own foreign policy for the entire Pacific. If his ideas were adhered to, said MacArthur, that small ocean would turn into "a peaceful lake." And just to begin, he proposed a United States defense line that would stretch from Vladivostok to Singapore, all of which would be protected by United States air, naval, and ground forces, presumably with himself in complete charge.

Then, once again swearing eternal fealty to Chiang, he said that Chiang should be encouraged, not discouraged. Anything less was "appeasement . . . a fallacious and threadbare argument."

Mr. Truman was reported at the time as being in "a cold fury."

More than ten years later I asked him, *Mr. President, how can you explain a man like that?*

Mr. Truman, who was then seventy-seven, said of MacArthur, who in 1950 was seventy, "I've given it a lot of thought, and I have finally concluded . . . decided that there were times when he . . . well, I'm afraid when he wasn't right in his head.

"And there was never anybody around him to keep him in line. He didn't have anybody on his staff that wasn't an ass kisser. He just wouldn't let anybody near him who wouldn't kiss his ass. So . . . there were times when he was . . . I think out of his head and didn't know what he was doing, and I'm sorry as I can be about a thing like that.

"That's the day I should have fired him, though. And I'll tell you this. After that day, I knew it was only a matter of time before there'd be a showdown."

The next morning there was an emergency conference at the White House with the Secretaries of State and Defense and the Joint Chiefs of Staff.

"I told them I wanted to fire him, and I wanted to send over General Bradley to take his place. But they talked me out of it. They said it would cause too much of an uproar, and so I didn't do it, and I was wrong."

Mr. President, suppose you had done it that morning in August instead of the following April?

"I don't know. I do not know. We might have got out of Korea six months earlier and not been at one time on the brink of a third world war. But I don't know for sure.

"The only thing I learned out of the whole MacArthur deal is that when you feel there's something you have to do and you know in your gut you have to do it, the sooner you get it over with, the better off everybody is.

"But one thing I did do that morning. I got him [MacArthur] to withdraw that statement. I said to Lou Johnson [Louis Johnson, who was in his last days as Secretary of Defense], 'I want that damn thing withdrawn immediately, and you tell MacArthur that's a direct order from me and make sure he understands it.' "

MacArthur did "recall" the statement, but since it was already in print in newspapers all over the world, that didn't really matter much.

For a time the hostility between the President and the general quieted down. In mid-September MacArthur made a surprise landing on the west coast of Korea at Inchon. His troops made a victorious march toward the thirty-eighth parallel, and within two weeks almost 130,000 North Koreans were taken prisoners. MacArthur's generals were in complete control of the area below the thirty-eighth parallel.

Truman sent the general a telegram:

"Few operations in military history can match either the delaying action where you traded space for time in which to build up your forces, or the brilliant maneuver which has now resulted in the liberation of Seoul. . . . Well and nobly done."

Truman made it clear, at least thought he had made it clear that while ". . . we have to fight a while longer in order to convince the North Koreans that they are vanquished and that further aggression doesn't pay," MacArthur was to go north of the parallel only if he was sure there were no large-scale Red Chinese or Soviet forces there. He was not to cross the Soviet or Manchurian borders by land or by air and he was to rely solely on South Korean troops near those borders.

That was a very complex order, particularly for a general who no matter what the condition of his head at any given moment had never fought less than a total war for anything less than total victory. And almost immediately there were rumors, not yet accredited to MacArthur himself, that his effectiveness was being limited. True, it was supposed to be a limited war for a limited objective, but there is no evidence anywhere that the general ever understood that or that he even tried to understand it.

Up to that time President Truman and General MacArthur had never met.

"I decided it was about time that we do so. The damn fool hadn't been back in the United States for fourteen years or more, and the messages I'd sent him through other people he somehow or other never seemed to understand. And so I decided that he ought to come back to the United States. To Washington. I thought we'd meet in the White House.

"I talked to General Marshall about it. [General Marshall had just returned from his retirement to become Secretary of Defense.] But the general advised me against having him come to Washington. He said, 'That man has become a kind of living legend with certain groups and especially with certain members of Congress, and if you brought him back here, I think it might do more harm than good. He'd stir up the China Lobby and all those people, and I don't know what all might happen.'

"He was right, of course; I told you. He was always right, ninety-nine percent of the time anyway. So we decided . . . I decided to meet him at some halfway point, and that's why we chose Wake Island."

Actually, the President had to fly more than 4,700 miles from San Francisco, while the general flew only 1,900 miles from Tokyo.

Dr. Wallace Graham, Mr. Truman's personal physician when he was President and after his return to Independence until his death: "I was with the President when he was going to meet MacArthur on Wake Island. And MacArthur was always a showman type. He deliberately tried to hold up his landing so that we would go in and land ahead of them.

"Harry caught it right away, and he told MacArthur, 'You go ahead and land first. We've got plenty of gas. We'll wait for you.' And that's what happened. That's what we did."

Mr. Truman: "MacArthur was always playacting, and he wasn't any damn good at it. I knew what he was trying to pull with all that stuff about whose plane was going to land first, and I wasn't going to let him get away with it.

"So I let . . . I made it quite clear that he was to go in first, and he did."

I understand that when you did get on the ground, there was another delay.

"There was. After we landed, there was a welcoming party there on the ground, but I looked out the window, and MacArthur wasn't there.

"Even after we stopped the engines and they opened up the door of the plane, the bastard still didn't show up.

"So I just sat there. I just waited. I'd have waited until hell froze over if I'd of had to. I wasn't going to have one of my generals embarrass the President of the United States.

"Finally, the son of a bitch walked out of one of the buildings near the runway there. He was wearing those damn sunglasses of his and a shirt that was unbuttoned and a cap that had a lot of hardware. I never did understand . . . an old man like that and a five-star general to boot, why he went around dressed up like a nineteen-year-old second lieutenant.

"I'll tell you this. If he'd been a lieutenant in my outfit going around dressed like that, I'd have busted him so fast he wouldn't have known what happened to him.

"But I . . . I decided to overlook his getup, and we shook hands and arranged . . . we had a meeting. I got there on time, but he was forty-five minutes late, and this meeting—it was just between the two of us, you understand, and was the only one like that.

"When he walked in, I took one look at him, and I said, 'Now you look here. I've come halfway across the world to meet you, but don't worry about that. I just want you to know I don't give a good goddamn what you do or think about Harry Truman, but don't you ever again keep your Commander in Chief waiting. Is that clear?'

"His face got as red as a beet, but he said . . . he indicated that he understood what I was talking about, and we went on from there.

"I didn't bring up what he'd written to the Veterans of Foreign Wars; I didn't have to. He did it. He said he didn't know what had got into him, and that it had been a mistake, and nothing like that would ever happen again.

"I didn't mention 1948* either, but he did. He says, 'Mr. President, I was just taken in by the politicians, and I apologize for that, too. It won't happen again. I've learned my lesson.'"

He seems to have been very apologetic and contrite that morning.

"He was. He was. When you were alone with him, he was a very different kind of fella. Butter wouldn't melt in his mouth. But . . . I've known a few other fellas like that, and when they're out in public, it's an entirely different story. They're always playacting out in public.

"I asked MacArthur point blank if the Chinese would come in, and he said under no circumstances would they come in. He says, 'Mr. President, the war will be over by Thanksgiving and I'll have the American troops back in Tokyo by Christmas,' and he went on like that.

"We must've talked for an hour or so, just the two of us, and I believe I made it more than abundantly clear to him that I was his Commander in Chief and that he was to obey orders and keep . . . not issue any public state-

---

* That year nobody knew much about MacArthur's views on anything, but the Chicago *Tribune* and the Hearst press thought they knew enough to be sure he wasn't one of your left-wingers and to start trying to drum up support for him.

In mid-March MacArthur, with his usual flair for understatement, allowed as how, "In this hour of momentous importance . . . I can say, and with due humility, that I would be recreant to all concepts of good citizenship were I to shirk any public duty to which I might be called by the American people."

Since he was on active duty in Japan, he couldn't do any active campaigning. His name, nevertheless, was entered in the Wisconsin Republican primary. He had, after all, once gone to school in Wisconsin and was appointed to West Point by a Congressman from that state, although he hadn't been in Wisconsin or anyplace else in the United States for eleven years. Some people even said he was the state's favorite son.

On primary day, however, the general got only eight of the twenty-seven delegates, and that more or less finished off talk about the duty the general wouldn't be able to shirk.

ments of any kind that hadn't been approved by me personally.

"He was just like a little puppy at that meeting. I don't know which was worse, the way he acted in public or the way he kissed my ass at that meeting." *

Mr. President, at the second meeting with MacArthur, the one with General Bradley, Dean Rusk from the State Department, Philip Jessup, Ambassador Muccio, and all the others, I believe he said that no more than sixty thousand Chinese troops could be got across the Yalu River because the Chinese didn't have any air power to protect them. And he also said that he had had complete cooperation. The official statement of what he said reads, "No commander in the history of war has ever had more complete and adequate support from all agencies in Washington than I have."

"I believe he did say something like that, yes."

The complete account of that meeting came in very handy the next spring after you'd relieved MacArthur and he was denying that he'd said, among other things, that the Chinese wouldn't come into the war with any force. It was very fortunate that a Miss Vernice Anderson was next door to the Quonset hut taking notes, although nobody knew that she was taking notes. Officially, that is.†

---

* In Mr. Truman's *Memoirs* the last of three paragraphs describing that meeting states: "The general seemed genuinely pleased at this opportunity to talk with me, and I found him a most stimulating and interesting person. Our conversation was very friendly—I might say much more so than I had expected."

I wanted to ask Mr. Truman about that discrepancy and many others, but I never did. The reason I never did was that I wanted our conversations to continue.

† Those notes worked out very well for everybody—except, maybe, the general, who claimed in April that he didn't know any such transcript was made, although a staff member had signed a receipt for the transcript at MacArthur's Tokyo headquarters.

The notes did not, however, surface until the general was appearing before a Senate committee that in April was looking

"No, nobody knew that she was taking notes; as you say, nobody *officially* knew it," said the President, and he smiled, and I believe he winked. The President was not

---

into the reasons for MacArthur's recall. Then the top-secret classification on them was somehow lifted, and they turned up in a front-page story in the New York *Times,* written by Anthony Leviero. Leviero received a Pulitzer Prize for his daredevil enterprise in the matter.

After all, he had been at Wake Island himself, and he described the meeting as giving the appearance of one between that of an "insurance salesman who has at last signed up an important prospect . . . while the latter appeared to be dubious over the extent of the coverage." Mr. Truman was the salesman, the general the insured.

In the *Memoirs* Mr. Truman and his ghost, Bill Hillman, say of those notes: "It was not until much later that I learned that Miss Vernice Anderson, the secretary to Ambassador Jessup, was next door and, without instructions from anyone, took down stenographic notes. This fact further became known during the hearings following General MacArthur's recall, and there was a good deal of noise about it. I can say that neither I nor Mr. Jessup nor anyone else had given Miss Anderson instructions to take notes; as a matter of fact, she was not brought along to take notes but merely to have a secretary available for the drafting of the communiqué that would have to be issued at the end of the meeting."

An awful lot of protesting about accidental note taking in those few words, and I yearned to ask Mr. Truman whatever happened to Mrs. Anderson. I hope at the very least she got a raise.

But, for reasons already noted above, I kept my silence on the subject.

As Bob Aurthur has written of the matter, "While the participant nods vigorously at Mr. Truman's injured denial that he had anything to do with stashing the secretary, or even knew she was there, the observer reflects how critical world events are sometimes conducted in Graustarkian, wondrous, and—dare I say?—simple minded ways. And why does Mr. Truman smile a little when he thinks back on how those notes suddenly surfaced when needed most?"

Bob's remarks were written back in those innocent days when Watergate meant nothing more than the name of a swank apartment house in Washington, D.C.

much of a winker, and when he did, the wink was always
so fleeting that you weren't sure you'd seen it.

"You run into good luck like that sometimes," he
added.

*Mr. President, I believe that at the very moment Gen-
eral MacArthur was telling . . . was saying that the Chinese wouldn't come into Korea in any force a hundred
and twenty thousand members of the Chinese Communist
Fourth Field Army had already crossed the Yalu, a lot of
them with Russian artillery and tanks made in Russia.*

"That's right, and of course, that was only the beginning."

*Mr. President, do you think the general was lying when
he made the assurances he made you, or was his intelligence just bad?*

"You'd have to ask him that, but I think . . . my feeling is that he just never learned the difference between the
truth and a lie. That was one of his troubles, and another
was. . . .

"Well, there's a story. On his ninetieth birthday, I think
it was, somebody asked Justice Holmes, Oliver Wendell
Holmes, how he figured he'd done all he'd done, been a
Supreme Court Justice and a soldier in the Civil War and
all of that.

"The fella that asked him, a newspaper fella, says,
'What's the secret of your success, Justice Holmes?'

"And Old Holmes says, 'Young man, the secret of my
success is that at a very early age I discovered that I'm not
God.'

"I told you. MacArthur never did find that out. And
that was his trouble. That was one of his troubles."

*Mr. President, before we're through with this series,
we're going to make you one of the great storytellers of
our time.*

"Now, no. Don't try that. Don't try anything like that
on me. Don't try to make a playactor out of me because
if you do, it'll fail. I'll tell you the facts, and I know what
the facts are because I was there. But that's all I'll do."

Yes, sir.

Only a few days after President Truman's return to Washington from Wake Island and from MacArthur's assurances of everlasting loyalty, the general directly countermanded the President's orders to use only South Korean troops near the northern borders. He personally ordered American forces into the vanguard of the drive north to the Yalu.

And on November 6, the day before the 1950 Congressional elections, which followed one of the bitterest campaigns in recent history, MacArthur sent a message saying that hordes of Chinese troops and matériel were crossing the bridges of the Yalu from Manchuria. He asked for permission to bomb the bridges and with characteristic rhetoric added, "Every hour that this is postponed will be paid for dearly in American and other United Nations blood."

Mr. President, do you think it was a coincidence that that message arrived just the day before an important national election?

"I leave that to you, whether it was a coincidence or not?"

Assuming that it wasn't, that it was deliberately done to affect the outcome of the election, has any other general in American history ever interfered with an American election in that way?

"Not to my knowledge, never. And it was a shocking thing."

In remembering the incident, the President still seemed to be in a state of shock. It was as if he were still feeling some deep personal sorrow over MacArthur's perfidy. Of course, I can't be sure what he was thinking. What is clear is that his resolve to avoid a war with Red China never wavered, election or not. In his answer he authorized attacks on the bridges only on the Korean side as a defensive measure. MacArthur wanted permission to invade China. Said permission was refused. "You are authorized to go ahead with your planned bombing in Korea near the frontier including targets at Sinuiju and Korean end of Yalu bridges. . . . The above does not authorize the bombing of any dams or power plants on the Yalu River. . . . Because it is vital in the national interests of the U.S. to localize the fighting in Korea it is important that extreme care be taken to avoid violation of Manchurian territory and air space."

The not-surprising result of that particular exchange was that the Republicans won sweeping victories at the polls the next day. Not only were the Democrats in general and Harry Truman in particular preventing a heroic general from using his full forces to defeat the Communists abroad, but they were at the same time conniving with and being supported by Communists at home. Joseph R. McCarthy, the United States Senator from Wisconsin, had said so. "The Democratic label is now the property of men and women who have . . . bent to the whispered pleas from the lips of traitors . . . men and women who wear the political label stitched from the idiocy of a Truman, rotted by the deceit of a Dean Acheson, corrupted by the red slime of a White [Harry Dexter White, a Treasury Department official]."

Of course, the voters turned large numbers of the treasonous bastards out. And in California they voted Richard M. Nixon in, electing him to the Senate and defeating Helen Gahagan Douglas, the Democratic "pink lady." Nixon claimed she was sympathetic to Communism, and his campaign manager, Murray Chotiner, issued the famous "pink sheet," which alleged that Mrs. Douglas' voting record very closely paralleled that of "the notorious Communist party-liner Congressman Vito Marcantonio of New York." In that campaign Nixon gave his full support to MacArthur, called for "unleashing" Chiang Kai-shek and his troops, and denounced Truman as being soft on Communism, both the domestic and the international variety. He did not actually get around to calling Mr. Truman a traitor until almost two years later.

In any case, if MacArthur's message was politically motivated, it was successful. But then an odd thing happened, very odd. On the day after the election, November 8, he sent another message. He'd been wrong. Hordes of Chinese troops and Russian matériel were *not* flowing across the Yalu on the still-unbombed bridges. Thus, although the general did not say so, no unnecessary American and other United Nations blood had been needlessly shed, not because of the bridges anyway.

But now the general said that "hostile planes are operating from bases west of the Yalu River against our forces in North Korea." He wanted to engage in "hot pursuit" of those planes and—yet again—to bomb bases in Manchuria.

President Truman, with the full approval of the Joint Chiefs of Staff, yet again denied him such permission.

MacArthur did, however, continue his drive to reach the Yalu, and by November 24 he announced that the final offensive was under way. "If successful," he said, "this should for all practical purposes end the war, restore peace and unity to Korea . . . and enable the prompt withdrawal of United Nations forces."

Not only that, the boys would be home by—well, not Thanksgiving but surely by Christmas.

As we all know, the Chinese do not celebrate Christmas, and they are notoriously unsentimental about American religious holidays. On November 26 more than 200,-000 of them poured across the Yalu, and the United Nations troops, most of them American, retreated in total confusion. Some observers said it was the worst military defeat in American history.

MacArthur said that what had happened was the result of Washington's, meaning Truman's, restrictions on him. He called them "extraordinary inhibitions . . . without precedent in American military history."

By January, 1951, not only had Pyongyang, the capital of North Korea, been captured by the Chinese Communists, but so had Seoul, the capital of the Republic of Korea in the south.

But then MacArthur, still smarting, still issuing complaints about his treatment in Washington, regrouped his forces and started north again. By March they were once more back at the thirty-eighth parallel, and it was here that the final, bitter showdown between the general and the President began.

Truman and the Joint Chiefs wanted MacArthur to stop at the thirty-eighth parallel so that the President, with South Korea now cleared, could, it was hoped, begin to negotiate a cease-fire.

. MacArthur was having none of that. He proposed not to stop the war, but to expand it; only in that way, he said publicly, would lasting peace be achieved. Otherwise, he would be fighting what he called "an accordion war," moving back and forth until first one side, then the other moved too far ahead of its supplies. As an alternative he proposed bombing China's industrial cities, blockading its coast, and, once again, using Chiang Kai-shek's army in Korea and to invade South China as well.

It was one of the most extraordinary long-distance confrontations between a civilian leader and a general in all history. Lincoln's troubles with the nine generals who preceded Grant seem pale by contrast.

Reminding the President of that moment, I said, *Mr. President, you have the reputation of being a somewhat impatient man, somewhat quick on the draw, but it seems to me, sir, under these circumstances, that you displayed Job-like patience. How did you manage to keep silent?*

"In the first place I knew what was at stake. I knew that if the slightest mistake was made, we would find ourselves in a third world war, and as I've told you time and again, I had no intention in any way of allowing that to happen. General Bradley said at the time that that would be the wrong war at the wrong place, at the wrong time, and with the wrong enemy, and he was absolutely right.

"If what MacArthur proposed had happened . . . had been allowed to take place, we would have wound up being at war not only with Red China, but with Russia, too, and . . . the consequences would have been . . .

it might have meant the destruction of a good part of the world."

Mr. President, considering what you said earlier about what you felt might be the condition of General MacArthur's mind at times, weren't you afraid of what might happen while he was still in charge?

"Yes, I was. I was very much concerned."

But you restrained yourself.

"I had no alternative. I had to act . . . whatever I did had to be done with extreme caution because I felt the fate of a good part of the world was at stake." .

Was that possibly your most difficult time as President?

Mr. Truman once again paused for a very long time, and then he said, "I believe it was."

On March 26 the Joint Chiefs of Staff informed Mac-Arthur that the State Department was "planning a Presidential announcement shortly that, with the clearing of the bulk of South Korea of aggressors, the United Nations is now preparing to discuss conditions of settlement in Korea."

MacArthur paid no attention at all to the advice from Washington. Instead, four days later he issued a statement of his own.* He said that he personally was ready to meet with the enemy [Red China] to discuss a settlement in Korea. Barring that, he threatened a general attack against China. And he suggested that if North Korea were to be surrendered, it be surrendered to him personally.

---

* "The enemy [Red China], therefore, must by now be painfully aware that a decision by the United Nations to depart from its tolerant effort to contain the war to the area of Korea, through an expansion of our military operations to its coastal areas and interior bases, would doom Red China to the risk of imminent military collapse. . . . Within the area of my authority as the military commander . . . I stand ready at any time to confer in the field with the commander in chief of the enemy forces to find any military means whereby realization of the political objectives of the United Nations in Korea might be accomplished without further bloodshed."

Even now, more than twenty years later, MacArthur's statement is almost unbelievable. One can't help wondering if Mr. Truman wasn't right. Perhaps MacArthur was mentally unhinged at times. Statements like that one certainly bear the marks of a man far gone in paranoia and megalomania.

The revisionist historians who see Harry Truman only as the most hawkish of cold warriors have generally ignored these particular exchanges between Mr. Truman and Douglas MacArthur, but it seems to me they demonstrate the very essence of the two men, a President who not only understood his position as Commander in Chief and who was determined to prevent a worldwide atomic conflict and did and an aging general who did in fact seem to confuse his identity with that of God, a wrathful, destructive God. Terrifying.

The other chilling thought that passes through my mind is what would have happened if Richard Nixon had been President at that time, a time when he was calling for full support of MacArthur, calling him "the greatest American patriot."

Sometimes I think we are luckier than we realize. But there. As Dean Acheson says in another part of this book, it's a waste of time to speculate on what might have happened if. . . .

Harry Truman waited two weeks.

I didn't ask how he managed, but I did ask why.

"I wanted, if possible, an even . . . better example of his insubordination, and I wanted it to be one that the . . . that everybody would recognize for exactly what it was, and I knew that, MacArthur being the kind of man he was, I wouldn't have long to wait, and I didn't. He wrote that letter to Joe Martin.* And you've read it. He

* Joseph W. Martin was the House minority leader, and on April 5 he read to the House a letter he had received from MacArthur. Martin, a reactionary Republican from Massa-

repeated that *he* wanted to use Chiang Kai-shek's troops and repeated that . . . all that stuff about there being 'no substitute for victory.' "

Whatever that means.

"Yes, yes. Whatever that meant."

And then what happened?

"We had a series . . . several meetings with what they called the war cabinet;* I never called it that, but that's what the papers called it. I called everybody together, and I said, 'I'm going to fire the son of a bitch *right now.*' And they all agreed. All except General Marshall. He said he was afraid . . . it might cause a lot of trouble with Congress as far as the defense budget was concerned. And

---

chusetts, had asked MacArthur how he felt about the Truman administration's refusal to use Chiang Kai-shek's army against the Chinese Reds.

Here, Martin told the House, was the general's reply; he had not asked that it be kept confidential:

"My views and recommendations with respect to the situation created by Red China's entry into the war against us in Korea have been submitted to Washington in most complete detail. Generally those views are well known and generally understood, as they follow the conventional pattern of meeting force with maximum counterforce as we have never failed to do in the past. Your [Martin's] view with respect to the utilization of the Chinese forces on Formosa is in conflict with neither logic nor this tradition.

"It seems strangely difficult for some to realize that here in Asia is where the Communist conspirators have elected to make their play for global conquest, and that here we fight Europe's wars with arms while the diplomats there still fight it with words; that if we lose this war to Communism in Asia the fall of Europe is inevitable; win it and Europe most probably would avoid war and yet preserve freedom.

"As you point out, we must win. There is no substitute for victory."

* It included, among others, Averell Harriman; Secretary of State Dean Acheson, General Marshall, Secretary of Defense; and General Omar Bradley, Chairman of the Joint Chiefs of Staff.

there were some other arguments, but not too many. The only question was how to do it with the least fuss."

There wasn't any way that wouldn't cause some fuss.

"With a man like that no way at all."

Mr. President, is it true that neither General Bradley nor General Marshall liked General MacArthur?

"Oh, no. No, not at all. I don't know anybody that liked him except maybe some of the people on his staff, and it was hard to tell with them because as I've told you each and every one of them was nothing but a damn ass kisser."

I reminded the President of something Heywood Broun once wrote about Herbert Hoover when Hoover was President. Broun wrote, "No one in the entire world really likes Herbert Hoover except Mark Sullivan [a conservative columnist of the time] and, possibly, Mrs. Hoover."

For the first and last time that day Mr. Truman laughed; then he said, "You be careful what you say about Mr. Hoover, because he's a friend of mine."

You said General Marshall had some doubts about discharging MacArthur.

"Yes, he did; he was concerned about the reaction of . . . certain Congressmen, and he wanted to think over what he felt the reaction of the troops would be. And so at the end of the meeting I asked him, I said, 'General, you go over there and you read all the correspondence that's passed between MacArthur and me for the last two years. Then be in my office at nine in the morning, and if you still feel I shouldn't fire him, I won't.' "

And you wouldn't have, if General Marshall had told you you shouldn't?

"I've told you. I knew the general very, very well; we'd been through a lot together, and I knew how his mind worked, and there wasn't a doubt in the world in my mind that when he saw what I'd put up with, that he'd agree with me.

"And the next morning at eight fifteen when I got to my office, he was out there waiting for me, which was very unusual. General Marshall was usually a punctual man, but he . . . I had never known him to be ahead of time. He worked on a very tight schedule.

"But that morning he looked up at me, and he says, 'I spent most of the night on that file, Mr. President, and you should have fired the son of a bitch two years ago.'

"And so we went right ahead, and we did it. There were . . . a good many details to be worked out. I asked General Bradley to be sure we had the full agreement of the Joint Chiefs of Staff, which he got; they were all unanimous in saying he should be fired. And we had to arrange to turn the command over to General Ridgway.

"And then of course, we wanted to be sure that Mac-Arthur got the news through official channels. We didn't want it to get into the newspapers first. But then . . . well, it was on a Tuesday I remember, and I signed all the papers and went over to Blair House to have dinner. Some of the others stayed behind at the White House to decide on exactly how to get the word to Frank Pace [Frank Pace, Jr., Secretary of the Army, then in Korea]. Pace was going . . . was supposed to notify the general.

"While I was still at Blair House, Joe Short [then White House press secretary] came in to where the others were, and he said . . . he had heard that the Chicago *Tribune* had the whole story and was going to print it the next morning.

"So General Bradley came over to Blair House and told me what was up, and he says if MacArthur hears he's going to be fired before he officially is fired, before he's notified, he'd probably up and resign on me.

"And I told Bradley, I says, 'The son of a bitch isn't going to resign on me, *I want him fired.*' "

As I've said, at the time of these conversations, Mr. Truman was seventy-seven years old, and while he was not noticeably enfeebled by age, he always struck me as being fragile. Not at that moment, though. At that moment his blue eyes blazed with fury. Harry Truman was right back there in the White House. He was ten years younger; he was once again President and Commander in Chief, and he wanted the son of a bitch *fired,* goddamn it.

The President continued, his eyes still angry, "And I told Bradley I wanted an hour-by-hour report of what was going on, and so he went back to the Pentagon, and he sent the message to Pace. But he couldn't get to him so General Bradley called me, and he asked my permission to send the message that he was . . . discharged right to MacArthur and telling him to turn his command over to Ridgway. I told him to go right ahead, the faster the better, I said, and he did it.

"And that's all there was to it. I went to bed, and Joe Short called a press conference and read my statement,* and it was all over but the shouting."

As I recall, there was plenty of shouting.

"No more than I expected. I knew there'd be a big uproar, and I knew that MacArthur would take every advantage of it that he could, but I knew that . . . in the end people would see through him, and it would all die down."

Mr. President, I'm not going to ask you if you slept that night.

"I'm very glad you're not going to ask me because if you did, I'd have to tell you the truth, which is that I did. The thing you have to understand about me is if I've done

* "With deep regret, I have concluded that General of the Army Douglas MacArthur is unable to give his wholehearted support to the policies of the United States government and of the United Nations in matters pertaining to his official duties. In view of the specific responsibilities imposed upon me by the Constitution of the United States and the added responsibility which has been entrusted to me by the United Nations, I have decided that I must make a change of command in the Far East. I have, therefore, relieved General MacArthur of his commands and have designated Lieutenant General Matthew B. Ridgway as his successor."

the right thing and I *know* I've done the right thing, I don't worry over it. There's nothing to worry over."

And in this case you were sure you were right.

"Didn't have a minute's doubt about it, and I knew that's the way history would judge it, too, and I guess you can say looking back on it now, that it has."

25

God Bless America

From the minute the news of MacArthur's dismissal appeared in the morning newspapers on April 11, there was a "fuss" that was unprecedented in American history. Never before and, for that matter, never since have so many millions of people been so instantly and deeply angry. And the man they were angry at was Harry S. Truman, who had fired the great man.

To a lesser degree, of course, Dean Acheson was blamed, but most people had known all along that he was a Communist, him and his haughty manner, his suspicious mustache, his phony accent, and his elegant tweed suits. Scarcely a day went by when Senator McCarthy didn't ask for *his* resignation.

I said, *"Mr. Secretary, I understand that in this period, during the uproar over MacArthur's dismissal, a group of citizens in Ponca City, Oklahoma, burned a dummy of you in effigy. Do you remember that?*

"I'm afraid not. It really would be a very difficult thing to remember all of the times things like that happened in those . . . troubled years. I became quite used to being vilified. It has its stimulating aspects, and for all I know, it may even be good for the liver.

"I believe it was sometime during this period that I got in a taxi someplace in Washington, and the driver turned to me and said, 'Aren't you Dean Acheson?'

"I said to him, 'Yes, I am. Would you like me to get out?' "

I told Mr. Acheson that I was in Europe at the time, working on a magazine piece about American troops stationed there, and one day in Marburg, Germany, I attended a lecture being given by the education officer on the dangers of Communism.

At one point he asked, "Who is head of the Communist Party in the United States?"

Only one hand was raised, that of a dark-haired young private who, judging by his accent, was from one of the states in the Deep South. Yes, he said; he knew who was head of the Communist Party in the United States. "Dean Acheson."

The dean was very pleased with that.

By noon of April 11 the Republicans had made plans to invite the deposed warrior to speak to a joint session of Congress the minute he got back to the United States. Did the Democrats object? Don't be silly. Most of them at the time were afraid to say anything really *mean* about Joe McCarthy, and the Senator from Wisconsin was at least human. To object in any way to the glorification of MacArthur—well, one might as well get up and blaspheme God on the floor.

Joe Martin said that in their meetings the Republican leaders had discussed "impeachments," meaning not only Harry Truman but, presumably, Acheson as well. McCarthy was less cautious, but that day he concentrated his fire on Truman. He said, "The son of a bitch ought to be impeached." And he added that the decision must have come "after a night of bourbon and benedictine."

The Gallup Poll found that only 29 percent of the people were in favor of what Truman had done, and the telegrams and letters pouring into the White House, 78,000 of them, were 20 to 1 against the dismissal. Most newspapers condemned what had been done, often vituperatively. And Harry Truman was burned in effigy by the indignant citizens of scores of towns in every part of the country.

And then, on April 17, MacArthur's Constellation, the *Bataan,* landed in San Francisco. He was back in his own, his native land for the first time since 1937. He was wearing a trench coat and a frayed battle cap; it may or may not have been the same cap that Mr. Truman found so objectionable at Wake Island. A man I know who was on MacArthur's staff insists that the general had an enlisted man, I believe a corporal, who did nothing but *fray* battle caps that had come straight from the Post Exchange, fray them so that they would look as if the general had just stepped out of some firing line or other.

Douglas MacArthur, the deposed Commanding General of the U.S. Armed Forces, U.S. Commander in Chief, Far East Command, Supreme Commander for the Allied Powers in Japan, and Commander in Chief, United Nations Command, paused dramatically at the head of the landing ramp, allowing the spotlights to play over the uniform, the jet-black hair, and the oddly unwrinkled face.

The crowd roared its approval, and the next day when the general went to a reception in front of the San Francisco City Hall, he spoke for the first time. He said, "The only politics I have is contained in a single phrase known well to all of you—God Bless America."

A hundred thousand people went wild at the wisdom of that remark; it seemed the cheers and shouts would never stop. Strong men were not ashamed to be seen weeping; women were hysterical, and hundreds of people were seen to cross themselves.

And when the general got to Washington, it was the same. Cheering crowds lined every street. It was estimated that there were 300,000 people on Pennsylvania Avenue alone, and there were another quarter of a million at the Washington Monument. Not a dry eye anywhere.

The general later appeared before the Daughters of the American Revolution and spoke to the ladies for about three minutes. "I have long sought personally to pay you the tribute that is in my heart. . . . In this hour of crisis, all patriots look to you."

As he spoke, all the daughters took off their hats so that their view of the mighty warrior would not be impaired by millinery. And the next day, when the recording secretary-general read from her minutes that the general's remarks were "probably" the most important event in the history of Constitution Hall, the word "probably" was immediately struck out.

When the general, Mrs. MacArthur (Jeannie), and little Arthur MacArthur went to New York, it was said that 7,500,000 people were out to greet them. Almost 800 tons of confetti and ticker tape were showered on them. The reception was bigger by far than that given to Charles A. Lindbergh when he got back from flying to Paris in 1927; it was greater than that accorded Dwight D. Eisenhower when he returned from victory in Europe in 1945.

As Eric Goldman points out in *The Crucial Decade,* MacArthur's welcome wasn't all cheers and tears. Writing of MacArthur's appearance in New York, Goldman says, "Amid all the uproar a quite different kind of feeling kept expressing itself. As MacArthur's limousine went by, men and women would cross themselves. The handkerchiefs came out. And sometimes there were patches of quiet, a strange, troubled, churning quiet."

The day after the conversation about the firing of MacArthur I said, *Mr. President, when you discharged General MacArthur, weren't you afraid that he might become a martyr, that in fact you might be helping him become President of the United States?*

"I didn't give a damn what became of him. He disobeyed orders, and I was Commander in Chief, and either I was or I wasn't. So I acted as Commander in Chief and called him home.

"I knew that he was one of those generals that wanted to be President, and there are a lot of them, more than you'd think. Some of them . . . one of them in particular that I can think of and I'm not naming any names. He thought he *deserved* to be President."

I believe the one you mean made it, didn't he? And recently, too.

"The one I'm thinking of was a . . . lived in the White House for eight years, but I don't think he was ever *President.*

"But about this general situation. What you have to

understand is that the President of the United States has to act as Commander in Chief at *all* times. A civilian executive just has to run the armed forces. The men who wrote the Constitution understood that, and it's been the same all through history.

"The Romans had the same sort of arrangement with two consuls who were in charge of running the army in the field. It just has to be that way. Other ways have been tried, but they never have worked. Somebody has to be in charge who has been freely and legally chosen by the people . . . by a majority of the people.

"France tried . . . you remember . . . tried a different way with the Committee of Five Hundred in the French Revolution. They couldn't make up their minds what they wanted to do. And Napoleon finally got tired of fooling around with them and took over and became the head of the French state.

"But about MacArthur. I'll say this to you. What I did I didn't do to injure anybody or head off any political opposition or anything of that kind. If he had had any background in politics at all instead of being completely military, he could have made good use of the situation, but he didn't do it."

How do you mean, he could have made use of it?

"Why, when he landed in the United States, he should have come in and reported to his Commander in Chief. That was the first thing he should have done, and then if people around over the country wanted to listen to him make speeches, that would have been all right. But he didn't do it.

"He made a lot of speeches . . . including that speech to both Houses of Congress. At the time of that speech . . . well, the minute I found out he was going to make it, I wanted to get a copy of it.

"So we were having a Cabinet meeting, and I knew somebody had to get it for me. So I looked around, and there was Frank Pace, and I said to him, I said, 'Frank, you get a copy of that speech and bring it to me.'

"Well, I've told you how he was. He was all right when

there wasn't any trouble, but the minute there was . . .
he'd be hiding in a goddamn tent someplace. So he started
stuttering and stammering, and he says [imitating Pace],
'Please, Mr. President, it would be very embarrassing for
me to ask the general or one of his aides. . . . I'd really
rather not.'

"I said to him, I said, 'Frank, I don't give a good goddamn what you'd rather. I want you to get me that speech
and bring it to me. On the double,' I said.

"He went and got it, and I read it. It was nothing but a
bunch of damn bullshit."

In *The Truman Presidency* Cabell Phillips says of that
speech, "one of the most memorable orations ever heard
in the Capitol, before a joint meeting of the House and
Senate and radio-television audience of untold millions.
He [MacArthur] was a stirring, romantic figure out of the
pages of a Kipling or a Richard Harding Davis as he
mounted the rostrum in the House of Representatives and
with a benevolent smile waited for the two-minute ovation
to subside. He was handsome, proud, resonant of voice,
confident of manner, and yet humble in a magisterial sort
of way. . . .

" 'I address you with neither rancor nor bitterness in the
fading twilight of life, with but one purpose in mind. To
serve my country. . . . "Why," my soldiers asked of me,
"surrender military advantage to an enemy in the field?"
[Long pause] I could not answer.

" '. . . I am closing my fifty-two years of military service. When I joined the Army, even before the turn of the
century, it was the fulfillment of all my boyish hopes and
dreams. . . .' "

Hunter S. Thompson, the political reporter for *Rolling
Stone,* author of *Fear and Loathing in the Campaign Trail
'72,* says that when he first heard a recording of the speech,
not knowing the circumstances or whose voice he was listening to, he rolled on the floor; he thought it was one of
Lenny Bruce's put-ons.

But it wasn't like that on April 19, 1951. According to

Phillips, "Nearly every sentence he spoke was punctuated by applause.

"There were tears in his eyes when, at last, he uttered his peroration:

" 'Since I took the oath at West Point, the hopes and dreams [of youth] have all vanished. But I still remember the refrain of one of the most popular barracks ballads of that day, which proclaimed most proudly that old soldiers never die, they just fade away.

" 'And like the old soldier of the ballad, I now close my military career and just fade away, an old soldier who tried to do his duty as God gave him the light to see that duty.

" 'Good-bye.' "

I said to Dean Acheson, *Mr. Secretary, I understand that after General MacArthur's speech before Congress there was a full-dress Cabinet meeting and that until you livened it up, it had been a pretty gloomy meeting.*

"Everybody, except I must say the President, was greatly upset by the speech; it was thought to have been extremely effective. But I could not agree. I thought it was more than somewhat bathetic, and this was at a time when bathos was less common and less popular in American political oratory than it is today.

". . . The President asked each of us what we thought the effect of the speech would be, and I said that . . . it was difficult to gauge with any precision, but I said that the whole thing reminded me of a man who had an extraordinarily beautiful daughter, and her father did everything he could to protect her. He let her go out only rarely and then only with young men of whom he approved and whose backgrounds were impeccable.

"At last, when she was twenty, she came to her father and said that she had a terrible thing to confess. She said, 'I'm pregnant.'

"At that her father threw up his hands and shouted, 'Thank heaven it's over. I've been afraid of something like this all my life.' "

I said, *Mr. Secretary, do you remember the President's comment on that speech?*

"No, no. You would have to ask him about that, but as I recall, it was a short comment. He described the speech with two Anglo-Saxon words, I believe, but as I say you must ask him about that."

Mr. Truman told me, "I said it was nothing but a bunch of bullshit. . . . There was a lot of carrying-on about that speech, and some of those damn fool Congressmen were crying like a bunch of women, but it didn't worry me at all."

Mr. President, did you listen to the speech on the radio or watch it on television?

"I'd already read the damn thing. And there wasn't any law that I knew of that could make me listen to it, too. Let alone watch it on television.

"It certainly didn't worry me, and neither did the ticker-tape parades they gave for him. Because I knew that once all the hullabaloo died down, people would see what he was.

"And somehow, wherever he went he just didn't make an impression on people that would make him President or much of anything else. Down in Houston, Texas—there are more damn fools down there than just about anyplace I can think of—they tried to raise five thousand dollars to buy him a Cadillac car. I don't think it's paid for yet."

After his triumph before both houses of Congress and the ticker-tape smash in New York, MacArthur retreated to a $130-a-day suite at the Waldorf, where for a week he said nothing, although an aide, when asked about the general's availability for a Presidential draft, referred reporters to the Book of John, especially the part where Thomas expresses some doubts about the Resurrection.

Reporters, most of whom are not vigilant Bible readers, hurried to their Gideons and to the Book of John, but about the best anybody could come up with was the part where Thomas says, "Except I shall see in his hands the print of the nails, and put my finger into the print of the nails, and thrust my hand into his side, I will not believe."

When Jesus finally shows up, He says to Thomas, "Reach hither thy finger, and behold my hands; and reach hither thy hand, and thrust it into my side: and be not faithless, but believing.

"And Thomas answered and said unto him, 'My Lord and my God.'

"Jesus saith unto him, 'Thomas, because thou hast seen me, thou hast believed: blessed are they that have not seen, and yet have believed.' "

That seemed to pretty much wrap up how MacArthur felt about the 1952 Republican national convention.

A few days later MacArthur emerged from his cave at the Waldorf and took off on a "crusade" that took him first to Chicago and Milwaukee and then to Washington again, this time for an appearance before joint hearings of the Armed Services Committee of the House and the Senate Foreign Relations Committee into the reasons for his dismissal. Simple disobedience of his Commander in Chief was not enough.

The hearings ran from May 3 until June 25, and there were many witnesses besides MacArthur, although he was clearly the star performer. In a three-day period he spent twenty-one hours and ten minutes on the stand.

Any oratorical flourishes were considerably diluted, however, because the hearings, despite Republican protests, were closed, and only what was supposedly nonclassified material was released each day. The total words spoken during the seven weeks were estimated at 7,000,-000, and, although newspapers devoted a good deal of space to them, they were almost universally unread.

MacArthur was not resurrected by the hearings. Indeed a nation of MacArthur idolators turned into a nation of doubting Thomases. As Harry Truman had predicted, people began to see MacArthur for what he was—vain, arrogant, jealous, petulant, more than a little foolish, and, above all, boring:

". . . the insidious forces working from within would
lead directly to the path of Communist slavery. . . . We
must not underestimate the peril. It must not be brushed
off lightly. It must not be scoffed at, as our present leadership has been prone to do, by hurling childish epi-
thets such as 'red herring,' 'character assassin,' 'scandal
monger,' 'witch hunt,' 'political assassination,' and like
terms designed to confuse or conceal. . . ."

Stuff like that was putting most people under sixty to
sleep wherever MacArthur appeared. And people who a
few weeks before had applauded when Harry Truman
was being burned in effigy now began to see him as a
plucky little man who had defended the Constitution,
their Constitution, against an old warrior who once may
have been powerful but was now only pompous.

When MacArthur first got back, Harry Truman had
told newspapermen that it would take about six weeks for
the "fuss" to die down, and that is exactly what happened.

In late May MacArthur returned to New York, and he,
Mrs. MacArthur, and little Arthur MacArthur went to the
Polo Grounds to see a Giant-Phillies game. A recording
of a seventeen-gun salute was played; the general stood at
attention in a box decorated with the Stars and Stripes and
a five-star flag. Then he paid tribute to "the great American game of baseball that has done so much to build the
American character."

At the end of the game, while the band played "Old
Soldiers Never Die," the three MacArthurs and the rest
of their party rose and started walking across the diamond
to the center-field exit.

Just before they got there, a man who had to be from
the Bronx shouted from the stands, "Hey, Mac, how's
Harry Truman?"

The spectators burst into spontaneous laughter and
applause, and that was it. That was the end. It was a
beautiful moment, and after that except for a few little
old ladies in tennis shoes and the Chicago *Tribune,* there

was no more serious talk about Douglas MacArthur and the Presidency.

I reminded the President of that afternoon, and he laughed and said, "Well, of course. The American people always see through a counterfeit. It sometimes takes a little time, but eventually they can always spot one. And MacArthur. I'll tell you. If there ever was to be a Counterfeit Club, he would have been president of it. That is one position he wouldn't have had to run for; he would have been elected, unanimously."

Mr. President, what was your overall impression of the general, besides the fact that he was a counterfeit and that he thought he was God?

Mr. Truman didn't have to give any thought at all to that one. He said, "He struck me as a man there wasn't anything real about."

26

On Generals in General

Mr. President, I gather you're not the only one of our Chief Executives who's had difficulties with generals.

"Oh, no. By no means. James Madison had a terrible time with his generals. He just sort of stumbled into the War of 1812. It never would have happened if it hadn't been for a few hotheads like Henry Clay."

Clay was a Congressman from Kentucky, Speaker of the House, and one of the leading proponents of the war.

"Clay was an expansionist, wanted to extend the country west, and wanted to take over everything that wasn't tied down, and . . . he even wanted to annex Canada, and that is the reason . . . one of the reasons he was so much for getting into war with Britain. He thought we'd gain a lot of new territory.

"But most of the people along the east coast, and that was a good part of the country at that time, they weren't for that war at all. Silliest damn war we ever had, made no sense at all.

"And like I say, Madison didn't want it, but he was a very weak President. A very valuable man when he . . . when they wrote the Constitution, but as President, he just couldn't seem to make up his mind about anything.

"And when he blundered into the War of 1812, except for Andy Jackson he didn't have a general who was worth a good goddamn. They not only weren't any good, they wouldn't do what he told them. And that's the reason the British were able to take Washington and burn the White House. When Madison heard the British were coming, he ran around like a chicken with its head cut off. It wasn't that he was a *coward;* he just didn't know what to do.

"What has always made me feel sorry for Madison is that he became President at all. The work he did on the Constitution and in writing the Federalist Papers with

343

Alexander Hamilton, that was more than enough to justify any man's life.

"But in the War of 1812 . . . Jackson won the only great victory, in the Battle of New Orleans, and it was fought three weeks after the peace treaty, the Treaty of Ghent, but because of bad communications, Jackson didn't know the war was over.

"That victory restored some of Madison's popularity, but he was still hurting over all those generals he'd had trouble controlling. So when the time came, he was very glad to retire to Montpelier [the Madison estate in Virginia], and as I told you, he died broke. And his widow, Dolley, she had to sell Montpelier, and she had to move to . . . had to move in with relatives in Washington, and Daniel Webster had to send her food. And Madison's son was a drunkard, his stepson that was, and he sold his father's papers to buy himself a drink.

"It was an awful thing to see. I don't know *why* this country isn't more grateful to its leaders."

Who were some of the other Presidents who had trouble with generals?

"James K. Polk, for one. He had trouble with 'Ole Fuss 'n' Feathers' [General Winfield Scott] during the war with Mexico. Couldn't get him to move. He stayed down there in Puebla in Mexico from April until August, wouldn't move an inch. Just sat on his ass. Churchill told me he had the same kind of trouble with Montgomery [Bernard Law Montgomery, British field marshal] in France in that other war. Couldn't get him off his ass.

"Of course, Scott finally got moving, and he finally took Mexico City, but he could have done it in May or June at the latest instead of in September, which is when it happened.

"One of the troubles with Scott was that he had in mind being President, which a lot of generals do. MacArthur, of course, was one, and Eisenhower was another, and he's the one I never would have believed it of. He's sat as close to me as you're sitting right this minute and swore up and down that he would never run for any political office and given me the reasons why a military man shouldn't be in politics, and I believed him."

But you didn't believe Lloyd Stark when he told you he wouldn't run against you for the Senate.

"I knew Lloyd was a goddamn liar; I thought I could trust Eisenhower."

You were saying that General Scott wanted to be President.

"He did, and he tried again and again, and, finally, in 1852, the Whigs nominated him. But he made a damn fool of himself every time he opened his mouth. So he didn't get very far. He retired in 1861, so Lincoln didn't have to put up with him during the Civil War. Retiring when he did was one of the few good things Scott ever did. Lincoln had enough trouble with generals without having to contend with 'Ole Fuss 'n' Feathers.' "

Did President Polk have any trouble with Zachary Taylor in the Mexican War?

"Not too much. Taylor, 'Ole Rough 'n' Ready,' he won the Battle of Buena Vista, and he was a pretty good general. Claimed he had no political ambitions. Just like Ike. Claimed he didn't want to be President, and he may even have meant it at one time. They say when somebody started to toast him as the next President of the United States, he told whoever it was, 'Stop your damn nonsense and drink your drink.'

"But later he sort of, apparently, changed his mind. That's the way it almost always happens. There are very few men who when they start thinking about the Presidency don't start thinking how maybe they'd do better at it than the fellow who's then in office, and then they start telling themselves that they'd probably be able to do the job as well as anybody else who's had the job except maybe for . . . oh, Washington and Lincoln and Jefferson maybe.

"And then the first thing you know they are . . . wondering what they are going to say when they get the nomination.

"In Taylor's case . . . finally, in 1848, he was nominated by the Whigs. They didn't know a damn thing about him, didn't know what party he belonged to even or how he stood on any of the issues, but they went ahead and did it.

"They always reminded me a little of some of those smart-aleck Democrats in 1948 who wanted to nominate Eisenhower for President without knowing a thing about him. Didn't even know what party he belonged to.

"But the Whigs nominated Taylor, and of course, he got elected because he was a great military hero. But he was no damn good in office. He was too old, and he didn't know anything about it. He only lived about sixteen months after he got in office, but that was plenty long enough to tell that he was very much out of place in the White House.

"Somebody, I forget who, said war is too important to be left to the generals, and that's true. But politics . . . we ought to try to devise a way to keep them out of politics altogether."

Tell me about Lincoln and his generals.

"Lincoln had more trouble than any President with the general proposition. He had to fire McClellan twice, and then he had to fire all the rest of them or demote them in rank until he finally got Grant in charge, and the war came to a successful conclusion."

Why did he have to fire McClellan twice?

"McClellan was a very difficult man. He was young, about thirty-five, thirty-six, I believe, and after the First Battle of Bull Run, when the streets of Washington were filled with stragglers and deserters, and nobody seemed to know what to do, why, McClellan organized the Army of the Potomac, and he did a very good job of it. He was always very popular with the soldiers.

"But as I say, he was a young, very young man, and just like MacArthur after he organized the Army of the Potomac, McClellan got blown up by the papers out of all proportion, and he got to thinking that the whole fate of the Union was on his shoulders. Lincoln liked him; they'd known each other back in Illinois when McClellan was head of one of the railroads there and Lincoln was one of its lawyers. The Illinois Central, I believe.

"But when he got to Washington, McClellan had a hard time getting it into his head that Lincoln was President. He seemed to think that Lincoln was still . . . that he was still Lincoln's boss somehow. He was very rude to the President, used to come late to meetings, and once when Lincoln went to visit him at *his* house, McClellan came in, and he saw Lincoln, but he didn't say hello or anything. He went straight upstairs and went to bed.

"But as you know, Lincoln was a very patient man, and he overlooked these . . . this rudeness. When some of Lincoln's Cabinet members objected to the way McClellan was acting, Lincoln told them . . . he said, 'Never mind.' He says, 'If he brings us success, if he brings success to the Union side, I will gladly hold McClellan's horse for him.' But that didn't happen. McClellan didn't *move*. Same trouble Polk had with 'Ole Fuss 'n' Feathers' and Churchill had with Montgomery. McClellan just sat on his ass.

"One day somebody in the War Department came and told Lincoln that there didn't seem to have been any firing in McClellan's sector since after sunset. And Lincoln says that that didn't surprise him a bit. He says what he really wanted to know was had there been any firing in that sector *before* sunset. He says it reminded him about the fellow who went around saying that he had come across a really unusual child that was black from the hips down. And when somebody asked him what color the child was from the hips up, the fellow said, 'Why, black, of course.'

"And it wasn't only that Lincoln couldn't get McClellan to *move*. The general was always issuing statements about . . . concerning political matters, and they always indicated that whatever it was, McClellan could do it a lot better than Lincoln was doing it.

"Of course that meant that McClellan was aiming to be

President, and they asked Lincoln if he was going to issue a reply to something or other McClellan had said.

"Lincoln said, 'No,' he wasn't. He said he wouldn't do that, but he said the whole thing reminded him of the fella whose horse started kicking around and got his foot stuck in the stirrup. The fella looked at the horse, and he said, 'Look here, if you want to get on, I'll get off.'

"Of course, in 1864 the Democrats nominated McClellan for President, and at the same time they adopted a platform saying that the war was a failure and that they were willing . . . would probably make a deal with the South.

"McClellan refused to support the platform, and then the Union victories at Mobile Bay and Atlanta lost him a lot of support. But Lincoln . . . Lincoln was a man who suffered greatly, and he was inclined, always, to look on the dark side of things. He was convinced that he would be . . . that he would lose the election in 1864, and he felt that that would mean the end of the Union.

"He drew up a statement that was signed by every member of his Cabinet saying that after losing the election, he would do everything he could between the election and the inauguration to save the Union. But he said after the inauguration, the successful candidate would have made promises to win the election that would mean the end of the Union.

"Of course that didn't happen. Lincoln was reelected, and afterward Lincoln told Seward [William Henry Seward, Lincoln's Secretary of State] that if McClellan had been elected, he'd have said to him, 'General, you are more popular with the American people than I am. Now let us both use our influence to try to save the country. I'll help you raise all the troops you need to end the war as quickly as possible.'

"Old Seward, who had never liked McClellan, said, 'And the general would have said, "Yes, yes," and kept on saying, "Yes, yes," and he would never done a damn thing at all.' Which is probably true. Because McClellan was a man who fought more with his mouth than he did with . . . than he used his troops to fight.

"Lincoln also had trouble with a fella named Pope [General John L. Pope]. He was another bombastic fellow who made all kinds of promises that he never did live up to, and he never had any intention of living up to them.

"When Lincoln put him in command of the Army of the Potomac, Pope said he wouldn't *rest* until the war was won. He said he would have his headquarters in his saddle. But after the Second Battle of Bull Run, which was one of the worst Union defeats of the war, there were hundreds, maybe thousands of wounded and dying men in the streets of Washington and on the floor of the Capitol and everywhere else where there was empty space.

"It was just an awful defeat, and Lincoln removed Pope from his command and sent him up in the northeast someplace to keep an eye on some tame Indians. And old Horace Greeley said in the New York *Tribune* . . . said that in the Second Battle of Bull Run, 'Pope evidently had his headquarters in his saddle, and he sat on his brains.' "

Mr. President, how do you explain the success of General Grant? Especially after all those other generals had been such terrible failures?

"Grant was a very . . . had a very simple idea of how you go about winning a war. He wasn't much . . . didn't know much about strategy. A lot of other generals on both sides, they had all studied the same books at West Point, and Grant . . . well, he wasn't much of a reader or scholar. There was one book by some Frenchman. I forget his name.* And the high-ranking officers on both sides of the fence were studying this book and using the same strategy, and it wasn't working.

---

* Baron Henri Jomini, actually Swiss, whose military writings attracted Napoleon, who gave him an important position in the French Army. The book which summarized all of Jomini's military theories was published in 1838 and was called *Précis de l'art de la guerre*.

And one day some young lieutenant asked Grant if he'd read that book, and Grant said, 'Hell, no.' Of course he hadn't. He said he didn't have to. He said what you have to do to fight a war, you have to find the enemy, and you have to hit him with everything you've got, and then you've got to keep right on going. And that's what he did. He never stopped to issue fancy statements about this and that. He just kept right on going."

Mr. President, last week when I was back in Brewster I was reading W. E. Woodward's biography of Ulysses S. Grant, and he says that when Grant went back into the service in 1861, he took over a very unruly regiment that I believe two previous officers had been unable to manage. This was in Galena, Illinois.

And when Grant arrived, wearing an old felt hat and a beat-up coat and his beard needing a trim, the men expected he'd give them a long lecture, eat their tails out, as they used to say when I was in the Army.

But Grant didn't. He just stood up in front of them, of the regiment, and all he said was, "Men, go to your quarters."

And that very much reminded me of what you said when under very similar circumstances you took over Battery D. All those men expected that you'd give them a very hard time, but all you said was, "Dismissed."

I hope you won't think my question is impertinent.

"I've told you before. If I think you're impertinent, I'll let you know."

I was just wondering if you'd read that about General Grant before in the First World War you said what you said to the troops in Battery D.

"Well, you might say that at that time I was familiar with the history of the Civil War or the War Between the States, whatever you want to call it, and so I *may* have happened on that incident. I've told you. One of the reasons for reading history is to learn from it and, if possible, make use of it."

That was the second and last time that I believe Mr. Truman winked.

I gather you feel some admiration for General Grant, as a general at least.

"Well, you have to remember that all my people were on the other side, were on Lee's side. But I have always felt that Grant was a very good general; they both were, and Lee was one of the kindest men who ever lived. After the war, he became president of Washington and Lee University down in Virginia. Only then it was just called Washington University, and they say he knew the name of every boy in that school.

"And he was a very gentle man, never got angry or, if he did, never did show it. When he was marching up the Shenandoah Valley on his way to Gettysburg, he kept waiting for Jeb Stuart to show up. Stuart was a fine cavalry officer but a very undependable sort of fellow. And he was another one of those who was always out to make as many headlines as he possibly could. Lee didn't know where he was when he was going to Gettysburg. Stuart finally did show up, on the first day of the battle, which meant that he hadn't done his job, finding out, as the cavalry was supposed to, how strong the enemy was. And I think that was a very big factor in losing that battle, if it was lost. More of a draw, I think.

"Anyway, when he did show up, Lee didn't say what he . . . all that he must have had in his mind. He just said, 'I see you are here at last, General Stuart.'

"Lee was a tactician and a scholar, and he had studied every battle in history, I think, and he'd learned from what he'd studied. If he'd been on the other side in that war, he'd probably have more the reputation he deserves. I told you. History is always written by the winners. And if Lee had been on the other side, he'd probably have wound up being President of the United States."

How do you think he'd have been as President?

"We've done about enough guesswork for one time. Lee was a professional military man and a West Point graduate. I've told you how professional soldiers are in politics, no damn good at all."

Mr. President, the way you feel about West Point, or

seem to feel, you don't seem to think too much of it, and yet you wanted to go there yourself.

"Yes, but that was because I needed to, wanted to, get a free education. I didn't necessarily say it was a good one. I'll tell you. It seems to give a man a narrow view of things, and if you're going to be a soldier and nothing else, that may work out all right. But not for any other line of work and especially not politics. They never seem to teach them anything at all about understanding people up there." *

Getting back to General Grant, he certainly seemed to demonstrate at Appomattox that he was a very generous man, wouldn't you say?

"One of the most generous who ever was. Lee was all dressed up fit to kill that day, you know, wearing his best uniform and wearing a sword. Grant showed up in . . . I believe it was an enlisted man's uniform, and his boots hadn't been shined, and as you were saying about that incident up at Galena, Illinois, his beard probably needed a trim. I'm not even sure he had a sword. They say that during the Battle of the Wilderness he just stood there whittling away on a piece of wood with a jackknife.

* I'm aware that we have already discussed Mr. Truman's feelings about a West Point education, but his answer this time was somewhat different and seemed to me to be worth preserving.

And there is this, from *The Man from Missouri*, by Alfred Steinberg; speaking of Mr. Truman's first term in the Senate:

"Despite his lack of major influence, requests for aid poured into his office. When he could do something, his approach was to favor the underdog. 'One morning,' Messall [Victor Messall, the Senator's Secretary] said, 'I brought him fifty folders of applications for appointments to West Point from Missouri boys. The folders were thick and contained recommendations from judges, state legislators, mayors, et cetera. We went through each folder methodically, and finally we got down to a folder that contained no letters of recommendation—only a single-page application written in pencil on a sheet of cheap, rough paper. Truman read it and then he turned to me and ordered, 'Give him the appointment.'"

"One thing you have to understand about Grant. He was very familiar with defeat, with failing at things, and he knew about being poor. His father was a tanner, you know, and he grew up working as a plain dirt farmer. They never had much money, the Grants, and after he'd been to West Point, he said that what he'd learned there wasn't nearly as important as what he'd learned as a boy, which was that if you undertake a job, you have to finish it. And of course, knowing that is . . . was why he was so successful in the war.

"After he finished at West Point, he was in the Mexican War and made a very good record for himself, and then . . . he finally wound up stationed out in California; he had to send his wife and children back to Ohio, and he missed them. He and Mrs. Grant, they were . . . very fond of each other.

"While in California, he and the colonel in charge, a Colonel Buchanan, they didn't hit it off, and Grant was drinking. He was always a drinking man his whole life through.

"The colonel was going to bring him up on charges, but instead, Grant resigned. He came back East, and his father-in-law gave him some timberland down near St. Louis, which Grant cleared, about sixty acres, I believe, and he built his own log cabin. Called it Hard Scrabble, and of course, it has since become a national monument.

"He tried to farm the land, but the panic of 18 and 57 and 58 wiped him out, and after that he never made much of a go of anything he seemed to undertake. When the war came along, he was working for his brother in Galena, working in a leather store. He was thirty-nine, forty years old, and nobody thought he'd ever amount to a tinker's dam.* Except his wife, Julia. Julia Dent her

---

* In speaking of this part of Grant's career, which he did with great warmth and understanding, I always felt that Harry Truman felt a real sense of identity with him. After all, at forty, Harry Truman, having already gone broke in the haberdashery, had just suffered his first political defeat, and Margaret had just been born.

name had been. She never lost faith in him, and in the war it turned out she was right.

"What I'm saying is that Grant was always a very humble, very understanding man, and down there at Appomattox he realized that he wasn't any different from those Southern boys who'd been on the wrong side. And he felt just the way Lincoln did, that the South should be treated as a disobedient child and not a conquered nation. Some of the Radical Republicans in Washington were talking about hanging Lee or convicting him of treason, but Grant said that nothing like that was going to be allowed to happen. The kids . . . the boys in Lee's army were hungry, and they had to be fed. That was the first thing. And it was spring; it was April the ninth, and the . . . those boys were going to need horses and mules to plant their spring crops. They were not going to be put in prison camps . . . the way some of the Radical Republicans were suggesting. They were going home. All they had to do was sign paroles, and as long as they lived up to them, they would be left strictly alone.

"That was all. It was a very good thing that he did. As I said, Grant was a very generous, kind man, and if he hadn't got into politics, he might not have gone down. . . . His place in history would have been . . . more secure. But when he got into the White House, he turned out to be the weakest President we have ever had, and his administration was the most corrupt in all our history up to now. He wasn't crooked himself, but everybody around him was.

"And the biggest trouble was that he just had no understanding at all of what to do. He didn't have the slightest understanding of free government.

"I've told you what happens with these generals. They think being President is some kind of reward for services rendered in the war, and they think the White House is like some Army post they can retire to and take life easy.

"Grant had the idea that Congress was supposed to run things, and he thought being President was just sort of . . . like that other fella we've discussed, some kind of ceremonial job where all you had to do was entertain visiting royalty and pin medals on people and shake hands and getting your picture taken with a big grin on your face.

"I'm pretty sure he'd never read the Constitution; he wasn't much of a reading man, and he'd only voted once in his life and that was in 1856, when he voted for the Democrats. After he'd had a misunderstanding with Andrew Johnson,* the Radical Republicans took him over, claiming he was one of them. which he wasn't. He wasn't one of anything, of any party. He just didn't understand what was going on.

"And after he got elected in 1868, why the people around him were stealing the country blind. Old Gould and Fisk [Jay Gould and Jim Fisk, New York financiers and scoundrels] wined and dined him and tried to convince him to keep the government out of the gold market so they could clean up on it, and for a while they did.

---

* In 1867 during the height of Andrew Johnson's troubles with Congress he appointed Grant to succeed Edwin M. Stanton as Secretary of War. Stanton was an ally of the Radical Republicans in Congress, who favored the severest penalties for the Southern states; Johnson and Grant agreed with Lincoln's policy, which was, as Mr. Truman says, to treat the Southern states as disobedient children. "Let 'em up easy," Lincoln once said.

At the time of Grant's appointment Congress, then in recess. had already passed the Tenure of Office Act, which asserted that no member of the President's Cabinet could be discharged without the Senate's approval, a clearly unconstitutional measure.

When Congress re-convened at the end of 1867 one of its first acts was to refuse to consent to Stanton's dismissal. Grant immediately resigned. He had no real understanding of the issues involved. He just thought that Congress was boss, no matter what, and that confusion was unfortunate then and even more so when he himself became President.

In any case, Johnson, a man of monumental rages at times, felt that he had been betrayed. It was his understanding that Grant would stay on until the Tenure of Office Act had been tested in the courts. Grant then felt that *his* honor had been impugned, and the two men became lifelong enemies.

And there was the Credit Mobilier scandal in which speculators made tens of millions of dollars by bilking the Union Pacific Railroad, which had been subsidized by the federal government. And it resulted in a great scandal that involved several members of Congress who had accepted gifts of stock as a bribe to keep their mouths shut.

"As I say, Grant wasn't involved in any of those things personally, but he has gone down in history as head of the crookedest government we have ever had.

"But he was reelected, mostly because the Democratic candidate was Horace Greeley, the fellow I've told you was editor of the New York *Tribune*. Greeley was also nominated by the Liberal Republican Party, but somehow he just didn't come across in the campaign. He just couldn't seem to project himself to the electorate the way he should have. For some reason I never have been able to figure out he came across as kind of a nut. People didn't care much for Grant as President, but they reelected him rather than take a chance on Greeley. His defeat and the death of his wife just before the election drove him crazy, and he died in less than a month. A very interesting man, though; he's worth reading about, because for one thing as you will see a lot of his ideas were way ahead of their time.

"But Grant got reelected, and his second term was even worse than his first. A lot more fraud and corruption were uncovered, and there was the panic of 18 and 73, and through it all Grant just sat there, not knowing what to do. It was just an awful period of American history. Grant's indecisiveness and his letting the Radical Republicans run things led to difficulties between the North and South that haven't been settled to this day."

After Grant got out of office, didn't he go on a round-the-world cruise?

"Yes, after he got out of office, he went over to see his daughter who'd been married in the White House to an Englishman, and they made quite a bit over him in England, which he liked, and so he just kept on going, and everywhere he went he was greeted by the kings and queens and prime ministers and what have you, and there were parades for him, and they gave him a lot of decorations.

"When he got back to the United States, he'd been gone two years or so, and he landed at San Francisco and was greeted with considerable enthusiasm. And then he tried to go back to Galena, Illinois, for a while, but somehow things didn't work out there. Nothing seemed to go right for him there."

Unlike your returning to Independence after being President. I mean, things seem to have worked out very well indeed.

"If you want to make that comparison, I suppose you could make it, yes."

And eventually didn't Grant wind up in New York?

"He went to New York, and he didn't have much money left, but then he went flat broke with a Wall Street firm named Grant and Ward. He was the only President who tried to promote the Presidency in business, and I don't like that fact in his history. That is exactly what he was doing, though.

"But Ward, Ferdinand Ward his name was, took him for every penny he had. And he'd borrowed money from old man Vanderbilt [William Henry Vanderbilt, son of Cornelius Vanderbilt], and since he couldn't pay it back, Vanderbilt took what little real estate he owned and everything else poor old Grant had, including even his ceremonial swords. I believe they ended up down at the National Museum.

"But that's an awful thing, to see a former President humiliated like that. It shouldn't happen. You might say Grant brought it on himself by acting like a damn fool, but it still isn't right. It shouldn't be allowed to happen to an ex-President.

"When Grant realized that Ward had taken advantage of him, he said, 'I have always trusted men long after other people gave up on them, but I never will trust another human being as long as I live.' "

And did he?

"Oh, I don't know. I suppose so. He was a trusting fella, and you either are or you aren't, and there's not much you can do about it.

"He seems to have trusted old Mark Twain. He was desperately in need of money, and that's when he got tied up with Twain and wrote his memoirs. In two volumes. I think Mark Twain helped him write them. Some of it. I don't know how much, but some of it sounds a lot funnier than Grant ever was, and a lot of what is said doesn't compare at all with what really happened. Those books are very. interesting reading, but they are very inaccurate." *

Do you think that's carelessness or deliberate?

"Oh, I think he told Mark the things, just like I'm talking to you, the things that he remembered the way he remembered them. And of course, no man's memory is absolutely perfect.

"I think the principal thing he was trying to do was to make a good front before the country because he was, even in that day, considered the worst President that ever was in the White House. Although he came very near to being nominated and elected a third time. Did you know that?"

No, I didn't. Tell me about it.

"It was in 1880, and the Republican convention was in Chicago, and there was . . . there were several different splits in the party. The first person nominated was John

---

* I couldn't find any evidence that Twain actually helped Grant write the two volumes of his _Personal Memoirs;_ indeed, the last pages, in Grant's own weakening hand, were written only forty-eight hours before he died.

There are places, though, where Grant does come through wittier than anyone ever suspected he could be. And Twain certainly had a hand in editing the manuscript.

In any case the memoirs are very good books, not much read any more, which is a pity. Harry Truman felt that Grant was, despite his failure as President, a complex and interesting man, and judging by the memoirs, he was right.

Sherman, who was a Senator from Ohio and a brother of the old general who took Atlanta. Sherman didn't have the chance of a snowball in hell, but he was nominated by James A. Garfield, who had just been elected to the Senate from Ohio, and he gave what turned out to be the best speech of the convention. He was quite a great orator, Garfield was. On the day Lincoln was shot he was in New York, and the crowds were running wild, and they asked him to speak, someplace down in Wall Street, I believe. Asked him to speak to quiet people down, and he did. He said that . —. told people that sad as Lincoln's death was, he said something like the Republic would survive. It's in one of the books in the library here. You could look it up.*

"The second person named was James G. Blaine, who was from Maine and had been Speaker of the House for several terms. And then he was elected to the Senate, and he almost got the nomination for the Presidency in 1876, but he was . . . he had been accused of making a personal profit out of the sale of some railroad stocks and bonds and using his position in Congress to swing it."

Railroad corruption keeps turning up, it appears, all through American history. Why is that, do you suppose? Is it because . . . well, there used to be a man named Willie Sutton who robbed banks, and they asked him why he did it, and he said, "Because that's where the money is."

"That's part of it. That's part of it. The railroads have always been subsidized by the government, and they have always made enormous profits, and as we were talking

* Lincoln's assassination inspired one of Garfield's most memorable speeches. He stood on the steps of the Sub-Treasury building in New York and to the uneasy crowd below said, "Clouds and darkness are around Him; His pavilion is dark waters and thick clouds; justice and judgment are the habitations of His throne; mercy and truth shall go before His face! Fellow citizens, God reigns and the Government at Washington still lives!"

. . . saying the other day, very little looking into it is ever done. It's not like Wall Street and the Securities and Exchange Commission. The railroads just keep on being looted, and the greedy do it and get away with it."

Maybe the railroads should be socialized.

"That may be."

I waited for more, but there was no more. I guess that Harry Truman at that stage of his life wasn't going to let himself be accused of being a Socialist, not again.

I didn't press the issue, and we continued.

What kind of man was Blaine?

"Well, I've never thought he was much of any kind of man. He was in the Senate in 1880, and he was known as 'The Plumed Knight' because of his very fancy way of talking. He was one of those men . . . who just seem to spend their whole lives doing nothing but running for President, and it's been . . . I've always felt that the ones who want it too much and let it show too much, they never do make it for some reason or other.

"That was what happened in 1948, among other things. The fella that was running against me wanted to be President so much his tongue was hanging out, and it showed.

"The trouble with people like that, and there have been a lot of them in our history, if they ever . . . if by some chance they ever do get *elected,* they don't know what the hell to do. A lot of them haven't thought beyond just getting elected. Grant was a good example of that type, and there've been others more recently. They get elected, and they don't have a program.

"Once you get in the White House those—what-do-you-call-them—those Madison Avenue fellas can't bail you out, not all the time they can't.

"Anyway, in 1884 Blaine finally did get the Republican nomination, and he might have made it, too; he was running against Grover Cleveland, and everybody thought he'd be elected until a few nights before . . . maybe the night before the election some minister* in New York City introduced him as the candidate who was against 'Rum, Romanism, and Rebellion' and, of course, Cleveland's people made good use of that, and Blaine never did repudiate it for some damn reason, and he was licked.

"He lost New York State, and that was the end, except he did serve in the Cabinet of Benjamin Harrison and didn't do too bad a job of it, especially in Latin American affairs.

"He was a lightweight, though; at least that's my opinion."

But getting back to the Republican convention of 1880, he did not get the nomination that year.

"No, he did not. You've got to stop me from getting off the beam here; I get carried away some times."

Keep going right ahead and doing it. I've learned more American history during the time we've been talking than all the time I was in school, including college. More world history, too. And I must say it's a lot more interesting.

"Well, I'm glad you feel that way. I told you. If I hadn't got mixed up in politics, I might have been a history teacher. . . .

"But at that 1880 convention of the Republicans it finally got down to a race between Blaine and Grant. The big city bosses, Conkling of New York† and the bosses from Pennsylvania and Illinois, I forget their names, they wanted Grant again because they were pretty sure they could reelect him, and they knew that once he got in again, they could control him. Just as they always had.

* On October 29, 1884, the Reverend Samuel Dickinson Burchard in a speech introducing Blaine referred to the Democrats as the party of "Rum, Romanism, and Rebellion." The following Sunday Catholics in every church in New York City and a great many other places heard about that speech. Very few of them voted for Blaine.

† Roscoe G. Conkling, a U.S. Senator from New York who controlled all the federal patronage of the state when Grant was President. He placed the general's name in nomination at the convention.

They were called the Stalwarts, and the other side, the folks that were supporting Blaine, were called the Half-Breeds.

"The convention was completely deadlocked. They had thirty-five ballots, I believe, and finally Hayes [President Rutherford B. Hayes] got in touch with the fella that was running the convention and suggested to him that Garfield had made the best speech of the convention and why didn't they nominate him. And so on the thirty-sixth ballot they did.

"Garfield made the first of the front-porch campaigns; people came down to that little town in Ohio, whatever it's called [Mentor] to see him, and he got elected but by a very small margin, about ten thousand votes, I believe.

"And then, of course, after he was inaugurated in March, he only served until July, when he was shot in the back in the Baltimore and Ohio station in Washington. By a disappointed office seeker.

"And he was succeeded by Chester Arthur, the guy with the side whiskers and striped pants."

The one that was supposed to have kept a whore in the White House.

"That's what they tell on him, yes. . . . But getting back to where we started out, you can see how near Grant came to being nominated for a third term and, as I say, automatically practically reelected.

"But of course that didn't happen, and that's . . . after that he and Twain got together on his memoirs, and while they were working on them, Grant got cancer of the jaw, and he died a very painful death. But he was a stubborn cuss; he was in great, great pain, but he wouldn't . . . you might say he wouldn't *allow* himself to die until he'd finished. It's just like he was in the war and everything else he undertook. He wouldn't give up. He said once someplace in the war that he'd fight it out if it took all summer on the same front line, and that's the way it was with the memoirs.

"Of course, the funny thing about it. Grant. He was

living on borrowed time, you might say, for the last twenty years of his life, because if he'd . . . Lincoln asked him to go to the Ford Theater with him the night he was assassinated, but Grant and Mrs. Grant didn't go. They went up to visit their children someplace in New Jersey.

"If they had gone, though, Grant would have been shot because he was on the list of John Wilkes Booth."

I believe those memoirs turned out to be very successful, didn't they?

"Yes, they did. They made a lot of money for Twain, though he managed to lose it later, but they made a lot for Mrs. Grant, which always pleased me very, very much. Because otherwise, she'd have been under very hard circumstances. As she had been a good part of her life."

Mr. President, what really astounds me—if Grant had been nominated again in 1880, you say he'd have been reelected. Even though everybody knew that he'd been a very bad President.

"That's right."

How could such a thing happen? How could they even consider nominating him when he'd had such a poor record?

"How could they nominate Eisenhower for a third term and elect him? And that's what would have happened if the Republicans hadn't cut their own throats with that amendment [the twenty-second] they passed to stop another Roosevelt and limit the President to two terms. The damn thing wasn't ratified until 1951, and only nine years later, when 1960 came along, if it hadn't been for that damn amendment, they could have had Eisenhower in the White House for another four years. So instead they had to make *do* with somebody like Nixon.

"I would like to have been a mouse in the corner at some of the carrying-on I'll bet they did in private. I would just like to have been there and heard it."

Mr. Truman thought over that delicious possibility for a moment, and then he started laughing. He laughed for quite a long time. Or else he was chuckling dryly.

One thing I am sure of. He was enjoying himself hugely.

A little later I said, *Do you think Eisenhower could have defeated Jack Kennedy? We may have discussed this before; at the moment I can't remember.*

"Yes, I do. If Nixon came as close as he did to doing it, Eisenhower could have done it in a walk."

Mr. President, you said earlier this morning that you thought General Grant had never read the Constitution. Do you think Mr. Nixon has?

"I don't know. I don't know. But I'll tell you this. If he has, he doesn't understand it."

A Few Further Observations
on "Ike"

Mr. President, yesterday you said that if it hadn't been for the Twenty-second Amendment, Eisenhower would have been nominated in 1960 and reelected for a third term. Do you think the Republic could have survived another four years of him?

"Oh, yes. We survived those five poor Presidents that I'm going to tell you about, even though if they'd been stronger, we might not have had a Civil War. But what you have to understand is that the system we have under the Constitution that was set up by those fellows in Philadelphia has survived worse things than Eisenhower. Not much worse but some worse."

Getting back to Grant for a moment, do you think there are other parallels between Grant and Eisenhower, beyond the fact that they were both professional Army men and poor Presidents?

"For one thing, Grant was a hell of a lot better soldier than Eisenhower. What they never seem to say about Eisenhower is that he was . . . very weak as a field commander. When they had to fire that general* at Kasserine Pass, after the Kasserine Pass, Ike was in charge, but Marshall had to do the firing. Ike didn't have the guts to do it.

"Bradley was a great field soldier, but Ike wasn't. That job he had over there in London and in Paris [Supreme Allied Commander in Europe] what he was, what he did,

---

* After the fiasco at Kasserine Pass Major General Lloyd R. Fredendall was relieved of duty as commander of the II Corps. He was returned to the United States, actually fired. The official reason was that he would be of more value as a trainer of troops. I was unable to track down exactly who did the firing, although, again officially, it was Eisenhower. In any case he was replaced by General George C. Patton. Omar Bradley became Patton's deputy.

he presided at meetings mostly, and he approved strategy that had been drawn up by other people, but he never did *originate* anything. General Marshall was just the kindest man that ever was or ever will be, but he told me that Eisenhower had to be led every step of the way.

"But he, apparently, did well enough at that presiding job. They seemed to like him, but that's one of his troubles. He wanted, as President he wanted everybody to like him, and you can't have that.

"A President who's any damn good at all makes enemies, makes a lot of enemies. I even made a few myself when I was in the White House. And I wouldn't be without them. I wouldn't be without them."

Mr. President, as you know, there has been considerable debate about what was said between you and General Eisenhower at his headquarters in Frankfurt in 1945, at the time of Potsdam, about your volunteering to support him for President in 1948 if he wanted it.

"There's no reason for any debate about it. I saw him there in Frankfurt, and I told him how grateful the American people were for the job he'd done, and we talked about the fact that a lot of wartime heroes get into politics and get elected. And he said that under no circumstances was he going to get into politics at any time. And that's all there was to it. He said I said it, but I didn't.

"I've told you time and again how I feel . . . how I've always felt about professional military men in politics. It wouldn't have made any sense for me to promise a thing like that, would it? It would be against my whole philosophy, wouldn't it?"

Yes, sir. Totally against it.

"And it was the same thing in 1948; he said I offered him the Presidency, which I didn't. In the first place, it wasn't mine to offer. What happened, before he retired as Chief of Staff to go up there to Columbia we had a talk, and *again* he assured me he had no intention whatsoever of going into politics. I told him I thought that was the right decision, and it was. If he'd just stuck to it.

"There's a letter in my file in here which was written

by Eisenhower to the old man who runs the paper in
Manchester, New Hampshire,* that is the best analysis
I know of on why a military man can't possibly make a
good President. I never pulled it on him, but it's the best
possible analysis of why a military man can't be an executive in a republic. It's a crackerjack. It's just exactly what
the facts are.

"But I wouldn't have *ever* supported Eisenhower under
any circumstances for President even if I didn't . . .
hadn't known about his personal life."

*I'm sorry, sir. What do you mean about his personal
life?*

"Why, right after the war was over, he wrote a letter
to General Marshall saying that he wanted to be relieved
of duty, saying that he wanted to come back to the United
States and divorce Mrs. Eisenhower so that he could marry
this Englishwoman."

It took me a moment to recover from that one, and
then I said, *Do you mean Kay Summersby, who I believe
was his jeep driver?* †

---

* Leonard Finder, then publisher of the Manchester *Union
Leader*, placed Ike's name in the Republican primary, but
Eisenhower wrote him: "I could not accept nomination even
under the remote circumstances that it would be tendered
me. . . . The necessary and wise subordination of the military to civil power will be best sustained when life-long professional soldiers abstain from seeking high political office."

† Miss Summersby, a member of the British Women's
Auxiliary Corps, which later became the Women's Army
Corps, began her association with General Eisenhower as his
jeep driver. In *Crusade in Europe*, his single mention of her
comes when he discusses putting together his personal staff
in Algiers in December, 1942. He states, "Kay Summersby
was corresponding secretary and doubled as a driver."

But he does go on to pay tribute to women in wartime:
"Until my experience in London I had been opposed to the
use of women in uniform. But in Great Britain I had seen
them perform so magnificently in various positions, including
service in active anti-aircraft batteries, that I had been con-
verted. . . . From the day they first reached us their reputation as an efficient, effective corps continued to grow. Toward

"I think that was her name, yes. But I don't care what her name was. It was a very, very shocking thing to have done, for a man who was a general in the Army of the United States.

"Well, Marshall wrote him back a letter the like of which I never did see. He said that if he . . . if Eisenhower even came close to doing such a thing, he'd not only bust him out of the Army, he'd see to it that never for the rest of his life would he be able to draw a peace-

---

the end of the war the most stubborn die-hards had become convinced—and demanded them in increasing numbers. At first the women were kept carefully back at GHQ and secure bases, but as their record for helpfulness grew, so did the scope of their duties in positions progressively nearer the front."

In any case, Miss Summersby stayed with the general until November, 1945, and in 1948 her book was published— *Eisenhower Was My Boss*. On the jacket it says, "Hers is a portrait of General Eisenhower as few could see him, continuously, at moments of tension, making great decisions, during long hours of routine work, and while he relaxed at bridge or horseback riding.

"As the General's chauffeur, she was the guide who introduced him to wartime London and conducted him safely through pea-soup fogs. With him in Africa, Italy, France, and Germany, she first piloted his car to important conferences and on arduous inspection tours over roads scarred by battle and crowded with the matériel of war. Later, at headquarters, she was his receptionist, personal secretary, and aide."

Miss Summersby describes the end of their long relationship rather cryptically: ". . . on the last day of October, he gave me the nicest present of the war . . . or the peace: an empty seat on his plane, headed for Washington on official business.

"I took out my first papers toward becoming an American citizen.

"Arriving back in Germany after the short trip, I found the General packing. He was taking over from General Marshall [as Chief of Staff], who had postponed his retirement in order to carry out a Presidential assignment in China.

" 'I'm going to Washington tomorrow,' General Ike said as I entered the office. 'But I'll be back.'

"He didn't come back."

ful breath. He said it wouldn't matter if he was in the
Army or wasn't. Or even what country he was in.

"Marshall said that if he ever again even mentioned a
thing like that, he'd see to it that the rest of his life was a
living hell. General Marshall didn't very often lose his
temper, but when he did, it was a corker."

Mr. Truman was silent for a moment, and then he
said, "I don't like Eisenhower; you know that. I never
have, but one of the last things I did as President, I got
those letters from his file in the Pentagon, and I destroyed
them."

That was the first mention and the last of Miss Summersby and the exchange of letters between Generals
Marshall and Eisenhower.

A little later I said, *Mr. President, the other day when
we were making our first tour of the library, you showed
me the copy of* Crusade in Europe *that General Eisenhower inscribed to you. I'm sure you've read it, but I
was wondering, of the things you know about, how accurate is it?*

No answer. That was the only time in all our conversa-
tions that Mr. Truman didn't respond at all to a question.
So I waited a moment, then said, *Have you read General
Bradley's book* A Soldier's Story?

"Yes, I have, and that is a very good book. Bradley was
perhaps our greatest field general in the Second World
War, and in his book, he has . . . so far as I can make
out, he hasn't told a single lie. Of course he's a Missourian,
so maybe I'm prejudiced."

*Mr. President, were you surprised when Eisenhower
finally did become a Presidential candidate in 1952?*

"No, no. I could see it coming a long way back. I told
you. Once the bug bites a man, there are very few, generals or not, who can resist. And I never thought Eisenhower was one of those who could. He had . . . a very
high opinion of himself. Somewhere along the line he
seemed to forget all about the fact that he was just a poor
boy from Kansas."

After he got the nomination, did you think he'd be elected?

"When I saw the way the fellow that was running against him acted, I did. That fellow didn't know the first thing about campaigning, and he didn't learn anything either. He got worse in 1956."

Still you helped . . . Eisenhower's opponent out in 1952.

"Yes, I did. After Eisenhower got his picture taken with that fella from Indiana—what's his name?—the one that called General Marshall a traitor?"

Senator William Jenner.

"He got his picture taken with him, and then when he was in Milwaukee, he took out what . . . he was going to pay a tribute to General Marshall, but he took it out rather than stand up to McCarthy. It was one of the most shameful things I can ever remember. Why, General Marshall was responsible for his whole career. When Roosevelt jumped him from lieutenant colonel to general, it was on Marshall's recommendation. Three different times Marshall got him pushed upstairs, and in return . . . Eisenhower sold him out. It was just a shameful thing." *

---

* On October 3, 1952, Eisenhower made a speech in Milwaukee, Wisconsin, the home state of Senator Joseph R. McCarthy, then at the height of his influence and popularity.

Eisenhower spoke of freedom; he was all for it. He said, "To defend freedom . . . is—first of all—to *respect* freedom. This respect demands, in turn, respect for the integrity of fellow citizens who enjoy their right to disagree. The right to question a man's judgment carries with it no automatic right to question his honor."

Then, according to Emmet John Hughes, who wrote the speech, the general was to have said, "Let me be quite specific. I know that charges of disloyalty have, in the past, been leveled against General George C. Marshall. I have been privileged for thirty-five years to know General Marshall personally. I know him, as a man and a soldier, to be dedicated with singular selflessness and the profoundest patriotism to the service of America. And this episode is a sobering lesson in the way freedom must *not* defend itself."

Did you ever discuss it with General Marshall?

"Oh, no. Oh, my, no. You didn't discuss things like that with General Marshall. He would have been very much embarrassed if you'd even try."

I understand there were a few controversies between you and General Eisenhower about the inauguration in 1953.

"Yes, there were. . . . Eisenhower's got a reputation —and I don't see how it happened—of being an easygoing fella, but he isn't. He is one of the most . . . difficult. people I have ever encountered in my life. I'm told that when he was in the White House, he treated the staff worse than a bunch of enlisted men.

"But on this inaugural business. He wanted . . . he was going to treat the President the way MacArthur did at Wake Island, and I was still President until he was sworn in, and I wasn't going to stand for it.

"He wanted the President to pick him up, to come to the *Statler Hotel* to pick him up, and he hadn't even been inaugurated yet. A thing like that had never happened before in American history, and it indicated to me that not only didn't *he* know anything about American history, he didn't have anybody around him who did either. And as events developed in his administration, I guess that was about right.

"Why . . . the only time in history the President-elect hasn't come to the White House to pick up the new President was in 1801, when John Adams and Mrs. Adams left the White House before Jefferson was sworn in. And of course, Roosevelt didn't come in to escort Hoover out because he couldn't walk up the steps.

"But those were the only two times.

"Of course, you know what happened with Ike. He came to the White House to pick me up, but he wouldn't get out of the car. So I had to go out and get in. It was a

---

But Eisenhower never got specific. He never spoke those words. On the advice of unnamed Republicans in Wisconsin who persuaded him that they would be an *insult* to McCarthy, he deleted them. So much for his respect for freedom.

very shameful thing, and as you know, we didn't have much of a conversation on the way to the Capitol." *

Why do you think he was so rude?

"I think his conscience hurt him on the way he'd acted toward General Marshall. I'd let him know in no uncertain terms how I felt about it, and I think he was ashamed."

Maybe also he was nervous, realizing that he didn't know enough to be a good President.

"Maybe so, but I don't think he had the sense to know that he didn't know enough. The trouble with both of the

---

* In *Mr. Citizen*, which Mr. Truman wrote with the help of William Hillman and David M. Noyes, that ride is described as follows:

"The journey in the parade down Pennsylvania Avenue was quite restrained—as far as the occupants of the Presidential car were concerned. We began our trip in silence. Then the President-elect volunteered to inform me: 'I did not attend your Inauguration in 1948 out of consideration for you, because if I had been present I would have drawn attention away from you.'

"I was quick to reply: 'You were not here in 1948 because I did not send for you. But if I *had* sent for you, you would have come.'

"The rest of the journey continued in silence."

Also from *Mr. Citizen*:

"It was January 20, 1953, when it became my time to take part in the ceremonies of turning the office of the President over to Dwight D. Eisenhower. Washington, on that day, was cold and clear but not uncomfortable. The President-elect and I were sitting in the room of the sergeant-at-arms in the Capitol, waiting to go out through the Rotunda to the Inaugural platform.

"Suddenly General Eisenhower turned to me and said: 'I wonder who is responsible for my son John being ordered to Washington from Korea? I wonder who is trying to embarrass me?'

"I answered: 'The President of the United States ordered your son to attend your Inauguration. The President thought it was right and proper for your son to witness the swearing-in of his father to the Presidency. If you think somebody was trying to embarrass you by this order then the President assumes full responsibility.' "

candidates in 1952 and again with the same ones in 1956, they just couldn't make up their minds about things. I don't think the one who was on our ticket would have been a good President, but at least he knew something about the office. Ike didn't know anything, and all the time he was in office he didn't learn a thing.

"I'll give you an example. In 1959, when Castro came to power down in Cuba, Ike just sat on his ass and acted like if he didn't notice what was going on down there, why, maybe Castro would go away or something. Of course what happened, the Russians didn't sit on their ass, and they got him lined up on their side, which is what you have to expect if you've got a goddamn fool in the White House. He was probably waiting there for his Chief of Staff to give him a report, and he'd initial it and put it in his out basket. Because that's the way he operated.

"He came to see me. I invited him in not long after the election, and he didn't want to come; I think he didn't want to interrupt his golf game down in Florida or Georgia or wherever it was, but he finally did come. And he looked around a little, but I could see that nothing that was said was getting through to him. He got there mad, and he stayed mad. One of his troubles . . . he wasn't used to being criticized, and he never did get it through his head that that's what politics is all *about*. He was used to getting his ass kissed.

"At one point he says to me, 'Who's your chief of staff?' I held my temper. I said to him, 'The President of the United States is his own chief of staff.' But he just could *not* understand that. In all the years he was in the White House he never did understand that the President has to *act*. That's why the people of the United States elect you. They don't elect you to sit around waiting for other people to tell you what to do.

"Now when Castro came into power, if I'd been President, I'd have picked up the phone and called him direct in Havana. I wouldn't have gone through protocol or anything like that. I'd have called him up, and I'd have said,

'Fidel, this is Harry Truman in Washington, and I'd like to have you come up here and have a little talk.'

"He'd have come, of course, and he'd have come to the White House, and I'd have said, 'Fidel, it looks to me like you've had a pretty good revolution down there, and it's been a long time coming. Now you're going to need help, and there's only two places you can go to get it. One's right here, and the other's—well, we both know where the other place is. Now you just tell me what you need, and I'll see to it that you get it.'

"Well, he'd have thanked me, and we'd have talked awhile, and then as he got up to go, I'd have said to him, 'Now, Fidel, I've told you what we'll do for you. There's one thing you can do for me. Would you get a shave and a haircut and take a bath?' "

Mr. Truman, whose sense of timing was as good or better than any stand-up comedian I've ever heard, waited for the expected laugh, and when it was over, he said, "Of course, that son of a bitch⋅ Eisenhower was too damn dumb to do anything like that. When Castro decided to go in the other direction for support, Eisenhower was probably still waiting for a goddamn *staff report* on what to think."

As you may have observed, Mr. Truman was often a profane, a mildly profane man to me anyway, but "staff report" were the two dirtiest words he uttered in all our talks together.

I said, *Mr. President, what happened after the inauguration in January, 1953?*

"We had lunch at Dean Acheson's house, and then we got on the train and came home, and that was all there was to it."

28

Five Weak Presidents

Mr. President, you were saying the other day that you had great faith in the future of the Republic, that we had five weak Presidents before the Civil War, and that, having survived them, you feel we can survive almost anything. Could you tell me about them?

"That was one of the very worst periods in our history, the twenty-some years before Lincoln was elected, before the Civil War. And if we hadn't had those weak Presidents, we might not have had a Civil War, although that's just a guess on my part.

"What I do know is that when you have weak Presidents, you get weak results.

"There's always a lot of talk about how we have to fear the man on horseback, have to be afraid of the . . . of a strong man, but so far, if I read my American history right, it isn't the strong men that have caused us most of the trouble, it's the ones who were weak. It's the ones who just sat on their asses and twiddled their thumbs when they were President.

"It started out . . . this whole period started out in 18 and 40 when the Whigs nominated William Henry Harrison, the old fella we talked about the other day. Harrison was another one of those who was great for getting his name in the headlines and treating the truth with considerable carelessness. He was of the same ilk as MacArthur in that regard, although not so much so.

"The campaign of 1840 was the first one in which the Madison Avenue people took over. Only, of course, it wasn't Madison Avenue; it was just that the campaign was run by people who didn't know or care what Harrison's policy was. And anyway he didn't have any policy. He wouldn't of known what a policy was if he'd seen one.

"They made a very big thing out of the Battle of Tippecanoe in Indiana, which had taken place almost thirty

375

years before. In 1811, I believe it was, and it wasn't much of a fight, just a few hundred soldiers under Harrison's command and some Shawnee Indians, and some historians seem to feel it ended more or . . . in what might be called a draw, although the Indians withdrew.

"But Harrison wrote back to the Secretary of War in Washington saying practically that he'd won one of the greatest battles against the Indians since the Pilgrims landed at Plymouth Rock.* And he said he'd defeated the great Shawnee Indian chief Tecumseh, which wasn't the case at all. Tecumseh wasn't even there at the time; it was his brother, an Indian by the name of . . . he was called the Prophet.

"Harrison got away with it, though, because there wasn't anybody around to check up on him. There's a lot wrong with the newspapers and the radio and television and all of that, and we've talked about it. But in

---

* In *The Patriot Chiefs* Alvin M. Josephy, Jr., writes of the Battle of Tippecanoe: "The number of Indian dead . . . was never known, though it was estimated to be between 25 and 40. Harrison lost 61 killed and 127 wounded, but on his return to the settlements he announced that he had won a great victory and wrote to the Secretary of War that 'the Indians have never sustained so severe a defeat since their acquaintance with the white people.' The importance of the battle was soon exaggerated beyond reality, and in the flush of excitement many of the western settlers began to think that Harrison had beaten Tecumseh himself. The facts of what had been little more than an inconclusive swipe at a small segment of Tecumseh's followers never fully caught up with the legend of a dramatic triumph, and in 1840 the magic of Tippecanoe's memory still worked well enough to help elect Harrison to the Presidency."

I could find no sound evidence that Harrison himself claimed he had defeated Tecumseh, probably the greatest Indian chief in American history. Harrison's followers did make that claim, though, and General Harrison never denied it.

In 1813 in the Battle of the Thames River in Ontario Harrison's men actually did kill Tecumseh.

the long run, like Jefferson said, about newspapers, that is, we'd be worse off without them.*

"So as a result of Tippecanoe, Harrison got a somewhat inflated reputation as a general, and it kept him going for thirty years and finally got him into the White House, although not for long.

"The campaign slogan in 1840 was 'Tippecanoe and Tyler, Too.' I'll tell you about Tyler in a minute.

"And the people who were running the campaign claimed he'd been born in a log cabin, which was a damn lie. His family had . . . were very large landowners in Virginia, and his father, Benjamin Harrison, was one of the men who signed the Declaration of Independence.

"And Harrison himself had a big farm in Ohio, down near Cincinnati, I believe it was.

"But in the campaign that was never mentioned, and they sent out a log cabin on wheels around to various parts of the country. They also claimed he drank hard cider and wore a coonskin cap. It reminds me a little . . . and I wouldn't want this to get out . . . I wouldn't want to hurt anybody's feelings, but it reminds me of that fella from Tennessee that was aching to be President and went around getting his picture taken in a coonskin cap.†

---

* In a letter to Edward Carrington in 1787 Jefferson wrote: "The basis of our government being the opinion of the people, the very first object should be to keep that right; and were it left to me to decide whether we should have a government without newspapers, or newspapers without government, I should not hesitate a moment to prefer the latter. But I should mean that every man should receive those papers and be capable of reading them."

And in a letter to Elbridge Gerry in 1799 he wrote: "I am for . . . freedom of the press and against all violations of the Constitution to silence by force, and not by reason, the complaints or criticisms, just or unjust, of our citizens against the conduct of their agents."

† Estes Kefauver, a Senator from Tennessee, gained a national reputation in the early 1950's as chairman of a Senate committee investigating organized crime. He did a lot of cam-

"Of course the idea was that Harrison was a plain man of the people, while the fella that was President and he was a good, strong President, too, Martin Van Buren, they claimed he put perfume on his whiskers and ate on gold plates in the White House. That wasn't true either, but in that campaign, like at least one recent one that I could mention, the true facts didn't matter much.

"And, of course, Harrison won the election. He was sixty-eight years old, and on inauguration day he was showing off. It was raining cats and dogs, but he insisted on leading the inaugural parade back to the White House on horseback. He wouldn't wear a hat or coat or anything, and that was on March 4, 1841, and exactly one month later, on April 4, he was dead of pneumonia. So he . . . so I'm not counting him as one of the five. It's like he never had been President, and it's just as well. He wouldn't of had any notion at all of what to do.

"John Tyler, who succeeded him, was the first Vice President to become President, and he was the brother of my great-grandmother's father, and so he's kinfolk of mine in an indirect way. Margaret's got his nose. His picture's hanging in the family dining room, and I used to say, 'Margaret, look at your nose up there.'

"And she'd say, 'Turn that old man around; I don't want to see him.'

"Old Tyler. He was nominated for the Vice Presidency by the Whigs, although he was really more of a Democrat if he was anything. I never could figure out what he stood for, and I don't think the Whigs ever did either. I don't think they ever asked him. All they were interested in was getting Harrison in the White House. It just never seems to have crossed their minds that he'd catch pneumonia by acting like a damn fool—and die.

"Of course Tyler had been in the Virginia legislature

paigning for the Presidency posing as a kind of frontiersman in a coonskin cap. He was nominated for the Vice Presidency by the Democrats in 1956 but was defeated in the Eisenhower landslide, along with Adlai Stevenson.

and in Congress, and he was governor of Virginia and then was in the Senate. And he resigned from the Senate because the Virginia legislature wanted him to expunge a censure of Andrew Jackson from the Senate record. He wouldn't do it, and so you can't say he was . . . that he didn't have principles, but that's about all you can say for his record. In none of those jobs did he leave a record so that you could figure out what he stood for.

"And in the White House about the best thing you can say for him is that he was a stubborn cuss. The Whigs wanted him to let Daniel Webster, who was Secretary of State, and Henry Clay, who thought he ought to have got the Whig nomination in 1840 and been President . . . let those two run things. Tyler said, no; he said he wasn't about to be an acting President, and eventually he won out, and Webster resigned.

"But when that had been accomplished, Tyler couldn't seem to figure what to do next, and in the meantime the War Between the States was getting close to being inevitable, and Tyler and the ones that followed him just watched it happen. They were all one-term Presidents, and not one of them was able to fill the office they held."

I was reading about them last night, and as nearly as I can make out, they seemed to feel that if they just kept quiet and didn't rock the boat, the differences between the slave states and the free states and the opponents of slavery and the proponents would just disappear.

"That's right, and that's the one thing that won't ever happen, not in a million years. That's the *meaning* of government. If you're in it, you've got to govern. Otherwise, you're in the wrong business.

"Now Tyler, about the only thing he's gone down in history for, his wife died while he was President. He was in his fifties, and he married a rich young girl in her twenties. It was quite a scandal at the time.

"And so after those . . . after his years in the White House, he went back to Virginia, and he finally tried to call a last-minute peace conference of those other weak-

lings that had been in the White House. That was in
February, 1861, but, of course, it was too late, and nothing ever came of it.

"Tyler finally turned up in the Confederate Congress,
and that was the end of him."

Mr. President, it seems to me in the Memoirs *you spoke
rather more favorably of Tyler.*

"Did I? I don't remember. . . . Well, if I did, I must
have learned something since."

After Tyler came Polk.

"Yes. And Polk [James K.] was nominated by the
Democrats in Baltimore in 1844. He was a real dark
horse, and he was only nominated at all because the delegates to the Democratic convention in Baltimore in 1844
were deadlocked, and the Southerners didn't want Van
Buren.

"Of course during Polk's administration we fought and
won the Mexican War, which gave us more . . . a larger
area of new territory than at any time except for the
Louisiana Purchase. Polk had a good deal of trouble with
his Cabinet, though; he just couldn't seem to keep it in
line, and Mrs. Polk . . . she wouldn't allow any dancing
or cardplaying in the White House, and they say there
were times when she got it into her head that she herself
was President. She was a very strong-minded woman.

"Polk . . . after his term in office he went back to
Nashville, and he died within a month or so after leaving
the White House.*

"The next man . . . we talked about him the other
day was 'Ole Rough 'n' Ready,' old Zack Taylor, the
hero of Buena Vista, and he was another of those damn
fool generals that didn't know anything about politics,
nothing at all in any way, shape, or form, and so Daniel
Webster, who was Secretary of State, and Henry Clay ran
things, and after sixteen months in office, on July 4, 1850,

---

* Polk lived a little less than fifteen weeks after leaving
the White House and was buried in the dooryard of his home
in Nashville; his wife outlived him by forty-six years.

he went to an Independence Day celebration, and they say he ate too much watermelon and died.

"And the fella that took his place, the Vice President, was Millard Fillmore, who had started at the very bottom and worked his way up, and I think I told you, his son was ashamed of his father's origins, and after the old man's death, his son burned all his papers.

"Not that I mean to indicate that Fillmore was much of a President. He forgot all about his origins. He'd been born in a log cabin someplace in New York State and was apprenticed to a wool carder. He married a schoolteacher and started working his way up, but at the same time he started toadying to the rich, which he continued to do all the rest of his life, including when he was President. As a result, he was never any kind of leader. He did just what he was told, and what he was told was not to do anything to offend anybody. Which, of course, meant that he ended up by offending everybody.

"But he was just a no-good; he took to having his bath water perfumed, and he surrounded himself with every kind of luxury you could think of.

"As President he was . . . well, I'll tell you, at a time when we needed a strong man, what we got was a man that swayed with the slightest breeze. About all he ever accomplished as President, he sent Commodore Perry to open up Japan to the West, but that didn't help much as far as preventing the Civil War was concerned.

"And, of course, he was followed . . . Fillmore was followed to the White House by Franklin Pierce, finest-looking man who I guess ever was President. He's got the best picture in the White House, Franklin Pierce, but being President involves a little bit more than just winning a beauty contest, and he was another one that was a complete fizzle. He signed the bill that repealed the Missouri Compromise, and that did it. That started the Civil War. There just wasn't any holding it back after that because that's when the two-state war we were talking about began, the border raids on both sides of the border that separated Kansas and Missouri.

"Pierce was a friend of the fella that wrote *The Scarlet Letter*, Nathaniel Hawthorne, and when he was elected President, Hawthorne said to him, 'Frank, I pity you from the bottom of my heart,' and that's just about right. That's about what he should of done, felt sorry for him because Pierce didn't know what was going on, and even if he had, he wouldn't of known what to do about it.

"The last of them, of course, the last of these weak Presidents that brought on the Civil War, that at the very least allowed it to happen, was James A. Buchanan, and he was just like the fella that followed me into the White House. He couldn't make a decision to save his soul in hell.

"He was an old bachelor, and the only reason he got the nomination was that he'd been out of the country; he'd been the American ambassador to England, ole Pierce had sent him over, and as a result, Buchanan hadn't made any enemies to speak of on the slavery question.

"Another reason he got the nomination, he was from Pennsylvania, and in those days the Pennsylvania election was held in October. They figured if he could carry Pennsylvania in October, he could carry the whole country in the November election, and he did both.*

"When he was inaugurated, he was sixty-five years old, and he was another one of those fellas, he'd been trying to *be* President for twenty years, but when he got it, he didn't have the first idea what to do. By the time his four years was over he was in disgrace just about everywhere, and he died a very unhappy old man.

"But there you are, five men, Tyler, Polk, Fillmore, Pierce, and Buchanan, not counting Harrison and Taylor, and the five of them coming one right after the other made the Civil War inevitable. Not that I'm saying it might not have happened if we'd had strong men in office, but there's a chance that it wouldn't.

* In accepting the nomination, Buchanan said that he was really too old to enjoy it, that ". . . all the friends I loved and wanted to reward are dead and all the enemies I hated and had marked for punishment are turned my friends."

"They were no damn good at all, but they were all honorable men. It's a most interesting study to find out that the Presidents of the United States have all up to now been honorable men, whether you like them or agree with them or not. Not a corrupt man among them."

How can we have been so lucky? Or is it luck?

"No. Luck had nothing to do with it. It's due to the fact that we've got the best Constitution in the history of the world, and one of these days I'm going to read it to you and explain how these men who met in Philadelphia in 1787 made it great."

29

What Ruins a Man

We were sitting in Mr. Truman's office at the library during one of the interminable waits for film to be changed in a camera. It was after lunch, and I believe he had had a "libation" or two. His eyes were a little brighter than usual, his complexion a little pinker.

In any case, without warning, he said, "Do you want to know what I think causes the ruination of a lot of men?"

I said that I most certainly did. The question is one that has occurred to me now and again.

"Well," Mr. Truman said, "I've made a great, long study of these things, as you can see up there if you've looked."

He pointed to the bookshelves, which, as I've said, mostly contained biographies and histories.

"Three things ruin a man if you want to know what I believe. One's power, one's money, and one's women.

"If a man can accept a situation in a place of power with the thought that it's only temporary, he comes out all right. But when he thinks that he is the *cause* of the power, that can be his ruination.

"And when a man has too much money too soon, that has the same effect on him. He just never gets to understanding that getting enough money to eat and getting a roof over his head is the thing that throughout history most people have spent their lives trying to do and haven't succeeded. . . . If you've got too much money too soon, it ruins you by setting you too far apart from most of the human race.

"And a man who is not loyal to his family, to his wife and his mother and his sisters can be ruined if he has a complex in that direction. If he has the right woman as a partner, he never has any trouble. But if he has the wrong one or if he's mixed up with a bunch of whores, why, then he's in a hell of a fix. And I can name them to you, the ones that got mixed up in that way. But we won't do it now.

"Those three things, though, in my opinion, power, money, and women in that order, are what most often contribute to the ruination of a man. You read your history and you'll find out."

Like a great many of Mr. Truman's maxims, it is easy to dismiss these particular observations as hopelessly corny, especially the part about women. I think it can be safely said that Mr. Truman never got mixed up with a bunch of whores, not even when he was in France during the First World War. So far as I can make out, his only erotic experience Over There was in Paris, France, where he went to the Folies Bergères, which he found, and I quote, disgusting. I hesitate even to think how he would have reacted to the carryings-on of Miss Linda Lovelace in *Deep Throat*.

No, I think his knowledge of women was limited to his mother, his sister, Bess Truman, and Margaret. He was so painfully shy with all other women that he seemed to pretend they simply didn't exist. In our first meetings one of our party was a woman who fancied herself, I guess, a director, and Mr. Truman never once looked at her or addressed himself to her. In conversations with me he referred to her as "that other one." He would say, "I hope that other one isn't coming today."

Fortunately, she didn't last long. Not only did she make Mr. Truman nervous, she was a total incompetent. Like so many others in the project, she drifted off after putting together an hour of film that was totally incomprehensible.

Jane Wetherell, whom I have elsewhere described as "a girl who dresses in clothes you'll see in next month's *Vogue*," was coordinator of the television project, and if Mr. Truman absolutely had to address her it was as "young fella."

Ms. Wetherell is now the wife of Robert Alan Aurthur, and he described two occasions when she had to deliver material to Mr. Truman's suite at the Carlyle: ". . . he opened his door a crack, peered suspiciously at her for a moment before admitting her into the sitting room, and then very deliberately left the door wide open for as long as she was there. Both times, Jane reported, after Mr. Truman had nervously hustled her out, she heard safety bolts snapping closed behind her. A fella from Missouri never knows what kind of badger games New Yorkers will pull next."

So Mr. Truman didn't know much about women, but then during his tenure in office, Women's Lib was as outlandish as a suggestion that man might someday land on the moon. But what Mr. Truman has to say about power, its causes and effects, is both shrewd and sophisticated, and *that* was something he had to know about to be able to govern.

Mr. Truman never made the mistake of thinking that he was the *cause* of power.

The last time I was in Independence, in the fall of 1969, I talked as I had many times before to Miss Sue Gentry, who, as I've said, had been writing about Independence and the Trumans since 1929 for the Independence *Examiner*.

I said that the President must have been very upset a few months earlier when [in March 1969] Richard Nixon stopped off in Independence with Mr. Truman's old White House piano as a gift for the Truman Library.

Mr. Truman, then eighty-four, went to the library for the first time in several years, and he and Richard Nixon shook hands. The whole of the journey and the ceremony that followed must have been an effort, not only physically but mentally as well. But if an incumbent President of the United States was so crass and unfeeling as to carry out such hypocrisy, what was an old man who was an ex-President of the United States to do except go through the motions with a man he despised?

And then, to add to the insult and injury, Mr. Nixon sat down at the piano and played "The Missouri Waltz." Neither he nor anyone on his staff had apparently taken the trouble to find out that Mr. Truman hated that particular piece of music.*

Miss Gentry said, yes, it must have been a trying time for the President, but she added that Mr. Truman had been very hard of hearing in recent years and that when Nixon finished playing, Harry Truman turned to Bess and in a loud stage whisper asked, "What was that?"

It becomes increasingly difficult to know when to laugh and when to cry.

---

* In a television interview in 1962, when we still had some hope for the series, David Susskind interviewed Mr. Truman on *Open End,* and David said to him, " 'Missouri Waltz' isn't really your favorite song, is it?"

Mr. Truman said, " 'Missouri Waltz' was composed in 1911 or 12 or maybe as late as 1914 by a man from Iowa. And it was called 'Hushabye, My Baby.' And the Foster Music Company in New York bought it, changed the name of it, called it 'The Missouri Waltz,' and didn't take the words of it. You ought to read the words, and then you'd see why it's kind of obnoxious as a state song."

Susskind, "It's not your favorite number?"

Mr. Truman, "No, no. My favorite number is Chopin's A-Flat Opus 42 Waltz."

30

Of Painting and B. Berenson

It is easy to dismiss Harry Truman's taste for painting, nothing surprising about it. He was fond of Rembrandt's "Descent from the Cross." His favorite painters were Frans Hals, Rubens, Leonardo da Vinci, and Holbein. He liked Gilbert Stuart's portrait of George Washington. He thought as little of modern painting as he did of modern architecture. He was quoted as saying, "I love beautiful pictures, landscapes and portraits that look like people. We see enough of squalor. I think art is intended to uplift the ideals of the people, not pull them down."

Strictly George Babbitt, depressingly predictable, and yet . . . and yet. I had read that when Harry Truman and Bess were in Europe in 1956 they went to see Bernard Berenson, that awesome and feisty old man, who was then ninety-one. Incredible. Harry Truman at I Tatti? You have to be kidding.

One day I asked Mr. Truman about the visit, and he said, "Oh, yes, when we were in Europe, we just had to look him up. He was the best in his line, and if I've learned one thing in life, it's that you have to pay attention to what the experts say. You don't have to agree, but you have to listen.

"Old Berenson was one of the nicest fellows I've ever met, and he took us all over the house and explained to us what to look for in a painting. And when we got to those museums in Florence and elsewhere, we knew a little about it.

"When I found out that the Boss and I were going to be able to see him, I took the trouble to read up on him. If it's possible, I always do that before I meet somebody. The more you know about a person, the better you can judge him. Of course, you can't *always* depend on what you read. In the end, you have to make up your mind. You have to depend on your eyes and ears and your good

sense, and nine times out of ten you're right. Especially if
you give the other fellow the benefit of every doubt, and
I've always done that, always *tried* to anyway. . . . But
Berenson. He was really a remarkable fellow, and I wish
I'd got to know him better.

". . . Of course I already knew a *little* something about
painting. When I was a young fellow, I used to go to a
museum in Kansas City, and they always had a pretty
fair collection. . . . I never told anybody about it, my
going there I mean. In those days that was not the kind
of thing you talked about, not around here anyway."

I asked the President if during the years he was in
Washington he had spent much time in the National
Gallery.

He said, "When I was in the Senate, I used to go there
pretty often, but after I got into that other job, I just . . .
never could. In *that* damn job I couldn't even go to the
bank to cash a check without a crowd following me
around. Asking for autographs. And it's just like I told
you. Those folks who want autographs. They're just like
a bunch of pups. Once one of them pisses on a fire hydrant
then they've all got to do it."

In 1963 Bernard Berenson's *Sunset and Twilight* was
published, selections from his diaries for the years 1947–
58. By that time he had been putting down what he
thought of people for more than seventy years, and he
was not easy to please. Earlier in his life he had complained that Bertrand Russell and George Santayana never
really *listened;* André Gide, he felt, was too solemn and
quite unwilling "to recognize me as an equal." Henry
Adams was only interested in sounding off about im-
becility—"his own and the world's, in that order."

And only ten days before the Trumans came to I Tatti,
he had taken Mary McCarthy "to Gricigliano, back by
the Sieci and along the Arno. Tuscany at its most enchant-
ing moment, a wonder and a joy for my eye. But Mary
scarcely opened her eyes to all this beauty."

But on May 28, 1956, Bernard Berenson wrote:

Harry Truman and his wife lunched yesterday. Came at one and stayed til three. Both as natural, as unspoiled by high office as if he had gone no further than alderman of Independence, Missouri. In my long life I have never met an individual with whom I felt so instantly at home. He talked as if he had always known me, openly, easily, with no reserve (so far as I could judge). Ready to touch on any subject, no matter how personal. I always felt what a solid and sensible basis there is in the British stock of the U.S.A. if it can produce a man like Truman. Now I feel more assured about America than in a long time. If the Truman miracle can still occur, we need not fear even the McCarthys. Truman captivated even Willy Mostyn-Owen, aged twenty-seven, ultra-critical, and like all Englishmen of today hard of hearing anything good about Americans, and disposed to be condescending to them—at best.

On Evangelists

"It used to be you couldn't go downtown in the evening without running into a half dozen evangelists ranting and raving and carrying on; some of them put on their shows in tents or at camp meetings, and some of them just stood around on street corners and worked up a crowd. They'd stir people up for a while, but they always got over it.

"But now we've just got this one evangelist, this Billy Graham, and he's gone off the beam. He's . . . well, I hadn't ought to say this, but he's one of those counterfeits I was telling you about. He claims he's a friend of all the Presidents, but he was never a friend of mine when I was President. I just don't go for people like that. All he's interested in is getting his name in the paper."

An Attempted Assassination

On November 1, 1950, while President Truman was taking a nap at Blair House, the Presidential residence while the White House was being renovated, two Puerto Rican nationalists tried to break in to assassinate him. In three minutes thirty-two shots were fired, and one White House policeman was killed, as well as one of the Puerto Ricans.

I asked *Mary Jane Truman* about her memory of that day, and she said, "At the time . . . the day they attempted to assassinate my brother, I was the Grand Matron of the state in the Order of the Eastern Star, and I had two chapters to constitute down in what we call the boot heel of Missouri.

"And we had been driving that day down from Springfield, down into the boot, and we didn't have a radio in the car. So when we arrived there . . . the telephone rang just as I got there, asking for me. It was a call from St. Louis, and it was the FBI calling, but when they told me it was the FBI, I was sure they were mistaken. I was sure it was the Secret Service, and I was . . . you might say I was somewhat apprehensive, and when I got to the phone and they informed me that they . . . that an attempt had been made to assassinate Harry . . . they said it just like that, and, well, I was . . . I'm afraid I just kind of went to pieces. I was sure he had been hurt, but then they told me that he hadn't been, but they insisted on sending several guards . . . several guards were put on the place where I was. They thought . . . they seemed to think that other members of the family might be in danger, but I just pulled myself together, and I went ahead and constituted the chapter that night. And the next night we constituted another one in a little town about twenty miles from Pottersville and then went on into St. Louis from there."

Weren't you nervous?

"Oh, yes, I was nervous, but I went ahead and did what I . . . what had been set up for me to do. It certainly wouldn't have done my brother Harry or anyone else any good to worry about something that hadn't happened, and I knew that he felt very strongly about not losing sleep over that *kind* of thing.

"When they saw the guards, some of the others were much more upset than I was."

In speaking of the assassination attempt Mr. Truman told Admiral Leahy, "The only thing you have to worry about is bad luck. I never had bad luck."

I asked Mr. Truman about that remark and the assassination attempt, and he said—this was almost two years before John F. Kennedy was assassinated—"Well, I'll tell you. Getting shot at was nothing I worried about when I was President. It wouldn't have done the slightest good if I had. My opinion has always been that if you're in an office like that and someone wants to shoot you, they'll probably do it, and nothing much can help you out. It just goes with the job, and I don't think there's any way to prevent it." *

What did you do afterward . . . after the attempt?

"Why, I went and got dressed, and I went ahead and went out to Arlington Cemetery and made a speech dedicating a statue out there, and then I proceeded with the rest of my schedule. If you are President of the United States, you can't interrupt your schedule every time you feel like it. The people who put you there have a right to expect that you will carry through with the job."

Going ahead and doing your job seem to be characteristic of Trumans.

About luck Mr. Truman said, "You asked about being

---

* When Mr. Truman lectured at Columbia, he was asked his opinion of capital punishment, and he said, "Why, I've never really believed in capital punishment. I commuted the sentence of the fellow who was trying to shoot me to life imprisonment. That's the best example I can give you."

lucky, and I'd say, yes, I have been. To have gone as far as I did—a lot of it has to be luck.

"I told you. Around here I was never considered anything special. They never kept any records on me because they didn't think I'd amount to much.

"Around here they're like—a lot of people are like that old fella in New Salem, I forget his name, but he'd been a friend of Lincoln's, and after Lincoln was assassinated, they asked this old man what he remembered about him, and he said, 'Well, I had no idea he was going to be President, so I didn't take as much notice of him as I might have.' "

Mr. President, you may have been lucky, but you never . . . there's no point in your life when you seem to have trusted to luck.

"No, no. I was always out there pushing."

The Dean Resigns

I read only this afternoon that yet another book by a revisionist historian has been published, saying that Dean Acheson was a bloodthirsty cold warrior, and maybe that's true. The dean certainly believed in Russian containment and both as Undersecretary, and as Secretary of State he was an advocate of a hard-line policy against the Soviet Union.

Moreover, as you have seen, except for Harry Truman himself, no man was more responsible for the United Nations "police action" in Korea. So if, as the revisionists insist, guilt must be assigned, I guess Harry Truman and Dean Acheson were as guilty as anybody for the fix we're in, and any day now sainthood will be conferred on the late, beloved Joe Stalin, who was Christ-like by comparison.

Speaking of revisionists, Bob Aurthur has written: "It has been said that Mr. Truman reversed the Roosevelt philosophy of tolerant accommodation toward the Communist world, setting us a hard-line, anti-Communist, counterrevolutionary course, resulting in hot and cold wars, a trillion dollars spent on armaments, and a reversal of priorities that has virtually plundered and wrecked our planet. Yes, this charge can be made, if not proven, and in all of it Mr. Acheson concurred."

Yes, the revisionists may be right, although it seems to me far too early to tell, and I am always suspicious of those who would rewrite history to fit their convictions of the moment.

After reading Charles Beard's *An Economic Interpretation of the Constitution,* which takes a dim and narrowly Marxist view of the Founding Fathers and what they did in Philadelphia that hot summer in 1787, Justice Oliver Wendell Holmes wrote to his friend, the English jurist, Sir

Frederick Pollock, "You and I believe that high-mindedness is not impossible in a man."

Mr. Acheson, a friend and great admirer of Justice Holmes, was a high-minded man.

The dean was always controversial, of course. When he was in office, he was, as I have observed elsewhere, probably more hated than any Secretary of State in our history. Of course, then his detractors were of the right. They found him not too hard but too soft on Communism and the Communists, both the domestic and the international variety. If, in fact, he was not a Communist himself.

In his own account of his years as Secretary and before, *Present at the Creation,* Mr. Acheson reports on a meeting sponsored by the National Council of Soviet-American Friendship to which he had been assigned to speak in place of James F. Byrnes, then Secretary of State.

The tone of the meeting was best indicated by the fact that the keynote speaker was the Very Reverend Hewlett Johnson, the "Red" Dean of Canterbury Cathedral. The meeting was in Madison Square Garden, and Johnson received "a tumultuous ovation as he sashayed around the ring like a skater in the long black coat and gaiters of an English prelate, his hands clasped above his head in a prize fighter's salute."

Johnson's speech "became an antiphony, the Dean shouting the rhetorical questions, the crowd roaring back the responses. After an ovation, as much for themselves as the speaker, or for him as one of themselves, my hour had come," Mr. Acheson writes.

I felt like a bartender announcing that the last drink before closing time would be cambric tea. Fortunately mine was a short speech, but between me and the end of it was a paragraph of my own devising—one of the few. It followed an acknowledgment of the Soviet Union's reasonableness in desiring friendly governments along her borders. Then this: "But it seems equally clear to us that the interest in security must take into account and respect other basic interests of nations and men, such as the interest of other peoples to choose the general surrounding of their own lives and of all men to be secure in their persons. We believe that that adjustment of interests should take place short of the point where persuasion and firmness become coercion, where a knock on the door at night strikes terror into men and women."

I hurried on, trying to outrun the pursuing boos and catcalls, tossing to those wolves a quotation from Molotov and one from Stalin. But I had shown my colors; those who took their red straight, without a chaser of white and blue, were not mollified. When I finished, protest drowned out even polite applause. At the end of the ramp, a policeman touched me on the arm. "Come," he said. "I can show you a quiet way to your car." Nothing could have been more welcome, except possibly, the quiet scotch waiting for me at the friend's house where I was staying.

Some years later, during what has come to be known as the "McCarthy period," my presence at the Madison Square meeting was adduced as evidence of sympathy for communism. This seemed to me to add a companion thought to Lincoln's conclusion of the impossibility of fooling all the people all the time, the difficulty of pleasing any of the people any of the time.

Mr. Acheson seemed to infuriate people without half trying, and while his friends insisted that he was serious, he was irritatingly unsolemn, and as we all know, a solemn man is a man who can be trusted.

As Undersecretary he was asked how it had happened that Soviet Ambassador Nikolai Novikov had been held incommunicado at LaGuardia Airport for refusing to sign a customs declaration which, as a diplomat, he did not have to sign. Mr. Acheson replied, "I will have to give you the celebrated answer of Dr. Johnson—'Ignorance, madam, pure ignorance.' He was likely to begin an address at a solemn meeting of State Department officials from this and other countries by saying, "All I know I learned at my mother's knee—and other low joints."

Once when helping with the manifesto for a United Nations program to help feed postwar Europe, he suggested that a phrase be changed from "expectant mothers" to "pregnant women."

He told the delegates, "A maiden aunt of fifty-one once told me that she was an expectant mother. What you mean here is 'pregnant women.' "

As I have said, scarcely a week went by when Senator Joseph McCarthy did not demand his resignation, and a great many less hysterical members of both houses of Congress broke into a rash at the mere mention of his name. Senator Hugh Butler, one of the Neanderthal men that Nebraska with depressing regularity seems to send to Congress, once said, "I watch his smart-aleck manner and his British clothes and that New Dealism, everlasting New Dealism in everything he says and does, and I want to shout, 'Get out, get out. You stand for everything that has been wrong with the United States for years.' "

Once at a press conference when such attacks were at their most hysterical he was asked how they affected him, and he said that he was reminded of the man found on the Western plains during the days of Indian fighting. He was brought to a fort hospital and in examination found to be scalped and, among numerous other injuries, to have an arrow sticking in his back.

As the doctor prepared to take out the arrow, he asked, "Does it hurt very much?"

"Only when I laugh," said the man.

I'm inclined to think that the historian Douglas Southall Freeman best summed up the dean's lack of easy popularity. Mr. Freeman wrote, "Acheson found it difficult to conceal his contempt for the contemptible."

When I met Mr. Acheson, it was easy to see why he unnerved a great many people. He was tall, broad-shouldered, carried himself like a British cavalry officer, wore a precisely trimmed mustache that still bore some traces of red, and had deep-blue eyes that I at first thought

were cold, possibly even cruel. I later changed my mind
about that. His eyes were amused more often than not,
and they were extraordinarily warm when he was discussing his association with Harry S. Truman or George Catlett
Marshall.

Dean Acheson's father had been the Episcopal Bishop
of Connecticut, and his mother was the heiress of a
wealthy Canadian distilling family. He had gone to Groton,
to Yale, and to Harvard Law School, where he was graduated near the head of his class.

In confronting the dean it always gave me some slight
comfort to remember that a friend at Yale and his room-
mate at Harvard was a witty young man from Indiana who
never quite made it in the law, Cole Porter.*

One of Acheson's professors at Harvard, Felix Frankfurter, recommended him as a clerk to Louis D. Brandeis,
Associate Justice of the U.S. Supreme Court, and he spent
two years in that capacity, soaking up a good deal of
Brandeis' libertarian philosophy as well as the liberalism
of Brandeis' close friend and associate Justice Oliver Wendell Holmes.

Acheson was fond of quoting Holmes' advice on the
way to achievement: "If you want to hit a bird on the
wing, you must have all your will in a focus. You must
not be thinking about yourself, and, equally, you must not
be thinking about your neighbor; you must be living with
your eye on that bird. Every achievement is a bird on the
wing."

And that, he once told me, was what Harry Truman and
George Catlett Marshall had in common. They lived with

---

* More accurately they were housemates. In: *The Life That
Late He Led: A Biography of Cole Porter* George Eells writes
of that time: "In various ways, all during his sojourn at
Harvard, Cole persisted in trying to turn it into a little patch
of Yale. The fall of 1915, he joined a number of Scroll and
Key men from New Haven, including Dean Acheson and
T. Lawrason Riggs, in renting a house at 1 Mercer Circle. To
care for the place, they hired a man who cleaned, prepared
one meal daily, and served tea for them and their guests every
afternoon at four."

their eyes on the task at hand. He would not, Mr. Acheson said, place himself in that category; that would be presumptuous.

Most of those who knew him well would have so placed him, though, including Harry Truman. I asked Mr. Truman why it was that he, a man suspicious of Eastern intellectuals and in particular those with what he contemptuously called Ha-vud accents, had got along so well with such a one as Dean Acheson.

Mr. Truman said, "Because I knew . . . I sensed immediately that he was a man I could count on in every way. I knew that he would do what had to be done, and I knew that I could count on him to tell me the truth at all times.

"I've said this before, but when you get to be in a position of authority, which I was at that time, that's the most important thing there is. You've got to be able to count on a man's word, and if you can't, forget it. . . . I've had experience with the other kind as well, and that's the *worst* thing there is. A liar in public life is a lot more dangerous than a full, paid-up Communist, and I don't care who he is."

An odd combination those two, the plainspoken man who was a dropout after two years of night classes at the Kansas City Law School and the austere Grotty and honors graduate of Harvard Law. Mr. Acheson has written: "In the last analysis Mr. Truman's methods reflected the basic integrity of his own character. He could have said of them what Mr. Lincoln said of his: 'I desire to so conduct the affairs of this administration that if, at the end . . . I have lost every friend on earth, I shall have one friend left, and that friend shall be down inside me.'"

There is a kind of rueful satisfaction in writing those words, as I am, on the final day of John Mitchell's testimony before the Watergate Committee.

It is impossible to imagine Mr. Truman and Mr. Acheson telling less than the truth to each other.

At first Mr. Acheson refused to have anything at all to

do with the television project. He was furious when he heard that David Susskind's company was in charge of the project. Not long before David, the eternal Candide, had conducted a haphazard television interview with Nikita Khrushchev during which Nikita proved, among other things, that he was a very smart cookie. David proved that he was more than somewhat naïve where international affairs were concerned.

But, otherwise, their hardly historic exchanges seemed to me innocent enough. Not to Mr. Acheson. His eyes glowering, his mustache bristling, the dean said, "Susskind almost started the third world war with that *insane* interview. I decline to be associated with him in any way."

Bob Aurthur explained that David was not directly involved in the project, and I nodded vigorously. No matter. We were, as Bob later wrote, "sent, if not flung, out into the snow."

But two days later, after a telephone call from Mr. Truman in Independence to Mr. Acheson in his Dickensian law offices in Washington—I always felt like Pip the first time he went to Mr. Jaggers' offices in London, fresh from the country—the dean agreed to cooperate with us. After that I spent, sometimes with Bob, more often alone, several afternoons with him, mostly talking about Korea and about Mr. Truman.

I didn't tape any of those conversations; if you want the truth, I was afraid to ask for permission. But immediately after each session I hurried back to the Statler and typed up all of Mr. Acheson's stately sentences; they are not easily forgotten.

I should add that while I always apologized for taking too much of the dean's time, despite the fact that he was a highly successful lawyer, as well as a very visible social figure in Washington, he always urged me to stay just a little bit longer, and I always did. I had the feeling, very likely wrong, that he was lonely, not so much lonely for other people as lonely for the power he once had, lonely for the days when, for good or ill, he and his friend Harry had the fate of what in those days was called "the free world" in their hands, almost alone in their hands.

One thing for sure. He loved talking about those days, and I don't think that there was a single doubt in his mind that what he and Harry had done was right, that, indeed, it had saved the world, all of it, not just the free part, from total disintegration. The regrets were, as he says in *Present at the Creation,* only those of Holmes who on his fifty-ninth birthday spoke at a meeting of the Massachusetts bar, summing up his years on the supreme judicial court of that state:

"I ask myself what is there to show for this half lifetime that has passed? I look into my book in which I keep a docket of the decisions of the full court which fall to me to write, and find about a thousand cases, a thousand cases, many of them upon trifling or transitory matters, to represent nearly half a lifetime. . . .

"Alas, gentlemen, that is life. . . . We cannot live our dreams. We are lucky enough if we can give a sample of our best, and if in our hearts we can feel that it has been nobly done."

To which Mr. Acheson adds:

Of the years covered in this book the first five were for me preparation for the last seven. Those seven, the period of Mr. Truman's Presidency and of the immediate postwar years, saw the entry of our nation, already one of the superpowers, into the near chaos of a war-torn and disintegrating world society. To the responsibilities and needs of that time the nation summoned an imaginative effort unique in history and even greater than that made in the preceding period of fighting. All who served in those years had an opportunity to give more than a sample of their best. Yet an account of the experience, despite its successes, inevitably leaves a sense of disappointment and frustration, for the achievement fell short of both hope and need. How often that which seemed almost within grasp slipped away. Alas, that is life. We cannot live our dreams.

I do not know if, before Mr. Truman's death, Mr. Acheson was aware of the revisionists or, if he was, what he thought of their conclusions.

I am sure, though, that he would have deplored their prose. Without exception they write as if English was a second language that they will never quite master.

Of course, the fact that they are ponderous may account for their popularity.

One afternoon I told Mr. Acheson that I might someday write a book about Harry Truman, and I paraphrased Jonathan Daniels' comment that so far as Mr. Truman was concerned, "never has so little been rewritten by so many."

Mr. Acheson said, "I have never understood why the press did such an *abysmally* poor job in writing about the President. . . . *That's* something you should consider in your book. It's as if the correspondents had made up their minds when Mr. Truman became President that he was a country bumpkin, and I am afraid a great many of them never changed their minds.

"I have read over and over again that he was an *ordinary* man. Whatever that means . . . I consider him one of the most extraordinary human beings who ever lived.

"The difference between the public image of him and the private man that I knew was vast, greater than for any public figure I have ever known."

Mr. Acheson had for a short time in 1933 been Undersecretary of the Treasury in Franklin Roosevelt's administration, but he had resigned over a disagreement over the devaluation of the dollar. Roosevelt was furious with him, although seven years later, in February, 1941, after a lengthy courtship on Roosevelt's part, Acheson returned to the fold as Assistant Secretary of State.*

* Mr. Acheson has written that his feeling toward Roosevelt was one of "admiration without affection."

In his book *Morning and Noon* he adds: "The impression given me by President Roosevelt carried much of this attitude

I said, *Mr. Secretary, was there a greater difference between Mr. Truman's public image and his private self, greater than the public and the private Franklin Roosevelt?*

"Indeed yes. So far as I could ever discover, there was really very little difference between Roosevelt the public figure and Roosevelt the private man. Roosevelt was all surface. If there were hidden depths in him, I never discovered them, although I suppose it could with justice be said that I did not spend too much time searching for them.

"Roosevelt had great *charm* [Mr. Acheson made the word an epithet], but I have never thought highly of charm in a man; for that matter, I have never thought particularly well of charm in a woman.

"I have never been an admirer of the work of Sir James M. Barrie, and I believe him to have been wrong in what

of European—not British—royalty. The latter is comfortable, respectable, dignified, and bourgeois. The President could relax over his poker parties and enjoy Tom Corcoran's accordion, he could and did call everyone from his valet to the Secretary of State by his first name and often made up Damon Runyon nicknames for them, too—'Tommy, the Cork,' 'Henry, the Morgue,' and similar names; he could charm an individual or a nation. But he condescended. Many reveled in apparent admission to an inner circle. I did not; and General Marshall did not, the general for more worthy reasons than I. He objected, as he said, because it gave a false impression of his intimacy with the President. To me it was patronizing and humiliating. To accord the President the greatest deference and respect should be a gratification to any citizen. It is not gratifying to receive the easy greeting which milord might give a promising stable boy and pull one's forelock in return.

"This, of course, was a small part of the man and the impression he made. The essence of that was force. He exuded a relish of power and command. His responses seemed too quick; his reasons too facile for considered judgment; one could not tell what lay beneath them. He remained a formidable man, a leader who won admiration and respect. In others he inspired far more, affection and devotion. For me, that was reserved for a man of whom at that time I had never heard, his successor."

he wrote about charm.* As he was in so much else that he wrote.

I said—this is known as White House dropping—*I had* substitute for intelligence in persons of both sexes. Thus, I have always been and will remain wary of it."

I said—this is knowin as White House dropping—*I had dinner at the White House twice while Mr. Roosevelt was President, and it seemed to me that he was incapable of listening. Perhaps that's unfair. He didn't seem to me to listen. Would you agree that that was usually the case, sir?*

The dean smiled, and his eyes were very pleased.

He said, "The ability to listen is very rare. I have known very few men, particularly men in high places, who have been able to do it. Most public men I have known were not accustomed to the sound of any voice save their own. And Roosevelt was very high among them.

"I must add that Mr. Truman not only had the ability to listen, he could *hear*, which is quite another thing. And at the end of a conversation, he not only remembered what he had heard, he understood and made use of it."

Mr. Secretary, how would you define the difference between the public Harry Truman and the private Harry Truman?

"One difference is that the picture of Mr. Truman that has emerged through the press is that of a man who, to use that questionable phrase that I believe originated in what is known as the Old West, was inclined to 'shoot from the hip.'

"And indeed, very often in his press conferences it was difficult to restrain Mr. Truman. Once he was asked a

---

* In his play, *What Every Woman Knows*, Sir James M. Barrie wrote:

"*Alick.* What *is* charm, exactly, Maggie?

"*Maggie.* Oh, it's—it's a sort of bloom on a woman. If you have it, you don't need to have anything else; and if you don't have it, it doesn't much matter what else you have. Some women, the few, have charm for all; and most have charm for one. But some have charm for none."

question, he was inclined to answer it when it might have been the better part of valor to maintain silence. Perhaps, however, that was the price to be paid for his utter lack of guile. Mr. Truman was perhaps the most guileless man ever to reach such high office.

"His answers to the press were never calculated, never, for that matter, calculating. But as a result, he earned the reputation of being a *peppery* man, an impatient man.

"In his private associations with the people in his administration, he was perhaps the kindest and most patient man in my memory.

"But to me his greatest quality as President, as a leader was his ability to decide. General Marshall, who also had that quality, has said that the ability to make a decision is a great gift, perhaps the greatest gift a man can have. And Mr. Truman had that gift in abundance. When I would come to him with a problem, the only question he ever asked was, 'How long have I got?' And he never asked later what would have happened if he had decided differently. I doubt that that ever concerned him. He was not a man who was tortured by second thoughts. Those were luxuries, like self-pity, in which a man in power could not indulge himself.

"I would say that Mr. Truman had an Aristotelian understanding of power. He had not only read the Greek and Roman philosophers, he understood them. And by understanding what men had done in the past he was able with a sometimes terrifying reality to anticipate what a man would do in the present. He had an almost unbelievable ability to judge character.

"And he was as near to being totally unselfish as any man I have ever known, with the possible exception of General Marshall.

"Mr. Truman was a good friend of Justice Brandeis, and when he was in the Senate, he used to go, almost every week, I believe, to the Justice's at-homes. On Monday evenings.

"It may have been Justice Brandeis who told him, as

the Justice once told me, that: 'Some questions can be decided even if not answered.' He meant by that that it isn't always necessary for all the facts on a given situation to be available. They almost never are, perhaps never are.

"And it isn't necessary that one side be wholly right and the other totally wrong, because that seldom happens either.

"It is enough, the Justice used to say, that the scales of judgment be tipped in one direction, and, *after* a decision is made, he would say, 'One must go forward wholly committed.'

"I have been with Mr. Truman through a great many decisions, foreign policy decisions, decisions about war, peace, whether or not to go through with a difficult, unpopular operation, and never once have I seen him pause to consider whether or not he ought to do something because of its possible effect on his electoral future or the political future of his party.

"Now I can understand that many people would think this isn't a compliment, and it isn't really meant as a compliment. It is meant as an analysis of the man.

"I suppose that a President has to remain President in order to do great things, and therefore he ought to do *sensible* things to be reelected. But I am also perfectly certain that if too many things get between the President's vision and the target he's shooting at, his vision is going to be deflected. Ambition is one of the great things that intervenes. Political considerations. Will this get me votes or will it lose me votes? That deflects the aim.

"Ego is a great deflector of aim. One of the major elements of Mr. Truman's greatness is that these matters did not get between his eye and the bull's-eye. He looked at what he was doing without the myopia of ambition or extraneous events or any of the other weaknesses of important people.

"I hope you will be able to get some of that feeling about Mr. Truman into your book.

"As you know, I have been associated with some extraordinary men, but to me, of them all, Harry Truman was the most remarkable, the most extraordinary."

Mr. Secretary, I read someplace that several years ago you said you had known two great men in your life and one who was near great. And that the first two were Justice Holmes and General Marshall.* You were quoted as saying that the third was Justice Brandeis.

"Oh, dear, did I say that? I must say I don't remember saying it, although I shouldn't wish to deny that I *may* have said it. In any case, if I *did* say it, it must have been early on, very early on in my association with Mr. Truman, and I would now amend what I may have said to place him in the very front ranks. With General Marshall . . . his greatness was immediately apparent. With Mr.

---

* In his book *Sketches from Life* Mr. Acheson has written: "The moment General Marshall entered a room, everyone in it felt his presence. It was a striking and communicated force. His figure conveyed intensity, which his voice, low, staccato, and incisive, reinforced. It compelled respect. It spread a sense of authority and of calm. There was no military glamour about him and nothing of the martinet. Yet to all of us he was always 'General Marshall.' The title fitted him as though he had been baptized with it. He always identified himself over the telephone as 'General Marshall speaking.' It seemed wholly right, too. I should never have dreamed of addressing him as 'Mr. Secretary'; and I have never heard anyone but Mrs. Marshall call him 'George.' The General expected to be treated with respect and to treat others the same way. This was the basis of his relationships.

". . . President Truman has put his finger on another foundation of General Marshall's character. Never, wrote the President, did General Marshall think about himself. . . . With General Marshall self-control came, as I suppose it always comes, from self-discipline. He was, in a phrase that has quite gone out of use, in command of himself. He could make himself go to bed and go to sleep on the eve of D Day, because his work was done and he must be fresh for the decisions of the day to come. He could put aside the supreme command in Europe in favor of General Eisenhower because it was his plain duty to stay in the Pentagon dealing with that vast complex of forces which, harnessed, meant victory."

Truman it was less immediately apparent, but that did not in any way detract from its existence.

"But should we not get into other matters? I have no taste for playing God, I leave that to others. The world is filled with people who like nothing better."

Being certain that I knew the answer, I said, *Mr. Secretary, have you ever had any regrets over what you said about Alger Hiss after his conviction in January, 1950?*

Mr. Acheson must have been expecting that one because he hesitated for just a moment; then he said, and at no time had he sounded more positive, for that matter more eloquent, "I have in common, surely with all other human beings, surely this is the universal experience, even among the highest and most mighty, many regrets. Decisions that were wrong, decisions that were evaded, words that I should have spoken and did not speak, words that I did not speak that I should have.

"In short, like every man, I have many regrets, but what I said on that day is not among them. I could wish that I had said it better, but what I said came close to what I intended saying, and that is, I imagine, enough to ask.

"I had, of course, given a great deal of thought to what I would say about Alger Hiss if I were asked, and I knew I would be asked. I even consulted Mrs. Acheson on the matter, and she said, and rightly, that there are some decisions, the loneliest decisions, I suppose, the most important, that *no one* can share. And so that morning, feeling naked and most vulnerable, I said what I felt I had to say."

One of the discomforts of being fifty or so is that what I expect everyone to remember a great many people do not remember, in many cases, alas, because they weren't born at the time. Thus, for those who missed the case that was to my generation what the Dreyfus case was to that of Emile Zola, a few words about Alger Hiss.

Like Acheson, Hiss was a graduate of Harvard Law

School. Acheson received his degree in 1918, Hiss in 1929. He had been a brilliant student, and Felix Frankfurter, then a professor, recommended that Hiss become the secretary to Justice Oliver Wendell Holmes, which for a year he was. Later he was one of the young New Dealers in the Agricultural Adjustment Administration and the Justice Department. In 1936 he joined the Department of State, and he was an adviser at a good many foreign conferences, among them the one at Yalta among Roosevelt, Churchill, and Stalin. He was never, however, in the first echelon of State Department officials, and in 1947 he resigned to become president of the Carnegie Endowment for International Peace.

The next year Whittaker Chambers, a vast, untidy man who had become a senior editor at *Time* magazine, accused Hiss of being a Communist. Later he said that Hiss had turned over some confidential documents—they turned out to be of minimal importance—to him, and he in turn, he said, had turned them over to the Russians. This had all happened, if it happened, in the thirties, just when in the thirties was a matter of some dispute, but that need not concern us here. What matters is that too much time had elapsed for Hiss to be charged with espionage, but he could be and was tried for perjury.

And while his two trials were going on—the first ended with a hung jury—it was impossible to go anywhere, in Washington or New York anyway, without getting into an acrimonious discussion about whether Hiss or Chambers was telling the truth. Chambers was not easy to love. Not only was he untidy, but he had had an erratic career and was clearly far gone into paranoia.

Hiss, on the other hand, seemed to have been a model public servant. He was an outwardly gentle, undeniably brilliant, rather elegant man of whom, according to Murray Kempton,* a Harvard classmate once said, "I remem-

---

* In *Part of Our Time,* a book about the thirties that was published and widely admired in the fifties, Mr. Kempton writes: "Alger Hiss and Whittaker Chambers are two ex-

THE DEAN RESIGNS 411

THE DEAN RESIGNS 411

ber Alger Hiss best of all for a kind of distinction that had
to be seen to be believed. If he were standing at the bar
with the British Ambassador and you were told to give a
package to the Ambassador's valet, you would give it to
the Ambassador before you gave it to Alger.

"He gave you a sense of absolute command and absolute grace. . . ."

Even Chambers described him as having, among other,
less admirable qualities, "an unvarying mildness, a deep
considerateness and gracious patience."

As the Hiss trials progressed, those on the lunatic right,
and at the time that seemed to include a good part of the
Republican Party, became more and more persuaded that
not only were Acheson and Hiss both Harvard men, but
they were both too piss-elegant for comfort, and they were
undeniably fellow traitors.

Actually, their association, both personally and profes-
sionally, was scarcely more than casual. Mr. Acheson has
written: "I had known him since his graduation from Harvard Law School . . . but had no close association with
him until in 1946 his work in charge of United Nations
liaison in the Department brought him under my supervision. His brother, Donald, however, had served as my
assistant from 1941 through March 1944, and was, in
1949, as he is at the time of this writing, one of my
partners in the practice of law. This is the first appearance
of the Alger Hiss affair in this book. It is enough to say
of it here that at the time of the hearings [on Acheson's
confirmation as Secretary of State by the Senate Committee on Foreign Relations] what had seemed in the beginning incredible and bizarre had moved into personal tragedy. It was destined to go on to something approaching
national disaster, lending, as it did, support to a widespread attack throughout the country upon confidence in
government itself."

traordinary men; yet it has been their fate, accepted by
Chambers and forced upon Hiss, to be treated as typical of
the decade through barely three years of which they were
drawn together and so inextricably involved."

So much for the Hiss-Acheson connection. What concerns us here is that the second jury chose to believe Chambers, warts and all, rather than the impeccable and unflappable Hiss. On January 21, 1950, Hiss was found guilty of two counts of perjury, and at his weekly press conference four days later Dean Acheson was asked if he had any comment on the case.

Acheson said that he would not discuss the legal aspects of the case because it was still in the courts. But then with a passion rare, perhaps unprecedented in an American Secretary of State, particularly one who was the son of an Episcopal bishop, Mr. Acheson leaned forward in his chair and said, "I take it the purpose of your question was to bring something other than that out of me. I should like to make it clear to you that whatever the outcome of any appeal which Mr. Hiss or his lawyers may take in this case I do not intend to turn my back on Alger Hiss. I think every person who has known Alger Hiss or has served with him at any time has upon his conscience the very serious task of deciding what his attitude is and what his conduct should be. That must be done by each person in the light of his own standards and his own principles. I think they were stated for us a very long time ago. They were stated on the Mount of Olives and if you are interested in seeing them you will find them in the 25th Chapter of the Gospel according to St. Matthew beginning with verse 34.

"Have you any other questions?" *

* On the night of January 25 Dean Acheson wrote to his daughter: "This has been one of those days easy in the intrinsic tasks, but hard and exhausting because of what was added. Today Alger Hiss was convicted and today I had my press conference. Alger's case has been on my mind incessantly. As I have written you, here is stark tragedy—whatever the reasonably probable facts may be. I knew that I would be asked about it and the answer was a hard one—not in the ordinary sense of do I run or do I stand. That presented no problem. But to say what I really meant—forgetting the yelping pack at one's heels—saying no more and no less than one

In *Present at the Creation* Mr. Acheson adds: "After the press conference was over, Mike McDermott, Special Assistant for the Press, who had served secretaries since Mr. Hull, walked with me in silence to my door. 'I am going to ask a favor of the Secretary of State,' he said, 'which I have asked only once before in my service. May I shake your hand?'

"We shook hands and parted."

Eleven years later, almost to the day, Mr. Acheson looked at me and said, "I remember that occasion very well, and I remember going to the President in the late afternoon in great despair. As I told you, I had been asked a question I had long expected, and I had answered it as I felt I had to, but I had not anticipated the . . . the intensity of the reaction. Within an hour the newspapers were filled with headlines about my statement, and I felt that I had perhaps made it impossible for me to continue in office, that quite possibly my usefulness was at an end, and so that afternoon I went to the President to offer my resignation.

"The President already knew what had happened; he had seen the ticker tape.

"He looked at me, and he said he understood why I said what I had said. He said he knew all about friendship, that not too long before he had flown to the funeral of a friend, Tom Pendergast, and he said, 'You should have seen the headlines and the carrying-on when I did that, but Tom Pendergast was a good and loyal friend, and he

truly believed. This was not easy. I felt that advisers were of no use and consulted none. I understood that I had responsibilities above and beyond my own desires. And all this one had to handle dependent upon the fall of some fool's question at a press conference.

"At the end of the day I am tired, but I have no idea that there was any better way, though one could have wished for better words and thoughts in that crowded and slightly hot and sweaty room."

never asked me to do a dishonest deed, and so I went to his funeral, and, eventually, it all blew over, and this will, too. In the long run, after all the hullabaloo is over, people will remember that you're a man who stuck by his friends, and that's what counts.'

"Then he looked up at me, and he said, 'Dean, always be shot in front, never behind.' And then he said, 'You'd better get back to work. We've got a lot of *important* things to do.'

"And, of course, that is what I did, and the matter of my resignation was never mentioned again."

I didn't tell the dean, but I had discussed that afternoon with Harry Truman some weeks before, and his memory of what was said was somewhat different. Mr. Truman said, "When I appointed Dean Secretary of State, I said to him that as I understood the Constitution, the President ran the foreign policy of the United States, while the Secretary of State was his principal adviser in the field, and I said that I assumed that it was understood between us that that was the way our relationship would work. He said that it was.

"And I remember I told him, I said, 'Now, Dean, if there is an important decision to be made, always bring it to me in the morning so I'll have time to think it over. If you bring me a decision in the afternoon, that will mean you've already made up your mind and only want me to okay whatever it is.'

"Well, when he came to me that afternoon and talked about resigning, I told him that when my friend Tom Pendergast died, I got in a plane and flew out to Kansas City to attend his funeral. He was my friend, and he never asked me to do a dishonest deed, and that's what I told Dean, and I said, 'If you think there's a big hubbub over this Alger Hiss thing, you should have seen all the carrying-on there was then.'

"But I said these things don't last. I said, 'A month from now, all of this won't mean a thing.'

"And then I said, 'Now, Dean, about this resignation

business, this is the first time you've brought me a decision late in the afternoon. Don't do it again.' He said he wouldn't, and he didn't."

A month after his famous press conference Mr. Acheson was asked to appear before the subcommittee of the Senate Committee on Appropriations. Ostensibly, that summons was for him "to clarify" his statement on Hiss. Actually, of course, the hope was to stir up more hostile headlines. The chairman of that particular subcommittee, Senator Pat McCarran of Nevada, was, as Mr. Acheson gently puts it, "not a person who in the eighteenth century would have been considered a man of sensibility."

Mr. Acheson made several points that afternoon, but the one I like to remember was this:

"There were . . . personal reasons for stating my attitude. One must be true to the things by which one lives. The counsels of discretion and cowardice are appealing. The safe course is to avoid situations which are disagreeable and dangerous. Such a course might get one by the issue of the moment, but it has bitter and evil consequences. In the long days and years which stretch beyond that moment of decision, one must live with one's self; and the consequences of living with a decision which one knows has sprung from timidity and cowardice go to the roots of one's life. It is not merely a question of peace of mind, although it is vital; it is a matter of integrity of character."

On the last afternoon we talked, the last before the filming on the Korean decision began at Blair House, I said, *Mr. Secretary, I once wrote that Harry Truman may be the last human being ever to be President. I know it's far too early to make any definitive judgment on that, but would you care to make any comment on it?*

Mr. Acheson thought for a moment, and then he said, "Yes, yes. On the basis of our present, very limited experience you might say that. Mr. Truman may be the most *human* person I have ever known. He is completely without artifice.

"In public life he did always what seemed to him best to do. Now in my youth and, of course, in Mr. Truman's youth that would not have been considered so unusual a quality. One did what seemed to be the best thing to do without undue regard to the consequences to one's self.

"But it seems to me, as I look around me, and this may only be a sign of increasing age, it seems to me that this quality has become increasingly rare, especially in political life.

"We are increasingly urged to do what is pragmatic, what will work, what is popular, what has been approved as acceptable by the polls. I sometimes think that many men currently in public life would be hard put to commit themselves on whether or not it was raining without first finding out what reply would be most acceptable to the electorate."

Mr. Secretary, would you say that is true of the present administration, Mr. Kennedy's administration?

Mr. Acheson smiled. "I believe," he said, "that my meaning is quite clear without elaboration."

The Kennedy people talk a good deal about situation ethics, whatever that means. How do you think Mr. Truman would feel about that?

"You'd have to ask Mr. Truman, but I seriously doubt that he has ever found it necessary to place a modifying adjective in front of the word 'ethics.' "

As I've said, I don't know whether Mr. Acheson's international policies will eventually be found to have been right or wrong. I am sure that he was an honest and courageous man. And if there are men of such rectitude —it's been a long time since I've been able to work *that* word into a sentence—anywhere in public life today, I fail to see them.

I commend to the revisionists these further words of Mr. Acheson on the last afternoon we talked:

"I incline to go along with Winston Churchill, who said that among the deficiencies of hindsight is that while we know the consequences of what was done, we do not know the consequences of some other course that was not followed." *

* In the *Apologia Pro Libre Hoc* to his massive *Present at the Creation* Mr. Acheson adds this thought: "In the epigraph Alphonso X, King of Spain, is quoted to the effect that if he had been present at the creation he would have given some useful hints for the better ordering of the universe. In a sense the postwar years were a period of creation, for the ordering of which I shared with others some responsibility. Moreover, the state of the world in those years and almost all that happened during them was wholly novel within the experience of those who had to deal with it. 'History,' writes C. V. Wedgewood in her biography of William the Silent, 'is lived forwards but it is written in retrospect. We know the end before we consider the beginning and we can never wholly recapture what it was to know the beginning only.' "

On J. Edgar Hoover

Mr. President, what did you think of J. Edgar Hoover?
"To tell you the truth, I never gave him all that much
thought. He was, still is inclined to take on, to try to take
on more than his job was, and he made quite a few too
many speeches to my mind, and he very often spoke of
things that, strictly speaking, weren't any of his business,
but then a lot of people do that, especially in Washington.
As long as he did his job, I didn't pay too much attention
to him.

"One time they brought me a lot of stuff about his
personal life, and I told them I didn't give a damn about
that. That wasn't my business. It was what he did *while*
he was at work that was my business."

The CIA

I said earlier that Mr. Truman was not much given to second thoughts, and I learned not to expect any. But one morning as we were yet again waiting for a cameraman to change film, I said, *Mr. President, I know that you were responsible as President for setting up the CIA. How do you feel about it now?* A few days earlier we had been discussing the Bay of Pigs fiasco.

"I think it was a mistake. And if I'd known what was going to happen, I never would have done it. I needed . . . the President needed at that time a central organization that would bring all the various intelligence reports we were getting in those days, and there must have been a dozen of them, maybe more, bring them all into one organization so that the President would get *one* report on what was going on in various parts of the world.

"Now *that* made sense, and that's why I went ahead and set up what they called the Central Intelligence Agency.

"But it got out of hand. The fella . . . the one that was in the White House after me never paid any attention to it, and it got out of hand. Why, they've got an organization over there in Virginia now that is practically the equal of the Pentagon in many ways. And I think I've told you, one Pentagon is one too many.

"Now, as nearly as I can make out, those fellows in the CIA don't just report on wars and the like, they go out and make their own, and there's nobody to keep track of what they're up to. They spend billions of dollars on stirring up trouble so they'll *have* something to report on. They've become . . . it's become a government all of its own and all secret. They don't have to account to anybody.

"That's a very dangerous thing in a democratic society, and it's got to be put a stop to. The people have got a right to know what those birds are up to. And if I was back in the White House, people would know. You see, the way a free government works, there's got to be a housecleaning every now and again, and I don't care what branch of the government is involved. *Somebody* has to keep an eye on things.

"And when you can't do any housecleaning because everything that goes on is a damn *secret*, why, then we're on our way to something the Founding Fathers didn't have in mind. Secrecy and a free, democratic government don't mix. And if what happened at the Bay of Pigs doesn't prove that, I don't know what does.

"You have got to keep an eye on the military at all times, and it doesn't matter whether it's the birds in the Pentagon or the birds in the CIA." *

---

* I should add that publicly Mr. Truman continued to uphold the CIA. This was one of the few areas in which what he said publicly differed from what he said privately.

On a disastrous day at the Army Command and General Staff School that Bob Aurthur described in detail in the August, 1971, issue of *Esquire,* Mr. Truman was asked about the CIA by a young Army officer who was a veteran of Korea. On that occasion Mr. Truman said, "When I took over the Presidency he received information from just about everywhere, from the Secretary of State and the State Department, the Treasury Department, the Department of Agriculture. Just everybody.

"And sometimes they didn't agree as to what was happening in various parts of the world. So I got a couple of admirals together, and they formed the Central Intelligence Agency for the benefit and convenience of the President of the United States. . . . So instead of the President having to look through a bunch of papers two feet high, the information was coordinated so that the President could arrive at the facts.

"It's still going, and it's going very well."

On the other hand, now that I've looked at it again, that's pretty faint praise.

Moreover, it has recently been revealed that as far back as February, 1947, General Marshall in a memorandum to President Truman said of the agency five months before it was set up: "The Foreign Service of the Department of State is the only collection agency of the Government which covers the whole world, and we should be very slow to subject the collection and evaluation of this foreign intelligence to other establishments, especially during times of peace. The powers of the proposed agency seem almost unlimited and need clarification."

36

Some Friends and Neighbors, Too

Eddie Meisberger, a retired newspaperman, and a veteran of Battery D: "The thing about Mr. Truman is . . . he has never changed. He never changed at all. He was the same man in Battery D and as county judge and President and after. That was one of the things you could always count on; you always knew where you stood with Mr. Truman.

"I remember one time not too long after he got to be President, and he'd just been to Potsdam and met Stalin and Churchill and all of those, and he came out here to Kansas City, and, of course, there was quite a following of the press, and they had a press conference at the Federal Building here in Kansas City, to be followed by a luncheon. I was invited to the luncheon, but I got over to the courthouse a little ahead of time, and while I was waiting, a Secret Service man came in and said, 'There's a gentleman at the other end of the building who wishes to see you. Follow me.'

"I followed him, and we went to a corner office, and he opened a door, and there was the President behind a desk, standing up. He'd been to Potsdam and to San Francisco for the United Nations, and I don't know where all he'd been, but he hadn't changed a particle.

"There were some others there, Ted Marks I remember [also a veteran of Battery D] and one or two others, and the President opened a drawer in the desk, and he kind of grinned, and then he went over and locked the door. And then he went to a cupboard and reached up and got an old tumbler. It wasn't too clean, a heavy glass tumbler. And he took out a bottle of refreshment and poured each of us a drink. We told him we'd enjoy that, but where was his glass?

"He said, 'I won't take one right now because right in the next room is a delegation of Baptist ladies from Independence, and we have an appointment in a few minutes. So I can't join you now.

" 'But,' he said, 'I feel a bad cold coming on, and I'll just put this away and take it out at home tonight and use it.' And he folded up the carton around the bottle and put it back in the desk.

"And I said, 'Well, I'm on a government payroll, you know, and I don't know whether I should take one right now.'

He said, 'Well, as President, I'll give you fifteen—fifteen minutes of annual leave right now, and you can join the others.' So we said, 'Down the hatch.'

"And he told us stories about some of the vicissitudes and the problems of the Secret Service and how being President his privacy was not what it used to be. But he said that went along with the job and he'd just have to put up with it as best he could."

I gather from what you say that Mr. Truman has remained unchanged since he came back to Independence to live after being President.

"Oh, yes. He hadn't changed a bit after being President. And I'll tell you one thing, if you didn't know he'd been, he'd never tell you. It's not the kind of thing he'd ever mention. He's not proud in *that* way.

"One day after he got back we had a lunch at the hotel here in Kansas City, and during the luncheon for some reason or another he got a Charley horse or a kink in his knee.

"And when he was ready to leave the hotel to go back home to Independence, he told us he could hardly walk. So a couple of us helped him downstairs and got him into one of the boys' cars, and we took him over to Eighth and Grand, where he had his car parked.

"When we got there and the attendant got his car out, he still could hardly walk. And we said, 'Mr. President'—because we always address him as *Mr. President* regardless of how well we know him—we said, 'We don't think you should drive this car by yourself. We're worried about you.'

"And he said, 'No. Hell,' he said, 'turn it and point the damn thing towards Independence. I'll get there.' And we put him in the seat, and off he went bound for Independence. He got there safely, and I guess he always will."

Susan Chiles, retired schoolteacher and writer: "Of course, since they got back from Washington, we haven't seen so much of the Trumans, because they don't go out much. I think they're lonely in that big house. I think they think people would treat them . . . the way you'd treat a President and First Lady, and maybe people would. It's hard to tell.

"But almost nobody goes to see them. I think people would go to see them, but when a man . . . when a couple have been President and the First Lady, you hesitate just to go and call. They've met so many people, kings and queens, and . . . people just don't seem to call the way they might otherwise.

"But I know this. There must be some satisfaction for Harry Truman knowing he has been one of the great Presidents, and I believe that has already been proven.

"Mort, you know—Mort, Junior—was a special FBI agent in Washington in the first year that Harry was President. And I visited there six weeks, and I visited Mrs. Truman in the White House, but Harry was at the United Nations meeting. So I didn't get to see him.

"But while I was there, I attended a banquet of the National League of American Pen Women, and they were discussing Mr. Truman and his attitudes and saying very harsh things about him. I took it as long as I could, and then I got up, and I said, 'Now I don't know anything about the issues, but I know that Harry Truman is honest, and whatever he says will stand the test of time,' and I sat down, and they didn't discuss him anymore.

"In the time that has passed since, I believe it can be said that I was right."

Walter Bodine, a Kansas City television commentator: "While he was President, those of us who covered the

news here in Kansas City were kept at a distance from
Mr. Truman. When he would come back from Washington, there were always a lot of reporters around, and there
would be the Secret Service. You couldn't get to know
him then.

"But we did get to know him after he came home, and
I think I, like everyone else, thought that when Harry
Truman came home, he would stay a brief period and
then, like almost everybody else who goes to Washington,
he would find some reason to go back and live there.
Or maybe settle down at an Eastern college, an Ivy
League college as a lecturer or something like that.

"I couldn't really believe that after all he'd been and
all he'd done he'd come back and live in Independence,
but he has, and, actually, I think no man ever relished
being a private citizen more. He couldn't wait to start
driving his own car, and I remember one day, when a
newsman met him at Ninth and Grand—in those days he
had an office at Tenth—Mr. Truman was carrying a
briefcase.

"The newsman said to him, 'Mr. President, could I
carry your briefcase for you?'

"And he said, 'No, I'll tell you something. Before we
left Washington, I decided that when we got home, we
were going to do everything for ourselves, and that defi-
nitely includes carrying my own briefcase.'

"The way I'd sum it up is that Harry Truman never
left home, actually. He's a citizen of Independence, and
I think he just commuted to Washington for a while."

*Edgar Hinde, former postmaster of Independence and
a veteran of Battery D:* "I think when Harry came back
to Independence from Washington, he sort of hoped he
could live like everybody else. He'd been used to going
up around our old country square here, and he always
knew everyone there. But after he was President, he
couldn't do that, and it bothered him. I think it still does.

"Of course, Independence is no longer a small town;

it's a small city, and everywhere **Harry** goes now, it's just a nuisance, with people coming up and wanting him to autograph a piece of paper and shake hands with him.

"And there are all the visitors, all wanting to take a look at Harry Truman. I guess he's our most famous local product and maybe always will be.

"And he tells me . . . he says it's even worse when he's on a trip. It just always takes all the pleasure out of it because he is never left alone. People won't leave him alone. He'd go . . . he goes into a town, and somebody always says, 'There's President Truman,' and naturally, everybody follows him.

"He was telling me about one time when he was in Indiana in a motel, and this motel owner knew him, and he promised he wouldn't tell anybody Harry was there.

"But he and Mrs. Truman went out for dinner, and when they got back, he said there were about five hundred people waiting for him in front of the motel. And he said it was the same thing all the way back to Washintgon. His privacy, he has none."

Harry Truman: "I try to live the way I did before I went to Washington, try to live like I always did, but it's a hard thing to do. When you get to be a notorious character, people are always around with curious ideas of taking a look at the fellow who's been through what I have. And I'm patient with them because I know exactly what's affecting them. But it's not very good for privacy.

"I was told by the former President, Mr. Hoover, that souvenir hunters had even taken the doorknobs off his house, had taken some of the weatherboarding off his house. And when I became President, the Secret Service had found out all about this situation, and they decided that the property where Mrs. Truman and I lived ought to be protected. So they put an iron fence around it so people couldn't come in and pick up flowers and souvenirs around the place.

"On one occasion, when the back gate was left open, some old lady drove in and began pulling up the tulips that Mrs. Truman had set out, beautiful white tulips. And she was stopped by the guard who happened to be on duty and told that it was private property and she shouldn't do that.

" 'Oh,' she said, 'Mrs. Truman won't care if I take a few of her tulips,' and kept on pulling them up. So that's the reason we have to be surrounded by an iron fence, and I don't like it. Never did like it and never will like it, but it has to be done because of the souvenir hunters. They're not real Americans. They're just people who want to accumulate a lot of stuff and then throw it away. You find most of it in the attic when they die."

Miss Ethel Noland: "My picture window here pictures the Truman house across the street. Originally it was the Gates house. It's a very old house and an interesting house, and it is certainly a fine example of Victorian architecture.

"Of course, since Mr. Truman came back from Washington, the tourists are omnipresent. They're there when I first look out in the morning. They walk down Truman Road, and they survey the house from all sides. And finally, you find them standing out in front. And one *always* goes across the street and takes a picture of those at the front gate. It seems to me that's almost an unwritten law, that they shall do this.

"Sometimes if I go out, they will come across to ask me questions. They will say, 'Do you know Mr. Truman? Does he visit the neighbors? How do they like him?' And many questions like that.

"Fortunately, we can all speak well of him. I answer their questions as if I were just a neighbor, instead of telling them that he and I are related. Harry Truman and I are first cousins, my mother having been a sister of Harry's father, John Anderson Truman.

"However, he never complains because the tourists' attitude is always quite admiring. You'd surely have to admire a person to get up at five or six o'clock in the morning to go and see where he lives and try to catch a glimpse of him. . . . That does not, however, make it any easier for Mr. Truman. Although, as I have said, he does not complain. He comes from the kind of background and has the kind of upbringing where one is publicly cheerful at all times. One does not *discuss* one's dissatisfactions with life, as seems to be so prevalent with people nowadays.

"I am sure I am quite old-fashioned. When I ask someone how he or she is, I trust that they will say to me, 'I am fine. How are you?' And I will do likewise.

"I most certainly do *not* want them to tell me how they are."

Mrs. W. L. C. Palmer: "I do not think that Mrs. Truman ever liked any part of it. She just never learned to enjoy public life in any way . . . the politics of it and some of the people that at one time or another Harry had to . . . with whom he was associated. I had that feeling here when Harry was judge and, later, when I visited them in Washington. At the White House when he was President and she was First Lady.

"I think Mrs. Truman would have been just as content with life if she had never left Independence, but I doubt that she has ever mentioned it, even to Mr. Truman. She has always been a woman of great understanding, and in recent years, since they have come home from Washington, Mr. Truman has seemed to be very much dependent on her.

"But the important thing is, being First Lady was just never anything that was *necessary* for her."

Do you suppose it was rather like Rachel Jackson who, after Andrew Jackson was elected President, said, "Well, for Mr. Jackson's sake I am glad, but for my part I never wished it"?

"Very much so. Mrs. Truman is a person who would do what she feels Mr. Truman wanted her to do, but she has

always been a person of great privacy, and politics is not
a life she would have chosen for herself." *

Edgar Hinde: "Of course Harry likes people, and that
shows. He is very fond of people, I'd say, and he takes
time with them.

"After the library was built, I took my sister over to
visit him. He chatted with her; he played the piano for her,
and he showed her around the library.

"Later on the way back from the library she said to me,
'I can see why Harry Truman has been so successful in
politics. He takes time with people.' "

I mentioned to Mr. Truman what Edgar Hinde had said
and added, *I understand you did the same thing when you
were President, that you always took time with people. I
wonder, sir, does that have anything to do with the fact
that when you were first elected to the Senate, you had
considerable difficulty getting in to see President Roosevelt
at all?*

* Bob Aurthur has written of one "dinner" he had with
Mr. Truman at twelve noon in Independence: "As the limousine left the parking area, Mr. Truman suggested we eat at
the Howard Johnson's just outside the Library. 'I could take
you home,' he said matter-of-factly, 'but the food at Howard
Johnson's is much better.'

"I regretted the opportunity to have lunch chez Truman,
however poor the fare, but as Mr. Truman checked his coat
in the painfully familiar Howard Johnson's, Bill Hillman revealed sadly that the offer had been an empty gesture. Except
for an afternoon during the shooting of the first film, Hillman
and the other cronies had never been invited to the house.
Other evidence gathered over my time with Mr. Truman led
me to the conclusion that sometime early in their marriage
Bess Wallace Truman had made a deal.

" 'Harry,' I imagined she'd said, 'be a judge if you want.
Get to be a Senator, Vice-President, or even President . . .
but *never* bring those people you hang around with into *my*
house.'

"Or words to that effect."

When Truman first came to Washington in 1934, he almost immediately called at the White House to pay his respects to Roosevelt, but for five months he was stalled off by Steve Early, Roosevelt's press secretary. When he finally did get in to see Roosevelt for the first time, the appointment lasted only seven minutes, and nothing of importance was discussed.

The truth is that during Truman's first term in the Senate, while he supported Roosevelt and the New Deal almost totally, Roosevelt ignored him. The White House took him and his vote for granted.

At one point, having started to drive back to Independence, he was brought back to the Capitol by state highway patrolmen to break a tie on a major bill. He was in a fury, and he called Steve Early and said, "I'm sick and tired of being the White House office boy. This is the third time I've come back here to bail you guys out on a vote. You tell that to the President!"

I mentioned that incident to Mr. Truman, who said, "Oh, yes. I was angry, and I was hurt, but I got over it, and Roosevelt and I became . . . quite close.

"But the whole thing taught me a lesson. People are always very nervous when they meet the President of the United States, and they can be . . . they can have their feelings hurt if he is . . . less than kind to them. And courteous. Courtesy is the cheapest thing in the world, and it's a wonder to me that people aren't that way more of the time.

"When I was President myself, I never ran anybody out. If you're willing to work a little extra, you can see everybody it is necessary for you to see, and you can spend as much time with them as need be. There's always, almost always plenty of time. There are always twenty-four hours in a day if you make use of them. I think I mentioned that that's one of the lessons I learned from reading old Benjamin Franklin's *Autobiography*. He gives you some very good hints on how to make the best use of your time.

"The main thing isn't *time*, it's *people*, and I have al-

ways tried very hard to keep that in mind. In the White
House it was never . . . almost never that people
wanted to stay too long. They were always embarrassed
at taking my time, and they wanted to leave too soon.

"And it's the same here at the library. The main thing
I have to be concerned with is to be sure that my visitors
are at ease and not worried about whether they are going
to stay too long and that kind of thing.

"When you get into a conversation and it lasts over the
time they're supposed to stay, I always tell them to stay
and finish, and of course, that's the way it ought to be
done, and as long as I'm around, it always will be. It's
very, very easy to hurt people, and if you don't have to
do it, you should do everything possible to avoid it."

In 1964 Eric Sevareid in a conversation with Mr. Truman got on the same subject, and he quoted him as saying, "What you don't understand is the power of a President to hurt."

Sevareid added, "An American President has the power
to build, to set fateful events in motion, to destroy an enemy civilization, to win or lose a vast personal following.
But the power of a President to hurt the feelings of another human being—this, I think, had scarcely occurred
to me, and still less had it occurred to me that a President
in office would have the time and the need to be aware
of this particular power among so many others.

"Mr. Truman went on to observe that a word, a harsh
glance, a peremptory motion by a President of the United
States, could so injure another man's pride that it would
remain a scar on his emotional system all his life."

Then Sevareid recalled an episode that the President
had also told me, shortly after it happened, in the late winter or spring of 1962. He had given a lecture at, I believe,
the University of Southern California, in any case at a
college or university in Southern California; the lecture was
on the subject he loved best, the Constitution and the
Presidency.

During the question period a boy got up and said, "Mr.

President, what do you think of our local yokel?" He meant Pat Brown, then governor.

Mr. Truman told the boy that he should be ashamed of himself, that to speak of the governor of a state in such a disrespectful way, even if he disagreed with him, was a shameful thing. The boy, close to tears, sat down.

When the question period was over, Mr. Truman went to the boy and said that he hoped he would understand that what he had said had to do with the principle involved and that he meant nothing personal. The boy said that he did understand, and the two shook hands.

Afterward Mr. Truman went to see the dean to ask him to send reports from time to time on the boy's progress in school. The dean said he would and had.

I asked Mr. Truman if he had ever heard from the boy himself, and he said, "He's written me two or three times, and I've written him back. He's doing very well."

Sevareid said of the incident, "The simple point here is that Mr. Truman had instantly realized how a public scolding by a former President could mark and mar the boy's inner life and his standing in the community.

"I feel gratified to have heard this story. It has given me an insight into the responsibilities of a President that I did not have, and it has immeasurably added to my own residue of memories about the man from Missouri. He is nearly eighty now. He may live to be a hundred—his is a strong stock—but this, I know, is the specific memory that will return to me when his time does come."

Earlier Sevareid had written: "A man's character is his fate, said the ancient Greeks. Chance, in good part, took Harry Truman to the presidency, but it was his character that kept him there and determined his historical fate. He is, without any doubt, destined to live in the books as one of the strongest and most decisive of the American Presidents." *

* From *Eric Sevareid: An Unknown Side of Truman.* From the Washington *Evening Star.* February 4, 1964. Also reprinted in Cabell Phillips' admirable book *The Truman Presidency.*

Captain Mike Westwood of the Independence police department, a companion, sometime chauffeur, and long-time friend of Mr. Truman: "I don't recall the date, but it was after Mr. Truman got back from Washington, from being President, and we took a trip down south to Jefferson City. That was on Highway Forty before it was a double-lane highway. And all of a sudden Harry told me to pull over to the side of the road, and there was a woman trying to herd a bunch of hogs that had got loose, and he said, 'Let's help that lady get her hogs in.'

"So I went out and stopped traffic, and he helped her get those hogs off the road. Can you imagine a President of the United States, a former President of the United States, doing a thing like that?

"Well, when we got to Jefferson City, there was a reporter there to meet us. Someone on the highway had recognized the President and called Jefferson City saying he'd seen Harry Truman out there herding hogs. The reporter asked him, I don't think he could believe it, thought there was a mistake of some kind, but he asked Harry, and Harry said, yes, he'd done it. He said somebody had to, and he said anyway he'd been a farmer long before he got to be President."

37

The Library Tour

Except for the lectures in the auditorium I think what Mr. Truman enjoyed most in the years when he could manage it was taking people on tours of the library. I must have gone on the tour, say, twenty times, and Mr. Truman's comments never varied much. He just edited his remarks some when there were ladies—to him all women were ladies—and children on the tour. I am sure that in his entire life he never swore or uttered an obscenity in what he called "mixed company."

When we left Mr. Truman's private office, he would stop for a moment at the piano in the large reception room, pounding out a few chords. Then, if the company were strictly male, he would say, "My choice early in life was either to be a piano player in a whorehouse or a politician."

He would pause; as I've said, he was a skilled stand-up comic, albeit with a somewhat limited repertoire, pause, then say, "And to tell the truth there's hardly a difference."

I laughed just as heartily the dozenth time I heard that Rotarian joke as I did the first, and so did the dejuicers, Noyes and Hillman, who must have heard it many more times than that. So did Harry Truman, who'd heard it more than anybody.

On the first day and the last and on a few occasions in between Mr. Truman stopped first at a glass case in which was a mint copy of Dwight D. Eisenhower's book *Crusade in Europe*.

"That's the first copy he gave to anybody outside his immediate family," the President would say. "Take a look at what he wrote in it."

On the flyleaf the general had written to the man who was then his Commander in Chief, "To Harry S. Truman —with lasting respect, admiration, and friendship, Dwight D. Eisenhower."

"I sometimes wonder if the son of a bitch knows the

meaning of any of those words," Mr. Truman would say, walking on.

We would come to a framed copy of that issue of the Chicago *Tribune* that on November 2, 1948, had the headline DEWEY DEFEATS TRUMAN.

Mr. Truman always looked at that headline as if he had never seen it before. He never said anything about it. No need to. He just stood there and grinned, and at that moment he never seemed to look much older than he had that memorable night in 1948. Few men in history have known such a victory, and it was all his, all, and he knew that and relished it. One of his more attractive qualities, to me anyway, was that just as he was never arrogant, he was never falsely modest either. He took the knocks, and hard knocks they were, without complaint, and he felt he was entitled to enjoy his triumphs. And he did, by God, and it was fine to see.

That first day I said, "Mr. President, were you really able to go to sleep that night without knowing for sure whether you'd won the election?"

"Of course," said the President. "I knew I was going to win. Never had the slightest doubt about it. Besides, it was all over but the shouting. What would have been the point in not getting a good night's sleep?"

How do you explain your remarkable ability to go to sleep like that?

"Because I don't drink coffee for one thing. Another thing is that whatever I've done I've done the best I can. So I don't go to bed and worry."

The President stopped at a photograph of himself, General MacArthur, and several administration officials on Wake Island.

Mr. Truman identified the other people in the picture, saving MacArthur until last.

"And, of course, we all know who that is," he said, pointing. "That's God.

"We'll talk about him some other time, but if you think I'm rough on him you ought to hear what General Wainwright had to say about him." Major General Jonathan M. Wainwright, Jr., succeeded MacArthur as commander of the U.S. forces in the Philippines after MacArthur left for Australia early in the Second World War.

"Wainwright said he wasn't any better than a common coward, and General Marshall gave me a rundown on MacArthur that was the best I ever did hear. He said he never was any damn good, and he said he was a four-flusher and no two ways about it.

"I'll tell you about the trouble I had with MacArthur. Why, hell, if he'd had his way, he'd have had us in the Third World War and blown up half to two-thirds of the world."

We walked on, and the President said, "People who think they are God are bound to get in trouble sooner or later."

One entire section of the public part of the library is filled with gifts Mr. Truman had received from various world leaders, a display of coins, medals, even a solid gold dinnerware set sent by some Arab potentate. Mr. Truman never thought any of those things were *his,* though. "They were given to the President of the United States, which is what, for a time, I was, but I never thought they were meant for my personal use. The only exception—"

He stopped in front of a jeweled sword given to the President by King Saud of Saudi Arabia, and Mr. Truman said, "The only exception. I told Bess I'd give *that* to her if she'd kick Bricker [a reactionary Republican Senator from Ohio] in the ass, but she wouldn't do it. So it's still here."

We came to a corner of the library in which were photographs or drawings of all the Presidents. Mr. Truman pointed to the picture of Abraham Lincoln.

"Lincoln was a great President," he said, "and I'll tell you why. He had nerve enough to save the Union under the most difficult circumstances. And if he hadn't saved the union of the United States, we would have been divided into half a dozen countries like those Central American countries and I wouldn't have any influence in the world. That's the reason I admire him. He had the guts to go ahead and do what he thought was the right thing at a time when he had a great big opposition. He was roundly abused for it, but he did the right thing."

How do you suppose he knew what the right thing was?

"He knew the history of this country. He'd been in the Congress, and he didn't like to serve there. And he'd also been a local politician. He knew things from the ground up. And he knew that if the United States as a country couldn't be saved it would end up in a division of the various states into various governments which would never get together and do the job. That's the reason."

The President started on, then stopped. "Lincoln was a great man all right," he said, then added: "Of course, heroes know when to die."

Was he making an analogy between Lincoln's death and that of Franklin Roosevelt? I thought so and was even more sure of it when he turned back and pointed out the photograph of Andrew Johnson.

He said, "It took about eighty years for the truth about Andrew Johnson to come out, but it finally did, and now people know what kind of President he was."

I said, "Why did he get into so much trouble, coming so close to getting impeached, by one vote, wasn't it?"

"One vote less than the necessary two-thirds in the Senate. I'll tell you why it happened. Johnson tried to carry on Lincoln's policy. Lincoln was going to treat the South not as a conquered nation but as a sinful child. Johnson tried that, and what happened was a case of the power of Congress ruining a President of the United States. Old Thad Stevens was the cause of that. He just wasn't any damn good. Period.*

"There never was a man in the White House who was more thoroughly and completely mistreated than Johnson. He was a Democrat from Tennessee. An Andy Jackson Democrat. That's what he was. So when the Republicans after their first administration found out they couldn't win

---

* Thaddeus Stevens was a Republican Congressman from Pennsylvania. After the war he was one of the organizers of the effort to treat the Southern states as "conquered provinces" and was a leader of the effort to impeach Johnson.

without some other approach, they set up the American Union Party with Lincoln as the Presidential candidate and Johnson as the Vice President.

"They got elected, and, of course, after Lincoln was shot, Johnson being a Tennessee Democrat was abused and mistreated, but he was a tough old guy. He didn't have any diplomacy at all, but he finally wound up at the end of his life by being reelected Senator from Tennessee. He fought from one end of the damn state to the other, and you know it was divided into three parts the way Gaul was. . . .

"Anyway, he finally won and made one of the finest speeches that has ever been made in the Senate on what a public servant ought to do. You ought to read it." ·

If Lincoln had lived. . . .

"If Lincoln had lived, he would have had the same experience, but like I said, heroes know when to die."

One of the tours of the library was with Bobby Kennedy, then Attorney General. It was a hurried tour, and it was clear to me, though probably not to the Attorney General, that the President wanted to get it over with as quickly as possible.

After Kennedy had left, Mr. Truman said, "I just don't like that boy, and I never will. He worked for old Joe McCarthy, you know, and when old Joe was tearing up the Constitution and the country, that boy couldn't say enough for him."

He stopped for a moment, and there was an inaudible sigh.

"The whole Kennedy family, as nearly as I can make out, about all they're interested in is *getting* the power. They don't care a hoot in hell about using it. They're afraid to use it for fear it might not be *popular*. I've told you what happens if a President worries too much about winning popularity contests every day . . . every other day or so. You simply can't do it.

"I wouldn't want this to get out, because I hope the boy in the White House will do a good job, but so far it

looks to me like power for itself is the only thing that interests any of them, and they've spent the money to buy it.
I don't like that. I told you the other day . . . the minute
you can buy an *election*, this country is in big trouble.
The biggest it's ever had.

"Now they say young Bobby has changed for the better.
They never say anybody's changed for the worse. They
say he's changed for the better, and maybe he has, but
what I can never understand and never will if I live to be a
hundred is why it takes so long these days for somebody
to learn the difference between right and wrong. A man
who hasn't learned that by the time he's thirty is never
going to learn.

"They say Nixon has changed, too, but they'll have to
prove it. They'll have to prove it to me. Where that fella's
concerned, you might say I'm from Missouri."

When we finished the first tour of the library, it was late
afternoon, and the sun was beginning to set.

We stopped off in the office of the President's secretary,
Miss Rose Conway, who had been with the President since
1945 when he became Vice President.

Mr. Truman started toward his own office, stood in the
doorway for a moment, then turned back, smiled, and said
that he looked forward to seeing us the next day.

"About this television series," he said, "you fellows
keep in mind that I have no idea of selling a bill of goods
to anybody. I just want to give people—especially the
youngsters—some idea of what a President has to do,
what he has to go through from the point of view of a
man who's been there."

We were silent for a time after he went into his own
office. Finally, I turned to Miss Conway and said that it
must have been quite an experience working for so many
years with a man like Harry Truman.

Miss Conway, the gentlest of women, said that it had
been.

"And in all this time," she added, "he has once to say
a harsh word."

38

The Cause and Cure of Hysteria

Mr. President, we've talked about hysteria in the United States several times, and I know it's a subject that concerns you very much, and I wonder if we could go back to it, at least briefly, today?

"Yes, and I'll tell you why it interests me. I may already have told you. I feel that if our constitutional system ever fails, it will be because people got scared and turned hysterical and someone in power will demagogue them right into a police state of some kind. That's what I've always worried about. And still do."

Last night I was reading a statement about a man I know you admired—we've discussed him before—Justice Brandeis. It was his dissent in a wiretapping case at the time the Prohibition Amendment was still in force. I believe the government, probably through the Justice Department, claimed that in order to catch some bootleggers it had to do some wiretapping. Or else it had done some wiretapping. I'm not sure which.

Anyway, the majority of the Supreme Court went along, agreed, but Justice Brandeis dissented. I'm sure you're familiar with it, but could I read you what he said, in part anyway?

"Go right ahead. I've probably read it at one time or another because I think I've read every one of his decisions, but . . . I'm sure whatever he said was right. Because he was a man who always thought his way through to the right conclusion."

Well, sir, he wrote, "Our government is the potent, the omnipresent teacher. For good or ill, it teaches the whole people by example. Crime is contagious. If the government becomes a lawbreaker, it breeds contempt for law; it invites every man to become a law unto himself; it invites anarchy. To declare that in the administration of the criminal law the end justifies the means—to declare that the government may commit crimes in order to se-

cure the conviction of a private criminal—would bring terrible retribution." *

I really don't have to ask, but I will anyway. Would you agree with that, sir?

"Oh, yes, right down the line. You see, if you study the history of this country, you'll discover that there have always been certain people who felt that to get a certain law to work—and I think I told you the Prohibition Amendment was a big mistake, shouldn't have been passed in the first place and couldn't be enforced—but there are always people with a certain kind of mind who

---

* Brandeis' dissent was printed in Jonathan Daniels' biography of Mr. Truman, *The Man of Independence*, a book of which, as has been mentioned earlier, Mr. Truman didn't think highly. Mr. Daniels also quoted Max Lowenthal, a civil libertarian whose acquaintance with Mr. Truman went all the way back to his investigations into railroad finances during his first term in the Senate.

" 'What I think is deep in him,' said Max Lowenthal who had discovered Truman's integrity on the railroad committee, 'is a sense of the atmosphere of the American tradition. That sort of atmosphere was pervasive and a part of men's feelings for America in the eighties and nineties and 1900's when Truman was growing up. I know it of the Middle West where my own childhood and youth were spent in that atmosphere. While there was much economic injustice at the time, there was a quality of freedom—an absence of any aspect whatever of the modern police state—that some of the younger generation today may not know of except in a limited way through their reading.' "

And on the same subject Daniels quotes a man he identifies as an "old liberal":

"Nothing is more important than the grasp of fundamental American principles shared by such liberals as Truman and old-time conservatives, too. I think we find it in Truman, not because he is for liberalism in economic matters, but because he senses the spirit of the American political system. That has something to do with the way he ran his investigations. It is an innate part of his personality to be fair and to know what is fair, and to exercise restraint when he possesses great power, particularly the power to investigate and detect, and the power to police."

say that you've got to violate the Constitution or the Bill of Rights or both in some way or another to make sure some new law works or take care of some new threat.

"I've always thought that the democratic system can survive any threat at all from the folks, it doesn't matter who they are, the Jacobins, who everybody thought was the enemy in Jefferson's time, or the Communists now.

"It isn't any different now than it was when Jefferson became President. Read his first inaugural speech;* you'll see what I mean. And you must remember how young this country was then, young and didn't have too many friends in the world, but Jefferson said, I've got it right here, I'll read it to you, said, '. . . let them stand undisturbed as monuments of the safety with which error of opinion may be tolerated where reason is left free to combat it.'

"And read that letter he wrote to Henry Lee† saying

---

* At his first inaugural on March 6, 1801, Jefferson said, ". . . If there be any among us who would wish to dissolve this Union or to change its republican form, let them stand undisturbed as monuments of the safety with which error of opinion may be tolerated where reason is left free to combat it. I know, indeed, that some honest men fear that a republican government cannot be strong; that this government is not strong enough. But would the honest patriot, in the full tide of successful experiment, abandon a government which has so far kept us free and firm, on the theoretic and visionary fear that this government, the world's best hope, may by possibility want energy to preserve itself? I trust not. I believe this, on the contrary, the strongest government on earth. I believe it is the only one where every man, at the call of the laws, would fly to the standard of the law, and would meet invasions of the public order as his own personal concern. Sometimes it is said that man cannot be trusted with the government of himself. Can he, then, be trusted with the government of others? Or have we found angels in the forms of kings to govern him? Let history answer this question."

† In 1824 Jefferson wrote to Henry Lee: "Men by their constitutions are naturally divided into two parties: 1. Those who fear and distrust the people and wish to draw all powers from them into the hands of the higher classes. 2. Those who

that there always have been two kinds of people, the ones
that trust the people and the ones that don't. It's been true
all through the history of this country, all through the
history of the world."

*And wiretappers, people who want to wiretap are
among those who don't trust the people, would you say?*

"That's right. Any attempt to invade the privacy of a
private citizen, doesn't matter what it is, is in violation of
the Bill of Rights, and those who propose such a thing
are more of a danger to the country than the ones they
want to listen in on."

*Didn't you have something to do with the consideration
of wiretapping when you were chairman of a Senate subcommittee that considered all wiretapping bills?*

"Yes, I was. There's always somebody around, Congress, somewhere, that thinks the country won't last until
day after tomorrow unless there's a lot of wiretapping
allowed. And of course, before they invented wiretapping,
they depended on other means to pry into people's personal lives. And I have always been against it, when I
was in the Senate and when I was President.

"I am happy to say that none of the wiretap bills ever
got out of that subcommittee when I was chairman."

*And as you say, you continued to feel the same way all
through the time you were President.*

"I did. There were all kinds of hysterical bills, legislation that the people who were so scared of the Communists said would take care of the matter and forget about
the Constitution. The Mundt-Nixon bill was one, you

---

identify themselves with the people, have confidence in them,
cherish and consider them as the most honest and safe, although not the most wise depository of the public interests.
In every country these two parties exist, and in every one
where they are free to think, speak, and write, they will declare themselves. Call them, therefore, liberals and serviles,
Jacobins and Ultras, whigs and tories, republicans and federalists, aristocrats and democrats, or whatever name you
please, they are the same parties still, and pursue the same
object. The last appellation of aristocrats and democrats is the
true one expressing the essence of all."

remember, and then there was the McCarran Act,* which was finally enacted into law over my veto, but I spoke out against things like that every chance I got. They tried to stop me; it was just before the Congressional elections of 19 and 50 I think it was, and they all tried to stop me, keep me from vetoing it, saying a veto would

* As Cabell Phillips in *The Truman Presidency* describes the bill, "What McCarran [the powerful chairman of the subcommittee of the Senate Committee on Appropriations] came out with in the end was a well-nigh undecipherable bill . . . which did *not* prohibit membership in the Communist party but *did* require that all who belonged to it proclaim that fact by registering with the Attorney General. . . . A Subversive Activities Control Board was called for to enforce these registration provisions. In addition, the bill denied employment to Communists and their 'dupes' in defense facilities; prohibited the issuance of passports to them; called for the deportation of any alien who had ever been a Communist; and provided for the detention in wartime 'of any person as to whom there is reason to believe he might engage in acts of espionage or sabotage.' This meant Communists, obviously. It could also, presumably, mean anybody whom a McCarran (or an Un-American Activities Committee chairman) found to be, by the rule of guilt by association, a sympathizer or fellow traveler of the Communists. It was a dragnet such as any dictator might envy."

The bill passed—the year was 1950, you remember—the House by a vote of 354 to 20 and the Senate by a vote of 70 to 7. It was not a brave year, 1950, but Harry Truman vetoed the bill. He said: "It's just like the Alien and Sedition Bill of 1798, and that didn't work either."

He tried desperately to have the veto sustained in the Senate, but the veto was overridden, 57 to 10.

According to Mr. Phillips, "It was a good fight, a typically Truman kind of to-hell-with-where-the-chips-may-fall fight. He had stood his ground against overwhelming odds for what he believed to be right. His enemies gloated over his defeat, but he won new respect with the more dispassionate editorial writers and columnists. And just as he had prophesied, the McCarran Act did prove to be a legalistic and administrative monstrosity, destined to be fought over in the courts for more than a decade and adding little to the net security of the nation."

cause the Democratic Party to lose votes, a lot of votes, and it may have. It may have, but just because the country is hysterical, and there was a lot of hysteria at the time, why, that is all the more reason the President has to speak out for what is right. Otherwise, he's got no reason being in the White House. The President has to do the leading in a case like that.

"I've said before, the President is the only person in the government who represents the whole people. There are some who can afford to hire lobbyists and others to represent their special interests, but the President isn't elected to pull strings for anybody. He's elected. I've said it before, to be the lobbyist for everybody in the United States. And he is, too, if he's any good.

"And when there's a moral issue involved, like any violation of the Constitution, the President has to be the moral leader of the country. Right now we've got this Birch Society, this John Birch business, and it's just another example of hysteria, and it's fooling some people, the same class that was fooled by the Ku Klux Klan and the other wild things that have come along. It'll work itself out.

"And if the politicians have got the guts, they help shape public opinion, but some of them, a lot of them, are like Mark Hanna said about William McKinley, they've got their ears so close to the ground they're full of grasshoppers. They can't tell what's going on."

Would you say, off the record, Mr. President, that that's somewhat true of the man who's now in the White House [John Kennedy]?

"Yes, I would, and I'm sorry to say it, but all the time he was in the Senate, all the time he could have provided some leadership as far as old Joe McCarthy was concerned, he never did do it, and it's a shame. I hope he learns. He wrote that book, you know [*Profiles in Courage*], and I hope he learns to be a little more outspoken about issues, but I have yet to see it."

Mr. President, early in 1948, when hysteria over the Alger Hiss case was at its height, you were asked if you thought the whole thing was "a red herring" to divert the country's attention from more important matters. And you said that you did think it was. And, of course, as you remember better than anybody you were greatly criticized for that remark. I wonder if in the years since you've changed your mind.

"I wouldn't say they criticized me for that. I've been criticized by experts, and it doesn't bother me, but they carried on a campaign against me that was as bad as any this country has ever known. Those men, McCarthy and that fella Jenner and Nixon [then a Congressman from California], they stirred up a hysteria as bad as any this country has ever known. We're lucky to have pulled through it, and I'm not at all sure we're over it yet.

"But about Hiss. I never knew him, of course. I met him once out in San Francisco when we were setting up the United Nations, but that's the only time.* I'll tell you something, though. They never proved it on him."

Proved that he was . . . had been a Communist spy, you mean?

"That's right. They tried, twice you may remember, they tried to do it, but they never did."

Wasn't that because the statute of limitations had run out so that he couldn't have been convicted on espionage charges; so they convicted him on perjury charges instead?

"That's what they said, but I never did believe it. I think if they'd had the goods on Hiss, they'd have produced it, but they didn't. All it was was his word against the word of that other fellow [Whittaker Chambers]. They didn't come up with any proof. That's the way I felt at the time anyway.

"What they were trying to do, all those birds, they were trying to get the Democrats. They were trying to get me out of the White House, and they were willing to go to

---

* Actually the President saw Mr. Hiss again after the San Francisco conference ended. Hiss, who had been Secretary of the conference, flew back to Washington in a government plane and presented the charter to Mr. Truman at the White House.

any lengths to do it. They'd been out of office a long time, and they'd have done anything to get back in. They did do just about everything they could think of, all that witch-hunting that year, that was the worst in the history of this country, like I said. The Constitution has never been in such a danger, and I hope it never will be again."

Hiss's name was mentioned once again. Mr. Truman said that the best biography of Andrew Johnson had been written by Lloyd Paul Stryker, and I said that, as the President no doubt knew, Stryker had been Hiss's lawyer in the first trial.

Mr. Truman said, "I'm not a bit surprised. He was a man who was never afraid to take on an unpopular cause."

Mr. President, do you think the United States is particularly susceptible to hysteria, more than any other country, I mean?

"I don't think so. You read your history and you'll see that from time to time people in every country have seemed to lose their good sense, got hysterical, and got off the beam. . . . I don't know what gets into people. The first go-round if you remember was in Massachusetts at Salem."

Let's talk about that.

"It was back in 1692, and some of the girls up there started saying they'd been haunted by evil spirits. They wanted to create a sensation, and of course, they did. It took fire. And they even brought a defecting minister back from Maine or wherever it was and hanged him as a witch. Altogether I think twenty people were hanged, and one man was pressed to death. And they used dunking stools, that kind of thing. It was awful, what happened.

"And of course years later, back in 1954, the state of Massachusetts said it had been a big mistake, the whole thing, and they passed a law pardoning all the people that had been put to death, but that didn't do them much good. It's not much good to apologize for hanging a man after the deed's been done."

Tell me about the Alien and Sedition Laws.

"They were passed in 1798, passed by the Federalists to stay in office, and old John Adams signed them into law. That was a phase of the situation brought about by the Jacobins in the Jefferson campaign. The Alien and Sedition Laws were absolutely unconstitutional. You ought to read them. Damnedest things you ever saw. One of the first things Jefferson did was to repeal them. They couldn't enforce them."

What did they say?

"Well, it was a totalitarian approach to things. They made it a crime for a man to say anything about the prevailing powers in government, and they made it a crime for an alien to take a hand in any affairs of the American government, and that included foreigners who had been made citizens of the United States. You ought to read them. You wouldn't think it could happen in this country, but it did.

"And what lay behind it was that people were afraid, the way I said earlier, it was the fear of the French Revolution, fear of the Jacobins. And the Federalists exploited that fear to stay in office, just the way the Republicans at the time we were talking about exploited people's fears of the Communists to *get* themselves in office.

"They accused Jefferson of being a Jacobin, which he wasn't, and after he was inaugurated, one of his first acts was to free all the people that'd been put in jail because of the Alien and Sedition Laws. Mrs. John Adams was very upset. She thought people who had criticized her husband ought to be in jail. At least that's the way it looked, but Jefferson wrote her a letter that set out his feelings in the matter in no uncertain terms. You ought to look it up. It's a crackerjack.*

---

* Jefferson's letter to Mrs. Adams said, "I discharged every person under punishment or prosecution under the Sedition Law, because I considered and now consider that Law to be a nullity, as absolute and provable as though Congress had ordered us to fall down and worship a golden image, and that it was as much my duty to arrest its execution in every stage as it would have been to rescue from the fiery furnace

"And then when old Andy Jackson came along, he had been a past Grand Master of the Masons in Tennessee, and they organized an anti-Masonic outfit at that time, in the campaign of 1832, and the anti-Masonic party got seven votes. Jackson won by a bigger majority than the first time, of course, but they still got seven votes."

What did they have against the Masons?

"Nothing. Nothing. They claimed that some fella was going to give away the secrets of the Masons and that the Masons up in New York had thrown him in Niagara Falls to prevent it. I've got every degree in the Masons that there is, and if there are any secrets to give away, I'll be damned if I know what they are.

"But it turned out to be a situation that was made to order for the period, and it was another example of hysteria that lasted, as I say, through a Presidential campaign.

"And then those same kind of people, after the anti-Mason thing petered out, they became anti-Catholic. And they burned churches and tarred and feathered priests all over the northern part of the country.

"And then it became the Ku Klux Klan, of course, and we've talked about that. Those birds were against everything.

"And of course after the First World War there was an hysterical period. These things always seem to happen after a war. I've never quite figured out why. But after the First World War we had J. Mitchell Palmer. Woodrow Wilson had appointed him Attorney General of the United States, and it was one of the worst mistakes Wilson, who was otherwise a great President, ever made.

"Because Mitchell, instead of enforcing the law, which was his job, started seeing Communists everywhere, and people got in a panic, and everybody was afraid of everybody else. People got thrown in jail for no reason at all

those who should have been cast into it for refusing to worship the image. It was accordingly done in every instance without asking what the offenders had done, or against whom they had offended, but whether the pain they were suffering were inflicted under the pretended Sedition Law."

except they parted their hair on the wrong side according to their next-door neighbor.

"It was a terrible thing, a terrible thing. These hysterical periods always are."

You had some hysteria right in Independence with the Mormons, didn't you?

"We did, very much the same sort of thing. The Mormons got chased out of Illinois, Nauvoo, Illinois, on account of the polygamy situation. And when they left there, they came to Independence, and the same sort of situation developed. They even called out the militia to help chase them out, and then they went to a town called Fair Play north of the river about halfway to the Iowa line.

"And, finally, they came to Council Bluffs, Iowa, and Brigham Young marched them out to Utah, and it's the most remarkable march, I think, in the history of civilization. Some of them were pushing carts, and some of them, those that could afford it, had wagons. And they set up the Mormon state of Utah. They were exceedingly hard-working people, and they built Salt Lake City, which is one of the most beautiful cities in the country."

Why do you think people in Independence in those days hated them so much?

"People in Independence haven't changed a bit. The old people hate them just as much now as they did then. It's a violent prejudice. I don't feel that way, and a great many of the people of Independence do not, but you take the old-timers, the old Independence families, they won't have anything to do with Mormons."

Why?

"Well, why does a South Carolinian hate to eat at a table with a nigger? It's the same feeling exactly. It's a prejudice, and it doesn't make any sense, but it's there. And some people in public life take advantage of those prejudices."

Mr. President, a few minutes ago you said that the same kind of people are always behind these movements. What kind of people do you mean?

"Well, of course, a great many of them are not mentally complete, and many of them have prejudices of the kind we talked about, and with some of them it's a case of their having lost everything. You remember how in the deep Depression, when the farmers were having such a hard time, particularly in Iowa and northern Missouri, the corn belt, and a judge in Iowa made an injunction against the farmers' organization that had spilled milk on the road when they didn't get the right price for it.

"And those farmers didn't pay any attention to the injunction, and they came close to hanging the judge. But then Roosevelt came along with that lovely voice of his, and he made Henry Wallace Secretary of Agriculture, and they wrote a farm bill that worked, and the farmers calmed down.

"But what it always is, the people who are hysterical are afraid of something or other, and somebody's got to lead them out of it."

And speaking of hysteria, in your time, of course, there was a man named Joe McCarthy.

"Oh, yes, and I've told you he was just a no-good son of a bitch. And he was a coward. You take a damn demagogue, and he's always a coward. And what you have to do with a coward, you have to fight him, and I did. I cussed him out every chance I got.

"And of course, it wasn't just McCarthy. A fella like that couldn't have got anywhere if he'd been fought from the very beginning. They didn't do it, though. A man like that—it's like a sickness. It isn't going to disappear if you just ignore it. If that was the case, we wouldn't need doctors, would we?

"And the others, the people who know a man like that is up to no good but who encourage him for strictly partisan reasons. People like Taft [Senator Robert A. Taft, a Republican Senator from Ohio, father of the present Senator], he knew that what McCarthy was saying wasn't true, that he was demagoguing the issue for all it was worth, and he knew that was a dangerous thing to do because while I never did agree with him on much of anything at all, I think he understood the history of this country. But he said, you know, that if McCarthy didn't have the facts in one case, he should keep on making accusations until he got to one where he could come up with the facts.

"Now that's where the real danger comes; it isn't only the demagogues. It's the ones who encourage them, who'll do anything in the world to win an election. They're just as bad."

Mr. President, when you were at Columbia,* you were asked about the Japanese on the West Coast being relocated during the Second World War. You said that was another example of hysteria. Could you comment on that?

"They were concentration camps. They called it relocation, but they put them in concentration camps, and I was against it. We were in a period of emergency, but it was still the wrong thing to do. It was one place where I never went along with Roosevelt. He never should have allowed it."

Nobody ever suggested that Americans of German descent or Americans of Italian descent be put in concentration camps, be relocated.

"Well, it may have been suggested, but it didn't get very far."

Do you suppose it was because Americans of Japanese descent looked different?

"It may have been. But the reason it happened was just the same as what we've been talking about. People out on the West Coast got scared, and they panicked, and they decided to get rid of the Japanese-Americans. That's how it happened.

* In April, 1959, Mr. Truman gave the first Radner lectures at Columbia University; he spoke on the Presidency, on the Constitution, and on hysteria and witch-hunting. The lectures were published by Columbia University Press in a book called *Truman Speaks*.

"That's what I've been telling you. A leader, what a leader has to do is to stop the panic. I've told you a time or two before, I guess; a leader has to lead, or otherwise he has no business in politics. At least that's the way I've always looked at it.

"What you have to understand is that most people in this country are men and women of common sense, and when somebody gets too far out of line, like that McCarthy fellow, the people take charge and put him out of business.

"In the long run people with common sense always take over, and we don't have to worry about people whose opinions are out of line with the rest of us.

"And there have always been men who understood that, from the time this country began there have been. Take a look at what Jefferson had to say on the subject:

" 'Reason and experiment have been indulged, and error has fled before them. It is error alone which needs the support of government. Truth can stand by itself. Subject opinion to coercion: whom will you make your inquisitors? Fallible men, men governed by bad passions, by private as well as public reasons. And why subject it to coercion? To produce uniformity. But is uniformity of opinion desirable? No more than face and stature. Introduce the bed of Procrustes then, and as there is danger that the large men may beat the small, make us all of a size, by lopping the former and stretching the latter. . . . Is uniformity attainable? Millions of innocent men, women, and children, since the introduction of Christianity, have been burnt, tortured, fined, imprisoned; yet we have not advanced one inch toward uniformity. What has been the effect of coercion? To make one half the world fools, and the other half hypocrites. To support roguery and error all over the world.' " *

I said, "I've never read that before. It's very beautiful, and I thank you for introducing it to me. Among so much else."

---

* From *Notes on Virginia*.

"Well, the point is we've been very, very fortunate in this country up to now; we've had men like Jefferson who were reasonable and responsible and who understood our past and been concerned with our future.

"There's been such men in the past when we needed them, and I see no reason why there won't be in the future. That's why I'm an optimist, and I think you'll agree with me that the facts bear me out."

39

Afterword

The last time I was in Independence, in the fall of 1969, the old man who drove me there from the Kansas City airport asked if I had come to town on business or pleasure. I said a little of both, and he said—people in Independence tell you things; you don't have to ask—"If you've come to see Harry Truman, and nine out of ten strangers, that's why they come, you won't be able to. Mrs. Eisenhower was here day before yesterday, and she talked to Mrs. Truman on the phone, but that's all. He don't see people anymore, don't even go on his walks half the time. Neither of them go out much since that sickness. Four years ago it was."

He stopped the taxi in front of the gate at 219 North Delaware. The house had been repainted the previous summer, and it glistened clean and white in the late afternoon sun. The wide lawn was neatly trimmed. A black man was sweeping the sidewalk, and there were the sounds of his broom and of copies of the Independence *Examiner* being tossed onto neighboring front porches by a boy on a bicycle. Otherwise there was silence, awesome in its way and welcome. We were only six miles from the smoke-blackened skyline of Kansas City, but it could have been a million.

The taxi driver got out, looked at the house for a moment, deposited some tobacco juice on the sidewalk, and said, "This used to be the summer White House, and there'd be reporters around. By the hundreds they were. And even when he and the missus came back from Washington, there was the tourists always around. But you don't even see many of *them* anymore. They forget. That's the damn trouble with people. They forget."

He jammed the Stetson lower on his forehead and for a moment wobbled precariously on the high heels of his cowboy boots. "You get old. It don't matter a good god-

455

damn who you are or what you did, they don't pay you
no mind. Especially the kids. Their long hair and dirt an
inch thick on their faces—they can't wait for you to die.
I'd like to get ahold of just one of them. I'd take him by
the hair, and I'd—".

He looked at me and then, as if dismayed by the anger
within him, closed the pocketbook mouth over a single
yellow tooth and got back into the taxi.

"Don't usually talk that much, especially to a stranger,"
he said. "But I'm a friend of Harry's. Never been in the
house, but I'm a friend all right. Everybody in town is, I
guess, or think they are, and there isn't practically a building that don't have a picture of him, unless maybe it's the
Republican headquarters."

I paid the fare, including a tip. He rejected the latter.
"Can't take that, wouldn't feel right. Now you take Harry
there. Harry'd understand. We're old men, the both of us,
but by God neither one of us took nothing we didn't earn.
And we don't owe anybody in the world."

For a while I was alone in front of the house, which may
some day be a national monument like Monticello or
Mount Vernon or the Hermitage, where old Andy Jackson
is buried. Miss Sue Gentry of the Independence *Examiner*
told me later, "No one knows what will happen to the
house. It is a question no one has asked."

Just before dusk a young man and his wife and their
three children, two boys and a girl, started taking pictures
of the house and of each other standing in front of it. They
were all blond and blue-eyed and handsome. Not surprisingly, their car had Minnesota license plates.

The young man asked if I'd mind taking a picture of
all of them, and they stood in a rigid line, displaying an
extraordinary number of perfect white teeth.

"Except for the Bomb, I mean his dropping the Bomb,
I don't really know much about him," said the young
man, "but we were in Kansas City, and I thought, what
the hell, we're this close. It'll give the kids something to
remember."

He glanced somewhat nervously at the house. "Are they in there now, do you think?" I said I thought they were, and he said to the children—who, if not the most knowledgeable, must have been the cleanest children ever— "Do you realize there's a former President of the United States in there? And a First Lady?" The kids nodded. So?

Finally the wife, who looked a little like the very early Ingrid Bergman, asked a question that has occurred to me from time to time. She said, "What in the world do you suppose they talk about?"

They drove off, the question unanswered, unanswerable.

It was dark now. The only light in the house was in the small sitting room downstairs. Harry Truman and his First Lady were two old people, alone, lonely. The house was peaceful at last. Harry Truman once called the White House a big white jail, but now the house at 219 North Delaware was a prison, too. Mrs. Truman was still a member of the Tuesday Bridge Club, but it had been years since she had attended, and a couple of years earlier, when she was invited to Kansas City to be done some honor or other, she said, "I can't. Mr. Truman won't go to bed until I get home."

I watched the light go off in the sitting room, and a moment or so later another one was turned on in the Truman bedroom upstairs. Finally the house was in total darkness, and there was not a sound anywhere. It was ten minutes after nine.

Independence is no longer a small town; it is a city with a population of 116,000, and, to be sure, there are the inevitable developments, Manor Oaks and Virginia Heights and Monticello with the tired modern houses that Harry Truman disliked so much. And there are the equally unlikable flossy apartment houses, most of them with the look of displaced Beverly Hills Renaissance. One has two swimming pools but not a single palm tree. And the motels; I stayed at Howard Johnson's.

But, happily, until the end of Mr. Truman's life there

was a kind of nineteenth-century oasis around 219 North
Delaware. The streets cannot be so very different from
what they were in 1890, when the Trumans moved to
town from Grandview. They are wide and lined with
trees, elm and cottonwood and oak, and on that crisp
autumn afternoon the leaves were just beginning to turn.

They are the kind of streets we remember or would
like to remember from our childhood, free of smog, free of
wars and confrontations, free of insoluble problems. Even
the names are nostalgic: Linden, Maple, Walnut, Cottage,
Liberty.

The houses are large and well kept, and between forty-
five and fifty of them were built just before or just after
the War Between the States. Houses like Miss Cammie
Johnston's, for instance, at 305 South Pleasant, built in
1850, vaguely English, in a style of architecture called
Missouri River Gothic. In the north wall is a cannonball
left from the First Battle of Independence.

Mr. Truman spent most of the last twenty years of his
long extraordinary life in the oasis, surrounded by the
houses and the people he grew up with and who loved
and respected him.

Only a block away from the house at 219 North Delaware was the site of the high school from which he and
Bess were graduated in 1901; the building itself had long
since burned to the ground. I had read that he had carried
some lines from Tennyson's *Locksley Hall** in his wallet

* The lines were:
      "For I dipt into the future, far as human
              eye could see,
      Saw the Vision of the world, and all
              the wonder that could be;
      Saw the heavens fill with commerce,
              argosies of magic sails,
      Pilots of the purple twilight, dropping
              down with costly bales;
      Heard the heavens filled with shouting,
              and there rain'd a ghastly dew
      From the nations' airy navies grappling
              in the central blue;

ever since his graduation, and one day I asked him about that.

He said, "Oh, yes, and the paper I copied it on kept wearing out, and I kept recopying it. I don't know how many times, twenty or thirty I expect.

"That poem made a very strong impression on me, because, although it was written in 1840 or thereabouts [1842], it predicted a great many things that happened during my lifetime and some other things that haven't happened yet but will happen someday. Tennyson knew all those things and wrote them, and that's one of the reasons I've always—and I hadn't ought to say this—had a lot more faith in poets than in reporters. Reporters just tell what has happened, and they don't do too good a job of it a lot of the time, but poets, some of them, they write about what's going to happen.

"Now Tennyson knew there were going to be airplanes, and he knew there was going to be bombing and all of it. And someday there'll be a parliament of man. It stands to reason, and that's what I was doing when I went ahead with setting up the United Nations and when I kept it from being torn apart by what happened in Korea. The United Nations is the first step.

"I guess you might say Tennyson had some influence on my career, such as it was, and I could have had worse examples to follow."

Did you read Morte d'Arthur *when you were a boy?*

"Oh, yes. I read the complete works. Everything he

Far along the world-wide whisper of the
    south-wind rushing warm,
With the standards of the people plunging
    throw' the thunder-storm;
Till the war-drum throbb'd no longer,
    and the battle-flags were furl'd
In the Parliament of Man, the Federation
    of the world.
There the common sense of most shall hold
    a fretful realm in awe,
And the kindly earth shall slumber, lapt
    in universal law."

ever wrote. That's what I'd do. I'd read something I liked
by a fella, and then I'd go to the library and get . . .
take out everything else he ever wrote and read it straight
through. He wrote another poem about the same time as
*Locksley Hall, The Golden Year,** it was called, and
there's a lot in there about peace, too. I can't remember
what it was, but Tennyson was a man very much concerned with stopping wars, and I guess you might say I
was, too.

"We went about it in different ways, of course."

*Mr. President, I understand from reading Mr. Citizen
that you were offered a number of high-paying jobs after
you left the White House and that you turned them all
down.*

"Oh, yes. I could have been a millionaire and then some
I guess. But they weren't interested in hiring me. They
were hiring an ex-President. They wanted to cash in on
that, and they offered me, oh, a lot of six-figure salaries
to do nothing much at all except let them use the name
of an ex-President. I wouldn't let them do it, though. I'd
rather die in the poorhouse than do a thing like that."

*I was reading last night that when you were chairman
of that committee we've talked about you turned down
something like fifty thousand dollars for some lecture
tours. Was that another example of your not wanting to
cash in on your position?*

"You've got to be careful. You've got to be careful.
It was the same sort of thing. They were putting up the
money for the chairman of what was called the Truman
Committee, and I wasn't going to take advantage of the
others who were on the committee and were working just
as hard as I was and deserved just as much of the credit.
It wouldn't have been fair to them.

"Besides, my job, the job I was elected to fulfill was to

* "Ah! when shall all men's good
Be each man's rule, and universal peace
Lie like a shaft across the land?"

do my job in the Senate, and that meant doing a lot of homework and not gallivanting around the country and being half-dead tired all the time, as well as not being prepared to ask the right questions and get the facts we were after."

Mr. President, another thing I didn't know until last night when I was reading about it in the book about the library here, you had a chance to go overseas to investigate transportation and supply, but you wouldn't do it. Would you mind explaining why?

"That's right. I could have gone, but two members of the committee had boys that were in the service over there, and I didn't. So I sent them instead. They wanted to see their boys, and I thought they ought to be able to do so."

Wouldn't you have liked to go?

"Oh, yes. Oh, my, yes. But I think I've told you a time or two. You can't always do what you'd like to do, and the sooner you learn that, the better off everybody is."

Mr. President, it constantly amazes me that you seem always to know what is the right thing to do.

"Oh, I don't think knowing what's the right thing to do ever gives anybody too much trouble. It's *doing* the right thing that seems to give a lot of people trouble."

After a moment we went on to other matters.

Mr. President, could I ask you a very personal question?

"Go right ahead. I've told you before, if I want to stop you, I'll stop you."

You said the other day that Justice Holmes attributed his long and successful life to the fact that he discovered at an early age that he wasn't God. To what, sir, do you attribute your long and remarkable life?

"Well, I never thought I was God; that's one thing for sure. I grew up wanting to be as good a man as my father was and as my mother wanted me to be. I never had the notion that I was anything special at all; even when I got that job in the White House, I didn't. And I never had the notion that there weren't a lot of people who couldn't do whatever it was better than I could.

"But that never worried me. All that ever concerned me was that I wanted to do it as best *I* could. So I guess I'd have to say to that, to your question, that I always tried to be satisfied with what I was and what I was doing. My father used to say that a man ought to leave the world a little better than it was when he came into it, and if that can be said about me, I guess you'll have to say I lived a successful life."

Did it bother you, leaving the pomp and circumstance of Washington? Of the White House?

"Never gave me any trouble at all. I always kept in mind something old Ben Franklin said at that meeting in Philadelphia we were talking about. They had a big discussion about what should be done about ex-Presidents, and Alexander Hamilton I think it was said that it would be a terrible thing to degrade them by putting them back among the common people after they'd had all that power. But old Ben Franklin didn't agree. It's here someplace . . . I've got it, what he said. . . . Here, read it."

Franklin said, "In free governments the rulers are the servants and the people their superiors and sovereigns. For the former therefore to return among the latter is not to degrade them but to promote them."

Mr. Truman smiled, and he said, "I kept that in mind when I was in the White House, and I've had it in mind ever since I got my . . . promotion."

Index